THE LAWS
of GARTSHERRIE

A novel by AJ Morris

Published by

McAlpine Media

First published in 2015 by
McAlpine Media
www.mcalpinemedia.co.uk

ISBN: 978-0-9934468-0-1

British Library Cataloguing-in-Publication Data
A catalogue record for this book is available
on request from the British Library.

Designed & Typeset by McAlpine Media, Glasgow.

CONTENTS

DEDICATION

With all my love to my Mum and Aunt Mary
who prepared me for life.

And, to Rebecca, my precious granddaughter.
The future comes from the past.

ACKNOWLEDGEMENTS

I offer my heartfelt thanks to:

My publishers, Gary and Joanne McAlpine of McAlpine Media. They also provided wonderfully sensitive design work, as well as reading the early draft. Great sounding boards, clever computer boffins - and pals to laugh with.

The Scottish 'girls' who read my early draft and gave me the confidence to tell the story: Liz, Jane and Pearl - the pals of my youth.

My teenage friend Laura who read my finished manuscript, gave me wise advice. And, the perspective of youth.

My long suffering husband, Paul, for absolutely everything.

And, not forgetting Chronic Peripheral Neuropathy for forcing me to sit and write.

CHAPTER 1
March 1899

A young woman sat opposite her husband in the third class carriage of a steam train travelling from Glasgow, it was heading towards the biggest coal, iron, chemical and industrial town in the whole of Scotland, Coatbridge.

The population of the town was a huge melting pot, like the blast iron furnaces. Coatbridge attracted poor, displaced and job hungry people, from Ireland, the Highlands and Islands of Scotland, Lithuania, Russia and Poland.

It seemed as though the poor of the world were all rushing towards this Lanarkshire town, that until as recently as 1830 had been nothing more than a small country village.

In the black of night the furnace fires lit the sky like erupting volcanos so that the town was never without a fearsome red glow.

The town was also overshadowed by an enormous bing of waste dross standing like a black mountain threatening to engulf the population in a mantle of coal slurry.

Coatbridge might look like, and smell like, a medieval image of hell, but the people who inhabited it were like people everywhere. Good, bad, jealous, spiteful, generous, plain, handsome, the whole gambit of the human condition.

What united this mixture of religions and nationalities, with a very few exceptions, was poverty.

As the people of Coatbridge headed towards the new century and the end of the Victorian era, life for them was one of hard grind and extreme poverty.

Although slavery had been abolished throughout most of the British Empire in 1833, the people who worked in the mines and foundries and other heavy industry in Lanarkshire at the beginning of the twentieth century, were as much a slave to the company owners as any plantation worker cutting sugar cane in Jamaica or toiling in the cotton fields of the Americas.

Darkness was falling on the chilly March afternoon, as the train from Glasgow passed the outlines of the many giant monuments to industry that dominated the skyline.   In a cloud of sulphuric steam it drew into Sunnyside Station, a misnomer, a name which in no way reflected the reality of its surroundings.

Among the many people who alighted from the train were the Law family, a middle aged man and his young wife, together with a dark haired toddler and a tiny red haired baby.

Agnes Law had been born and brought up in Glasgow, so she was no stranger to industry, but the atmosphere of this sooty, noisy, busy place with its gigantic structures, disgorging red flames, terrified her.   Coatbridge, might look like Hell, but Agnes would eventually learn it also housed Angels.

Agnes was a pretty girl in her twenties.   Petit with small neat features, a flawless complexion and striking blue eyes, she had beautiful long dark silky hair, which was kept tied up in a knot under her winter felt hat.

Rab, her husband, was a good deal older than Agnes, but despite years of toil he was still a fine looking man.   His dark hair contained a sprinkling of grey and his grey blue eyes held a steely determined look.   He was holding the hand of a little girl, who was snugly wrapped in shawls to keep out the biting March wind.   Between them they carried their few possessions in an old black leather portmanteau bag and wrapped in a bed sheet, which was tied together at the corners.

Rab had said nothing to Agnes on the train journey as to where they were going, or where they would be staying.

They left the station, still smelling the acrid steam from the engine.   As they emerged into the busy road, Agnes was taken aback when a tall man rushed forward to greet them and, in a broad

Ulster accent, addressed Rab.

"How goes it my man? Little did I think when I was your lodger and we worked in the metal foundry in Glasgow that you, and your wee wife here, would be my lodgers. Come on Rab, it's a tidy walk to the Rows, so it is. Now what would I be calling your good lady and the fine wee bairns?"

Robert Law introduced his wife Agnes to his friend Alex Johnstone.

"And this is my fine little stepdaughter wee Charlotte, the babby is our newborn Mary Ann."

Alex welcomed the family to Coatbridge, saying.

"We best get you back quickly to the Gartsherrie Rows, for a warm by the range fire, and a bite to eat. Jessie, my wife, will take good care of you Agnes, she is used to wee bairns we have three, two girls and a lad."

The walk seemed to take a very long time, even with the men taking it in turns to carry Charlotte, while Agnes carried the baby at her bosom. In reality it was less than half an hour but a combination of the chilly air, the strangeness of the town and a baby, who badly wanted to suckle, made the journey seem like hours to Agnes.

They passed the Monkland canal with its barge boats, carrying their cargos of black coal; the railway lines with wagons in the sidings; and then the huge structures and chimneys that was "The Works", Wm Baird & Sons.

Alex shouted above the noise, the noise that would eventually become second nature to Agnes, so that she barely even heard it.

He offered an explanation to his new lodgers.

"We are nearly at the Rows now. That big grey sandstone building is the Gartsherrie Institute. It was built aboot ten years back by the Baird family, probably to keep us oot of mischief. It has swimming baths, reading rooms and lecture rooms, that's where the Lodge meetings are held. The brass band practice is also held at the Institute. We have dances on a Saturday night, even a pigeon fancier club; all Gartsherrie life meets at the Institute, so it does."

They turned into the Long Row, walking along a cobbled road past a long terrace row of grey stone cottage style houses. On the opposite side of the road there were outhouses, which Agnes would later learn were coal cellars, wash houses with big copper boilers and toilets blocks. There was also drying greens with poles for hanging out washing and some of the houses had plots of land, which could be used for growing vegetables. Families lucky enough to own rugs used the fences along the perimeter of the greens to beat their carpets with curved bamboo paddles.

Alex and Jessie lived near the top of the Row at 130, making it quite a long walk over the cobbles to reach their little house, set within the long cottage like terrace.

At last they arrived at their destination and Alex turned the door handle; the house was only ever locked at bedtime. Nobody locked doors during the day in the Rows. They entered through a small scullery, which held a sink and a wooden workbench. Several pails and a butter churn were under the bench, a pot and a large cast iron frying pan on top. There was also a pile of chipped stoneware plates and bowls and a large jug containing an odd assortment of cutlery, cooking implements and wooden spoons. On the wall, resting on two large nails, hung a zinc bath.

They gladly tumbled into the living room, lit by an oil lamp and the glow from the range fire, which was the heart of the Johnstone home. There was a black cast iron pot hanging over the range, from which came a tempting aroma.

As soon as he entered the house three children ran towards Alex, putting their arms around him.

"Paw, paw, who have you brought home?" they chorused.

"Give me a minute bairns, be quiet now till I talk to your Mammie. Jessie, let me introduce you to the Law family, our new lodgers. This is my good pal Rab, or Robert, if we are using his Sunday name, and his wife Agnes, the wee lass is Charlotte and the babe Mary Ann.

Rab and Agnes, these three mischiefs are Samuel or Sam, Agnes and Mary, our three bairns. We are going to be having a big Agnes and a wee Agnes and a big Mary and a wee Mary, so we are. Thank goodness the other lass is called Charlotte."

"Please, can I go into the other room and feed wee baby Mary?"

Agnes asked Jessie.

"Surely," she replied, "but it is frozen cold in there, just sit here by the warmth of the fire and suckle the wee wean under your shawl. That is how we all feed the bairns here in the Rows."

After Mary was fed Agnes took stock of her surroundings. The walls were whitewashed and clean. The furniture was poor, a plain wooden table that was scrubbed clean. To one side of the table was a bench, on the other side there were three stools. In the middle of the table sat a brass oil lamp. There was a wooden rocker type chair on one side of the fire and another rough built chair on the other. The rocker and chair had folded plaid blankets over them and blue ticking cushions, the only visible signs of comfort. Either side of the fire were cupboards, one of which contained the family's store of food. There were two recess beds on the left hand side of the room. On the back wall was a door, made from planks of wood, which were battened together. This led to the bedroom where the Law family would sleep, or as Alex would say 'ben the hoose'.

It was a comfortless bedroom, two more recess beds, the only furniture a large wooden chest or kist and a low chair. There were a number of hooks on the wall to hang all the family's clothing. No curtains graced the window, just a piece of sacking which had been nailed to he window frame to keep out draughts and provide a degree of privacy.

The floors were all stone, without the comfort of a rug to warm them. Agnes thought of her parents' home in Glasgow, she had always thought they were poor, but compared to this abject poverty they lived in luxury.

Jessie sat the four children at the table and dished them each a plate of soup rich with vegetables, peas and barley, which they ate with a slice of bread. After the children finished eating they all took turns going for a wee wee in the zinc pail, as it was too cold to go out to the toilet block. The three Johnstone children, Samuel, Agnes and Mary all said their prayers and were then put to bed, top to tail in one of the recess beds in the kitchen.

Charlotte was taken by Agnes into the bedroom and settled

down to sleep.   After her nappy was changed Mary too was snuggled down beside Charlotte.   Charlotte cuddled into her little sister, using her like a hot water bottle for warmth.

Jessie now dished up soup with a slice of bread for the four adults.   After finishing their soup the men were given a piece of flank mutton from the pot, together with some whole potatoes.

When the meal was finished the women cleared away the dishes and went out to the standpipe to fill the kettle and a jug with water. Jessie then put oatmeal in a pot to soak with warm water.

"It makes the porridge making in the morning much easier, she explained to Agnes."

Tired from their journey the Johnstone's new lodgers, Rab and Agnes, went to their bed in the back bedroom while Alex and Jessie slept in the kitchen and enjoyed the residual warmth from the range after it had been backed-up with damp coal dross.

Morning began for Jessie with the 6.00am siren.   Her first job of the day was to put on the porridge oats to cook.   Meanwhile, she spread slices of bread with beef dripping for Alex and Rab's break and put them in their tin piece boxes.   A large pot of tea was brewed, a mug for the men with their breakfast and the remainder poured into their enamel tea cans.

The menfolk were now up and busy washing in the scullery.

There was no conversation, Alex and Rab sat at the table Jessie served them with great steaming bowls of oatmeal porridge, seasoned with salt and mugs of black tea.   There would be no sugar to sweeten the tea until payday.   As the men prepared to leave for their shift Jessie handed each of them a piece box containing their bread and dripping together with an enamel can full of black tea.

After the men had left for work Jessie went through to the bedroom to waken Agnes, she found her lying feeding baby Mary while Charlotte hid under the covers.

Jessie spoke firmly, but kindly.

"Agnes, am I right in thinking you have lived a much better lifestyle in Glasgow than the one you see now in Gartsherrie?"

"Yes" she replied. "I always thought we were poor.   My Paw is a master bricklayer and my mother used to take in sewing and do a bit of dressmaking. But the flats we lived in always had flush toilets on the half landing, and we had wooden floors and rag rugs and running water and, and, and."

Agnes started to sob uncontrollably. Jessie put her arm around her as her three bairns stood watching through the open door. Jessie, allowed Agnes to shed her tears for a few minutes, then she spoke to her in a firm, no nonsense, manner.

"Look Agnes the Rows are a way of life and the quicker you accept life here the better for you and your wee bairns. Every spare bed is used. Every family has lodgers; we used to have two lads, Eck and Archie. They were all right but Alex knew I would prefer another woman to share the load with. Washing cooking and cleaning for three men and looking after the bairns on my own was a real struggle. Then Alex heard that his auld pal Rab had got a job at the Works and wanted a place for him and his wee family, so he found other digs for the two boys.

Agnes, two households sharing can be a living hell, or we can support each other. There are houses in the Rows where the two women living together argue constantly, they even fight each other. I have seen women with black eyes; hair pulled out in handfuls, while the other women and weans gather round and egg them on. Women can be worse than men when they get started, especially if the argument is about their weans.

I don't want it to be like that with us, I want us to be friends. I will show you the ropes here. And Agnes, you must learn quickly. No nonsense of pining for how it was in Glasgow, you must just get up now, dry your eyes, and feed Mary. The Long Row hooses are no mansions but they are a great deal better than the hovels of the Rosehall Rows that the miners live in, just count your blessings Agnes Law."

Agnes was no fool, she realised how lucky she was to have a woman like Jessie in her corner. Yes, her life had certainly taken a turn for the worse but she was also responsible enough to know that her first thought must be for her two wee girls. Working together with Jessie was the best way to ensure their survival. Too many babies died from disease, overcrowding, poor food and just plain neglect. Jessie's bairns were clean and looked healthy, that was a good starting place.

Jessie herself had a pretty heart shaped face and violet blue eyes, her hair was a soft brown and like most of the women in the rows tied up in a knot at the nape of her neck and held in place with pins. Petit, like Agnes, although her figure was softer and she had a rounded bust. What made Jessie exceptional was the warmth of her nature and her sense of humour. Jessie had a ready smile and could always find a kernel of goodness in everything that befell the Johnstone family.

Agnes came into the warmth and sat by the hearth on the rocker chair feeding Mary while Jessie backed up the fire and gently reheated the porridge. The four older bairns started playing with some shiny ball bearings which they used like marbles.

Jessie briskly dished the porridge; after they had all eaten breakfast, she poured some water into a bowl and washed the hands and faces of the four bairns. Then they had to take it in turns to dip their fingers in a cup of warm water with a little baking soda added and use their fingers to rub their teeth clean.

Jessie was firmly in control, issuing orders.

"Right Agnes get wee Mary wrapped up to go out. You four get into your outdoor shawls, Sam put on your balaclava and you three girls get into your bonnets, I'll help you fasten your button boots. We all have to go down to the Store, now."

Damping down the fire with wet dross Jessie then shooed them all out into the cold dank morning.

As they walked over the cobbles down the Long Row Jessie started Agnes's tuition.

"We are going down to the Store, always the first job of the day. It is the only way to be sure you get a nice new baked loaf of bread. If you are not down early and miss the bread you have to give your man fried porridge that has been set from the morning with his dinner, also you won't have any bread for his piece and dripping the following morning. Not a good idea, I have seen women with two black eyes for missing the bread delivery. Not that my Alex would ever raise a hand to me, or our bairns."

Doors were opening, women and children walking back and forth to the toilet block; there were queues at the standpipes for water; children out playing. Friendly cries greeted them as they walked.

"How do Jessie? Bitter cauld one this morning?"

"New pal Jessie?"

"Have you heard Jessie, Sammy the Pole has been fighting again at the Works and he has been suspended for three 12 hour shifts. God knows how that wee wife of his will manage."

"I know how she will manage." Jessie confided in Agnes. "One neighbour will give her a couple of onions, another a cup of oatmeal, another a few tatties. That's how we survive here. Ninny, God knows what her real name is, but that's what she gets called here, is a Catholic. All the Polaks are Catholics, so are the Lithuanians. But believe me, the men might talk their talk about Billies and Tims, and join their Orange or Hibernian Lodges but we all have to help each other here in the Rows if we want to survive. So her Protestant neighbours and her Catholic neighbours between them will do their best to make sure that Ninny and Sammy's weans are fed."

They reached the Store; it was really a Shop owned by Gartsherrie Works'. The men earned their money, they paid their rent for their Work's House and their wives bought the messages at the Work's Store. What precious little money was left they used to buy porter or beer, again at the Store, in order to forget the hell of Baird's Work for a few hours each week.

The Store was divided into sections, general groceries, butchery, drysaltery, and a wine and spirits department. Adjacent to the Store was another shop with the grand name of 'The Emporium', this shop sold material, clothes, shoes and haberdashery. On a Friday fresh fish was sold from a horse drawn cart, in the Store's backyard.

Jessie chose two large white loaves from those piled high on the long wooden trestles. They each had a black crust on the bottom and a rounded brown crust on top and smelt yeasty and delicious.

Then she moved over to join the butchery queue.

"Can I have a knap bone for soup please, Mr Clark?"

"Certainly Mrs Johnstone I've got a nice one here with your name stamped on it, and will this be a new neighbour with you today?"

"Yes, this is my friend Mistress Law, no doubt she will be coming into the Store for her messages when she is settled in the Long Row."

"Excellent, just take Mistress Law over to see Miss McDougall in the office and she will sort her out with a Store Number, and explain how the system works."

The office was a closed rectangular mahogany structure in the centre of the Store, wood at the bottom with glass panels fitted on two sides and wood on the others; inside were two women, wearing brown linen coats. One woman was sitting facing a solid wood panel, working on ledgers. The other facing a glass window with an opening at the front; she marked down the women's purchases in their Store Book. Bills were settled on a Saturday morning, after the men had been paid.

Together they waited in the queue while the other women had their purchases marked up. Jessie handed over her book and Miss McDougall entered her purchases.

Jessie then introduced Agnes.

"This is Mistress Law, can you please give her a Store Book Miss McDougall, her man's name is Robert Law and he is working beside my husband."

Miss McDougall took a new book from the pile under the counter and filled in Agnes's details, she then informed her.

"Your number is 7550 Mrs Law, and the dividend is paid on the quarter days."

Jessie and Agnes then gathered up the children, who had been playing quietly in the sawdust which covered the floor.

Walking back to number 130 they again ran into a number of neighbours with whom they had to pass the time of day. When they eventually arrived home, Jessie announced.

"Don't settle yourself Agnes, we are off out again. We'll just leave the food in the scullery, and pick up the milk cans. This time it's up to Shanks's Farm, and I'll be able to show you the Rows proper, Agnes."

As they walked Jessie explained to Agnes the system and the names of the Rows.

"There are quite a number of different Rows, built as the Works expanded and more and more people came to live in Gartsherrie. The South Square, we passed that going down to the Store. Then there is North Square, Heather Row, The Dandy Row, Herriot Row, Wee Row, Quarry Row, Cornish Row, Stable Row, and The Long Row, where we live.

Even within the Rows there is a pecking order, The Square and Long Row are higher up than Wee Row or Dandy Row, and Herriot Row is one step up on them but not as high as The Square and the Long Row; complicated isn't it. But you wouldn't believe the snob value associated with the name of the Row, even when you consider we are all as poor as church mice, it does make me laugh.

A lot of people live here Agnes, and we are all bound to the Works in one way or another. No work at Baird's Works and we all starve, or we move on to pastures new."

It wasn't a very long walk to the farm. When they arrived they walked through the yard to the Dairy and Jessie warmly greeted the lady working in the milk parlour. Jean Shanks was Farmer Shanks' sister, a plump, rosy-faced woman, who enjoyed the company of the women who came to buy produce from the farm.

Jessie introduced Agnes to Jean, who then endeared herself to Agnes by admiring wee Mary.

"My she is a bonny wean with all that lovely red hair, she'll certainly steal the boys hearts one day."

Jessie bought a quart of milk, a sack of onions; half a stone of potatoes; two turnips, some carrots and parsley. Her purchases cost one shilling and twopence, which she paid with money from her well worn purse.

Jean then asked the children if they had been good and helped their Mammies'. Jessie's three started to shout.

"Yes, Miss Jean we are very good," Charlotte soon got the idea and joined in. "We are all really, really good."

"Right, right, I get the message." said Jean. "Now wait there, and I'll see if there is anything to be found in my Special Tin."

She disappeared into the farmhouse and returned with four home baked biscuits.   The children's' eyes lit up as she gave them one each.

"Mind, be good now, or never another wee treat will you get from my Special Tin." said the kind hearted Jean.

They said their thanks and started the walk back home.   Agnes carrying the milk and wee Mary; Jessie with the sack of potatoes and vegetables on her back; with the four children munching on their home baked biscuits.

As they walked back to the house there were the inevitable greetings from neighbours.   Everybody seemed to know everybody. Having lived in a big bustling city Agnes was used to having lots of people around her but not the level of intimacy she found in the Gartsherrie Rows.

Jessie greeted everyone with a cheery smile, introducing Agnes to the women, and then giving Agnes potted histories as to who they were.

"That's big Isa, heart of gold but if she has a wee drop of porter on a Saturday she gets as drunk as a puggy and you can hear her singing Orange songs from here to the Whitelaw Fountain down in Coatbridge.

Alice is a quiet wee woman, she is a rarity here, nae weans.   Her and her man Hughie have about four lodgers so they are certainly not short of a bob or two.

Come on now Agnes hurry up here comes Jenny Baxter, she is not the full shilling, if she sees us we will never get away."

They fell into the house laughing at their dodging of poor Jenny. "Lets have a piece and a cup of tea." Suggested Jessie.   "I don't know about you but I'm ready for something."   Agnes suckled wee Mary while Jessie cut slices of bread for all of them, spread them with a little jam and shouted for the children to come in from their play outside the house.

"Get your hands washed wee ones, and come and eat your bread and milk."   The word "eat" galvanised them and they all ran into the scullery to wash.   Only then did they all sit at the table to enjoy their jammy bread and milk.

Agnes noticed how well mannered Jessie's children were.   They might not be rich but they certainly knew how to sit quietly at the table while eating and drink without slurping. When they finished each child said, "Please may I leave the table?" They then took their cup and plate into the scullery to wash them up.

The longer Agnes spent in Jessie's company the more she realised how lucky she was to have been taken under the wing of this fine woman.

As the two woman ate their bread and enjoyed a cup of tea Jessie questioned Agnes.

"Tell me, what are you good at Agnes, any wee skills that can make a few pennies are always good. Also we can sort out how to divide the work between us most effectively."

Agnes responded by saying.

"Jessie I want to thank you so much for all your kindness. I just don't know how I would have coped in a strange new place, what with Charlotte into everything and Mary just being a few weeks old. I am so grateful...."

Jessie cut her off in mid sentence.

"Come on Agnes enough of all the grateful nonsense, we are all here on God's earth to help each other. Now come on tell me, what are you good at?"

The two women laughed, and they both instinctively knew that they were going to be friends.

"Well," said Agnes, "I can cook quite well. My Maw taught me and I worked in service for a time. I can also sew a bit. I can knit and I can scrub a floor with the best of them. Oh, and I can change a nappy."

"Funny," said Jessie,

"We never say nappy here, we all say hippen. Nappy is a Glasgow word."

"Aye Jessie, I've a lot to learn about life in the Rows." said Agnes. "So what are we going to do now? You just tell me what you want me to do and I'll be your pupil."

"Me a teacher," laughed Jessie. "You can certainly blether Agnes Law but that's not going to get the work done.

You must stay inside in the warm today with Mary, and you can keep an eye on the other bairns, they will be fine playing outside with their gird and cleek.   Make the soup for the dinner.   I'll go up to the bing with the bogie and get some dross."

"What's a bing?" asked Agnes.

"You really are a city girl Agnes Law," laughed Jessie.   "It's a mountain of waste where we go to get the dross to back-up the fire with, if we are lucky we can also sometimes find bits of coal.   The only problem is it's a good two-mile walk to the bing.   Four miles walking for a bogie of dross, but at least it's free.   We keep the bogie, which Alex made from bits of this and that from the Works, in the coal cellar.   I'll away and get it now, the quicker I get away the quicker I'll be back.   I'm Lady Jessie now with my cook Agnes making the evening meal."

They laughed together as Jessie lifted her shawl and flounced out of the room, leaving Agnes alone with wee Mary.

Agnes set to work; getting fresh water from the standpipe. Using the knap bone they had bought she made stock in the big pot hanging over the fire, Agnes then prepared the soup with care.   She peeled and chopped carrots, onions and potatoes, added lentils, salt and pepper, then the pot was set on a really slow simmer.   It was now one o'clock, the soup should be done to perfection by the time the men returned from their shift and they ate, around seven o'clock that evening.

The next few hours were filled for Agnes by doing some hand washing; changing and feeding Mary; and, unpacking their few possessions.   Most of their belongings she put into the kist but her portmanteau she pushed under the bed, as far back as she could, in it was secreted Agnes's private memories, together with some money. Not much money, but a bridge against starvation.

Jessie returned and the children came in from their games, just as it was getting dark.

"I've stowed the dross in the coal cellar." said Jessie, "Now I need a good wash before we have our tea.   Right weans, I'm first in the scullery for a wash and then its you four to get scrubbed up. Agnes, what's that lovely smell, and it's no just the soup?"

"It's called skirlie, responded Agnes.   My mother used to make it, you get oatmeal and chopped onions, fry them slowly in beef dripping with salt and pepper, it tastes just like haggis."

"Well I really am Lady Jessie coming home to this feast. You are spoiling us Agnes, but don't you stop mind."

The women got the children fed and into bed; then Agnes washed, changed, and fed Mary, and the bairns were put down to sleep before the men arrived home after their hard days toil.

The Johnstone house provided a warm welcome for the returning workers, with the savoury smells from the cooking and the heat from the glowing fire. In the lamplight the room looked cosy, despite the plain furnishings and bare walls.

Alex and Robert were exhausted after their day's labour. They washed and sat at the table, no words were spoken until after they had all eaten their soup and bread. The skirlie and mashed potato meal went down well, finished off with a big mug of tea.

"That was a rare feast ladies," said Alex.

"I found a newspaper in the bothy today Jess. Will you read us a wee bit, I'm dog tired and I expect Rab here is tired out as well".

The men settled themselves on the chairs and lit clay pipes, filled with their favourite baccy. Jessie laid the newspaper over the table, while she glanced through it looking for an article of interest.

"More trouble in South Africa between the Empire and the Boer Republics, by the sounds of it there could be another Boer War. Terrible thing to say but it would certainly keep the Works busy. What else, lets see now, she turned the pages.

Oh there is a funny advert here for Pears Soap with a photograph of some missionary type." Jessie put on her best upper crust voice.

' The first steps towards lightening the White Man's Burden is teaching the virtues of cleanliness. Pears Soap is a potent factor in brightening the dark corners of the earth as civilisation advances, whilst among the cultured of all nations it holds the highest place - it is the ideal toilet soap.'

What a laugh, with our burdens and living in this dark corner, the best we can afford is carbolic soap. Pears Soap indeed, fine for them with money and highfalutin ideas."

Rab stood up, tapped out his pipe on the grate and said. "Right Mistress Law, bedroom."

Agnes followed him through into the bedroom. They quickly undressed in the chill of the room and got into bed.

Rab then lay on top of his wife and they had sex. They did not make love, no showing of care or affection, no tender kisses. There was no gentleness in this coupling. He entered her and used her, like as two animals would mate. Thankfully for Agnes the act did not last long and Rab immediately turned over and fell soundly asleep.

Agnes lay quietly in the dark, sleep would not come. She listened to the soft breathing of her daughters and knew this was now her life, she could not leave Gartsherrie. Rab, her man, had the Works and his Lodge, she had the weans and the Rows. The only bright light so far was her friendship with Jessie Johnstone. And, the only thing between her and destitution was a little money, and some gold jewellery, carefully hidden in the lining of her portmanteau.

CHAPTER 2
Hogmanay 1899

Agnes, Robert and their bairns had been living with the Johnstone family for about eight months. Agnes was now familiar with the Rows and their people. It was surprising how quickly she had got used to the constant battle for cleanliness against the stoor from the Works; buying the messages at the Store or Shanks Farm; getting water from the standpipe; collecting the dross from the bing; making sure that the meals were well cooked and on time for the men at the end of their shifts.

Life on the Rows also meant that Agnes lived with the constant knowledge that nothing, but nothing, could ever be wasted. Even the sacks from the farm containing the vegetables were washed and fashioned into suits for the men to wear in the tar pit where they worked. Or sewn together in layers to make extra blankets for the bed.

As Jessie's friend, Agnes had got to know a number of the neighbours. The Murphy Family at 135. Mr Murphy was an invalid and his wife not only looked after him but cooked and cleaned for their four sons who were still living at home; the Smiths who lived opposite in 129 and who's three children played with the Johnstone bairns and Charlotte; Miss Jean Shanks at the Farm; Miss McDougall at the Store. Even Jenny Baxter, that Jessie always said was 'only eleven pence ha'penny in the shilling' did not seem too bad and Agnes always tried to make time to have a wee blether with her.

The days were fine and were often full of laughter. Jessie was a great mimic, she could do everything from the Polish, 'an I says to im, eat a yer beetroot soop'; to Miss Wilson who worked at the Works office and was ever so, ever so, gentile.   Agnes's two wee girls were thriving, alongside Jessie's brood; and although poor, they never starved.

Agnes's dread was the nights.   Unlike many of the other men in the Rows, Robert never lifted a hand to his wife, or the children. To Charlotte he often showed a little kindness and she would always run to meet him when he came home from work.

He would sometimes try to hold wee Mary's hand, but the little girl, who was as good as gold during the day with Agnes and Jessie, would invariably cry when her father came near her.

Rab was not a bad husband, he was a cold husband.   And, his word was law.   Agnes used to think, Law by name, Law by nature. Never could she argue or stand up to him.   They did not share jokes like Alex and Jessie, or enjoy the same kind of easy affection. No hand on the shoulder or compliment on her cooking for Agnes. Sex was demanded, and given, refusal was unthinkable.   But always the dread of another pregnancy, and yet another mouth to feed.

There was a great excitement in the air, this wasn't just another Hogmanay.   No, this was the moving from 1899 to 1900.   What would the new century bring for everyone living in the Rows?

Once again Britain was at War with the Boer Republic.   Some of the young men had joined up with one or other of the Scottish Regiments.   The young lads saw going to South Africa as an exciting adventure: and their mothers spent their days dreading a telegram from the dark continent.

The women's suffrage movement was getting reported more and more in the newspapers but the rights of women seemed a million miles away from daily life, as lived in the Rows.

Agnes and Jessie had been cleaning and cooking all day.   The children were to be allowed to stay up to see in the New Year, they were jumping with excitement, especially as Agnes had baked some shortbread and they were also to have bread spread with butter and home made blackberry jam at midnight and mugs of cocoa made with warm milk.   The women had been saving their pennies for weeks to buy some delicious treats to help bring in this special New

Year, a new century.

Jessie had left to go down to the Store and buy some jugs of porter for the menfolk. She was also going to buy a gill of sweet sherry wine for her and Agnes, a gill of whisky for the two men and ginger wine for the children and any visitors who called to first foot. Tradition dictated this should be someone tall, dark and handsome, to ensure good luck for the incoming year.

Agnes used the time alone to make her special little potato cakes, she grated potato, squeezed out the water and added finely chopped onion, a little flour, seasoned well and fried the little patties in beef dripping. They were delicious and Agnes only ever made them for special occasions.

Suddenly Jessie burst into the little house like a whirlwind.

"Guess what, it's Hogmanay, the end of the auld year and excellent, excellent news for the New Year. Agnes, you know that Gartsherrie Academy is full and we have been waiting for the new school to be built for what seems like forever. Well the Work has decided that meantime they will pay for two teachers to teach the weans down in the Institute.

Hurrah, oh Agnes we can leave them there in the morning on the way to the Store and take turns with Ena Smith next door collecting them. What a lot of time we are going to have; no watching they don't get into trouble and no more having to teach the wee ones ourselves when we get an odd half hour. I can't tell you how excited everyone is down at the Store. I got in quick and put the names of my three and your Charlotte down on the register.

Jessie grabbed her friend around the waist and danced her around the room. What a start to the New Year. Oh, by the way, the teachers are sisters called Miss Jennie and Miss Margaret Mathieson. I expect they are grumpy auld maids but I so don't care. They will completely change our lives."

The men returned from work and bathed in the zinc bath in front of the fire before changing into their best suits, their only suits. The children, together with Agnes and Jessie, were already washed and had changed into their Sunday best.

As the witching hour of midnight approached the children were reaching a fever pitch of excitement; people were out and about in the Rows and the tension could be felt in the air. There was the sound of an accordion playing, voices singing, people laughing and joking.

In the Johnstone home Jessie stared to sing Aye Fond Kiss in her lovely clear voice. The bairns cried, "sing more Mammie, sing Charlie, please, Charlie, come on Mamie." So Jessie and Agnes sang Charlie is my Darling and the wee ones joined in.

Alex piped up, "Enough of these Scottish Rabbie Burns songs, let's go back to where we were born in County Fermanagh. Come on Rab my auld pal, we'll have the tunes of the Eniskillen Fusiliers, so we will."

To Agnes's surprise, Rab joined with Alex, they pretended they were holding flutes and tooted the tunes. Marching around the table, the children joined in and there was much laughter in the house as the minutes towards the new century ticked past.

Suddenly there was a cacophony of noise outside, they stopped their music, sirens sounded, not one but dozens from all the different works in the town. The blasts rang out to welcome the New Year, the New Century, and what everyone hoped would herald a better and more prosperous time.

The Johnstone and Law families toasted each other, the adults sharing the quarter gills of whisky and sherry and the children ginger wine, as they welcomed in the first day of the new century. The two families kept with tradition, they all held hands and sang Auld Lang Syne together, evoking memories of the past and hope for the future.

Agnes and Jessie dished out the food and Alex poured the mugs of porter. A knock came to the door. It was Archie Smith from next door to first foot, and wish them all a 'Guid New Year'. Thankfully he was tall and dark although handsome was stretching it a bit.

"Come in Archie my man, you'll take a drop of porter and a wee cake with us, so you will." said Alex. "As well as the New Year, our lasses are celebrating the opening of schoolrooms down at the Institute. Let's hope we all have something to celebrate in

1900 and beyond."

The noise in the Rows, the celebrations, drinking, eating and general goodwill went on long into the night, where as always the sky was lit with the glowing red of the furnace flames, an everlasting dawn or sunset, dependent on your view of life.

In the early hours of the morning, Agnes lay in bed beside Rab, who was now sated with porter and sex, fast asleep beside her.

Thoughts, aided by the sherry, came tumbling into her brain. Agnes allowed herself a little reminisce into her past, but opening that door brought silent tears. No, best to sweep those thoughts up and put them into a tidy little box, tie them up in ribbon and leave well alone, together with the gold trinkets in the portmanteau.

Think instead about the education the wee ones were going to get at the improvised school in the Gartsherrie Institute, until the new school, long promised, was built. Agnes berated herself, think safe thoughts, only think safe thoughts, for a new future, in the new century.

January 1st was a day, when apart from essential work, the great Works was missing it's thousands of ant workers. The men were at home with their families recovering or sobering up from the revelry of the night before.

Agnes and Jessie rose early, as normal, backed up the fire and prepared the porridge. As the children arose they made sure that each was quietly washed, dressed and fed. The two men they let sleep on, until they themselves were ready to waken and get up to eat. After they had eaten breakfast Alex and Rab put on their outdoor clothes and prepared to leave the house.

"We are just having a wee walk, then a meeting today with some of the lads, before the Lodge Meeting proper later tonight. Nothing for you ladies to concern yourselves about."

Alex offered by way of explanation. Rab just looked at him in amazement.

"Come on Alex, let's be away. No need to give the womenfolk reasons for what we are doing, have you gone mad man." muttered Rab under his breath.

The men set out to walk the two or three miles to The Lochs.

The stretches of water between, Gartsherrie and Gartcosh, were really the Drumpellier Lochs, part of the Drumpellier Estate. To the Gartsherrie folk they were simply, The Lochs.

As they walked out through the Rows in the quiet of the New Year morning they heard the first stirrings from the houses. Children coming out to play with their gird and cleeks; Auld Willie with his handcart selling milk to the women, ladling it into their quart enamel cans; some of the men were surfacing, looking worse for wear, after the celebrations of the previous night. The Rows were awakening to a New Year, and a New Century.

They walked in companionable silence these two hard working men. Over twenty years difference in age but they shared a religion and a country. They were both Protestant Ulstermen through and through. The other thing they shared was a childhood on the land. Neither one could fully accept that they now spent their days labouring in a tar pit, inside an iron works that looked, and sounded, like a scene from a biblical hell.

Alex broke the silence.

"The lasses put on a good show last night, so they did, Rab. They certainly did well considering how little money they have to run the house. Your Agnes makes lovely pancakes and girdle scones and those wee fried potato cakes of hers are well tasty."

Rab replied. "Aye, I'll give her that she is no a bad wee cook and she is good with the bairns, but Alex, she is a cauld, cauld wuman. A man wants more than a good meal at the end of the working day. I might as well lie over a log as lie over that one, there's nae passion for a man in her bed."

"Look Rab, I know this is your own business but you are not exactly warm to Agnes. You come in from the Works and never a pleasant word to her, she is hard working, a good cook, good mother, and right bonny. Where is she going wrong?" asked Alex.

Again they walked in silence for some minutes before Rab murmured in reply.

"She is wrong because she is not Mary Ann McGuire, that is where she is wrong. You met my beautiful Mary Ann when you lived with us in Glasgow, was there ever a more bonny, loving, Ulster lass? Do you know Alex, we had seven bairns, seven, and each of them was conceived in passion and deep deep love.

How could Agnes give and receive that kind of love with nothing but a bowl of soup and a tattie cake. Naw man, my wife, my beautiful Ulster lass died in my arms and no other will ever take her place.

But a man needs a wife and Agnes is that wife. I have given her respectability and I'll no raise a hand to her but Alex, auld pal, she is not, and never can be, my lovely Mary Ann."

"Rab, I know it is none of my business but while we are talking man to man on this new century day. Why did you call wee Mary after Mary Ann?" asked Alex.

Once again there was silence for some minutes as they walked and puffed their pipes. They were now well out in the countryside bordering the Drumpellier Estate. They stopped and looked at the beautiful snow dusted view and marveled at the fresh cleanliness of their surroundings. At last Rab spoke.

"Two reasons really. Firstly to punish Agnes, and don't ask me why Alex but I sorely wanted to punish her and her stuck up family. I wanted her to always remember who was boss in the marriage, every day of her life. But there was another reason, wee Mary is the image of my sister Mary and she has the same beautiful red Ulster hair of my Mary Ann McGuire and the green eyes, like the green County of Fermanagh. I suppose you could say she was named in Love and in Hate. Don't talk of this again Alex, it's finished. Love and Hate two sides of the same bloody coin, not that we see many coins in this damned place.

Now come on man enjoy God's good fresh air, a day away from the hell hole that is Baird's Works is a day to be relished to the full, so it is."

While the men were out Agnes and Jessie decided that they too would enjoy a day off work. The four older children, well wrapped against the cold of the day, went out to play.

The two women made tea and luxuriated in enjoying the hot drink with some shortbread while sitting in front of the fire. Mary cuddled up on her mother's knee.

"Tell me Jessie" asked Agnes. "Where do you come from originally and how come you ended up in the Rows?"

"Not much to tell really. I was born in the East End of Glasgow, when I was a toddler my Paw got a job at Clydebridge Steelworks at Cambuslang, Paw worked there as a time served tradesman. As well as looking after me Maw worked from home as a milliner so we were quite comfortably off really. I was fourteen before my wee brother Archie was born and two years later another wee boy Jimmy came along, by that time I had a job in a fancy hat shop in Rutherglen. All was well in the life of the Clark family, then there was a tragedy. Both the boys caught scarlet fever and died within days of each other. Maw never got over the loss of her wee lads and she died the following year.

After he lost my mother Paw just had to get away from Cambuslang. He got a job in Colvilles in Motherwell. I left my job in the hat shop and moved with him. I kept house for him and a lodger and I also had a job assisting the cook in a local public house that served food.

When I was about eighteen Paw met a woman called Annie, within months they were married, I never really liked her, 'too sweet to be wholesome' if you know what I mean. Around the same time our lodger left and Alex was the new lodger.

Alex and I just clicked, we were the same age and liked each other from the start. You have to admit Alex is tall and handsome, with those big blue eyes and his dark curly hair and he was a bit of an Irish charmer.

Paw was married to Annie by this time, so we just upped and married and moved here. The attraction of Gartsherrie, if you can call it that, was getting a house.

Obviously we had to take in lodgers but we always managed to pay the rent, and not a penny of debt. Alex and I have never had to do the Monday morning visit to the pawn shop.

We've had our ambitions too you know but with every year that goes past the chances of the Johnstone family moving on to greener pastures gets less and less.

What really keeps us back is Alex is only a labourer, not a time served journeyman. Unlike your Rab, he can read and write a bit, not as good as me but enough to manage. You know Agnes, the men from the bogs don't stand a chance here. What with no formal education, and so much prejudice, either religious or simply because they speak differently, they are marked men.

Another reason so many of them come here, is that there is safety in numbers, and they have somebody else to look down on. The Polish and Lithuanians are even further down the pecking order than the Irish.

Enough of our blethers we had better get the food ready before the men return, they will want fed before their Lodge meeting down at the Institute tonight."

The men returned to work the following day, the celebrations over for another year.

The first few days of January passed quickly with Jessie and Agnes spending every spare moment working with the children on their reading, writing and arithmetic. Their only aids being little slates and some sticks of chalk.

At last the great morning came Samuel, Agnes and Mary Johnstone, together with Charlotte were taken to the new temporary classrooms, which were laid out with blackboards; little desks and chairs; and a high desk and chair for the teacher.

The classrooms were made attractive for the new pupils with a number of brightly coloured friezes covering the walls, showing the letters of the alphabet, numbers, animals, birds, flowers and trees.

The children were beside themselves with excitement. Particularly Charlotte and Mary Johnstone, who were both five and had never been to school before. The pupils were divided between the two classrooms, 5 to 8 year olds and those aged 9 to 12.

The official age for leaving school was 14 but there were simply not enough resources, so until the new school was completed, those not lucky enough to go to Gartsherrie Academy, would just have to leave school aged twelve.

The Store was awash with gossip, the main subject being Miss Jennie and Miss Margaret Mathieson.

"Not the auld maids we imagined, aye" said Jessie.

"Indeed not, they are both absolutely beautiful, with all that lovely auburn hair and puff sleeve dresses; and, did you see how nice and clean and shiny their nails were. Goodness, they must be about the same age as us." said Jessie.

"Same age, but no the same worries," Agnes observed. "You can easily see they don't have men and bairns to care for, and I would guess they have a maid at home to do the cooking and cleaning for them."

"Exactly Agnes, just the way I always do for you." Jessie mimicked in a refined voice. They burst into companionable laughter.

"Well maid, this is no getting your work done, go and see that nice Mr Clark the Butcher and find our what he has cheap and tasty for soup. Or, you'll be getting your marching orders my girl." laughed Agnes.

The children soon settled into life at school. Every day they came home with homework and classroom tales. Agnes and Jessie were much relieved that the children were getting an education. The fact that Rab could neither read nor write was a sensitive subject and Agnes privately thought that part of his coldness towards her was resentment at his lack of education, and jealousy that she had attended school until she was fourteen.

Another year, a new century, not much changed, but still a little laughter and gossip to season the plain fare of life.

Now that the four children were attending the Institute School life at 130 Long Row had taken on a new routine but for Jessie and Agnes there was no respite from hard work.

CHAPTER 3
March 1900

By the March of nineteen hundred the celebrations to mark the new century seemed a distant memory to the Law and Johnstone families. It has been a hard winter, although it was now well into March it was still icy cold; the days were lengthening but spring still seemed a long way away.

The atmosphere in the house had taken on a gloomy air, as they waited for the warmth of the new season. The men worked long days and returned home at night exhausted and soaked through by the sleet and snow of what seemed, a never-ending winter.

Mary's first birthday passed with only a small celebration to acknowledge the day. Agnes made some pancakes for the children coming home from school and they all gathered around the baby to sing a birthday song. Jessie and Agnes cleared up the evidence of this small celebration and all was as normal, children fed and in bed, before the men came home. Alex, with his jolly nature, would have enjoyed sharing the birthday happiness, but Rab's gloom mirrored the weather.

Since the New Year celebrations Rab had been sharp with the children and even more demanding of his wife. Agnes knew it was imperative that she did not anger him, every day she ensured that all his requirements were met, porridge cooked long and slow, no lumps, milk served in a separate bowl; nightshirt warmed at the fire; soup piping hot and perfectly made; water freshly boiled for his daily wash; hot bath ready when he finished Saturday shift.

The worst times for Agnes were the nights. Sometimes he took himself off to bed after his meal and was sleeping the sleep of the exhausted when Agnes crept in beside him, quiet as a mouse, always fearful of disturbing him.

Other nights he would sit gazing into the fire and smoking his clay pipe from the comfort of the chair. Without warning he would suddenly raise his eyes, look at Agnes, and say,

"Mistress Law, bed."

Three words that inevitably filled Agnes with dread.

It was Agnes's turn to take the bairns to school at the Institute and then carry on down Gartsherrie Road to the Store to buy the daily messages. They walked their usual route, down the Long Row, the children chatted, they exchanged good mornings with the neighbours, they heard the noises, they smelled the smells but for Agnes nothing in her world felt, as usual.

All she wanted to do was go back to bed, curl up and shut out the feeling of dread that was slowly enveloping her. They reached the Institute and went into the large grey granite building where Agnes took the children to their classrooms. The heat and the smell of so many children in one place seemed to hit her like a wave.

The next thing she remembered was smelling salts under her nose and a faraway voice saying . "Come now Mrs Law, you have fainted. I have sent Samuel home for his mother. Mrs Johnstone will be here shortly to help you home."

As she opened her eyes Agnes was aware of a kind concerned face looking down on her and a gentle hand stroking her face. Agnes burst into tears, that kindly gesture of compassion and care was the final straw, the secret she was holding became too much for her to bear and the tears flowed unchecked.

Thankfully she was in a little room which the Mathieson sisters' used as a staff room, so there was nobody to hear her sobbing.

A few minutes later Jessie arrived, carrying wee Mary, who was enveloped in a checked plaid shawl to keep out the winter cold.

"What's the matter with you Agnes pet, you look dreadful?" enquired Jessie.

Agnes responded by being violently sick all over the polished wooden floor. Miss Mathieson was kindness itself, saying.

"Don't worry Mrs Johnstone I'll clean up the floor."

Much to Jessie's surprise she efficiently cleaned the floor and then made a cup of tea for everyone.

As they drank the welcome brew Miss Mathieson asked in a matter of fact voice.

"Mrs Law, are you pregnant?"

Jessie was astounded, the idea of an unmarried middle class women cleaning up sick, serving her tea and then coming right out with such a question; well, it was simply beyond belief.

Fighting back another flood of tears, Agnes said.

"Yes, I am going to have a baby and I am terrified. We are just about managing at the moment but another child to feed and clothe, where will we get the money? We don't even have our own home; we lodge with Jessie and her husband Alex. We have one little room for four of us, Rab, me, Charlotte and wee Mary who is just over a year old. Rab will be pure black with anger."

Miss Mathieson stood up. "Just a minute ladies, I'll go and set the children some work, then I'll be right back."

When she left the room Jessie whispered,

"Well Agnes, who would have thought it, a school teacher like Miss Mathieson and she is so kind, calling us ladies. I'll never forget her cleaning up that sick, she knew exactly what to do. Now she is a real lady that one."

Jennie Mathieson quickly returned to the staff room. Jennie was beautiful by any standards; perfect skin; rich thick auburn hair, coiled at the back of her head; tall, five foot eight or nine with a lovely figure. Her sapphire blue eyes however seemed to take in everything and she gave off an air of quiet efficiency. The kind of teacher that children absolutely love, but would never in a million years dream of crossing.

"We'll have another cup of tea, my sister will keep an eye on both classes this morning." said Miss Mathieson, while putting the kettle over the fire to boil and brewing another pot of tea.

As she poured, Jennie insisted Agnes try and eat an arrowroot biscuit to settle her stomach. Mary sat on the floor enjoying her biscuit. And, if it had not been for the serious nature of the conversation it would have been an enjoyable tea party.

Jennie Mathieson did not beat around the bush.

"Are you absolutely sure you are pregnant Mrs Law?"

"Absolutely" Agnes replied. "I have other bairns and I know my body, I am most definitely pregnant, probably about six or seven weeks."

"Are you going to have the child?" asked Jennie.

"What else can I do, of course I'll have the bairn but Rab is going to be powerful angry." sobbed Agnes.

At this comment Jennie's blue eyes took on a steely anger.

"Look Agnes, he is the one who made you pregnant, he could abstain or he could withdraw before he impregnates you. It is his desire that has made you pregnant. His action, his responsibility.

My dear woman, if you are going to abort, do it now, before you are any further forward. There are terrible cases of women getting infections and dying from abortions carried out by old harridans with knitting needles in the later stages of pregnancy."

Agnes and Jessie listened in horror to a single woman speaking so openly. Jessie spoke up.

"Miss Mathieson, you are unmarried, obviously from a good, well educated, family. How can you know about these things or how poor women manage life in the Rows. I am lucky I have a good kind man but many of the men hereabouts are themselves bowed down by work and they take out their anger and frustration on their poor wives. If you beg my pardon saying this but, either by violence or by sex, and sometimes the two are as one."

Jennie seemed to lower her voice an octave,

"Ladies have you ever heard of the Women's Suffrage Movement?"

"Oh yes" said Jessie, "That is the organisation where the upper class women want to get the vote."

"True" said Jennie, "But it is much more than that, we want women to have rights of education; rights over their children in divorce settlements, financial rights; even the right to say no to sex in marriage, if they so wish.

A vote for the Member of Parliament of your choice is only the start. We are small in number now but our ranks are growing with each passing year.

If we do nothing life will never improve for women.

Remember ladies; it is not only poor women who suffer under the yolk. Rich woman can also suffer and many hide pain and sadness under a cloak of respectability. There can be bruises under silk and lace dresses you know.

Mrs Johnstone, who is the person who helps the women in the Rows?"

Without hesitation Jessie said,

"Mrs Millar. Mrs Millar is a widow she earns her keep by laying out bodies, helping at births and in other ways. You know Agnes, Mrs Millar from the Herriot Row, the auld body who always wears a black mutch with a wee white frill around it."

"Well, Mrs Law" said Jennie, "Are you going to consult Mrs Millar or are you going to tell your husband? The choice is entirely yours but I suggest you make it within the next few days, otherwise your vomiting and white face will make it for you.

Ladies please keep me informed and I will do anything I can to help and perhaps when things are more settled you might like to learn more about the Movement."

Agnes was still too much in shock to say very much but Jessie thanked Miss Mathieson for her care and kindness and they set off for home.

As they walked back to the wee house in the Long Row Jessie whispered to Agnes.

"Mind now, if we meet anyone sniffle and say you have a rotten cold, probably flu, coming on. The women here are no daft if you are vomiting and fainting, you are pregnant."

At last they reached the safety of number 130. They took off their shawls and Jessie set the kettle over the heat.

"Can you believe what just happened at the Institute?" said Jessie. "I certainly can't, a spinster school teacher talking about sex, and pregnancy, and suggesting you have an abortion, that was certainly a turn up for the book.

Agnes, we can talk openly now. What do you want to do about this pregnancy? Because she is right about one thing there are no secrets hereabouts."

"How do I go about ending it Jessie? I'm at my wits end; I think another baby now would just about finish me. I just couldn't bear all that pain to bring a child into the world; a child that we can't afford. And worse, to a husband who would not care a tinker's curse if I lived or died in childbirth. You know what he is like, cold as ice."

"Well if you are absolutely sure that is what you want I'll go over and see Mrs Millar." said Jessie. "The sooner the deed is done the better. But Agnes, I have got to ask you something, do you have any money? I don't know exactly but I think her potion costs about four or five shillings and I just don't have that amount of extra money."

By way of an answer Agnes went into the bedroom and pushed her arm underneath the bed, near the back wall she found her portmanteau bag. Opening it with shaking fingers she found a little tear in the lining at the bottom of the bag inside which a ten shilling note was carefully hidden.

Still shaking she returned to the living room and handed the money to Jessie, saying.

"Please Jessie, you are my only real friend in this place, I am so frightened, please go and see Mrs Millar for me."

Jessie put on her shawl and bonnet, glad that the day was dark and wet. There would be few people about to see her and possibly repeat that she had visited Mrs Millar.

"Look Agnes, I have an idea, give me Mary. I'll take the bairn, happed up in a plaid, to Mrs Millar's house. Mary will be the excuse for my visit. If I meet anyone I'll say you are both unwell with a fever."

It was only a ten-minute walk to Herriot Row. Jessie knocked on the door of number seven, praying Mrs Millar would be at home, and alone. Luck was with her; Mrs Millar opened the door and immediately ushered Jessie into her home.

"Come away in dear, what's the matter? Is the wee one unwell?" asked Ella Millar.

Jessie lowered her voice, there was nobody except her and Mrs Millar in the room but somehow the words were too private and secret to be said loudly.

"Mrs Millar you know my lodger, Mrs Law, well she is going to have another baby and well it would be better if she doesn't and well, do you have any of your special medicine?"

Mrs Millar pulled the kettle on the range, saying.

"Firstly, how far on is Mrs Law my dear?"

"Six, seven maybe eight weeks at the most." said Jessie.

"That's good, early stages are always much better, and a whole wheen safer."

Confirmed Mrs Millar, in a brisk businesslike manner.

"Honestly Jessie, you would not believe the lasses who come to me nearly at their full term. Not much I can do at the later stages, but at six or seven weeks she should miscarry naturally with a little help from the herbs. Pennyroyal in my special solution should work fine.

Now Jessie I will give you a bottle of tincture, you must give her half the medicine tomorrow morning on an empty stomach. Afterwards she can have a cup of weak tea but no food. The pains should start within three or four hours, then give her the second half of the tincture. When she bleeds it should be like a monthly but much much heavier; she will then need to rest and eat a light meal. All going well she will be as good as new in a couple of days."

"There is just one problem." said Jessie

"Her man would be furious if he knew what Agnes is going to do so I've brought wee baby Mary here today. I am going to say that she has a fever and you have given her some medicine. I am also going to tell the men that Agnes has a fever tonight."

"That sounds like a good idea, the least information the men know, the better for the women. I will give you a wee bottle with some sugary water with a taste of cold tea in it, give that to the wee one. It won't do her any harm; in fact if it helps her mother to keep her secret it will do her a lot of good.

Now Jessie I hate to ask but I am afraid pennyroyal and the other herbs don't come cheap. I have to charge you five shillings.

I know it is a lot and if you need to you can pay me in instalments, but I need two shillings today."

"No need to worry," said Jessie.

"I have your money in full." She handed over the tightly folded ten-shilling note. Mrs Millar took it and put it into a wooden biscuit barrel and gave Jessie two half crowns in change.

After Jessie had left for the Long Row Mrs Millar drew her faded red velvet curtains, which she had bought at Tinker Jimmy's Secondhand Store. They served the dual purpose of keeping out draughts and keeping out prying eyes.

The ten shilling note was carefully removed from the biscuit barrel and rolled into a cigarette shape, Mrs Millar then knelt down on the floor and carefully pushed the note inside the hem of her curtains, to join the many other ten shillings, pounds, even five pound notes in their secret hiding place.

Ella Millar was not a miser but she did think that people should always pay for her services. Her mother and grandmother had taught her well, not only about herbs and healing but about human nature. As she poked the note along Ella could almost here her granny saying. 'Mind now, always make a charge for your services. People only really appreciate what they have paid for and it gives them more confidence in your ability'.

While Mrs Millar had always taken heed of her grandmother's wise words she sometimes made an exception, and did not charge, where the medicine was for a child, and she knew the parents were genuinely poverty stricken.

The next forty eight hours were tense indeed for Agnes and Jessie. They followed Mrs Millar's instructions to the letter and around eleven o'clock Agnes started to bleed, the pain started shortly afterwards. Fortunately the children were at school and talk of Mary running a fever kept the other women with small children well away.

By the time Alex and Robert came home from the Works Agnes was laying in bed with wee Mary beside her.

In her usual efficient manner. Jessie dished out the meal for the menfolk.

"I've sent Agnes to bed with Mary." she said

"The medicine to reduce the bairn's fever that I got from Mrs Millar seems to be working, they are much better tonight, but I thought it might be an idea to keep Charlotte with my brood for another night. I'll just take a wee bowl of broth through the room for Agnes, she has been demented with worry about baby Mary."

The rouse worked, Rab slept alone in the girls bed, while Agnes cuddled Mary in the marital bed.

Sleep did not come easily for Agnes she spent most of the night crying silent tears. A few hours sleep in the early hours of the morning was not enough to hide her pain, mental as well as physical. Rab had no problem believing she was indeed a sick woman nursing a sick child.

Jessie got up and made the men's breakfast, she too had passed a sleepless night. With the menfolk safely off to work she fed the bairns and walked them down to school.

After she had taken the children into the classroom Jessie sought out Jennie Mathieson.

"Miss Mathieson I just wanted to thank you for all your kindness to Mrs Law and myself when her and her wee one, Mary, were taken badly with the fever."

Miss Mathieson spoke with equal formality.

"Glad to have been of assistance Mrs Johnstone. Tell me, how is Mrs Law keeping now? Well I trust."

"Much better thank you, I think the worst of her trouble is over now."

"Good, I am so pleased to hear she has recovered. Do give her my best wishes and perhaps we can have a little talk about the children when she is fully recovered."

The conversation was conducted in such a manner that nobody would ever have guessed they were discussing an illegal abortion.

Jessie quickly left the Institute and headed for the Work's Store. Whatever else was happening in her world she still needed to buy the bread and find something tasty for the soup pot.

Back in the Long Row Agnes got out of bed and started to get herself and the bed cleaned. It was all over now, time to tidy up and get on with life in the Rows.

Jessie burst into the house calling.

"Guess what Agnes, I got a sheep's heed from the Store Butcher, Mr Clark. Great what a wee bit of eye fluttering will do, and it wisnae the sheep's eye either.

Luckily I cleaned out the big pot this morning, a whole heed will keep us all well fed for days and days.

And, another thing, that Miss Mathieson was real nice this morning, and she said she wants to see us about the bairns. Bairns my foot, she wants to recruit us for her Suffrage Movement, if I'm not mistaken."

"We can't possibly get involved in any kind of Suffrage Movement." said Agnes.

"The men would kill us if they found out, besides when would we get time to march through the streets carrying banners?"

"Why not?" replied Jessie. "The men have been making a complete muck of things for years. I bet you and me could do better. I think we should talk to Miss Jennie Mathieson. As well as telling us about her Suffrage Movement maybe she could tell us how to get our nails nice and polished and looking like hers."

They both laughed aloud.

Despite the laughter, the seed was sewn in Jessie's mind with regard to getting involved in the Suffrage Movement. Without saying much to Agnes she kept thinking about the conversation with Jennie. Much as she tried to put it out of her mind, at unexpected moments the seed would worry her, like a pebble in her shoe. Eventually she decided to speak to Jennie Mathieson on the subject.

One morning, after dropping off the children, she bucked up her courage and spoke to Jennie. Jessie had rehearsed all sorts of ways to approach the school teacher, but when the moment finally came she simply said.

"Miss Mathieson I was just wondering if I could have a word with you regarding Samuel's reading homework?"

Jennie instinctively knew the real purpose of the request. "Certainly Mrs Johnstone, if you would like to step into the staff room I would be pleased to have a word with you."

Jessie wasn't quite sure how to start the conversation so she just jumped in.

"Miss Mathieson all those things you said when Agnes had her trouble, well I can't get them out of my mind. I would love to get involved with your movement but it is difficult. My man is quite easy going and I think he would agree to me going to a meeting, just as long as his mates at the Work did not find out. But Rab, Agnes's man, now he is quite another story. There is no way he would let her disappear to meetings. In his opinion he is boss and he makes every decision in their family.

Agnes is a very clever lass, but she hides it to keep the peace. Sad isn't it, that's why I would love to join your Movement for all the women like Agnes in Gartsherrie, in fact for all the women like Agnes in Scotland."

"Well spoken" said Jennie.

"Mrs Johnstone you are exactly the kind of lady we need to recruit to our ranks, not in ones and twos but in their hundreds, thousands even. It is the only way to progress. At the moment most woman who become involved are middle class and have received a decent education, also very often their fathers and mothers even husbands actively support them. My own father is a great advocate of Women's Suffrage.

I know you have to get on with your work now, as do I. However, I will write my address down on a piece of paper. A small group of ladies are meeting at our home on Saturday morning around ten o'clock. If you can, please join us. I promise you will get a warm welcome, there will be no pressure to join but at least you will get a better idea of what we are about."

Jessie lifted the paper, her heart was beating faster just at the very idea of taking a small brave step towards joining the Suffrage Movement.

As always the daily round of chores continued but over the next few days Jessie hugged her secret and whenever she had a few moments to herself she would dream of a different society, one where everyone had equal voting rights.

Jessie had told nobody of her intention to attend the meeting,

not even Agnes.   After breakfast on Saturday morning she
announced.

"My friend Jean, the one who used to live near us with her Maw
and Paw, she married a lad from the Whifflet.   Well, I've heard she
is not keeping very well and I just thought I would take a wee trip
over to see her.

Agnes, do you think you could keep an eye on the bairns for me
for a couple of hours and if I give you the money will you go down
and pay the Store bill?"

Agnes, immediately agreed, saying.

"Aye, of course I will, and while I am there I'll get some link
sausages and stew them with onion gravy for the meal today, if that's
fine with you.   Don't worry about things here, just have a good visit
with your pal."

Jessie wrapped her shawl around her and set off on her adventure.   Through the Rows, past Shanks Farm and up the hill to the
leafy suburb of Blairhill, where the Miss Mathiesons' lived with their
parents.   Her heart was beating ten to the dozen but she was determined to go to at least one meeting of the Suffrage Movement.

Eventually she found the house and rang the brass door pull.
Jennie Mathieson answered, saying.

"Welcome, welcome Mrs Johnstone, do come through to the
morning room.   My sister is just making some tea."

Jennie led Jessie through to a lovely room, decorated in a pretty
shade of Wedgwood blue with fine mahogany furniture and heavy
dark blue drapes.

Four ladies had already arrived; Jessie was astounded to see that
two of their number were known to her, Miss McDougall from the
Work's Store and Miss Jean Shanks from the farm.

Margaret brought in a tray of tea and biscuits, saying

"We'll all drink a cup now while we chat, as this is just an informal meeting.   Setting the tea tray on a mahogany side table she
handed the ladies tea in fine china cups and saucers."

Jennie opened the proceedings by saying.

"Ladies, firstly you will have noticed we never have any maids
working when we have meetings in the house, this is to provide local

ladies with a measure of discretion, should they not want their families to know they are attending a meeting of the Suffrage Movement in our home.

Jessie, Mrs Johnstone, has never had any involvement with our aims in the past so I think before we start I would like to give her a little background.

As far back as 1893 women over twenty one have been extended voting rights in New Zealand, a year later the same right was granted in Southern Australia. Some of the American States granted women voting rights considerably earlier. Without the right to vote women cannot determine who will govern and have a say in the legislation passed in Parliament. We, the so called Mother Country are far from being granted the franchise, very far indeed.

Our group in Coatbridge are not only interested in obtaining the vote, we are also interested in the next step, generally improving the rights of women in society.

The National Union of Women's Suffrage Societies was founded in 1897 as an umbrella to the many small local groups with the same aims. The union is led by a lady called Millicent Fawcett; she believes that the best way to attain suffrage is by campaigning through petitions, having meetings and issuing leaflets to encourage people to talk about women's rights, in a nutshell working and campaigning through peaceful routes.

Now we need to talk about recruitment within our branch. In this area of Lanarkshire we are having difficulty recruiting for two main reasons.

As you probably all know many ladies in our movement nationally are from the ranks of the middle and upper classes. In the Coatbridge area the population is mainly working class. The small amount of middle class ladies who live here tend to take the attitude that they are pillars of the community and they don't want to rock the boat. In fact, with few exceptions, they are actively against suffrage in any form.

The movement needs as it's backbone sensible working class women who want to fight for better rights not only for themselves but for their daughters, and for that matter, their sons. Human rights should extend to a fair and just life for all.

As we have two new ladies here this morning, I thought it would be useful if we each say a few words explaining who we are and what we hope to gain from the Suffrage Movement."

Margaret opened the proceedings by speaking on behalf of her and Jennie.

"My sister and I have been very lucky we enjoyed a good education and are now able to work as school teachers. Our parents, particularly my father, have always encouraged us to think of others as well as ourselves. However what we can do as individuals is very small and in the scheme of things will not make a huge difference to the society in which we live. The only way to make meaningful and lasting change is through the parliamentary system, in other words, the ballot box.

As a family the Mathiesons' believe that the vote is only the first step and then the really hard work begins. We must change legislation which keeps women downtrodden and dependent on the will of men.

Now Jean can you please say a few words."

Jessie had known Jean Shanks for many years and always saw her simply as the kind lady, the farmer's sister, who sold her vegetables. Jean's emotional words both shocked and saddened Jessie.

"I was brought up on a farm with my younger brother and two elder sisters. As children all four of us were expected to labour equally hard on the farm as well as carry out our school work. We were given no options on further education or what type of work we would like to do. As soon as we finished school we all worked full time on the farm.

Sadly, my eldest sister died of diphtheria when she was in her early twenties. My other sister married a farmer's son from an adjoining farm. It wasn't a love match, it was arranged by the two sets of parents much as if they had been joining the cow to the bull.

As the youngest girl I was required to stay at home, work on the farm and look after my parents. No chance of career, marriage, or children for me. When I was in my thirties my parents died within a few years of each other. My brother, Archie, inherited the farm, the house, the animals, everything, lock stock and barrel. My sister and I got the princely sum of five pounds each, can you believe, five pounds the price for a lost life.

So here I am at fifty, a spinster, totally dependent on my brother and his wife for a home and work. And, do I work, sixty hours a week at least. Do I get paid? Do I hell. I get my board and lodging and five shillings a week pocket money.

Can you not wonder I support the Suffrage Movement with all of my heart and soul."

The next woman to speak was a smartly dressed, thin bird like woman in her sixties.

"I am Isa Fullerton and if my late husband was still alive I would certainly not be sitting here. George was a thoroughly pompous nasty little man. His public face was George the prosperous grocer, hail fellow well met. In the privacy of his home he was a wife beating nasty little piece of work. I had two daughters by him and he never forgave me for not giving him two sons.

Thankfully both my lasses married decent men, one was widowed early in her marriage and is now financially independent and a keen supporter of the movement. The other is also a member, with the full support of her husband.

When George died I was thoroughly glad to be rid of him. Encouraged by my girls I have joined the Suffrage Movement in the hope other woman will be spared the violence I was subjected to for nearly forty years. I could not leave him, to have done so would have been saying goodbye to my wee girls.

The movement must, absolutely must, grow in strength."

Miss McDougall then told her story. Clever at school she would have loved to go to university and study. The family were not particularly rich but they sacrificed to send her younger brother, who was not nearly as bright as her, to Glasgow University to study as an engineer. He then graduated, promptly emigrated to America, married a girl from New York, and was now enjoying a successful career. Her final words brought tears to Jessie's eyes.

"And me, me. I am a spinster, in a boring job at the Store, providing for elderly parents. My brother, what of him? Him and his fancy American wife send a letter at Christmas with a calendar depicting American States. And, you know what? He is still the wonderful golden son, and I am the tin daughter. Do you wonder why I want to be part of the Movement."

Jennie then addressed Jessie.

"I know this is your first step towards involvement with the Suffrage Movement but would you like to say a few words Jessie?"

Afterwards Jessie was not sure where she found the words or the courage to speak but her thoughts just tumbled out.

"My name is Jessie Johnstone and I live in the Gartsherrie Rows. Listening to you ladies has made me realise how very lucky I am. I have a decent husband who would do anything for me and for our three children. Our problems are to do with poverty, through lack of education and opportunity in life.

I can't tell you all the reasons for my attendance this morning because they involve other people. However, just being here today has made me realise that the Suffrage Movement has to be about a lot more than getting the vote. After we get it we have to use it for the benefit of all, starting with woman.

My mother used to say, 'the hand that rocks the cradle rules the world'. As women we must all try our best to rock the cradle for our daughters equally with our sons."

The final woman to speak was tall, plainly dressed, without ornament. Her hair was pulled back in a tight bun and she was wearing gold rimmed spectacles.

Jessie, who missed nothing, thought 'If that girl made an effort she would be quite attractive, but she doesn't give a biscuit how she looks'.

"My name is Elizabeth Agatha Wallis-Banks. Liz to my friends. I have received an excellent education, mainly because my mother was widowed at an early age so there was no male interference in our household.

I have done all the work necessary for degrees in English and Philosophy but I have never attended a degree ceremony. Why, because a woman does not graduate as a man does. A woman going to university is treated as someone who wants an intellectual hobby, her efforts are not considered automatic entrée into a worthwhile career. In the rarified world of academia there is absolutely no place for women.

The Suffrage Movement must become more vocal in society, we have to become a force to be reckoned with otherwise it is going to take another fifty years before we get the vote, never mind learn how to use it effectively."

Jennie then took the floor.

"Thank you ladies for allowing our two new ladies, Jessie and Liz to know a little bit about our backgrounds and aims.

We must have a serious recruitment campaign in Coatbridge. At the moment we have around forty members, ten of that number must maintain considerable discretion regarding their involvement. Their families, or more particularly husbands and in one case father, would severely disapprove.

Ladies, I want you to please think about ways in which we can galvanise the women of Coatbridge. Next Saturday we will reconvene at the same time and place. The meeting will be open to as many members as can attend.

I will go through to the kitchen now and make a fresh pot of tea, before you all go out into the cold. Once again ladies, thank you for your support of the Women's Suffrage Movement."

While Jennie and Margaret made the tea the other women chatted amongst themselves.

The two newest recruits to the Coatbridge Branch were polar opposites. In normal life they would have had absolutely nothing in common, neither class, financial position, intellect or education. Liz approached Jessie.

"It was interesting to hear you say that you had a good marriage Jessie, a great many women join because they have dominating husbands or fathers, or are simply men haters.

I was involved in the movement when I was at Oxford. I can hear you thinking, Oxford is a long way from Coatbridge. Well I have moved back here because my mother has had a stroke and I felt I had to provide some support for her while I am studying for my doctorate. It was mother's financial support which enabled me to get an education in the first place, so the least I can do is be around when she needs a bit of help.

You were reluctant to openly state your reasons for coming along today. I am not involved in your community so would you like to tell me why, in the strictest confidence of course."

Jessie lowered her voice.

"Liz, without being specific I have watched friends having abortions, or struggling with umpteen weans because their husbands are too damned inconsiderate. I won't say any more, but I am sure you get the idea."

Just then Jennie and Margaret brought in the tea. The conversation became general as the ladies all drank a cup of tea and then left the comfort and warmth of the Mathieson household in Blairhill, and made their way back to their own homes.

Jessie was emotionally drained by the time she turned the handle of number 130 Long Row.

Agnes called out to her.

"That you Jessie? Are you in need of a cuppa? I got the messages down at the Store and the sausages are simmering away nicely on the range."

Jessie replied.

"No thanks Agnes but I do have a bit of a headache. Would you mind if I lie down in your room for an hour or so to draw myself together?"

Jessie lay on the bed and let all the words she had heard over the last few hours overwhelm her. The knowledge of how other women felt about their lot in life, women she had known for years, and yet did not know. Round and round the thoughts chased each other, Jessie simply could not find an oasis of calm.

Eventually Jessie heard the sound of Alex and Rab returning home from their Saturday shift. Not wanting questions to be asked she came through to the kitchen but used the excuse of the headache not to eat a meal with the family.

"The food smells lovely Agnes but I think I'll just have a wee cup of tea and then I think I'll go out for a walk, sometimes the fresh air helps."

Later that night while laying in bed beside Alex, with the children sound asleep in the other bed, Jessie whispered to her husband. "Alex I've got something to tell you about today. I didn't have a headache, it was just that my brain was all of a confused muddle."

"Jessie my sweetheart, your brain is never in a muddle, you are the sensible Glasgow lass, I'm the Ulster romantic with the head full of dreams and muddle." whispered Alex.

"Alex love, I'm going to tell you something, we've never had any secrets from each other, and I don't intend to start now. However, you must promise me you won't tell Rab and Agnes, especially not Rab."

Jessie poured out her heart to her husband, she told him everything that had transpired at the meeting in Blairhill, missed nothing out.

"Alex, can I get involved with the Suffrage Movement?"

He put his arms gently around her and whispered.

"Jessie my love, you must do what you think is right, you are my darl'n lass. Now cuddle up and give your Alex a kiss.

CHAPTER 4
October 1901

Now that Mary was a toddler and the other children were spending most of the day at school Agnes and Jessie sometimes went to the bing to collect the dross together.   It was more companionable and gave them an opportunity to have a good blether, away from the men and the bairns.   One day as they were shoveling dross into the bogie Jessie spoke out.

"Agnes you are a lot quieter than usual, knowing you like I do, I have to ask you the question, but I think I already know the answer.

Agnes Law, are you expecting again, because there is no fooling me. You don't need to answer me, I know by the look on your face I am right.   Oh lass, how far are you on?   And, do you want another visit to Mrs Millar?"

"You miss nothing Jessie Johnstone, and yes, I'm going to have another bairn." confirmed Agnes.

"Tell me Jessie, how did you and Alex manage to stop at three weans?   I can hear you two canoodling from our room sometimes, so you can't have given up entirely." enquired Agnes.

"Easy" said Jessie.   "Just marry a considerate man. We stop before completing and if he does go inside me he comes out before he discharges.   We have been doing that for years and no more wee Johnstone bairns.   But Agnes, I can't see you ever asking Rab to behave like my Alex."

"You are so right" laughed Agnes.

"Can you imagine me saying that we should only cuddle, he would explode."

"That is the whole point." said Jessie. "He is no meant to explode, just enjoy the canoodling."

They both burst out laughing.

"What funny Ma?" asked wee Mary.

"Nothing my wee lamb, nothing at all." Her mother replied.

"Seriously Agnes," asked Jessie, "What are you going to do about this pregnancy?"

Agnes thought for a few moments and then replied.

"Jessie I don't have any money left, I have used the other five shillings I had in the portmanteau. You know what Rab is like, I never get my hands on any cash. Rab pays Alex our rent and dig money directly, the only money I ever get is a few coppers to buy slate pencils for Charlotte or suchlike, and I needed wool to knit the girls socks and wintergreen ointment and other odds and ends, the money just seemed to go.

You know I was a widow when I married Rab, well the only thing I have of any value is my gold band from my first husband. I would never sell his wedding ring to pay for an abortion, that is one thing I would never do."

However Agnes did not mention to Jessie her other treasure hidden in the portmanteau, the little pendant on the golden chain.

"I could let you borrow the money" said Jessie. "The only problem is I would need it back. I could not explain a missing five shillings to Alex, one bob maybe but not five besides Mrs Millar may have increased her charges for all we know."

"So there is no option, I have to give birth to another Law bairn, another life that we can scarcely afford to feed. You know Jessie, there is not a day goes past that I don't wish I would have a miscarriage. Having said that, I felt really bad about getting rid of the baby the last time, so maybe it is just as well that the decision is out of my hands."

A few days later when Agnes bucked up the courage to tell Rab about her pregnancy his reaction was unexpected.

"Aboot time too, so it is, there was me thinking I had not done my duty by you Mistress Law. I hope you give me a wee laddie this time."

The weeks wore into months and with her growing belly Agnes felt a growing tiredness.   She knew better than to complain to Rab and if it had not been for Jessie taking on more than her fair share of the household duties she did not know how she would have managed.

The New Year came and went, they bought porter and ginger wine, Agnes made shortbread but somehow there was not the jollity there had been at the turn of the century when everyone felt that moving into the twentieth century would bring better times.

The death of Queen Victoria in January 1901 had truly seen the end if the nineteenth century.   The Coronation of Edward VII and Queen Alexandra in August 1901, after being postponed from the June due to his ill health, heralded in the Edwardian era.

However, bells to see out 1901 had not brought any real change for the better to the lives of the Law and Johnstone families and they did not expect that their lot in life would greatly improve.

Agnes had worked out that her confinement date should be around mid April, a springtime baby.

One cold morning at the beginning of March 1902 Jessie returned with the shopping to find Agnes crying her heart out. Jessie put her arm around her.

"What on earth is the matter Agnes? I know you haven't been feeling great but there is no need to cry so sore."

"Oh Jessie I just feel all wrong and I also feel I desperately want to see my mother. I haven't laid eyes on her since coming to Gartsherrie and my heart says I must get in touch with her.

What do you think I should do?"

"If that is how you feel there is only one thing to do," advised Jessie "write a letter and I'll run down to the box at the Store and post it off for you. I'm sure your mother will come and see you Agnes. I'll go and look out a pen and paper right away."

Jessie found the writing paper, a pen and a bottle of ink and gave them to Agnes but she just dissolved into fresh floods of tears.

"Jessie, will you write to her for me, please?"

So Jessie wrote.

Dear Mrs Neilson
I am writing to you on behalf of your daughter, Agnes.
I am very concerned for her health. Agnes is pregnant
and she is most unwell.
We live at:
130 Long Row, Gartsherrie, Coatbridge.
Your grandchildren, Charlotte and Mary are doing
well.
I would be really grateful if you would contact me as
soon as possible.
Yours sincerely
Jessie Johnstone

Jessie got Agnes to address the envelope, wrapped her shawl around her and quickly ran down to the Store to post the letter.

The following afternoon by the last post a letter arrived addressed to Jessie.

Dear Mrs Johnstone
I was most concerned to receive your letter yesterday
evening.
However, you do not mention in your letter the situation
with regard to my daughter's husband.
While I would be happy to assist my daughter at her
confinement I fear that Mr Law would not welcome
me.
If Robert Law is agreeable I will certainly come to
Gartsherrie.
Thank you for your concern.
Yours sincerely
Martha Neilson

"Well Agnes, that is plain enough. Your Maw obviously has a real measure of Rab. So what do you want me to do now? I can hardly write to the poor woman and say. 'Your son-in-law Robert will give you a grand welcome', when we both know full well that he certainly won't."

Agnes confided to Jessie the feeling that had been haunting her since the New Year.

"I'm beyond caring about me now, all I can think about is the care of Charlotte and Mary if anything happens to me. You have enough to look after with your own brood Jessie. I have to know that my Maw will take the girls if I die having this bairn."

"Don't talk like that Agnes, you will get through this confinement, the women will all rally round and help you." comforted Jessie.

"I know you will support me Jessie," agreed Agnes "but this time I need my own flesh and blood.

Will you please write again and tell her the truth. My mother is made of stern stuff I think she will come, in spite of Rab's attitude, besides it's your Alex's house not Rab's so as long as Alex agrees she can come, Rab can't keep her out."

Jessie got out the paper, pen and ink and started to write another letter to Glasgow.

> *Dear Mrs Neilson*
> *I have to be truthful with you and say that Robert*
> *Law will not give you a warm welcome.*
> *However, Agnes has asked me to write and stress to*
> *you her need and ask if you will come to her assistance.*
> *I am sorry to have to write to you in this manner but I*
> *had to tell you the truth of the situation.*
> *I look forward to hearing from you.*
> *Yours sincerely*
> *Jessie Johnstone*

Nothing more was heard from Agnes's mother for two days. The two women had more or less given up hope of hearing further from Mrs Neilson.

"I really thought my Maw would come out to Gartsherrie, or at least write." said Agnes, as she helped Jessie prepare the vegetables for the evening meal.

"What's for you won't go past you." said Jessie "You must just be brave."

Their conversation was interrupted by a knock at the door, then it burst open and a smaller, older version of Agnes, marched into the kitchen, carrying a large parcel wrapped in brown paper.

Agnes cried out.

"Maw, oh Maw, I am so glad you have come."

Agnes jumped up from the chair and threw her arms around her mother.

Jessie pulled the kettle over the hob and got out the brown earthenware teapot; this visitor called for the brewing of a cup of Lipton's finest.

Mrs Neilson was brutally truthful, she certainly did not miss and hit the wall.

"Now come on Agnes I told you no to marry that bugger from the bogs, but you have and we need to make the best of a bad job, you have Mary and Charlotte to think about.

Now my girl, when is your wee babby due and where will I sleep the night."

Jessie's mind had been birling ten to the dozen. She knew full well that the idea of Mrs Neilson sleeping at number 130, under the same roof as Rab was not to be tolerated.

"Mrs Neilson I am going to go and see a friend, a Mrs Millar, who is a widow woman and lives nearby. Perhaps I can arrange for you to stay with her."

Jessie pulled on her shawl and was off to Herriot Row as fast as her legs could carry her, leaving Mrs Neilson and Agnes to make the tea.

By the time she reached Mrs Millar's house and rattled the letterbox, Jessie was breathless.

Ella Millar opened the door.

"Come away in Jessie, what is wrong, has Agnes gone into an early labour?"

"If only that was all I had to worry about." bemoaned Jessie.

"Agnes's mother, a Mrs Neilson, has turned up to help Agnes at her confinement. Rab absolutely hates her and she hates him. I can't possibly let her sleep at my place, murder would be done, we would have to call out the polis's Black Maria van.

Mrs Millar, can I ask you a huge kindness.   Can Mrs Neilson sleep at your house, please?"

"There, there girl," Ella Millar comforted Jessie.   "Of course she can stay with me.   Now you get right back to the Long Row and sort out things there before the men finish their shift.   After supper bring Agnes's Maw over to my place.   In fact you might want to bring her straight over to mine, she can join me for a bite of supper. Best we give things a chance to cool down."

Jessie ran back thinking.   Jennie Mathieson is so right, the only way woman can survive in this world is by supporting each other and for as long as I live I will never forget Mrs Millar's kindness today.

By the time she arrived back at the Long Row Agnes had confided in her mother her worries about the birth and about the abortion the previous year.

Jessie ran into her house, saying

"Mrs Neilson, our friend Mrs Millar will have you to stay with her and perhaps you would like to go over now and she will give you a wee taste of supper."

Martha Neilson looked straight at Jessie with her piercing blue eyes.

"My dear, I know you have been a good friend to my Agnes and you are doing your level best in what is a difficult situation but I intend to stay here until Mr Law arrives, tell him of my presence, and then, and only then, will I take up Mrs Millar's most kind offer."

Jessie knew when she was beat.   Removing her shawl she finished getting the meal prepared, and the children ready for bed; while all the time dreading the impending confrontation.

Rab's first words on seeing Martha Neilson sitting in the Johnstone's home were.

"You auld witch I thought I'd seen the last of you in Carnarvon Street.   What the hell are you doing in my house in Gartsherrie?"

Martha stood her ground.

"Your house, your house, I think not, you couldn't provide a decent home for my girl. No, you are only staying here under the good offices of Mr and Mrs Johnstone.

I am now going to bide with a lady called Mrs Millar but I will be here for my daughter's confinement. Neither you, nor an army of Ulstermen from the bogs will stop me."

Robert was white with anger.

"Well you auld crone you are going to the right place she is another auld witch. Now take your face out of my presence."

Thankfully Alex stepped into the fray.

"Mrs Neilson, please be getting your coat and I will walk you up to Mrs Millar's home in the Herriot Row, she is a respectable lady and she will look after you, so she will."

The tiny lady left the house escorted by the tall Alex, who carried her parcel, wrapped in brown paper, under his arm.

Mrs Millar welcomed her unexpected lodger.

"Thank you Alex, Mrs Neilson will be fine now. You had better get yourself away back to the Long Row, I think you might be needed there to keep the peace."

Mrs Millar ushered Mrs Neilson into her comfortable living room, saying.

"Well this is a sorry state of affairs is it not Mrs Neilson? Don't worry we will have a wee bitty supper and everything always seems better after a nice cup of tea."

Ella Millar had prepared a tasty plate of mince, mashed potato and sliced carrot for them both, followed by tea, served in china cups with a plate of home made shortbread.

"That was absolutely delicious." said Martha. "You really are very kind to take me into your home, and me a stranger."

"Nonsense," said Ella. "Agnes and Jessie are both good lasses. I would do anything I could to help them.

However, I don't envy you having dealings with Robert Law. From what I gather he is not an evil man, in some ways quite a decent hardworking man. But as far as his family is concerned he is the boss and he will brook no interference."

"Oh, I know that is his nature" agreed Martha Neilson. "He behaves with an arrogance as though he was the Duke of

Buccleugh, and him more like the Duke of the Bogs.

Mrs Millar, Ella, I just want to see Agnes safely delivered of her wee wean and then I will get out of his life."

Ella rose, opened her press door and took out a bottle and two glasses.

"You'll join me in a wee dram Martha?   I think we might need one before this business is finished."

Back in the Long Row Robert had turned on Agnes and was berating her for allowing her mother to come to help at her confinement.

"You stupid woman, Jessie was perfectly capable of helping you at the birth but no, you had to bring that auld bitch to Gartsherrie.   You know full well what I think of her.   I tell you now Agnes Law, that's Law mind, not Neilson; get her on the train back to where she came from the morrow.   When I return from my shift I want her gone, so I do."

Agnes was in tears, the children were all upset and crying for their evening meal.   Jessie was doing her best to organise food, and children, while staying out of the argument.

When Alex returned he was furious to see neighbours hanging around outside the house, listening to the raised voices.

He stormed into his kitchen and for once in his life, the easy going Alex raised his voice.

"Enough, all of you.   I have never had folks listening to arguments outside my house.   Stop the rammy this very instant.   Jessie, lay the food on the table.   We will all eat our meat quietly, Rab and Agnes you can sort your troubles out later, in the privacy of your own room.   You must discuss what is going to happen about Mrs Neilson between yer two selves, not so as the whole of the Gartsherrie Rows can hear your private business."

Agnes rose to help Jessie dish the soup.   As she stood up the knitting which was on her knee fell to the ground and she collapsed in a heap on the stone floor.

Alex and Jessie immediately lifted Agnes and carried her into the bedroom where they laid her gently down of the bed.

Jessie turned to Alex, saying.

"I'll get her undressed. Will you please run back up to the Herriot Row and get Mrs Millar and Mrs Neilson. We are going to have a night of it. Also, tell our wee Agnes to put all the bairns into their night clothes and get them all into the beds in the kitchen."

Within half an hour the two ladies had arrived from Herriot Row; the children were all in the recess beds and Alex and Rab had gone out to walk the streets.

As Agnes had slowly regained consciousness the labour pains had set in. It was a difficult labour and the three women took turns to assist Agnes. Jessie made regular pots of tea to keep them going and at one point Mrs Millar went home to get one of her herbal concoctions.

Mrs Neilson unwrapped the parcel she had brought from Glasgow, it contained spotless white bed linen, sheets, pillow cases, bedspread; also sheets and blankets suitable for a baby's bed. Martha addressed Jessie, as she unfolded the linen.

"Whatever else my Agnes will have a clean bed. This Gartsherie place is so full of stoor from the Works I don't know how you manage to keep the bairns clean, I really don't."

Alex and Rab did not return home, having secured a lodging for the night with the family of one of their brothers from the Orange Lodge. The following morning they went straight to the Gartsherrie Works to work their shift.

After a night and day, during which Agnes endured the pains of hell, the cord was eventually cut by Martha Neilson at four o'clock the following afternoon, Agnes had endured more than eighteen hours of hard labour.

The child was born, a sickly little girl. Ella and Martha tried every skill in their armoury but the wee soul gave up her fight for life after two short days.

Meantime Agnes burned up with fever, and Jessie had to help nurse her as well as run the house and look after all the children.

The night the baby died, Rab went into the bedroom where his wife was lying exhausted and said, in a quiet, controlled voice.

"Agnes, I have decided. You will register the child into and out

of this world as Martha Osborne Law.   Martha Osborne being the
birth name of your auld witch of a mother."

Leaving his chilling words in the air, he went into the kitchen and
said.

"Alex, come on let's away out of this place full of women, I'll
buy you a glass of porter man."

Martha Neilson left Gartsherrie the following day.   Before leaving she sat with Agnes for an hour.   What was said was never spoken of but Mrs Neilson gave Agnes something else to hide away in
her portmanteau.

Ella Millar walked Martha to the railway station at Sunnyside.

The events of the past few days had drawn the women together.
Ella and Martha had formed a bond of mutual respect for each
other's medical skills and they were sorry to say goodbye.   They had
met as strangers a few days previously and now they parted as
friends.

Over the following years they carried on a regular correspondence which enabled Agnes to retain a tenuous link with her family
in Glasgow.

CHAPTER 5
April 1904

After the loss of wee Martha, Agnes fell into a depression. She became convinced that baby Martha's death was her punishment for deliberately miscarrying the previous child, and for being so angry at conceiving Martha.

Jessie tried her best to cheer her friend but her impersonations of the neighbours, or stories from the Store, no longer had the power to set them into fits of laughter.

When she discovered that she was yet again pregnant Agnes sunk further into her depression and Jessie was seriously afraid that this pregnancy would kill her.

With so much extra work Jessie, much to her chagrin, had to abandon any idea of getting seriously involved with the Suffrage Movement for the time being. Although, she continued to dream her dreams and attend the occasional meeting at the Mathieson house in Blairhill.

Agnes had about six weeks to go until the birth of the latest Law baby. It was a Friday night, the end of a long week, and the woman had finished their usual work for the day.

The meal was prepared awaiting the men returning from their shift and the two women were sitting in front of the fire. Agnes was turning the heel on a pair of socks for Charlotte and Jessie darning a pair of Samuel's socks. There was absolutely nothing to warn them of the impending change in their settled lives.

The men came in from work and immediately Rab announced.

"Well Agnes, you are getting a house of your own. The Laws'

move to Herriot Row tomorrow morning."

Agnes turned white, stammering.

"But Rab the bairn is due in a few weeks, how am I going to manage without the help of Jessie?"

"Maybe you depend too much on Jessie." Robert retorted. "I have made the arrangements, after my shift tomorrow I'll collect the keys and Alex will help us move our bits and pieces over to the new place. I have also arranged that we will have the beds, and the other furniture, of the folks who are leaving. It is done Agnes, tell the bairns in the morning."

He then proceeded to wash and eat his dinner as though absolutely nothing untoward had happened.

The following day was a nightmare for Agnes and the children. They saw their few possessions loaded on to a hand cart and pushed by Alex and Rab the ten minute walk up to Herriot Row.

The women followed on behind with the children. Growing up together the children saw themselves as a family of five and the older Johnstone children felt they were losing their two little sisters.

The house was similar in size and layout to the Johnstone's it had a small scullery, a kitchen with a range fire for cooking and heating, only here there were two bedrooms.

The house was filthy, and the grate looked as through it had never seen black lead polish. Guessing that the place would not be particularly clean Agnes had gone to the Store early in the morning and bought a supply of hard carbolic soap, soda crystals, strong disinfectant and some vinegar, together with two new scrubbing brushes a broom and an enamel bucket and basin. The money for these purchases came from some of her mother's parting gift, hoarded in the portmanteau.

"The lodgers will arrive shortly lass." announced Rab. "But you will have plenty of time to get the place ship shape clean, just like we have enjoyed at our lodgings with Alex and Jessie."

"What do you mean lodgers? Who are we going to have staying with us?" enquired Agnes.

"Don't be daft wuman, we can't possibly afford a place of our own without taking in lodgers and a man wants to be master in his home. The Johnstones' have been right good to us but it's no the same as having your own family name on the Rent Book."

Agnes knew better than to argue with him there was nothing else for it, at almost eight months pregnant, she had to set to work cleaning her new home.

Jessie and the children all helped with the backbreaking work. Both Jessie and Agnes were fearful about what their new lodgers would be like. Jessie knew full well that with the Laws moving out Alex would have arranged for new folk to move into her back room.

Meantime Robert and Alex left to take the handcart back to it's owner, who was one of their fellow brothers in the Orange Lodge. No doubt Robert would repay the favour by treating him to a pint of porter, the chosen drink of the Ulstermen, and they would share a pipe of Erinmore, their favourite pipe baccy.

It was about eight o'clock in the evening when the men returned, a bit worse for wear. The house and furniture were as clean as the women and children could make them but nonetheless Agnes was terrified that there would still be fleas in the mattresses, even although they had beaten them outside and sponged them with Lysol disinfectant.

Even with all the cleaning Agnes and Jessie knew they would still need to provide some food for the menfolk. Charlotte had peeled a large pot-full of potatoes. As soon as the men returned the women got the tatties on to boil and the slice sausages into the frying pan.

The two families ate their food together; after the meal ended the Johnstone family left to return to their home in the Long Row. And, the Laws settled down for their first night in their new home in the Herriot Row.

Agnes was sure that she would not sleep a wink with the worry of being in a strange place; and soon to have strangers staying as lodgers, not to mention a confinement in a few weeks time. However exhaustion took over and she was asleep almost before her head hit the pillow.

The following morning Rab announced he intended to work an extra shift starting at noon.

"Have my meat ready for eleven o'clock Agnes." he announced.

Putting on his tweed bunnet, muffler and jacket he went out the
door, without giving any explanation as to where he was going.

He returned around half past ten with two strange men and
introduced them to Agnes.

"These are our two new lodgers lass, Tam and Sammy Weir, they
are two brothers recently arrived from County Fermanagh. They
will have the back room, you will cook for them and do their washing. I'll give you a bit of housekeeping for the food and suchlike."

He turned round and addressed the Weir boys.

"There are two house rules, never come into my place drunk
and always respect my wife Agnes and the weans. If you don't obey
your arses will hit that cobbled road outside the house, so they will.

Now Agnes, serve the food. I've a shift to work, starting at
noon, and the boys will want a taste of your cooking, so they will."

Agnes served the meal, afterwards the three men left together.
Robert for the Works, and Tam and Sammy for a walk then a pint of
porter with the lads.

The following weeks passed in a blur of work for Agnes;
between looking after Charlotte and Mary, sorting out the new
house and looking after three men. All this in an advanced state of
pregnancy.

Perhaps all the extra work helped, but this delivery was the
opposite of the struggle she had endured with Martha. One morning, a few weeks after the move to Herriot Row, her waters broke,
and the contractions started. Agnes sent Charlotte to tell Janet, her
new next door neighbour.

Janet came running in, saying. "What can I do for you lass?
The bairn says you've started to have your baby."

"Aye, the contractions are coming quite quickly, can you get
Charlotte to go down to the Long Row and ask Jessie Johnstone to
come. And Janet, would you be kind enough to look after Mary
until the new bairn arrives?"

"Of course lass," answered Janet. "Now away into bed with
you. I'll organise the soup for the men coming home tonight, and
look after wee Mary, never fear."

Jessie arrived within half an hour and immediately put the kettle on and made some tea. They drank the tea and chatted between contractions.

"How long since you started Agnes? asked Jessie.

"The waters broke before eight o'clock this morning and the contractions started shortly afterwards. That's the twelve o'clock horn going off now, so that's about four hours."

"Well you are dilating quickly. I'm going to get Mrs Millar. I think this one is going to be quick but I would like another opinion." said Jessie, as she pulled her shawl about her and headed out to find Ella Millar.

By the time she returned with Mrs Millar it was almost over. Agnes had given birth to a handsome little boy, with a mop of coal black hair.

The women then did what had to be done to ensure the wellbeing of Agnes and the newborn child.

When Rab returned from the Works Agnes was sound asleep and the little boy was wrapped snugly and laying in a wooden box beside the bed, covered in the linen brought for Martha.

Jessie and Janet had cooked a meal for Rab and the lodgers, and got the girls ready for bed. When the three men arrived back from work the ever practical Jessie said.

"Right Rab, there is the soup and tatties, for you and the boys. The bairns have been fed and settled in bed. You must let Agnes get some sleep until she has to feed your new son. I'm away home now to see to my lot. Tell Agnes I'll come over in the morning."

With that, she drew her shawl around her and marched out. As she walked over the cobbled road home Jessie thought about the Suffrage Movement and the lot of women in the world, especially those with husbands like Rab.

In that short walk she made up her mind that she would seriously get involved in the movement, not just tinker on the outskirts, as she had done up until now.

The following morning Rab addressed Agnes.

"Well lass, I see you have given me my wee lad. I want you to register this bairn William James Law." He turned on his heel and headed off to work.

Agnes knew her confinement was now over, today she would have to get started with her work of; cooking, cleaning and washing, as well as breast feeding a new born baby.

A few days after making her decision to take a more active part in the Suffrage Movement, and after talking her feelings through with Alex, Jessie went up to Shanks farm early one morning to buy her vegetables. There was no one else around so she was able to talk openly to Jean Shanks.

"Jean the happenings I have seen in my life over the last few weeks have decided me. I want to play my part, even if it is just a wee one, in the fight for the rights of women. Even Robert Burns spoke of our rights all those years ago, The Rights of Woman, what a poem. When is the next meeting?"

Jean replied.

"Jessie a lot has been happening since you last attended a meeting. Tell you what, I have a wee sitting room for my own use at the farm. Come over tonight for a cup of tea and we can talk properly, say about eight o'clock, after you have fed the family."

Seeing another few customers arrive Jean became her normal kindly self.

"Right Mrs Johnstone, there are your tatties, roots and onions, I've put in a wee bunch of parsley, it just adds that something, don't you think. That will be a shilling please. Jessie handed over the money and took her leave.

Later that evening, with Alex's blessing, Jessie left her home and walked up to the farm.

Jean gave her a warm welcome, and ushered Jessie into her comfortable little sitting room.

"Come away in Jessie pet, it's good to see you. The kettle is on and I have a new type of biscuit in my tin, they include oats, raisins and almonds. I think you will enjoy them."

Jean disappeared into the farm kitchen, returning shortly with a groaning tea tray. She set it down on a side table, saying.

"We'll let the tea infuse for a few minutes. Now let me update you as to the goings on in the movement.

The Mathieson girls travel into Glasgow now several times a

week, we have developed a link with a group in the city, and we hope to be able to form support networks throughout Scotland.

You may have heard that last year Emmeline Pankhurst formed the Women's Social and Political Union together with her two girls, Sylvia and Christabel, this is probably the way forward, working more effectively in larger groups.

Although their methods in England are far more radical than we have previously known, they are militant and intend to take much stronger action than we would ever have previously dreamt possible in a place like Coatbridge.

As you know our group has always tried to look at the big picture on women's rights and not just at getting the vote, important as that is. The ladies in the Douglas Street Branch in Glasgow are of a similar opinion.

Our stand is, we are not simply out to organise jollies for upper class girls who have nothing better to do with their time than kick over the traces.

Unfortunately the new Pankhurst organisation is attracting a fringe group who enjoy drawing attention to themselves, rather than the cause, but that is altogether another issue which we are going to have to deal with.

Jessie, Coatbridge recruitment has not greatly improved. We get a few ladies interested and then their men find out and that's the end of that. The only women who really stay the pace are either spinsters or widows.

Well educated characters like the Mathiesons are few and far between at our branch. Coatbridge is poor, working class and full of immigrants. Can you imagine any of the Polaks or the other foreigners joining?

The Irish women aren't interested, they would rather have a glass of porter and a good fight. The only working class involvement comes from the city Scottish lasses, people like you, people with a bit of gumption and ambition. That is where we have to concentrate all of our recruitment efforts.

I think the tea will be infused now, get pouring Jessie and I'll update you on another few things."

Jessie poured the tea and the two women sat back in the comfortable chairs and enjoyed a little respite away from work, with a cup of tea and a home made biscuit, or two.

"Remember Liz?" asked Jean.   "Well her mother died last year, she is down in London at the moment, studying as usual. However, as you can imagine she has got herself involved in one of the London groups.   Every week she sends a letter which is read out at the meeting, keeping us abreast with what our English sisters are up to.   You can't imagine how encouraging her reports have been and it is wonderful to feel that we are not working in complete isolation.

We still meet on a Saturday morning at the Mathieson's home in Blairhill. In addition to the Saturday meeting we have now organised ourselves into various Committees.   Each Committee meets at a time that is suitable for the members and we give an update at the weekly meeting.   We are much more organised than we used to be, we take minutes at meetings, work to an agenda, fund raise.   Jessie lass it's exciting, join us.

Jessie could hardly believe the changes since she had last attended a meeting some eighteen months previously.

Jean's enthusiasm was infectious.   There and then, over tea and oat biscuits, Jessie decided to seriously participate in the fight for female emancipation.

When she returned home Jessie and Alex sat in front of the fire and talked, in whispers, as their three children were fast asleep in the recess bed.

"Alex love, remember when we used to talk of emigrating to Canada or America, we used to save every spare penny and watch our savings grow?" Jessie reminisced.

"Aye Jessie, I remember, and I also remember how with each wee bairn we had the dream got dimmer."

"Well Alex, I suppose I see the women's movement in the same way, it is my dream.   We wanted to go abroad for a better, a fairer life.   If we can't find the wherewithal to travel for the better life I want to try and make it happen here in Coatbridge; if not for us, for our children."

"Jessie love, I emigrated once, from Ulster to Scotland.   It brought me to you and gave me our wonderful bairns but little else. The roads here are not paved with gold, and I doubt if they are in America. I think you are right, better to make this place better than to keep cutting and running, the grass is not always greener elsewhere.

But Jessie my darl'n, it is greener in County Fermanagh, I wish to God I could show you. Oh how I would love to walk with you in Ulster, to show you the islands on Lough Earn, and the County Town of Enniskillen, home of the Fusiliers.

Jessie, your Alex is blethering, let's get back to the here and now. You must do what you think is right, I will support you one hundred percent, I just hope all the aims of your movement come to pass because it would also make for a better world for us men; despite what my auld pal Rab might think."

They both laughed, the very idea of the words Rab and the Suffrage Movement in the same sentence was ridiculous beyond belief.

Alex yawned. "Come on Jessie my love, it's time we were in bed. I have just one question about your new found enthusiasm, so I have. Does this Woman's Suffrage Movement allow canoodling?" Jessie giggled. "Come to bed my handsome husband and find out."

CHAPTER 6
January 1906

After her supper at the farm with Jean Shanks, Jessie became more and more involved with the Suffrage Movement.

Living in the Rows it was never going to be easy for Jessie to be vocal about her membership of the women's movement. However, in her quiet determined way she managed to make time to attend meetings, get elected onto the committee which worked with abused women, and still keep a discrete presence. Even her best friend, Agnes, was not aware of just how strongly she felt about the cause, and how deep was her commitment. Her only confidante was Alex, her husband, her lover, her rock.

In the lead up to the January 1906 elections there had been much excitement in the ranks of the women's movement nationally. Victory for the Liberals was considered their best hope and they desperately hoped that a change of government would lead to a change in attitude and that their demands would soon be met.

During the previous year Christabel Pankhurst and Annie Kenney had been imprisoned. There was also a concerted campaign that women belonging to the Suffrage Movement should be treated as political prisoners, this had met with mixed success and many women who had been brought up in genteel circumstances found themselves languishing in prison, or worse still, those brave enough to go on hunger strike were horribly force fed.

Liz had returned from England just before the Christmas of 1905; she arrived full of enthusiasm for the cause, and brought news of the more militant tactics being used by the Pankhurst women.

January 1906 - The newspapers carried the banner headline.

'Victory for the Liberals, Asquith new Prime Minister'

Nationally the women were delighted, they were now ready to take on the government and the protests moved up to a new level. This militarism was brought on in part by the success of women in other parts of the Empire, in obtaining the franchise.

Women in the colonies were enjoying the vote while women in the mother country in the year of 1906 were no nearer being treated as equals.

In March of 1906 the Daily Mail coined the phrase Suffragettes.

The members of the movement promptly started to call themselves SuffraGETes, as they had every intention of GETing the vote.

While Jessie's family of three children were becoming more independent, allowing her the time to fulfil her ambitions with the Movement and enabling her to add to the family income by doing millinery work from home; Agnes was still adding to her brood.

It was a beautiful morning in the month of May. Agnes knew that her time was nearly due and she had been getting organised for the laying in for some days. Sure that she was going to have a little girl this time she had made two wee dresses from some muslin bought at The Work's Emporium.

Sitting by the fire in the evenings she had embroidered the frocks with flowers, using some pretty silk thread given to her by Jennie Mathieson. James was a fine wee lad but girls were definitely less work and she fervently hoped this baby would be another girl.

Her new neighbour, Janet, had taken Charlotte and Mary to school, which was a great relief to Agnes, as she knew her labour would not be far off. There were very few vegetables left in the house and she should be going up to Shanks Farm with wee James to buy some potatoes but she simply could not find the reserves of energy needed for the short walk.

Since moving to Herriot Row, and despite her growing family, Agnes had felt lonely. Desperately missing the camaraderie of daily life with Jessie and Alex Johnstone.

James was playing in front of the range with some wooden bobbins.   Agnes just could not pull herself out of the chair.   Then she felt the familiar pain, it eased, she sat quietly for ten minutes and thought it had been her imagination.   Just as she rose to get a cup of tea she felt another labour pain and fell back into the chair. Fortunately at that moment Janet knocked and opened the front door.

"The weans are safely at...;   Oh my God Agnes, are you all right?"   Janet rushed into the room as Agnes slipped off the chair on to the floor.   Her neighbour helped her back into the chair and tried to being her out of her faint.

"Have you started?"   Without waiting for an answer she said "I'll run away doon tae the Long Row and get yer pal Jessie."

With that she disappeared.

By the time Janet returned with Jessie, the baby's head was showing.   Jessie quickly took charge, issuing orders to Janet, who obeyed without question.

When Charlotte and Mary returned from school, there was a new addition to the Law family, a beautiful little blond girl.

Rab arrived home from his shift to find Agnes sitting up in bed holding her wee baby girl wrapped in a shawl.

Uncharacteristically Rab held out his hands to hold the little bundle, saying.

"My she is a fine wee babby, so beautiful and so blond.   Well done Agnes lass."

Agnes decided to use the moment.

"Rab, this bonny wee lassie, can I call her after Jessie Johnstone? I could never have managed during the early years here in Gartsherrie without her and she has attended me at all my confinements."

"Aye lass.   Call the bairn Jessie, the Johnstones' have been good friends, it would be an honour to give the wee one the name of a fine woman like Jessie Johnstone."

Early in June Agnes made the journey to the Registrar's Office in Coatbridge.   For the first time she was going to register a Law baby with the name of her choice. Sitting in the waiting room awaiting her turn to see the Registration Clark, Agnes picked up a newspaper. She read an article about a petition containing thousands of signatures being presented to Parliament requesting that women be given the vote. A combination of the article and the thrill of registering her daughter with her chosen name made Agnes think seriously about the Suffrage Movement once again, she knew her pal Jessie Johnstone attended meetings, although she was always very secretive about her involvement.

Agnes felt that she wanted her little Jessie to grow up in a better world. A world where women, if not equal, would at least have a chance to have some control over their existence.

As she got off the Baxter's bus outside the Institute, Agnes had an impulse to go into the school and speak to Jennie Mathieson, before going to Janet's house to collect baby Jessie and her wee lad James.

Agnes tentatively knocked on the classroom door. Miss Mathieson answered. "Well how are you keeping Mrs Law? I heard that you have a beautiful little girl and you are going to call her Jessie. Would I be right in thinking she is being named after your dear friend Jessie Johnstone?"

"Yes, this bairn has my choice of name. For some reason Rab was in a really good mood when she was born and I got in quick with my choice. In fact I am just back from the Registrar's Office in Coatbridge.

When I was waiting in the office I read a newspaper article." said Agnes.

"Apparently there is an enormous petition going to Parliament demanding votes for women. Your campaign really seems to be growing in strength."

"Yes" said Jennie. "We have an ever increasing support among the ranks of the middle and upper class women nationally but what we really need is to get more grass roots support from working class women. Any chance you could get involved? You know Jessie has been coming regularly to meetings. You two are just the sort of intelligent women we need in our ranks.

Think about it Agnes, if you want to know any more come in at lunchtime any day and we can talk and have a cup of tea."

"Thanks Miss Mathieson, I'll have a wee talk with Jessie and maybe, just maybe, I'll think about getting more information.   It's been nice to talk to you, thanks."

On her way back to Herriot Row Agnes decided to nip in to see Jessie for a quick cup of tea, and tell her about her chat with Jennie Mathieson.

Jessie was in the scullery peeling vegetables when Agnes knocked and then walked straight into the house.

"Hello Jessie" called Agnes.   "Just thought I'd see if you were in for a quick cuppa before I go up the road and collect baby Jessie and James from Janet's next door."

"Always pleased for an excuse to put the kettle on.   You make the tea Agnes, and I'll just finish here, I'm nearly done in any case."

They sat down with their cups of tea and Agnes told Jessie about her trip into the Registrar's Office in Coatbridge and her chat with Miss Mathieson on the way home.

"Do you think I could find a way to get involved in the Suffrage Movement?" Agnes asked.

"I am so angry today, I bloody well think you should be out there carrying a banner supporting Woman's Suffrage." replied Jessie.

"What are you so angry about, it's no like you to be angry, you are usually the one who always sees the best in everything." Agnes responded.

"I take it then that you haven't been to the Store this morning, and you don't know the dreadful news, Agnes.   Well, there is no best in this I can tell you.

You know that wee quiet girl with the pigtails, Emma Hart, she would be about fourteen or fifteen.   The family come from Heather Row, the mother is a pale faced wee woman, with umpteen weans. The father is a big man and apparently not feart to use his belt.   It appears that his belt was not the only tool he was using.   He was abusing his lass, not just hitting her, using her.   The poor bairn could take no more and committed suicide.   That wee lass jumped off the bridge into the canal.

If that isn't a reason to get involved in a movement for the rights of women, I don't know what is."

"My God Jessie, that man committed an unforgivable sin. Have the Police been contacted?" asked Agnes.

"Oh he is denying everything, apparently sitting weeping like a bairn. His wife and the other weans are too feart to speak out against him.

It appears Emma told her wee pal what was happening to her and her mother took her to tell the polis. Forby that, some of the men he works beside suspected it was going on, but that is not enough evidence for the police to take him to the jail."

"I hope he roasts in hell." said Agnes. "Jennie Mathieson is right we need power to stop this kind of wicked thing from happening. If his wife had no been so scared of him and what he would do to her and the other weans she surely would never have let him tamper with a wee lassie like Emma.

Look Jessie I have to get back now and collect wee Jessie and James. Janet has enough looking after her own two without mine as well.

Can you come up to see me tomorrow and we can have a talk about how I could get involved in Miss Mathieson's movement. It certainly won't be easy but I have to do something."

"Right you are" agreed Jessie "Now away up the road and collect your bairns. I'll see you tomorrow pal."

As Agnes hurried back to Herriot Row she met several women, whose first words were. "Agnes, have you heard?" Or "Agnes, you will never believe...." Agnes couldn't get away from them quick enough, she just didn't want to discuss such a tragedy as if it was the normal banter of everyday gossip. Even her neighbour Janet's opening words to her were.

"Agnes your bairns are both safe and sound, no like that wee Emma. Have you heard the terrible news?"

"Aye, I've heard Janet. It's just a pity that them that seemed to know what was going on didn't speak up about it at the time. There is no point in talking now with poor wee Emma Hart laying cold on a slab.

Thanks for watching the weans Janet. That's wee Jessie legal now, another Law wean.   Cheerio now, I'd better away and start the dinner, before Rab and the lodgers get back."

Charlotte and Mary arrived home from school and Agnes set about getting the four children fed and ready for bed before preparing the food for the menfolk.

The children were all settled for the night by the time Agnes was ready to serve the meal to Rab and their two lodgers.   First she served the men their soup and then the boiling beef from the soup pot with a great heap of potatoes and turnip.

"That was rare." said Tam.   "My but you're a lucky man Rab to have a beautiful wife that can cook like an angel."

"None of your Ulster patter." growled Rab.   "Besides Agnes is lucky to have a man like me who would not lay a hand on her or any of our bairns.   Not like that bastard Hart, I heard that some of the men who work at the furnaces knew what he was up to but they kept their mouths shut.   They are all feeling guilty now, so they are. I was talking to Big Wullie Murphy and the men are no going to let it rest."

Agnes said nothing, she just quietly got on with preparing the mugs of tea for the three men, while listening intently.

"I tell you this," said Rab.   "If it had been any of the Ulstermen from Fermanagh who had abused their bairn, me and the lads in the Lodge would sort him out.   Same goes if he had been a Pole or a Lithuanian; it's up to his own kind to sort him out."

Tam asked "Who are his kind in the Rows, Rab?"

"He is a Catholic, he comes from some village near Cork, so that makes it up to the lads from County Cork to deal with him. Mind, the other Irish lads wouldn't mind joining in.   Some of them are no beyond giving their wives or weans a slap or even a belting but sex with your ain wee lassie, that's something else."

After dinner the two lodgers went out for a glass of porter to a pub over in Coatbridge.

Suddenly out of the blue, Rab knocked out his pipe on the grate and said to Agnes.

"You know lass I can't get out of my head what that bastard did to his poor wee lassie. I'm going to take a walk and see if I can find out what the lads are going to do about that big bastard Hart.

Rab walked down to the Long Row, knocked on Alex's door and the two men headed down towards the Institute to find out the latest news.

They were met by Jimmy Clark and Harry Watson, two of their fellow brothers in the Lodge.

Jimmy hailed Alex and Rab.

"Guess you two are out to find out what is happening to big Hart. Well, the lads from Cork have booted him into next week. Apparently he'll no be given that poor wee wifie of his any mair bairns. He'll be lucky if he can ever pee again, so he will.

The police know full well what happened, so they are right pleased with the Cork boys. They acknowledge what the bastard did but it would have been difficult to prove. So as far as the polis are concerned, justice done.

That's the end of it now, except everyone is putting a few pennies into a collection, so that Mrs Hart can bury the wee lass decently."

A few days later Jessie called in to see Agnes. Over a cup of tea she asked.

"Agnes, did you mean what you said about getting involved in the Suffrage Movement."

Agnes answered diffidently.

"Well I did and I didn't. The men seem to have sorted out the big Hart business. Do you know I was quite proud of Rab and the stand he took on that one.

Jessie, the honest to God truth is, I don't have the nerve. I simply can't risk Rab finding out that I have attended a meeting without his permission. I know I should be brave but I just don't have your courage.

Jessie I am truly sorry but you must count me out."

A few years earlier Jessie would have snapped at Agnes and told her to get a grip of herself and show a bit of spunk. However, years of involvement with the Suffrage Movement had taught her that not every woman would find the courage to speak out against injustice. That did not necessarily mean that they did not support the aims of the movement it just meant that self preservation for themselves and their children was their higher priority.

Keeping her true feelings to herself Jessie said.

"I understand Agnes, really I do, don't give it a thought, maybe one day you will come along."

Then they talked of the increase in the price of meat at the Store, and how the children were doing at school and the new school, Gartsherrie Primary, which was presently being built, and was due to open later in the year. Ordinary, safe, conversation.

CHAPTER 7
April 1909

Agnes had a difficult pregnancy with her second son. This time she was much bigger than she had been with her previous pregnancies, she was also plagued with sickness, not just during the early months but for the whole term. It was a constant amazement to Agnes how she seemed to keep so little down and the baby seemed to get bigger by the day.

How she would have managed without wee Mary's help she just could not imagine. Although only ten she could cook and clean with the best of them and she was a real wee mother to Jessie, who was only three, and pretty as a picture.

Sitting by the fire darning, a welcome rest after another hard working day, Agnes suddenly felt an all too familiar pain; she called to her daughter.

"Mary it's started. Go down to the Long Row and ask your Auntie Jessie if she will come over later after she has fed Alex and her three. When you get back can you see to the dinner for your father and our bairns. Charlotte will help you when she gets back from her work.

After leaving school Charlotte had started work at the brickwork at Glenboig. At seven o'clock each morning several horse drawn carts came along the Rows and collected a large number of young people, including Jessie's boy Sam, and took them to their toil at the Glenboig Brickworks, it was hard graft, but it was a job, and a welcome extra income for the family.

Both Jessie and Agnes hoped that there would be an understanding between their two children and that one day when they were older they might marry.

Charlotte and Samuel were quite aware of their mothers hopes but had no intention of ever realising them. Not surprisingly, since they had grown up almost as brother and sister, and that was their feeling for each other. They used to laugh together about the idea of them wed, especially since Samuel had set his sights on a beautiful young lass who also worked at the Glenboig Brickwork.

The carts returned to the Rows in the evening around six o'clock, bringing the weary workers home, tired they might be but each young person was quietly carrying his or her own ambitions, plans and dreams for the future.

As soon as Charlotte arrived home Mary shouted.

"Charlotte the baby is coming, Auntie Jessie should be here any minute. Can you help me get James and wee Jessie fed and into bed before Paw comes home?"

Weary as she was Charlotte set to work and between her and Mary everything was ship shape before their father and Aunt Jessie arrived.

Children fed, food ready for Paw, the lodgers and themselves, Maw given tea and toast, children washed. Yes, Paw couldn't possibly have anything to complain about.

By the time Jessie arrived Agnes's contractions were every ten minutes. This was not such an easy birth as Agnes had experienced with Jessie, the contractions seemed never ending. Charlotte helped Jessie with the laying-in while Mary stayed in the background and watched in fascinated horror.

After he had eaten his meal Rab walked down to the Long Row and sat with Alex, together they smoked their clay pipes, filled with their favourite baccy, Erinmore.

"The night is wearing in Rab." said Alex "It's after two in the morning, this must be another hard birth for Agnes, not like with your wee Jessie."

At three o'clock in the morning Jessie sent Mary to ask Mrs Millar if she would come and help. Ella Millar arrived with a coat over her long flannel nightgown.

"What is wrong Jessie? It must be serious if you can't manage without me."

"It certainly is serious, the baby seems to be stuck and I just can't move it. Poor Agnes is exhausted, I don't know how much more she can take." said Jessie.

Mrs Millar went over to the sink and thoroughly washed her hands. Then she entered the bedroom to examine Agnes. Even she, who regularly attended confinements, was shocked at the state of Agnes, who was now chalk white and beaded in sweat. After her examination she whispered to Jessie.

"It's a breech birth, I don't know if I can turn it but it is the wean's only chance. If we call in the doctor at this stage he will ask his question; 'The life of the mother or the life of the child.' Normally only the Catholics say, 'the life of the child' but although he is a good Protestant you just never know with Rab, he is quite likely to say 'I want the bairn'.

We have to do our best to turn the babe around, regardless of how much it pains poor Agnes.

Before we start, Charlotte pet, run back to my house, the door is on the latch. If you go into the press on the right hand side of the fire you will see a blue glass bottle with a cork, bring it, and hurry yourself now."

Charlotte set off like the wind to carry out Mrs Millar's instructions.

Mrs Millar tried to explain to Agnes what she was about to do, but Agnes was well beyond understanding.

When Charlotte returned Agnes was given a dose from the blue bottle, they waited five minutes and then they started working on her. It was an excruciating process and only the laudanum from the blue bottle enabled Jessie and Ella Millar to make any headway. At last they pulled the baby out, and to everyone's surprise he let out a lusty cry. It was a little boy, who with his large head and broad shoulders, had made his mother suffer so much pain. Only the skill of Ella Millar had saved his life, and very possibly the life of his mother.

At around five o'clock, after Agnes and the baby had been cleaned up, Jessie returned to her home to tell Rab the news. Both men were asleep in front of the dying embers of the fire when she entered the kitchen.

"Wake up Rab, you have another son" Jessie announced. "Rab it was a real difficult birth, the wee lad is stocky built, if it hadn't been for the skill of Mrs Millar I doubt whether you would have a wife, or a son for that matter. Now take yourself home and see to your Agnes."

Rab left for Herriot Row and Jessie fell into the chair, exhausted after all the trauma of the night.

Alex said nothing, he just stood up, pulled the kettle onto the hob and made her a cup of tea.

"Drink it down lass, then go to bed." Jessie did as her man said and was deeply grateful that Alex was her husband.

Rab returned to the Herriot Row and then went into the bedroom to see his wife and child. Agnes was asleep and Charlotte was sitting cuddling her new born brother. Robert looked at the sturdy red haired child.

"Charlotte, when your mother wakes tell her this boy will be called Robert, so he will. Mary can take a day or so off school to help at home. I'll away now and get ready for my shift at the Work."

Charlotte had left for the brickwork by the time Agnes wakened however Mary told her mother of her father's decision regarding a name for her new brother.

This time it took Agnes much longer to recover from the birth and Mary had to stay off school for several weeks, not days, to help her mother.

Robert was almost a month old before Agnes felt well enough to make the journey into Coatbridge to register him.

There would be no visits to the Institute this time. The new school, Gartsherrie Primary, had opened in 1906 and Jennie and Margaret Mathieson were no longer teaching the local children.

Life had seemed so hopeful after Jessie's birth but now Agnes felt that she was nothing more than a brood mare and would probably die having yet another Law child.

Money was even tighter with a family of six to feed, as well as a new baby. Agnes seriously considered writing to her mother and asking for help but two things stopped her; her pride and memories of wee Martha's birth and death.

One morning while trying to make soup, feed a hungry baby and keep an eye on Jessie, Agnes heard a knock on the door. To her surprise, when she answered it, Jennie Mathieson was standing on the doorstep.

"Please come away in Miss Mathieson." said Agnes. "Will you take a cup of tea with me?"

"I'd be delighted to join you for a quick cup. Can I hold your baby while you get the kettle on?"

As Jennie sat holding Robert, young Jessie came over and said shyly.

"Hello, who are you, and would you like to meet my dolly?" Jennie took the little girls hand, saying. "My name is Jennie and of course I would love to meet your dolly, go and get her."

Jessie returned with a clothes peg with a face drawn on it. Mary had dressed it in a little outfit made with some scraps of material, that was Jessie's dolly.

Jennie's eyes filled with tears. Realisation dawned as to how utterly hopeless it had been to try to enlist Agnes, and some of the other women with young families living in such grinding poverty, into the Suffrage Movement.

"Mrs Law I hope you don't mind me coming to see you unannounced." said Jennie.

Agnes laughed. "Nobody is ever announced in the Rows. No privacy here Miss Mathieson. But now you are here let's drink our tea, it will be an excuse to sit down for ten minutes."

"Actually the reason I came." said Jennie "I just wanted to say Margaret and I heard you had a really bad time having your last baby. I have brought a bag of some nourishing foods to help you recover your health and strength. You really must eat well Agnes, the whole family are depending on you."

"Thank you Miss Mathieson, you are very thoughtful and I can't deny this birth has really taken it out of me. Also, Robert is a much more demanding baby than Jessie ever was. He wants to feed every few hours and I just don't have enough milk."

"If you top up your diet Agnes it will help you feed the baby and that in turn will make everything else seem so much better. Now remember use the foods to supplement your diet, not for the children.

I am sorry but I have to go Agnes, I am meeting Margaret and we are going into Glasgow to do some planning work for the Movement." Jennie made her goodbyes then headed off to the railway station to meet her sister.

After she had left Agnes examined the contents of the two large bags Jennie had left for her. They contained, four large jars of Bovril, four tins of condensed milk, four quarter pound packets of Liptons Finest tea, six large slabs of Cadburys chocolate, four packets of Arrowroot biscuits, two packets of Frys cocoa powder a tin of a new product called Horlicks, a packet of Farola and a gill of brandy.

Agnes was overcome by such generosity but what made her tears flow was, underneath the food supplies was a bottle each of rose water, almond oil and witch-hazel. It was many years since Agnes had been able to smell these feminine indulgences, never mind use them.

Knowing that Rab would not approve of any assistance given from the Mathieson sisters Agnes gathered up all the produce and carefully packed them into her portmanteau bag and pushed it back under the bed, as far back as she could reach.

The following morning Agnes had another visitor, her friend Jessie Johnstone. Jessie knocked the door, turned the handle and walked into the kitchen all in one movement. Wee Jessie ran towards her Auntie. Big Jessie gathered the bairn up in her arms saying.

"And how is my beautiful wee namesake today? Agnes, I do believe wee Jessie is the bonniest of all your bairns."

"Away Jessie, you are only saying that because she has your name. I'm real glad you came in this morning. I have some news for you, guess who called on the Law household yesterday?" asked Agnes.

"Well" replied Jessie, "Was it Janet from next door? Or, was it the new butcher's boy from the Store? Or, that daftie Jenny Baxter or, I know, I know, it was Queen Alexandra."

Agnes shouted, over her nonsense.

"Shut up silly, it was Miss Mathieson, you know, Jennie. She brought me a big bag of food, from her and Margaret, to supplement my diet while I am feeding wee greedy guts Robert.

I'll away and put on a wee pan of milk and we'll have a real treat this morning."

Agnes put some milk and water on to heat then she disappeared into the bedroom with three mugs.

Agnes and Jessie, together with wee Jessie sitting on a stool at Jessie Johnstone's feet, enjoyed Fry's cocoa and arrowroot biscuits, while Robert slept peaceably in the little wooden box that Agnes had used as a crib for all her bairns.

While Agnes and Jessie were enjoying their cocoa, a short distance away in Blairhill two other woman were enjoying a morning drink. Jennie and Margaret Mathieson were sitting in the Wedgewood blue Morning Room drinking tea from Royal Doulton china cups and enjoying home made shortbread biscuits, served by a maid called Sally.

"It was so thought provoking yesterday when I went to Herriot Row to give Agnes Law some food to supplement her diet." said Jennie.

"The last birth has really taken it out of her. Anyway, what was so moving was, you know that sweet little girl she has, Jessie, called after Jessie Johnstone. The wee thing wanted to show me her doll and it was just a dolly clothes peg with a face drawn on and some little clothes made from scraps of material. It really made me grateful for our lovely childhood."

"Yes" agreed Margaret "Mother and Father really spoiled us when you stop to think about it. China dolls with real hair and pretty dresses and petticoats. We even had a fully furnished dolls house, plenty of books, piano lessons, nice clothes. All that and a decent education thrown in for good measure.

Heavens, I hope Mother and Father never send us the bill. Talking of Mama and Papa, I hope they are enjoying their time with Aunt Anna and Uncle Herbert. Do you realise Jennie, we haven't had a letter from them for two or three days."

Just at that moment, Sally knocked the door, saying.

"Second post has just arrived, Miss Jennie, Miss Margaret."

She then presented Margaret with a little silver salver holding a number of letters, including one from their parents bearing a Harrogate postmark.

All was again well in the Mathieson household.

CHAPTER 8
December 1912

Since the night of young James Law's birth back in 1904 each
year Jessie Johnstone had become more and more involved in the
Suffragette movement. As year succeeded year the movement had
seen it's triumphs and setbacks but throughout Jessie had never lost
faith that in the long run she was doing the right thing. Surely
eventually the united efforts of thousands upon thousands, perhaps
millions of women would prevail and women would get the vote, in
what would be the first step to true female emancipation.

Men too were hoping to gain a full franchise and there was a
feeling within the country that the Government would have no
option but to extend the vote to all men, without restrictions, sooner
rather than later.

With the passing of Edward VII in 1910 and the Coronation of
his son George in June 1911 the Suffrage Movement hoped that the
reign of George V and his beautiful wife Mary would herald in an
exciting new era. So much so that around 40,000 Suffragettes from
all over the Empire and the home countries, marched in a
Coronation Pageant, many of them in regional costumes, to a rally
at the Royal Albert Hall.

By 1912 the W.S.P.U. had opted for a massive campaign of window smashing. As a result many women found themselves in
prison, hunger strikes by the Suffragettes led to cruel force feeding,
throughout the country.

However, in Gartsherrie the windows were still mainly intact
when Agnes knocked then opened the door of her friend Jessie's

home in the Long Row.

"Hello pal, I just thought I would call in on the off chance you would be in." said Agnes. "Besides I badly needed a wee walk out of the house."

Jessie welcomed her friend into her home.

"Come away in Agnes and take a seat, I'll get us both a cup of tea. You'll take a wee girdle scone, I just made them fresh this morning."

Agnes gratefully eased her bulk into the chair.

1912 had not been a easy year for her. In May she had discovered that she was once again pregnant. Agnes had hoped that her childbearing years were over with the birth of Robert but it was not to be, almost forty and yet another bairn.

"When exactly is the bairn due?" asked Jessie as she prepared the tea.

"Middle of December or thereabouts, and not a moment too soon. I'm getting too auld for all this nonsense. And besides, Rab is far too auld still to be making babies. Did you know he is over sixty now?

Seven weans by his first wife and now a fifth with me, six if you count poor wee Martha, it's not right is it?

You know Jessie the Mathieson girls were dead right, women need to take control of their own future. And, it does start with the vote. I wish to goodness I could have got more involved in their movement.

The only movement the Laws have got involved in is the Salvation Army. James and Robert never miss a Sunday and James loves going to the young peoples band practice, wee Robert is just desperate for his fifth birthday so that he can join the band with his big brother.

I was really surprised that Rab has let them get so involved in the Sally Army but he seems quite pleased that they are learning to play musical instruments.

Jessie goes with them to the Sunday School but I think she is more interested in the tea and biscuits than going to the meetings.

Our Mary sticks with the Maxwell Church and as for Charlotte she only goes to church when she takes it up her humph.

But I must tell you a laugh, I caught Jessie singing away the other day:

'Salvation Army free from sin
They all went to heaven in a corned beef tin
The corned beef tin was full to burst
So they all fell out and broke their aaaahahahaha'

James and Robert were furious with her teasing but the wee besom just laughed.

It was all I could do not to laugh as well, I just took myself off out to the coal cellar, so as I wouldn't need to give her a good telling off.

Now that the new school is opened in Gartsherrie it certainly makes life easier for me, and the bairns can all stay on until they are fourteen.

What do you think they are getting taught now? Country dancing, woodwork, art, and gym as well as the three R's. But I do miss the Mathieson sisters, don't you?"

"Talking of the Mathieson sisters. When was the last time you were down at the Store?" asked Jessie.

"Weeks ago" replied Agnes.

"Janet next door has been really good picking up bread and something at the butchers for me and if I need anything else Mary or James go down when they come home from school."

Jessie brought Agnes up to date on the latest news.

"So Agnes. you have been living in a gossip free hoosie then. Well, the gossip is that Margaret Mathieson has disappeared. Her sister Jennie says that she is away on holiday, but who goes on holiday in winter? Besides they have always been inseparable, why would Margaret go off for weeks without her sister Jennie.

You probably know that their parents both died at the beginning of the year, within months of each other.

Now, Agnes, you know what they are like at the Store, what they don't know they make up. The silly blethers have got Jennie down as a murderer, the motive being, she is now the sole inheritor of the family house and money."

Agnes couldn't believe her ears.

"The wicked auld gossips must be mad. There never walked a finer girl than Jennie Mathieson. How on earth can people make up such ridiculous stories. Let them say anything to me and I'll knock them down to size."

"I couldn't agree more." said Jessie. "It is all utter nonsense, but we can hardly go up to her door and say. 'Good morning to you Miss Mathieson and by the way did you murder your sister?' Don't be daft."

"It's not so daft Jessie" said Agnes. "You have got to agree Jennie has been right good to us. Both her and Margaret were great teachers for both our bairns and she has always given us her help and support in other ways.

No Jessie, Jennie Mathieson doesn't deserve to be badly mouthed. I am damned if I am going to let bad minded gossip circulate about her, without making her aware of it. I think we should go and see her and tell her exactly what is being said so that she can defend herself."

Jessie had every intention of informing her friend Jennie what was being said but didn't pass this information on to Agnes. Instead she asked.

"When exactly do we do this?"

"Right now." said Agnes decisively. Drink up your tea Jessie. Robert, get your coat, balaclava and muffler on, we are going out for a walk."

"Why are we going a walk Maw? It's nice and warm in Auntie Jessie's house and I've no finished my scone." moaned Robert.

"Do as you are told Robert, you really can be a wee scunner at times. All you think about is your stomach, you can eat your scone as you walk. Jessie Johnstone, get your coat on we are going a walk up to Blairhill."

Agnes mustered her troops and they were out of number 130 and on their way to Blairhill within minutes of Agnes deciding to enlighten Jennie Mathieson.

They walked up the hill, past Shanks Farm and at last reached the lovely properties in Blairhill. Red and grey sandstone edifices with lovely tree filled gardens, surrounded by walls with wrought iron fences and gates. Everything looked so green, clean and neat in this comfortable little enclave; so near and yet so far from the Gartsherrie Rows.

Agnes marched up the path to the Mathieson home and rang the brass pull doorbell. The door was answered by a young girl wearing a striped grey dress and a white mob cap.

"Can I help you?" the girl asked.

"Yes" said Agnes. "We would like to see Miss Jennie Mathieson please."

"What are your names and I will see if she is available?" asked the girl.

"Just tell her it is Mrs Law and Mrs Johnstone from the Rows that are here to see her, please." replied Agnes.

The girl disappeared upstairs.

A few minutes later Jennie ran down the stairs and warmly welcomed Agnes and Jessie into her home.

"Lovely to see you both and this must be wee Robert. Goodness how he is growing. Come away into the Morning Room and Sally will get us some tea."

Sally was instructed to prepare a tea tray while Jennie ushered Jessie and Agnes into the Morning Room.

When they were all seated Agnes was completely overawed, she looked around the beautiful room with its tasteful furnishings took in the style, then shrugged her shoulders towards Jessie.

After bravely getting them to Blairhill and into Jennie's home Agnes had completely run out of steam and was unsure of what to say or do next.

Jessie had been a frequent visitor to the Mathieson home for many years, through her involvement with the Suffrage Movement. Many times she had drank tea and debated the cause in this selfsame room, so the elegant Wedgwood blue Morning Room held no awe for her.

Agnes was completely unaware that Jessie was not in the least overawed by the house or it's opulence.

For not only had Jessie drank tea in this room she had cried tears; supported other women; participated in many discussions and planning meetings; organised demonstrations and imagined a time when women were truly emancipated, not only in the comfort of Blairhill, but in the Rows of Gartsherrie.

Jessie opened the conversation.

"I hope you don't think we are taking liberties coming to your house like this but we felt we had to speak to you about the nonsense gossip that is going around the Rows. Some people, and may I tell you, some that should know better, after all you and your sister have done for them, are saying.

Well, what they are saying, sounds too ridiculous to repeat to you in words. There is no easy way to put this to you but they are saying that you murdered your sister and your parents to get the family money. There I've said it."

Jennie burst out laughing.

"Oh Jessie, Agnes, you have no idea how you have cheered me up, what a laugh. Me murdering Margaret, if only you knew the truth. Actually the murder story is quite tame when you set it against the real truth."

The maid Sally, knocked the door, then entered the room wheeling a laden tea trolly. There was a silver pot of tea with a separate matching pot for the hot water; silver milk jug and sugar bowl, with little tongs for lifting the lump sugar; china cups and saucers and little side plates, decorated with a pretty floral design; but what made Robert's eyes light up, there were two large platters; one containing little scones and another with homemade shortbread fingers, liberally scattered with castor sugar. And, to top it off a glass of milk for him.

Robert thought it was the best day he had had in ages, first tea and a scone at Aunt Jessie's house and now here was a trolly laden with what looked like a real feast. 'Just wait till I tell Jessie and James about this' he thought.

Sally left the Morning Room and Jennie proceeded to hand around the tea and scones which had been liberally spread with farm butter and real home made strawberry jam.

Agnes bucked up all her courage and started to speak.

"I hope you don't think we have a real cheek in coming here but we just wanted you to know what stupid people were saying so that you could sort it out."

Jennie passed another scone down to Robert who was sitting with his plate on the floor, saying.

"Thank you both so much for coming. I know you are here because you genuinely care. Yes, I do have a problem and there soon will be some serious gossip about the Mathieson family but I have certainly not committed murder.

Look, I will tell you both what has happened but please do not repeat what I am going to tell you until it becomes general knowledge, and it will, you can have no fear of that.

As you probably know my mother died at the end of January from cancer and my father died about six weeks later. Father's illness was really a broken heart, my parents were very close and he just could not face life without Mama.

One of our neighbours, a single gentleman, called to pay his respects. Margaret happened to be in on her own when he called and they talked for some time. Over the following months the gentleman called regularly and soon his friendship with Margaret turned to love. They have eloped together, married in England and he has obtained a position lecturing at Cambridge."

"But that is lovely, so romantic" said Jessie. What is the problem, why can't we just tell the busybodies the truth."

"Ah but that is not the whole truth, the bit I have missed out is that the gentleman was in fact Father Martin Smith, a Roman Catholic Priest. The Priest's House for the chapel in Bank Street is just across the road from here."

Agnes and Jessie almost dropped their tea cups.

"Will he get excommunicated or defrocked or just, just flung oot the chapel?" asked Agnes in horror.

"To be perfectly honest I have no idea." replied Jennie laughing. But the Catholic Church are certainly not pleased about one of their own eloping with a Protestant.

The three of us concocted a plan together. Margaret went down to Harrogate to visit my Uncle and Aunt. Margaret told them that

she had fallen in love with Martin but that I disapproved of her
marrying so soon after our parents deaths. Martin then arrived in
Harrogate a few days later and they quietly got married from my
Uncle's house. They then travelled down to Cambridge where he
takes up his new position as a Lecturer next week.

Before he left Martin wrote to Rome renouncing the priesthood,
and left a letter for his bishop. And then, the two lovers left me to
face the music.

So there you are ladies what do you think the gossips at the
Store will make of that story?"

"Goodness you couldn't make it up for the Coatbridge & Airdrie
Advertiser. They will have a field day in Gartsherrie, they haven't
had a juicy bone of gossip like this in years. 'Catholic Priest elopes
with Protestant School Teacher'.

Is there anything Agnes and I can do?" asked Jessie.

"Not really" replied Jennie. "It was actually quite a relief to talk
about it with friends. The only other conversations I have had have
been with the Bishop's representatives. They were none too happy, I
can tell you. Interestingly they came to see me in pairs, probably
frightened to send a single one in case I seduced him." They all
laughed.

"Margaret has written me a beautiful letter. Her and Martin are
so very happy that truly I can't be angry with either of them. I just
intend to keep my head down and get on with my work."

As they talked Jennie passed more shortbread down to Robert.
'Best day ever' he thought.

"Well Miss Mathieson." said Agnes. "Jessie and I are truly sorry
to hear of your trouble, and I expect you are also missing your sister's company very much indeed. We won't say a word, but the
secret will come out soon. Don't worry we won't let anyone bad
mouth you or Margaret. The Mathieson sisters have been right
good to us and we don't forget kindness."

Jessie and Agnes stood up to leave and put on their coats.

Almost as though she could read Robert's mind working Jennie
called for Sally.

"Please make a parcel of shortbread, for my friends' other children. It's not fair if only Robert gets a treat today."

Sally returned with a parcel of the buttery shortbread to be taken home for the other children.

They then left the luxury of Jennie Mathieson's Morning Room in Blairhill and headed back, through the dreich December weather, to the Rows where brown earthenware teapots and thick pottery mugs, not silver and Royal Doulton, were the order of the day.

As expected the story leaked within a few days of Jessie and Agnes visiting Blairhill.

The Catholic version was, that a shameless Protestant hussy had lured their pure beloved priest into matrimony, except that it wasn't matrimony because, and heaven forbid, they had been married in a Protestant church, so they were now living in mortal sin.

The Protestant version was that a dirty Catholic priest had ruined the reputation of an innocent Protestant girl, the only saving grace was they were married in a Protestant church, except you could hardly count the Church of England as Protestant, too close to the Papists by far.

What they did agree on was that it was a huge scandal and the facts gave limitless opportunities for embellishment.

Agnes and Jessie did not get involved in the gossip and to be fair a number of the other women would also not hear a word against Margaret or Jennie Mathieson. The women with memories of the days of the school in the Institute and the caring acts of the two Mathieson sisters.

The weeks wore on towards the end of another year. Agnes grew even larger than she thought possible This babby was surely going to be the largest of all her children.

On 9th December she felt the all too familiar pain. Nothing else to do but make a cup of tea, while waiting for Mary to return from school with James and Jessie. Robert was playing on the floor with an assortment of metal pieces, bits of wood and stones. He turned to his mother and asked.

"Mammie can we no go and visit the nice lady with the jammy scones and shortbread again?"

Agnes answered.

"No son, that's not our life. We live in the Rows, we might not have gardens and fancy china but we are clean and respectable and we have our friends that support us, never forget that. As soon as I call your Aunt Jessie to come and help me she will, she might not be my blood sister, but she is my sister nonetheless."

Just then the door opened and Mary, James and Jessie returned from school, they ran into the kitchen, shouting and joking.

"How are you today Maw?" asked Mary, as she took Jessie's coat off and shook away the snow.

"Mary it's time. don't take your coat off, go straight down to the Long Row and ask your Aunt Jessie to come. I'll give the bairns some soup and then get myself into bed."

There followed another night of hard labour for Agnes, while Robert sat looking into the fire with Alex, both men smoking their clay pipes, packed with Erinmore.

"We have done this a fair few times Rab." said Alex. "It only seems like yesterday when I collected you and Agnes from Sunnyside Station and brought you all home to the Long Row. Charlotte was just a wee thing and Mary a tiny babby in Agnes's arms. A lot has happened since then."

"Aye" replied Rab. "A lot and bloody nothing. We are still toiling every day in the Works, coming home filthy at night with the ammonia smell on our clothes and skin. The only green grass and blue sky I see is when I am working over at the Miss Simpsons' garden, so it is. That at least gives us plenty of vegetables and tatties for the pot.

But Alex man it's no the same as spending every hour God sends in the open air. Do you know I hate that bloody Work more as each year goes past, so I do. I hope to God this is the last bairn from Agnes. I have had enough now."

"I'll bet no as much as Agnes has." said Alex. "Five weans, six pregnancies plus the one she is having right now. Rab you know the answer, stop having your way with your lass. You have enough bairns to look after you in your auld age, call a halt man."

They could hear Agnes's screams but it was too cold to go outside where the snow was laying thick on the ground, promising a white Christmas.

The baby was born around six in the morning, just as Alex and
Rab were preparing to go to their work. Jessie came through to the
kitchen and announced.

"Well Rab, you have another son. He is a big healthy lad.
Mary is just cleaning him up and then I'll bring him through for you
to see. Agnes is dog tired, at her age, and with such a long baby,
she has had a real hard time."

A few minutes later Jessie returned with the baby, wrapped in a
shawl, which had seen good service over the years. Robert
unwrapped the shawl and looked at his long, handsome son.

"Jessie tell Agnes this lad is to be called Alexander, after my
brother. Alexander Law, it's a good strong name, so it is."

With that he finished getting ready for work and left Herriot
Row to work his shift in the dank tar pit.

As soon as she had recovered from the laying-in Agnes took the
bus into Coatbridge and registered what was to be her last child,
Alexander Law.

CHAPTER 9
June 1914

Far away in a European town called Sarajevo, on the 28th day of the month of June 1914, an Austrian Archduke, Frans Ferdinand and his pregnant wife Sophia were assassinated. The repercussions from this act, perpetrated by a group calling themselves The Black Hand, caused the entire world to view a glimpse of Hell.

Meantime, the children of Gartsherrie were enjoying their holiday from school, which had started barely a week previously, in complete innocence of the cataclysmic events that were to shortly change the face of the planet, regimes would rise and empires fall.

The newspapers were full of War and talk of War. What was happening in countries and with people that the population of Gartsherrie had barely heard of, the Austrian Hungarian Empire; the old Queen Victoria's eldest grandson, Kaiser Wilhelm; The Balkans; Tsar Nicholas, Emperor Franz Josef. The talk grew louder and louder like a drum roll reaching a crescendo.

The moment when the adults living in the Rows realised that the situation was serious and a War could really be imminent was when everyday life changed for them personally.

Baird's Iron Works started to offer the men extra shifts. Not only Baird's, all the heavy industry plants were increasing production. This increase in output filtered down to the smaller foundries and engineering works, even to the small factories who supplied chemicals and suchlike.

The drums were beating faster and louder and the men and women of the Rows knew in their heart of hearts that there really was going to be a War and this War would affect them more than the Boer Wars in South Africa had ever done.

With a toddler to look after, as well as the other children, and a continuing fear of Rab ever finding out of her secret sympathy with the Women's Suffrage Movement, Agnes had steered clear of attending any meetings with Jessie.

As the likelihood of war grew the National Suffrage Movement was becoming more and more vocal. Never a day passed without articles in the press about demonstrations and protests, women chaining themselves to railings, force feeding. Women were starting to truly find their voice and even the politicians knew that the voice could not be ignored forever.

The local paper, the Airdrie and Coatbridge Advertiser, had now started to include articles about what was going on in the local branches of the movement.

With Alex's full support Jessie had now been involved in the campaign for around ten years. In the early years it was impossible for her to be an active member as she had too many commitments at home.

Now her bairns were all fully grown, working and contributing to the household, it was no longer necessary to take in lodgers and financially life was easier for the Johnstone family.

Gradually Jessie had been able to make 130 Long Row more homely, there was linoleum on the floors and the girls had made rag rugs. They had gradually bought some new furniture and Jessie had made cushions and curtains, at last a little comfort was entering into the lives of the Johnstone family.

Jessie still worked hard at home, and made a bit of welcome extra money by using her millinery skills, but her real joy was that she was now able to participate more fully in the cause.

It had been a tremendous boost to her self esteem to have been asked to Chair the Committee on Support for Abused Women a few years previously and she had recently been elected as Vice President of the Coatbridge Branch.

Alex was secretly very proud of his wife's achievements but they had an understanding that while he supported her choices she would be discreet with the neighbours. Alex dreaded the other men on his shift finding out that Jessie was such an active Suffragette, the ragging would be unbearable.

On making her way up the Herriot Row to hand some wool into Agnes, Jessie was caught by a sudden impulse to knock on Ella Millar's door.

Ella greeted her warmly.

"Come away in Jessie dear, hopefully you are no here to ask for help with yet another crisis."

"Not this time Mrs Millar, but there was something I wanted to discuss with you and that I would greatly appreciate your opinion about.

Ever sociable Ella said.

"Well before we start our blether Jessie, I'll mask a pot of tea and open my biscuit box."

They settled themselves down to enjoy their tea and biscuits. Jessie opened the conversation.

"Mrs Millar, Ella. Over the years you have helped hundreds of woman, very often from conditions and injuries inflicted by men. I was just wondering have you ever considered joining the Suffrage Movement?"

Mrs Millar burst out laughing.

"Oh Jessie pet, I think I am way too auld to go chaining myself to railings or ending up in prison. I do agree with their aims though and in my own small way I have tried to give support to the women of the Rows. I am not the only one living hereabouts who is a Suffragette in all but name. You have also given of yourself, as have many others that I could name.

But tell me lass why ask the question now? I have suspected you have been involved with the Suffragettes for years, a word here, a word there. I'm no daft you know."

"I suppose because I wanted your opinion, things are changing with all this talk of war. You must feel it's in the air Ella, for I certainly do." said Jessie.

"Yes I feel it, although there are plenty of folks that will keep going on in their own sweet way and ignore the signs, until it is all too late.

Look Jessie, If you want my honest opinion I'll give it to you."
said Ella Millar.

"I think this is going to be the opportunity of a generation, in fact
perhaps the opportunity of the century, for women to be taken seriously.
You need sensible realistic woman to come to the fore as lead-
ers. Not these rich, upper class flibbertigibbets who just want to
draw attention to themselves. Like that stupid woman who tried to
blow up Rabbie Burns cottage in Alloway, have you ever heard the
like, and her related to Lord Kitchener.
Jessie you are no flibbertigibbet. This could be your opportunity
lass. You want my advice? My advice is, grab it, the Suffragettes
must grab this chance with both hands, make yourselves indispensa-
ble to the country, then you really do have something to bargain with.
Now, Jessie Johnstone; another wee cup of tea?"
The weeks passed, daily the drumbeats rolled louder and louder.
On the 14th of August 1914 the Daily Mirror headline read;

Great Britain Declares War on Germany.

The initial reaction to the War was one of nationalistic fervor.
Thousands of young men rushed to the colours, just as they had ral-
lied to the flag for the South African campaigns, and countless wars
in the past, the boys saw it as an exciting ticket to the adventure of a
lifetime, not realising that in all probability it was their ticket to
deathtime.
It was many months before fighting started properly and even
when it did there were no large recruiting drives in the iron and steel
or mining communities, heavy industry being regarded as essential
for the war effort.
However, as the months passed, the net for recruits was flung
wider and wider.
Jessie was cutting out felt shapes for some hats she was making,
her hands were working but her thoughts were on the agenda for
the Suffragette meeting the following Friday evening, when a knock
came to the door.

The postman handed Jessie a letter in a brown envelope, addressed to Samuel Johnstone Esquire.

"Sorry Mrs Johnstone, I've seen too many of these envelopes, it's your son's call up papers." he said.

Jessie felt cold water pour over her heart. She accepted the envelope, thanked the postman, and sat down in front of the fire. The temptation was to take the damned thing and fling it into the depths of the fire and watch the flames gobble it up.

When Samuel left school he had managed to find himself a job in the Brickwork at Glenboig, at the time Jessie had been pleased that he wasn't going to be working at the Gartsherrie furnaces, where so many horrific accidents happened.

Over the past years he had worked hard and now he was a Supervisor and earning a decent wage, in fact considerably more than his father, who was still on a labourer's rate.

Fate is cruel, thought Jessie. If he had been working in the Works he would probably have been exempt from call up as his job would have been classed as, Essential War Work.

Jessie was still sitting nursing the envelope when her daughter, young Agnes came home from her work at the Co-operative offices.

What's the matter Mammie? How come you don't have the meal on, that's not like you at all."

"Agnes my dear, they've come," said Jessie, her voice almost a whisper.

"What on earth are you talking about Mammie? What has come?" asked Agnes.

"Samuel's papers have come, he will have to join the Army.

Agnes I am so bloody angry. I gave birth to that lad, I have brought him up, cooked for him, cleaned for him, loved him. Now a whole lot of daft auld men have taken us into War and I could lose my only lad. Me and how many more thousand women, and you know what Agnes, not one of us voted the government into power, we had no say whatsoever in who speaks for us.

Agnes, this War is going to change things. If we are going to win against the Hun, women will have to support the War on the home front, and for that support we will want payment, and that payment is a say in how we are governed.

You and Mary have always supported me in the movement and you have been discrete about it, because of your Paw and your jobs. But I think the time is nearly here when discretion will be a thing of the past. We will all be manning the barricades."

"Surely you mean womaning the barricades Ma." laughed her elder daughter.

"You are truly your mother's daughter." said Jessie with a smile.

"Come on lass, help me get a meal on the table, the call up papers aren't going to disappear if we all starve."

The following weeks saw not only Sam, but many other lads from Gartsherrie and the surrounding villages being waved off from the local station to journey to Maryhill Barracks in Glasgow, where they would be fitted out with uniforms and receive their basic training before being shipped off to France. The War had reached its grasping tentacles into the corner of the Empire that was the Rows of Gartsherrie.

CHAPTER 10
June 1915

The school holidays started on 19th June. James, Robert and Jessie Law came rushing home to Herriot Row, happy to have six weeks away from the classroom, and planning what they were going to do during the long summer break.

"What are you doing Maw?"asked Robert. "Are you making pancakes for our tea? "Can I have one now? Please Maw, go on, just one, please, please."

"No you are not having one, you greedy wee scallywag." Agnes snapped. "They are for tomorrow, when you are all off to help on a farm for the school holidays. As Lord Kitchener says 'Your Country Needs You'. Mind, God help it if it is depending on you Robert, you will probably eat more than you help.

Charlotte is having a week off from the brickwork to take you to the farm, it's out in the countryside near Condorrat, so it is quite a way to travel. She will work for a week, helping in the farm kitchen, then come home. You three will have four weeks on your own and then Mary will go to the farm to work for the last week and bring you all home. The pancakes are to eat on the train." explained Agnes.

Mary, who was now working with Charlotte in the brickwork, had originally come up with the farm plan, after reading an article in the Airdrie & Coatbridge Advertiser. It made a lot of sense, farms were looking for labour, so the children would be helping food production during the War. They would be paid and also receive board and lodgings. The money the children made would pay for new clothes for school, which were badly needed, and Maw would not have to feed them for six weeks. All in all a win win plan.

Mary had packed everything they would need into Maw's old portmanteau, including the pancakes, she gave Charlotte and the children instructions about the journey and their behavior, away from the discipline of home.

James, Robert and Jessie were really glad it was Charlotte who was going to accompany them on their big adventure, she was a great deal easier to manipulate than Mary and they reckoned that with Charlotte in sole charge fun times had arrived.

Charlotte walked to Sunnyside Railway Station with the children to catch a train to Kilsyth for the first part of their journey, they would then change trains and travel on the country line to Cumbernauld. When they eventually arrived at Condorrat Railway Station they would be met by someone from the farm and taken by horse drawn cart to Windy Hill Farm.

The Law youngsters boarded the steam train and settled themselves into a third class compartment. The three younger children were really excited at the adventure before them, although their mother had made it clear that they are were all going to have to work extremely hard.

The train had hardly left the station before Robert wanted to open the packet of pancakes. Charlotte, being easy going let him, he passed them around and they all started munching, savoring every tasty mouthful.

"Delicious" said Jessie, as she sucked the last crumbs from her fingers. "Maw can certainly make good pancakes. I wonder what the food will be like at the farm. What do you think Charlotte will it be as good as Ma's cooking?"

"I expect it will be fine, it had better be, or wee Robbie here will moan for the entire six weeks. And, you will have to look after him when I leave." replied Charlotte.

"Why me? James is the eldest why do I have to look after our Robert?" moaned Jessie.

"Because, wee sister, you are a girl and that's what girls do.

We look after the menfolk.   It has always been the same and it always will be, so you might as well get used to it now, and save yourself disappointment later in life."

Jessie was having none of it.

"I don't always want to be running after men, cooking and cleaning and having babies.   I want to get a good job when I leave school and earn lots of money and have lovely clothes and shoes and have my hair styled at the hairdressers."

The boys immediately started to mimic her.

"Have my hair styled by a hairdresser, oooooh."

"Shut up you horrible pair.   Charlotte how come I have to look after them? It's not fair." moaned Jessie

"It might not me fair but that's how it is Jessie Law.   So just eat your pancake and shut yourself up.   And, as for you two lads if you don't shut up and eat yours I'll give both of you a good cuff on the ears."

Charlotte regained control of her charges and the three youngsters settled down.

They reached Kilsyth, without Charlotte actually murdering anyone.   At Kilsyth they had the performance of changing trains onto the branch line for Condorrat.

Eventually they arrived and Charlotte shepherded her charges through the little country station.

The group from Gartsherrie stood outside the station as the other passengers dispersed.   Charlotte started to worry; 'What if nobody arrives to collect us, I don't even have the full fare to get them all home.' Five minutes passed, ten, fifteen.

The children had now moved beyond the restless stage and they were sitting on the ground, the boys flicking marbles.   Jessie, Jessie was dreaming of Marcel waves.

Just as panic was setting in Charlotte saw a cart, drawn by a dapple grey horse coming down the lane.   Relief poured through her, thankfully the children had not caught her earlier panic, they were just tired and bored.

"Are you the Law children?"   The young man driving the cart asked.

"Yes" said Charlotte. "Are you from Windy Hill Farm?"

"Well yes, if you are the Law children, get on board my fine chariot and I'll get you safely back to the farm. Mrs Baird, the farmer's wife will see you all right." said the driver, to the new band of workers from Gartsherrie.

He then helped them up onto the cart and they set off for the farm, the children at the rear with Charlotte sitting up-front beside the driver.

"What's your names?" the driver asked.

Robert started to speak but Charlotte quietened him.

"Shoosh Robbie. I'm Charlotte, my wee sister is called Jessie and the older boy is James and the wee red haired pest is Robert. I'm just staying for the week; my other sister Mary will come and collect them at the end of the school holidays. That's us all accounted for, now what is your name?"

"I'm Charlie Fyfe." said the young man. "I've worked for Farmer Baird since I left school at fourteen. I live in and I can do most of the jobs on the farm. The Bairds' are fairly decent folks to work for but the hours are long and the work is sure hard. The only really good thing about Windy Hill is Mrs Baird's cooking."

Jessie nudged Robert. "Hear that greedy guts you'll be fine."

"Shoosh you two," ordered Charlotte "I'm trying to find out about the farm. What kind of work exactly will we all have to do?"

"I think Mrs Baird wants you to give her a hand in the house Charlotte. With all the extra hands at harvest time she needs help with baking bread, making soup and doing the washing and ironing. The bairns will be tattie howk'n, in other words pulling up the potato harvest. I'll try and get the wee lass the job of collecting eggs and feeding the chickens and ducks. That would be nicer for her, rather than working out in the fields.

The boys will be sleeping in the barn with the other lads, there will be about twelve boys in total, some of them have already arrived and I have another trip to the station to get the others coming off the six fifteen train.

You and the lass are going to have my room and I will have to sleep in the attic. There is another lad, Bert, who normally shares the room with me but he is going to sleep in the barn, to keep an eye on all the lads."

Charlie pointed out Windy Hill Farm as it came into view on the road they were riding along. The farmhouse was a solid square house, built from blocks of grey granite, rather plain and unadorned, it looked as though it had weathered centuries of use and would stand for centuries to come, well after the present incumbents had gone to their long heavenly home.   The house was surrounded by outbuildings; an enclosed byre; an open barn; a dairy, that was kept spotlessly clean; and a number of labourers' cottages, roughcasted and lime washed white.

Charlie turned the cart off the road and along a rough track bordering the fields of potatoes. When they reached the farm yard, Charlie helped Charlotte and the children down from the cart and took them into the farm kitchen.

As they alighted from the horse drawn cart Charlotte noticed that Charlie had a brace on his right foot, giving him a pronounced limp.   Realisation dawned, 'so that's why a healthy young man hasn't been called up for service in the Army.' thought Charlotte.

"Mrs Baird" shouted Charlie.   "I've brought some mair help for the tattie howk'n."   He then introduced the four newcomers.

"Mrs Baird this is the Laws, Charlotte, James and Robert and the wee lass is Jessie."

"Hello everybody" said Mrs Baird.   Sorry I've got no time to blether just now. Charlie show the girls up to your room and take the lads out to the barn and introduce them to the other lads when they finish working.

After you have left your bag upstairs Charlotte could you and Jessie come down here and give me a hand.   Sorry to throw you in at the deep end but it has been pure mayhem here this week."

The girls quickly disposed of their bag and hurried down to the kitchen.   Where they were immediately under Mrs Baird's orders.

"Charlotte here are three blocks of sausages, can you slice and then fry them, as you get each batch done put them in the covered dish in the bottom oven of the range to keep warm. When you are finished the sausages slice these three cabbages finely and put them in that big pot. I've already washed the tatties.

Now Jessie my dear, can you take this big bowl and go into the garden, it's just through the back door. Fill the bowl with strawberries, bring them back, gently wash them, and slice them into another bowl and sprinkle with sugar.

I have made a nice big rice pudding, it's cooking in the top oven, strawberries will go fine with that. There now, dinner for the workers is organised."

Jessie didn't need a second bidding to go and pick strawberries. Working on a farm for the summer holidays was starting to look better by the minute.

Jessie ate quite a few strawberries as she picked, inside her head she chanted; 'five for the dish and one for me, five for the dish and one for me' and thought how she was going to enjoy boasting to Robert that she would be working in the farm's kitchen garden.

Everyone ate the substantial dinner sitting on benches at a long trestle table in the barn. As soon as the meal was over Mrs Baird, Charlotte and Jessie cleared away the plates back into the kitchen, washed the dishes and then started to prepare for breakfast the following morning, by soaking the oatmeal.

Mrs Baird explained to Charlotte.

"The lads work from early morning. I leave a big pot of porridge simmering and they all have a plate before they go out into the fields.

The workers all come back in around ten o'clock and we have a good cooked breakfast ready for them. Plenty of home made bread, butter, eggs, tomatoes, I also serve kidney, bacon or sausages and great mugs of steaming tea.

The men then work through until about four o'clock when I take big enamel cans of tea together with scones, or cake out to the fields. Supper is at around seven or eight o'clock.

It's too long a day for your wee brother Robert. We'll bring him back with us when we take the tea out, he can have a wee rest before we all eat our supper.

Jessie my wee dear, Charlie tells me you would like to help with the hens. In the morning I'll show you what you have to do with the poultry and that will be your main job for the summer. When you have attended to the poultry you can help me and Charlotte in the kitchen, shelling peas, buttering the scones, that kind of thing.

The men don't work on the Sabbath, apart from attending to the animals, we only keep a few cows for milk and in the summer when they give plenty I make a bit of crowdie cheese and butter. We also keep some animals for our own meat use, a few pigs and sheep and we usually raise a couple of steers every year.

Sadly, there is no day off for me, I still have to work on Sundays, there are always meals to cook and dishes to wash. We start with porridge for the men around seven and then we take the trap to church for the nine o'clock service. I do the cooked breakfast when we get back from the Kirk in the village."

When they eventually got into bed Charlotte and Jessie were so exhausted they were asleep before their heads hit the soft feather pillows.

By the time the girls came downstairs on Sunday morning Mrs Baird had the porridge on to simmer and she was slicing and coring kidney in preparation for the fried breakfast, when they returned from church.

The men and boys started to come in, a few at a time, and ate their porridge and milk at the big kitchen table. Another day was beginning at Windy Hill Farm.

James and Robert had also slept well after their long day. They had spent the night in the barn, with the other boys who were also holiday workers, laying on straw palliasses, covered with grey army style blankets. The barn was also home to a number of ferrel cats who kept the farm free of vermin in exchange for a basin of milk each day.

After the service, at the Church of Scotland Kirk in the village, everyone enjoyed the hearty Scottish farm breakfast, cooked and served by Mrs Baird and the girls.

Charlie managed to get in a few words with Charlotte, as he

helped her clear the table.

"Well Miss Charlotte from the big toon how are you enjoying working with Mrs Baird. Hard work on a farm isn't it?"

"It certainly is." replied Charlotte. But do you know what, I really like it here. Mrs Baird is very kind and although the work is hard it's better than the work I have to do at home."

"What kind of work does a pretty lass do in Gartsherrie?" asked Charlie.

Charlotte told him a little bit about her life.

"I work in a Brickwork in Glenboig and it is noisy, dirty and you never get out into the fresh air. At weekends I love to go to a dance at the Gartsherrie Institute with my younger sister Mary, but my Paw is very strict, so we have to be back home quite early.

I think I am going to enjoy my week on the farm; Jessie will be fine, I think Mrs Baird has taken a bit of a shine to her. I'm not so sure about the boys though, it seems awfully hard work in the fields."

"It is Charlotte." agreed Charlie. "But let's go for a walk and we can have a good blether. It is really great for me to have a pretty girl to talk to."

Charlie and Charlotte walked through the woods where the late bluebells were still flowering. They exchanged stories. Charlotte told him about her life as part of a big family living in the Workers Rows of an industrial town.

In return he told her how he had been brought up in a tied farm cottage. His father had also been a farm labourer and he didn't know any life other than working on the land.

"There wasn't enough work on the farm I grew up on to support another full time adult so when I was fourteen I got a job working for Farmer Baird, and I have been here ever since.

A few months ago Harry, who was the Charge-hand, left to get married. Two weeks later he left his new bride to march to War in France, sad really.

Farmer Baird promoted me to his job. Not bad for a twenty one year old. Most men are at least thirty before they get a Charge-hand job in farming. But I know full well the only reason

I've been promoted is because of this damned War taking away all the lads to serve in the army.

All the bairns have arrived now for the tattie howking but normally there is just Farmer Baird and his wife, their boys Tam and Eddie, they help out after school. Auld Hughie who is getting on now, and Bert who has taken on my old job.

But enough talk of work, there is a Barn Dance on tonight. It is going to be held at a farm a couple of miles away. I'll take the cart and drive us all over to Kirtle Farm. Have you been to a Barn dance before Charlotte?"

"No, but I've told you Mary and I do go to dances at the Gartsherrie Institute." Charlotte reminded him.

"I really love dancing, so Charles Fyfe, it's not all work and no play in the country."

"Oh, I think you will find there can be plenty of play in the country." said Charlie. "Come on townie, I'll race you to the dry stane dyke, look you can just see it through the trees."

He set of running with his limping gait, Charlotte on his tail, two youngsters enjoying each other's company and a long afternoon of freedom from work.

Charlie reached the wall first and Charlotte fell into his arms laughing. They fell on the ground and Charlie put his arms around her saying.

"Do you know Charlotte you are the best thing that has happened to me ever. As soon as I saw you waiting outside the railway station I knew you were the lass for me. I know we have only just recently met but can I kiss you?"

He held her close to him and gently kissed her on the lips. The kisses became more intense, he could feel her body through the thin cotton dress she was wearing.

Although she had gone out with a couple of boys in the past to the Institute dances, Charlotte had never let her emotions progress beyond a goodnight kiss. Part of the reason being she was too frightened of her parents to ever risk getting pregnant out of wedlock. She knew too many girls who had let their feelings go and ended up with their father insisting on a shotgun marriage, or

worse, ending up in the Workhouse, all chance of a respectable
married life gone for ever.

The warmth of the day, the skimpy dress, the feeling of being
with a handsome young man in a lovely place, all contributed to
letting her barriers down, she allowed him to caress her body.
Charlie removed his shirt and she felt his firm muscular body.
Charlotte wanted more she wanted the feelings to continue and
reach their climax but as he caressed her legs then tried to move
his fingers inside her drawers she stiffened and pushed him away.

"No Charlie, I really wish I could, but I can't, my Maw would
kill me if anything happened. We might not have much money but
God my parents are respectable with a great big R. I can't possibly risk a scandal."

He gently held her as tears of frustration fell down her cheeks.
Then he fastened her dress buttons, saying.

"Darling Charlotte I wouldn't do anything to hurt you, I want
to marry you. And, if you were to fall for a bairn with me, do
you know what, I'll be the proudest man in Scotland. Can you
imagine just how handsome a bairn would be with parents as good
looking as us?"

Charlotte laughed.

"Oh Charlie you do have a silver tongue. We had better be
getting back. I'll need to help Mrs Baird with the supper before
we go off to the dance."

The dance proved to be a great success. Charlie and young
Bert had harnessed up the big Clydesdale horses onto the dray
cart. Everyone who worked on the farm, including Farmer and
Mrs Baird, climbed aboard and settled themselves down on the
hay. The one exception being Auld Hughie, who firmly refused to
attend any such nonsense as a dance on the Sabbath.

Charlie drove with Charlotte sitting at his side, along the lanes
to Kirtle Farm and into the glorious Western sunset.

People from the surrounding farms had all started to gather,
greet friends and take up places inside the barn on the bales of
hay. The music was provided by two fiddlers and an old man on
the accordion. As soon as the music started the young people

were up on the floor dancing until there faces were red and they were exhausted.   The younger children played together and then eventually fell soundly asleep on the bales of hay.

At around ten o'clock a number of the farmers wives set up a make do table using the hay bales and a discarded door.   The ladies produced great piles of sandwiches wrapped in tea towels, and gallon flasks of their home made apple, blackberry and elderberry wines.

The dancers all made short work of the food and wine and sat on the hay gossiping, laughing and generally having a great time.

The older men in the company contented themselves with smoking their clay pipes, and an occasional snifter of whisky, while having heated discussions on market prices for livestock and animal feed, the state of the War and the favourite topic of farmers everywhere, the weather.

It was well after midnight when the fiddle music stopped and the weary revelers made there way back to their carts.

The children slept soundly on the way home and the adults quietly sang the songs of the day, including 'It's a Long Way To Tipperary'.   It sounded very poignant sung on a starry summer night in the Scottish countryside.

After their happy evening at the dance the singers were all acutely aware of the many local lads who were serving in France and would possibly never see their homeland again and their thoughts were drawn to the men and boys on the front.

Charlie carried Jessie, who was sound asleep, upstairs to the bedroom she was sharing with Charlotte.   Charlotte settled her sister down in the big brass bed, then came out onto the landing to say goodnight to Charlie.   One kiss led to another and it was not long before Charlie suggested they go upstairs to the attic where he was sleeping during the harvest.

They crept up the old twisted wooden staircase and into the dark attic room.   Charlie lit a paraffin lamp and they cuddled down on the rickety bed.

"I told you Charlie I simply can't risk falling with a baby, we can only canoodle, nothing more."

"Don't worry." Charlie said breathlessly, "we won't do anything you don't want, I promise."

But it did not stop at kissing and cuddling, Charlie and Charlotte felt such an attraction to each other it was magnetic. They made love and Charlotte lost her virginity in a camp bed in a farmhouse attic, after a barn dance.

In the early hours, as dawn was breaking, Charlotte quietly crept back downstairs and into the bedroom she was sharing with Jessie. Her little sister never knew she had spent the night all alone in the folds of the great feather mattress.

The following week sped past. Charlie working hard on the farm; the children out tattie howking; Charlotte helping Mrs Baird and Jessie, Jessie was having the time of her young life looking after the chickens, picking fruit and vegetables in the farm garden and generally being spoiled by Mrs Baird.

Mrs Baird had taken a real liking to Jessie. A mother of two sons, who were thankfully still too young to be called up. Alice Baird had always longed for a daughter, but fate had never given her the lass she desired. Her husband had been delighted with his two lads and as the years went by the possibility of a third child became more and more remote.

Alice Baird had reconciled herself that her family was complete and then, along came Jessie, and stirred up all her longings to be the mother of a little girl.

Charlie and Charlotte spent every free minute they could in each other's company during the working day. Their nights were spent together in the camp bed, with Charlotte making sure she always woke up beside Jessie in the morning. After leaving Charlie she slipped carefully into the great feather bed with its brass frame and headboard, which she had to be so careful not to rattle.

The friendship between Charlotte and Charlie had not gone un-noticed by her young brothers. One day as they were working, James said to Robert.

"I think oor big sister Charlotte is winching that Charlie lad, Paw would be beetroot faced if he knew, if we play our cards right she'll buy us caramels to stay quiet."

"Stoat'n idea William James" agreed Robert.   Mind you, they might be serious, and you know what our Maw says, 'every pot has got it's lid'.   Charlotte might just have found her tin lid."

The boy started to laugh, Robert had an infectious belly laugh and soon all the boy were laughing, even though they did not really get the joke.

Saturday came round only too quickly and Charlie had no option but to drive Charlotte on the cart back to Condorrat Railway Station, where seven short days before he had collected her.

As they drove Charlotte could feel the tears welling up in her eyes, but she was determined not to let Charlie see how upset she really was.   With her gaze fixed straight ahead she clung on to the box, full of good farm produce, which Mrs Baird had given her, to take home to her mother.

Charlie spoke, his voice breaking with emotion.

"Charlotte you know everything that has happened this week was meant to be.   I love you and I want to marry you.   I know I am not much of a catch, a farm hand with a gamy leg and no prospect of ever owning any land, but I would be a good husband to you and I would do my best to make you happy.   Oh Charlotte, you are so beautiful, I can't believe that we have had such a wonderful week together, it all seems like a dream.   I know it is probably too soon but please say you'll marry me, please, please say yes."

Charlotte's response was to laugh and cry at the same time.

"Oh Charlie I would love to say yes but I have to go back and speak to my Maw and Paw.   I am only nineteen so I would have to get their permission before I can marry.   Hopefully I can get them to agree and I can come back for the week at the end of the holidays to take the children home, instead of our Mary."

"Four weeks without you, it will be like four years" moaned Charlie.   "Could I not come to Gartsherrie after church tomorrow and speak to your parents?"

They were now within sight of the Railway Station.

"No Charlie, you don't know what my Paw is like.   I have to go home and talk to Maw first and see what is the best way to get him to agree.   Now look after Jessie and the boys for me until I come to collect them."

Charlotte jumped lightly from the cart and ran into the station, she bought her ticket to Coatbridge at the counter, quickly showed it to the Station Master and boarded the train.   There was no time for long goodbyes, just a blown kiss and a wave.

On the journey home Charlotte relived the previous week over and over again savoring every sweet moment.

It was not until she was almost at Sunnyside that she started to think about what would be the best way to approach her mother on the subject of Charlie.

Alexander was first to greet her when she arrived home, the little boy was so excited to have his big sister back that he ran towards her crying.

"Charlotte, Charlotte, where is Jessie and Robbie and James, where have you hid them?"

As she cuddled her little brother Charlotte reassured him.

"You wee silly, I haven't hid them, they are still working at the farm.   They will come home at the end of the summer.   Let's look inside my box at the something nice I have brought home from Mrs Baird, the farmer's wife."

Seeing her eldest arrive home Agnes crossed the road from the green where she had been hanging out washing.

"How did you get on in the country?   And, how are the bairns?" Agnes asked.

Without waiting for an answer she continued.

"Come away in Charlotte lass and I'll get the kettle on.   Mary should be back any minute, she has been out with her pal Ina, but she said she would be back for you coming home.   Your Paw is having a pint of porter with his pals but he'll be back for his dinner, or as he calls it 'the tatties".

"I've got a box for you from Mrs Baird, Maw." said Charlotte. "We worked hard on the farm but we were all really well fed, wee greedy guts Robert is in his element.   I thought that was really kind of her sending back some farm food for us."

They opened the box together and found it contained; a crowdie cheese, a hard cheese, farm butter, fruit cake, bannocks, home made farm sausages and a selection of soft fruits from the garden.

"Your Paw will fair enjoy this, especially the butter and crowdie with the bannocks, what a treat. I feel much better now knowing the weans are all being well fed."

Just then Mary burst into the kitchen.

"I saw you coming up the Row Charlotte, but I was too far back to catch up with you. How was the farm? Are the bairns all right? Is the place clean?"

"Good, yes. and yes" replied Charlotte. "Just take a look at the food in the box Mrs Baird gave me to bring home to Maw; that is an example of how we have been eating at the farm."

"Lucky you" said Mary. "I can't wait for my week in the country, when I go to Condorrat to collect the bairns."

For the next few days the Law family ate extremely well, and it was generally agreed that it had been an excellent idea of Mary's to send the bairns to Windy Hill Farm for the summer.

Agnes took some of the food down to Jessie Johnstone and over a slice of fruit cake and a cup of tea they had a blether while Alexander played on the floor alongside them.

"The farm idea seems to have worked well. You must send the bairns every year if that Mrs Baird is going to send you back food parcels. I wonder if another one will arrive with Mary when she comes home?" Jessie speculated.

"I can't deny the parcel has come as a nice surprise and Charlotte seems to think the bairns are right happy. Mind you I'm no so sure about Charlotte. That girl has been in a right funny old mood since she came home but I can't get anything out of her except how good life was in Condorrat."

"Pound to a penny it's a boy." stated Jessie. "I know with my Agnes, it's always a lad, and it's always such a worry. To be honest I will be glad when both my lassies are safely married off, preferably without Alex having to use a shotgun."

They both laughed it seemed quite like old times, Agnes and

Jessie drinking tea and having a laugh.

Although they had been joking, the idea of a lad being involved would not leave Agnes. There and then she made up her mind to tackle Charlotte on the subject at the first opportunity.

The opportunity came quicker than she had expected. Rab came home from work and announced that he was going to a meeting of the Orange Order.

The Laws' now had a father and son staying as lodgers, the father too old to be called up and the son too young. They too were Ulstermen, this time from Carrick Fergus in County Antrim.

The father, Jimmy, was going to accompany Robert to the Lodge meeting and young Jimmy was going out to play football with some of his young mates from the Works. Mary was out with her pal Ina, so the coast was clear.

Once she had wee Alexander settled for the night and there was just her and Charlotte, drinking a cup of tea, Agnes decided to make her move.

"Charlotte you haven't been your usual cheery self since you came back from the farm. Tell me is there anything bothering you?"

Charlotte knew that there was no point in lying to her mother, besides she had been trying to think of a way of telling her about Charlie ever since she had returned home.

"Well Maw there is something, I met this lad called Charlie, we've even got the same name. Anyway, we are in love and he has asked me to marry him. He has just been promoted to Charge-hand so he is going to ask Farmer Baird if he can have a cottage."

'I knew it, I flaming well knew it', thought Agnes.

"Charlotte will you slow down. Look you have known this lad for barely seven days and you are wanting to marry him. Tell me how come he hasn't been called up?"

Charlotte knew the best policy was to tell her mother absolutely everything. "He has a club foot Maw, so he is exempt from army service, besides he is doing important War work on the farm."

Agnes bristled. "This is getting worse by the minute Charlotte. Do you really think your Paw will let you move to Condorrat to marry a cripple? No he will not, and neither will I, that is the end of the matter. I want to hear no more talk about marrying this Charlie. Concentrate yourself on working at the Brickworks.

Besides, what about Samuel Johnstone? You wouldn't meet a nicer lad and you know we would all approve of that wedding, when he gets back from this damned War."

After making her thoughts on the matter clear Agnes quickly finished her tea, and then gave instruction to her daughter.

"Charlotte, clear away the tea things then stay in and keep an eye on Alexander. I am going out for a wee while."

Agnes hurried down to the Long Row to tell Jessie about this latest development. Fortunately Alex was also at the Lodge meeting so they had the house to themselves.

"Rab won't take too kindly to that idea." said Jessie, as she poured the tea. "He brings Charlotte up, and now she is earning good money and contributing to the household she wants to run off with a crippled lad to a farm in Condorrat.

If I was you Agnes, for the sake of peace in the house, don't encourage this romance between Charlotte and, what's his name, Charlie.

Besides we have always hoped that one day there might be an understanding between her and our Samuel. Nothing would make me happier than a wedding between our two bairns when my boy gets home from the War in France."

"I couldn't agree with you more." said Agnes. "I don't know what has got into the girl, she was brought up decently. All this 'we even have the same name' nonsense. I am going to keep a firm grip on that young lady I can tell you.

Agnes was as good as her word. When a letter arrived from Charlie she kept it in her apron pocket all day, as she stoked the fire to prepare the dinner she thought 'what the hell, it's going into the back of the fire', she then watched as the love letter turned to blackened flakes.

Over the following weeks a number of postcards and letters arrived addressed to Charlotte from Charlie. However, Agnes always made sure she got to the mail first and the correspondence always found it's way into the flames.

Charlotte wrote Charlie several letters but she stupidly left them for her mother to post and they too found their way into the back of the fire.

The summer wore on and Charlotte became more and more despondent that she had not heard from Charlie. Every day when she returned from work the first thing she asked was 'any mail?'. Agnes invariably quashed her hopes with phrases like 'Don't be daft it was nothing but a holiday romance' or 'What do you expect from a farm lad'.

Meantime, back at Windy Hill Farm, Charlie too was feeling totally despondent.

All the post for the farm was delivered to the Baird's Farmhouse. Every day Charlie would ask Mrs Baird if anything had been delivered for him and every day she would shake her head, saying.

"Sorry lad, nothing today."

Eventually they would just look at each other, she would shrug her shoulders and say 'sorry'.

The weeks rolled on, all the Law children thrived on the good country food provided by Mrs Baird; the outside work in the sunshine and the fun with the other children after work. The boys in the barn slung ropes over the rafters to swing on and staged battles using hay as hand grenades. Although by some way the youngest and certainly the smallest, Robert was very popular for his joke telling and tricks. He especially enjoyed winding up Charlie, besotted with Charlotte he was an easy target.

As for Jessie, Jessie was enjoying the best time of her entire life. The youngest Law girl loved feeding the poultry, gathering fruit and vegetables from the farm garden and helping Mrs Baird in the kitchen. In the evenings she would sit in the farm kitchen and regale Mrs Baird with stories of school and what she would like to do when she was grown up.

Mrs Baird enjoyed the company of Jessie more than she cared to admit and dreaded losing her when the children left for Gartsherrie and a return to home and school.

Charlie had been desperately hoping that Charlotte would arrive for the final week of harvest work and to escort the children back home to Gartsherrie.

Anticipating the best, but fearing the worst, Charlie drove the trap down to the train station to collect a Law girl.   From the lane Charlie watched the train pull into the station and then leave in a cloud of steam.

He desperately wanted to see his beautiful Charlotte but the Law girl who walked out of the station carrying her mother's portmanteau was indeed beautiful but she did not have black hair and blue eyes, she had thick red hair and green eyes.

Mary approached the driver of the horse drawn cart.

"Are you the Charlie Fyfe?   The lad who is going to take me to Windy Hill Farm?" asked Mary quite curtly.

Mary had decided that any young man who let her sister down was going to get short shrift from her.

"Yes I am." replied Charlie and can I say I was hoping it would be your sister who would come off the train."

"You hoped it would be my sister.   Some cheek you have, Charlotte has been so upset that you never contacted her or replied to her letters."

"Now just you wait a minute Miss Mary Law, I did write to your sister, cards and letters and never a word of reply."

Mary snapped at him.   "I think you have it wrong Charlie Fyfe our Charlotte wrote to you and I can assure you she has not received one missive from you since she came home, or are you calling me, and my sister liars?"

Mary did not have flame red hair for nothing and she could feel her temper rise at the injustice perpetrated on her elder sister by Mr Charles Fyfe.

The easy going Charlie had his limits and he raised his voice to this red haired harridan who was calling him a liar.

"Enough Mary Law, I don't know what happened to the letters but I am not lying and I can assure you I sent plenty of post and received nothing in return. If you don't believe me you can ask Mrs Baird, the farmer's wife, she will tell you the truth of the matter.

And, another thing, Miss High and Mighty, I just happen to be in love with your sister Charlotte and I would never break a promise to her."

Mary was about to snap back at him when she had a sudden thought, 'My Maw, I bet it was Maw. Her and Jessie Johnstone have been trying to pair Charlotte off with Sam Johnstone for years.'

Mary was silent for a few minutes while she tried to work out in her head what could have happened.

In a more subdued voice she said.

"Charlie, I'm sorry, but I think we may have got off to a bad start. Thinking about it, it may have been my mother who tried to make sure that you and Charlotte did not communicate with each other.

It is complicated to explain but my mother had plans for my sister and her plans did not include our Charlotte moving to a farm in Condorrat."

Charlie answered her, amazement in his voice.

"Mary are you really saying it's possible your mother is deliberately trying to keep Charlotte and me from getting together."

"Well I don't know for sure, but it's not impossible. My Maw is Mrs Respectable, we don't have much money but we have all been brought up well, no debt, no nonsense, and no gossip. I wouldn't put it past her to intercept letters to our Charlotte, if she thought it was in Charlotte's best interests.

Look Charlie, we can find out for sure. You write a letter to Charlotte tonight, and I will address the envelope to Charlotte. Ask her to reply to you, making sure she posts the letter herself and let us see what happens."

Mary arrived at the farm to a warm welcome from Jessie and the boys. They had all had a wonderful summer and were keen to share their news with their big sister.

Mrs Baird interrupted their reunion.

"You must be Mary the other working Law lass. Come away in my dear and I'll show you around. First of all Jessie pet, take Mary up to your room and let her get her bag unpacked. Then I'll have a wee cup of tea ready for you before we start making the dinner for the workers.

After a quick cup of tea and a slice of cake Mary was thrown in at the deep end. Cooking with good quality ingredients on a generous scale, Mary was in her element.

"Mrs Baird I feel as though we are cooking for an army. Is it always like this?" asked Mary.

"Pretty much at the potato harvest. Although, for the rest of the year I still do a lot of cooking every day. Farming wages are not very high but we also feed the workers and provide their accommodation. My husband insists that the men are all well fed, the workers eat the same fare as the family at this farm.

Not all farmers are as generous some of them are as mean as sin but my man says, 'good kitchen makes good workers'. Mind you I hardly get a minute to myself. I just finish one job and I start another."

Mary entered into the spirit of the work, with the energy of youth; then thoroughly enjoyed her supper and the camaraderie around the big table in the barn.

The following morning Charlie handed her a letter which she put into an envelope and addressed to Charlotte. Mrs Baird gave her a stamp and told her she would give the letter to Postie when he called later to deliver the farm mail.

On Tuesday evening, when Charlotte returned from work, she received a letter addressed to her from Mary. Opening the letter she found a note from Mary, together with another tightly folded missive from Charlie.

> Dear Charlotte,
> I suspect Maw has been destroying letters
> Charlie sent to you.
> Pretend this letter is from me, make something
> up, anything.
> Write back to Charlie, but remember and post
> the letter yourself. Tell nobody.
> Love, Mary

Charlotte had the presence of mind to babble on to her mother about how Mary had been welcomed at the farm and that the children were all well.

At the first opportunity she went into the bedroom, found the writing materials, and penned a note to Charlie. Fortunately there was a stamp in the writing box so she was able to slip the letter into her pocket and put her plan into action.

"Just going out for a wee while Maw. I might pop into Auntie Jessie's and see if Agnes Johnstone fancies a walk."

Charlotte was positive her mother would know she was up to something but all Agnes said was.

"Make sure you are back by nine o'clock at the latest, your Paw will be back around then and you know he likes you home at a decent time."

Charlotte posted her letter and said a prayer that this one would reach Charlie. It was now more important than ever that he would reassure her of his love.

Then she called into the Johnstone home and was given a warm welcome. All the family were out except her Aunt Jessie, who made a cup of tea for her unexpected visitor, they chatted about this and that for a time.

Suddenly, Charlotte felt she had to speak up, she had to let Jessie know the true relationship between her and Samuel.

"You know Aunt Jessie, Samuel and I would never have made a match. We have always been great pals, I was a bit of a tomboy and it was always more fun playing with him than the girls but that was all there was to it, we have always been like brother and sister."

"I now realise that Charlotte lass." acknowledged Jessie.
"I am afraid your mother and I always hoped that you and my Samuel would make a marriage. You always seemed so happy together and when he went off to the army I felt that there was something unfinished, something he wanted to deal with but felt he couldn't because he was going away to the War.

I wondered if it was you that was on his mind, perhaps he wanted to wed you but he did not think it right to risk giving you a wee baby when he might leave you a widow."

"No Aunt Jessie," confirmed Charlotte.

"It was never me. There might have been another lass but it certainly was not me. I just felt it was important that you don't continue to hold any false hopes."

"Thank you for being straight with me Charlotte. Over the last few weeks I have come to realise that I was wrong to see you as a daughter-in-law, besides I already love you as a bairn, sure I looked after you as a wee toddler, when the Law family first came to Gartsherrie.

Don't worry Charlotte lass, I'll have a word with your mother and tell her you must make your own decisions. I should never have allowed my heart to rule my head by encouraging her plans for a Law and Johnstone wedding.

Now my dear you had better get back to the Herriot Row before your Paw sends out the search parties."

Charlotte put on her coat and headed back home to the Herriot Row at a brisk pace, relieved that her Aunt Jessie understood her feelings and would support her when the time came, and Charlotte knew that the day of reckoning was coming soon.

Back at Windy Hill Farm Charlotte's letter arrived by the late afternoon post on the Wednesday. Mary handed it to Charlie after supper. It read:

My darling Charlie,
I was so relieved to get Mary's letter. I promise
you I never received one letter from you. I sent you
a few notes but stupidly I asked Maw to post them.
It is really important I see you soon. Charlie do
you still want to marry me? I wish I could tell you
this with my arms around you but I just don't know
when I will see you again.
Charlie, oh Charlie, I am going to have your bairn.
I am so frightened of Maw and Paw I just don't
know what to do.
Please tell Mary what has happened, she always
knows what to do, she is the sensible sister.

I love you my Charlie.
Your own Charlotte

Charlie held on to the knowledge from Charlotte's letter until after supper on the Thursday.   In twenty four hours his feelings had run the gambit of happiness, excitement, and abject terror.

He approached Mary as she was clearing away the dishes from the evening meal.

"Mary do you think I could have a wee word with you in private?"

"Certainly Charlie.   But I have to finish all my work first. Meet me at the bench in the garden around nine o'clock."

When Mary arrived Charlie was already waiting for her, she sat down beside him.   Charlie said absolutely nothing, he simply handed her the letter from Charlotte.

Mary read the letter carefully.   Angry as she was with Charlotte her main reaction was fear.   Fear of what her mother and father were going to say and do.

Mary turned to Charlie and snapped.

"Charlie I am furious with you and that daft sister of mine, but that is the least of your problems.   I need to think this one through.   I am going to bed now.   Meet me here same time tomorrow and we'll talk again."

Having bought a little time Mary climbed the stairs to the bedroom she was sharing with Jessie and got ready for bed.
It was still light outside and Jessie wanted to chat.   Mary was barely sixteen but she felt weighed down with responsibility and the last thing she wanted was an eight year old blethering on about her happy summer adventures.

Eventually Mary said.   "Jessie please wheesht, I have a lot on my mind I need to think, now turn over and get to sleep we have a busy day tomorrow.

Needless-to-say Mary did not fall asleep she turned the problems of Charlie and Charlotte over and over in her mind.
Reaching her decision she eventually fell into a fitful sleep.

The following day, after clearing up from the cooked breakfast

Mrs Baird said.

"Right Mary lass, let's sit down and have a wee half hour to ourselves and enjoy a cup of tea and a slice of cake in peace. You have been a great help to me, as was your big sister Charlotte. I could really do with one of the Law girls here permanently. In fact Mary I would like to ask you a question.

Do you think your mother would be agreeable to Jessie coming to live here on the farm? Both Farmer Baird and myself are well fond of the bairn and she would be treated like one of our own."

Mary was astounded, she had intended to take the, 'sit down for a cup of tea,' as an opportunity to ask Mrs Baird's advice on the Charlotte and Charlie escapade, not to be faced with yet another problem.

"Mrs Baird" said Mary. "I don't think my Maw and Paw would consider losing Jessie for one minute. And, I couldn't imagine life without my wee sister. I know Jessie has really enjoyed being here with you and I am sure she would love to come again next summer, if you are agreeable, but to live here permanently, never.

However, there is something else I would like to discuss with you. It's not easy but there is something I must tell you."

Mary launched into the tale of Charlotte and Charlie she finished by saying.

"So Mrs Baird if you would like a Law girl here at Windy Hill Farm perhaps it would be possible for Charlie and Charlotte to wed and she could work on the farm."

"Mary lass, you certainly have a problem on your hands." said Mrs Baird as she poured another cup of tea for them both.

"Obviously I would have to get my husband's agreement but we do have a farm cottage that Charlie and Charlotte could probably have. However, there are a lot of hoops to be jumped through before we get anywhere near that stage.

I suggest that after supper tonight, when the bairns are in bed, you and Charlie come into the kitchen and we will discuss the whole matter with my husband in attendance. After all Mary, it is his farm and he is the master.

Now lass we had better get on with the work, the fairies won't do the baking for us."

Mary could hardly eat her supper for thinking of the impending meeting with Farmer and Mrs Baird.

At last the moment came and Charlie and Mary joined the Bairds' in their homely kitchen.

Mr Baird, who was normally a man of few words, rounded angrily on Charlie.

"Lad, I gave you a home here and you have abused my trust by taking advantage of a young woman under my roof. I understand from my wife that Charlotte is now expecting your bairn, and at present her parents know nothing of her condition.

Charlie lad, what are your intentions? speak up now."

Charlie was clearly frightened, he held Farmer Baird in high esteem but he also knew that the family were God fearing Protestants and would not put up with any scandal surrounding those who lived and worked on their property.

"Farmer Baird, Mrs Baird." said Charlie. "Firstly I want you to know that I asked Charlotte to marry me before she returned to Gartsherrie and before I had any idea that there was a bairn involved. I love Charlotte and she loves me and we would be very grateful if you would allow us to wed and continue to live and work on the farm."

"That is all very well and good." said Farmer Baird. "But there is something you seem to have forgotten. Before you can marry Charlotte you must get her father's permission, I believe she is still under the age of consent.

From what young Mary here says it does not sound as though Mr Law would welcome a farm labourer as his son-in-law.

Mary and the children are due to return home on Sunday, I suggest you accompany them. You must then ask Charlotte's father for her hand in marriage and make the girl respectable.

Under the circumstances, Charlie, I have no option but to give you my permission to marry, it is my Christian duty.

You can live in the little cottage attached to the Dairy and in return Charlotte can work for my wife. We can sort out the details later but Mistress Baird could do with an extra pair of hands and this may well be the solution.

Understand this Charles Fyfe, Charlotte must come to Windy Hill Farm as your legal married wife, nothing else is acceptable to Mrs Baird and myself.

Now I am dog tired, it has been a long day. Go to your bed Charlie and stay out of my sight for the next few days, I am real disappointed at the way in which you have behaved.

Mary could you hold fire a few minutes, my wife would like a word with you lass."

Mr Baird went off to his bed and Charlie quickly retreated to his bed in the loft, grateful to have got off so lightly.

"Mary my dear" said Mrs Baird, "I know you are a sensible girl and I think you will agree with me there should be a little plan as to how Charlie approaches your family."

"To be honest Mrs Baird, I don't think any plan will help, my Paw, and my Maw for that matter, will be absolutely ropeable. You will be very lucky to get Charlie back in one piece."

"Well lass, we must just do the best we can." advised Mrs Baird.

"I think you should write to Charlotte and get her to meet you all at the railway station. Charlie should ask for Charlotte's hand without telling your parents that she is in the family way. The lass can only be six weeks gone at the very most, and babies can arrive early.

Your mother and father might have their suspicions at an early baby, but I suspect that your parents would rather believe the pre-mature baby story, at least for the benefit of the neighbours."

Mary thought, 'she has certainly got my Maw taped'.

"Now lass, get a letter written to Charlotte immediately and I will make sure Postie takes it first thing tomorrow. As soon as you are finished writing get to bed and forget all about this sorry episode until you return home.

Sunday morning dawned and Auld Hughie drove the Law children and Charlie, attired in his Sunday best suit, to the railway station in Condorrat.

The younger children sensed the tense atmosphere between Mary and Charlie. Even knowing he was lightly to get his 'head in his hands to play with' Robbie couldn't help saying.

"Charlie why are you all dressed to kill and coming to Gartsherrie with us? Anything to do with oor big sister Charlotte by any chance?"

Mary snapped at him.

"Shut up Robbie; I would advise you, and you too, Jessie and James to keep well out of the road when we get to the Herriot Row. No more questions now, just sit quietly until we get home, I have enough to worry me without you three prattling on and on."

Mary's tone brooked no argument so the three children had no option but to be quiet. However, this did not stop them giving each other looks and little signals. It took Jessie all her time not to laugh out loud, especially when Robert kept patting his heart and rolling his eyes heavenwards.

Charlotte was waiting at Sunnyside station to meet them. Seeing Charlie she ran into his arms and they embraced outside the busy railway station.

"I telt you," murmured Robbie to Jessie "They are winching and he is here to ask my Paw if they can walk out together."

Well he better be brave if he is going to take on Paw and Maw for permission to winch our Charlotte."

"What a homecoming, but it should be quite a laugh." agreed Jessie.

"Aye, a laugh, if we keep our heads well down." said James. "Mary is right, best we disappear nippy quick, and take wee Alexander with us before the fur starts to fly."

By the time they reached the Rows Mary's stomach was in a knot, she felt as though she would never be able to eat again. Even the large parcel of farm food Mrs Baird had given to her on leaving Windy Hill held no attraction.

They walked into the house, Mary, Charlotte and Charlie first and the three children lagging behind.

Agnes and Rab were sitting drinking a cup of tea while waiting

for their brood to return and little Alexander was sitting on the
floor continually asking.

"When Maw, will they be home soon Maw?"

Rab glared at the stranger, as Charlie came into the kitchen.
"What the hell is going on here?   Charlotte my girl, is this lad in
my home because of you?"

The three younger children grabbed Alexander and ran out of
the house.   Mary took the parcel and disappeared into the scullery
to unpack the food.   Leaving Charlotte and Charlie with her parents.

Without further ado Charlie formally addressed Charlotte's
father.

"Mr Law I would like to ask you for your daughter's hand in
marriage.   I have a job at Windy Hill Farm and I can get a farm
cottage for Charlotte and me to live in and well, I love your girl."

Before Rab could even reply Agnes started to shout.

"You want to marry my Charlotte.   My lass has been brought
up respectably in a good home.   Now you, a cripple with no
prospects whatsoever, want to wed her and take her miles from her
home and family.

Not half a mile from here lives another respectable family, they
have a handsome healthy son.   Where is he?   He is fighting for
King and Country, and when he returns he will take up his job as a
Supervisor at the Brickwork.   And, you dare to put yourself forward when Samuel Johnstone is fighting the Hun, for the likes of
you."

For once in his life Robert was in full agreement with Agnes.
He turned on Charlie saying.

"Get out of my home, I will not lose my lass to the likes of
you."

Charlie had been hoping to get their permission to marry without mentioning the pregnancy.   He now realised that there was
absolutely no alternative, they had to be told.   He bucked up every
bit of courage he could muster and said.

"Mr and Mrs Law, I asked Charlotte to marry me five weeks
ago when she left the farm.   I now understand she is expecting my

babby so it is important that we marry as soon as possible."

Standing in the scullery Mary heard her mother through in the kitchen yelling like a fishwife.

"You dirty little bitch. Charlotte Law, you were brought up decently and respectably and this is how you repay your father and me. You and, and that cripple are nothing better than the animals on the farm in Condorrat; and a dark day it was for this family when you went to that God forsaken place."

Charlotte was now weeping. To his great credit Charlie spoke up bravely.

"Mr and Mrs Law, what is done is done. I want to do the right thing by your girl. Please agree for us to see our ministers and have the Bans read in Coatbridge and Condorrat and we could set a date to marry for three weeks time."

Agnes was about to launch into another tirade when Robert stopped her and said in a voice carrying understated menace, that brooked no argument.

"Shut up lass. There is no more to be said, so there isn't. Let them marry and no longer darken my door."

He turned and addressed Charlie in a fearsome authoritative tone.

"Boy, return to Condorrat on the next train, see your Minister immediately, set a date for a marriage three weeks from today. Charlotte will go and see Rev Maxwell and the marriage will take place in the Maxwell Church Manse in Coatbridge.

We will attend as a family and then you will take Charlotte on the next train straight back to Condorrat.

Charlotte is not my blood daughter, her mother was a widow woman when we married. However, I have always treated her as my own lass and I am deeply disappointed by her disgraceful behaviour, so I am."

Listening from the safety of the scullery Mary was astounded at this information. Her mother a widow, Charlotte not her full sister. Well well, Maw kept that quiet, she thought.

Three weeks later Charlotte Fisher and Charlie Fyfe were married by the Rev. Maxwell in the local Church of Scotland Manse.

Charlotte's only ornament was a posy of hedgerow flowers picked by Jessie.

After the ceremony the bride and groom left to catch the five fifteen train to their new life at Windy Hill Farm.

The Law family had stovies for their evening meal, and the wedding they had attended earlier in the day was not mentioned at the dinner table.

CHAPTER 11
February 1916

1915 passed into 1916 and still the War continued.
The women of the Rows tried to fill their days with work and chatter so that they could forget the dread of the telegraph boy arriving at the door. The worst time was the night when sleep would not come, just the memories of a much loved son.

The women who had spent years longing for a son were now grateful for the blessing of daughters or childlessness.

There was one bright light on the horizon during the dark days of War for the Johnstone and Law families.

After leaving school at fourteen Agnes Johnstone had got a job working in Baird's Store office. Like her parents she was bright, and she took all the opportunities afforded to her by attending night school classes.

The Johnstone family were all very proud that her hard work was rewarded and she received a number of promotions. Agnes was now working as Secretary to the Accounts Manager of the Co-operative Society in Bank Street, Coatbridge. Quite a step up for a lass from the Rows.

At the age of twenty-two, Agnes had the same soft prettiness as her mother, together with her father's easy going, happy nature.

While working as Secretary to Mr Lauder, Agnes became friendly with one of the other Secretaries, an attractive girl called Catherine Coats.

Catherine and Agnes enjoyed each other's company, both in and out of the office. They started to go to the films together once a week and from there it was only a short step to visiting each other's homes for a meal.

The Coats family lived in a very nice Works house on the top section of the Square, bordering the Gartsherrie School playground. It was much larger than the run of the mill Row houses, enjoying it's own private garden, and joy of joys an inside flush toilet and bath. These houses were reserved for Managers and senior employees of the Works.

Catherine and Agnes, together with Mr and Mrs Coats had just finished Saturday night high tea of cold ham, salad and chips, accompanied by bread and butter, home made cake, and a large pot of tea.

The girls were about to get ready to catch the bus to go and see the latest film in Coatbridge when the front door opened. A tall, smartly dressed man, with a slight limp in his right leg, the result of childhood polio, entered the room.

"Sorry I'm late for tea Ma" he said in a soft well spoken voice. "There was a problem with the signals on the train home from Glasgow.   Any chance of being fed or will I go over to Coatbridge and buy some fish and chips?"

"Indeed and you will not." said Mrs Coats. "Sit yourself down and I'll get your meal, I just have to fry some more chips, it won't take me a minute."

Meantime Catherine introduced the newcomer to her friend.

"Agnes, this is my big, not only taller, but considerably older, brother Tom.   He is an Engineer in the Works; not of the hard working variety who get their hands dirty you understand; he wears a white collar, sits in the Work's Offices, and he has a fancy title."

Tom reposted.   "Excuse me, Miss Catherine, I worked my socks off to get my degree, that's why I'm a Manager, besides I do work extremely hard."

As he was speaking Tom shook Agnes by the hand, and then something very rare took place. They looked at each other and in an instant they fell, head over heels, in love.

Tom had worked very hard at school to overcome the disadvantages of his childhood polio. He knew that he would never be able to hold down a manual job, so he had no option but to use his brain if he was going to make his way in life.

Mr Coats worked as a Foreman Engineer and when Tom was due to leave school he managed to get him a job working in Baird's offices. Tom studied at evening classes and then he obtained a leave of absence from Baird's to study full time at Glasgow & West of Scotland Technical College in order to gain his degree in Engineering.

Tom was now in his mid thirties, although over the years he had gone out with a number of different girls he had never felt that he wanted to marry and settle down.

Now here he was staring open mouthed at this lovely young girl he had just met, who was probably ten to fifteen years his junior, thinking 'this is the lass I've been waiting for'.

Tom invited himself to join the girls on their outing to the cinema. He sat next to Agnes and they spent the first part of the movie programme quietly chatting rather than watching the screen.

During the interval Catherine whispered to Agnes.

"I am not going to spend my Saturday night playing gooseberry. Some of the girls from the office are sitting further down the aisle. I'm off to join them, just remember he is thirty five, bordering on ancient."

With this parting shot Catherine went off to sit with her other friends.

Agnes and Tom barely noticed Catherine's disappearance. They had a magical evening, they talked and talked and Tom could not understand how this beautiful, perfect girl had lived so close to him all his life and he had never met her.

Agnes did understand, she was well aware that although they both lived in the Rows, Mr Coats was a Foreman Engineer and her Paw was a Labourer in the Ammonia Pit, socially they lived a world apart.

Tom walked Agnes to her door in the Long Row, where they made arrangements to meet the following day. Before saying goodnight Tom took Agnes in his arms and gently kissed her on the lips.

The romance moved at the rate of a runaway train. Within a

month of their meeting Tom had proposed.

The Coats family liked and approved of Agnes, Catherine in particular was delighted at the prospect of having her friend Agnes as a sister-in-law.

Tom met the Johnstone family and liked them. Jessie's involvement with the Suffrage Movement had enabled her to interact with people of all classes so the idea of her daughter marrying a Work's Manager seemed perfectly reasonable.

Alex was more reticent about his daughter's upward social movement but his love for young Agnes and respect for Tom Coats soon won the day, besides if Jessie said it was fine, it was fine by him.

The date of 7th June was set for the wedding which was to take place in the Maxwell Church in Coatbridge, barely three months from the day Tom and Agnes met.

Wedding fever engulfed the Coats and Johnstone households. Mrs Coats invited Jessie over for tea and cake. Jessie asked Amelia Coats if she could bring her friend, Agnes, as she was an expert dressmaker, this was something of an exaggeration, but Jessie wanted her friend involved in the excitement.

Agnes and Tom could not have cared less about having a lovely wedding. They would have been quite happy to be married in Gretna Green wearing their working clothes so long as they could be together.

However, there was no chance that was going to happen. The ladies afternoon tea was a great success and plans were discussed in detail; flowers would not be a problem, the Coats had plenty in their garden and Rab also grew a surplus of flowers at the Miss Simpsons' garden which could be utilised.

Agnes offered to make the bouquets saying that while working in service she had learned a lot about presenting flowers.

Obviously the bridesmaids would be Catherine and Mary, the two sisters. Mrs Coats thought Tom would probably ask his friend Neil to be the best-man and his cousins Jim and Colin would serve as the two ushers.

Mrs Coats then announced that the reception would be at the Co-operative Hall in Coatbridge with a steak pie purvey, and perhaps trifle afterwards for around forty guests, naturally there would be music and dancing afterwards.

Jessie mentally gulped when Mrs Coats suggested this plan, knowing full well that her and Alex could never afford anything nearly so lavish. As she was about to make her feelings on the matter plain Mrs Coats said.

"Mrs Johnstone, my lad has been paying me dig money now for a considerable number of years, unlike your Agnes who is a great deal younger. I think it is only fair that the Coats family pay for the hall, the purvey and some music for the dancing.

Perhaps I could leave the wedding cake in your hands, that is if you can manage to get the dried fruit, everything seems to be in such short supply these days."

Agnes butted into the conversation.

"Talking of shortages, where on earth are we going to get material for outfits for a bride and two bridesmaids?"

Amelia Coats made a suggestion.

"Perhaps we could all look through our wardrobes and see if anything can be altered. And, there might be some nice material to be bought in Glasgow in one of the big stores."

Jessie agreed to have a think about the whole material question and suggested that they all have tea the following week at her house and pool ideas.

Mentally she was thinking. 'I can just imagine the cost of material nowadays, and it won't stop there, it will be gloves shoes, hats; what a nightmare. Just keep a smile on your face Jessie lass until you can come up with some kind of a solution'.

The women took their leave; Agnes thinking about cakes, Jessie thinking about clothes and Amelia quite oblivious to any problems, she would simply pay the Co-operative bill.

Since the outbreak of War there had been an upsurge of interest in the Suffragette movement. The membership in Coatbridge was now too large to meet at Jennie Mathieson's house. Premises had been secured above a workshop in Dunbeth Road, the location was central and the rent low so it suited the Suffragettes purpose admirably.

The Saturday after the Wedding Planning Meeting Jessie had arrived at the Suffragette H.Q. early, she was busy setting out leaflets when Liz arrived.   Her first words to Jessie were.

"What's this I hear that your eldest is shortly going to get wed, and to a Manager at the Gartsherrie Works no less."

Jessie laughed.

"No secrets in this place, is there.   Actually he is a very nice lad, quite a bit older than Agnes but it really is a love match, just like me and Alex, only with a bit of money.

Although I am really worried about the wedding Liz; the Coats family have been very generous, they are paying for the reception and the musicians.   However, I need to get something organised regarding clothes for the girls.

Mrs Coats thinks that the way to overcome the shortages and diabolical prices nowadays is to search through our wardrobes and re-model something.   What a laugh, she obviously hasn't seen my wardrobe."

Liz joined in the laughter.

"Well perhaps I am not the best person to give advice on fashion, you know me, only happy in plain and easy to wear clothes, haute couture was never going to be my thing was it?

However, I might just be able to help, my Mother liked to wear nice things when she was a girl and young bride, in fact, truth to tell, she liked good quality clothes all her life.   I have wardrobes full of lace and silk nonsense.   Obviously the outfits are hardly fashionable now, most of them date back to the days when Queen Victoria was a girl but perhaps you could rework the material, even I know that some of it is quite pretty."

Jessie impulsively threw her arms around Liz, saying.

"Are you serious, are you really serious, Elizabeth Agatha Wallis-Banks.   If you are, you are an answer to all my prayers.   Can I really have a nose through your mother's wardrobe?"

"Of course you can," agreed Liz, "perhaps you would like to bring the girls and have a good rummage.   How about tomorrow afternoon, I'll write down my address and give you directions, just don't hold my living in Airdrie against me, will you."

The rooms were starting to fill and the meeting about to commence but Jessie managed to whisper to Liz.

"Can I also bring my pal Agnes, she is a really good needlewoman so her advice would be most helpful."

Liz gave a typical Liz answer.

"Jessie, bring the Queen of Sheeba if it will help you, just don't expect home baking."

The following afternoon a party of five, consisting of Jessie and Agnes together with the bride and her two maids, Mary and Catherine set out from Gartsherrie. The adventure started on the blue Baxter's bus, travelling to Carlisle Road in Airdrie. Agnes Law had never been to Airdrie, the adjoining Burgh to Coatbridge, in all her years of living in Gartsherrie. The kind of poverty Agnes lived with did not allow for gadding about on un-necessary bus journeys.

Mary and Jessie Law were disappointed to be left at home, they would have loved to delve into wardrobes full of beautiful clothes but Jessie had decided that taking them to Airdrie was taking one liberty too far.

Liz, who had never met any of Jessie's friends or family before greeted them kindly.

"Do come in and I'll show you upstairs to my Ma's treasure trove of clothes. Have a good rummage around and take absolutely anything you want. I mean it, anything, you would be doing me a favour. Jessie here will tell you I am absolutely not interested in fashion. What you don't take the moths will probably gobble up.

After you have sorted out your loot we can enjoy a sherry, together, you will probably all need one."

Since the death of her mother, Liz had lived by herself in the family home, a large detached Victorian villa in Airdrie, What the ladies from Gartsherrie did not know was that Liz was in fact the Rt Hon Lady Elizabeth Agatha Wallis-Banks, and heiress of a considerable fortune.

The large bedroom she took them into, was furnished with a four poster bed, the coverlet made of a rose coloured pink silk, with pink Jacquard drapes. The furniture was mahogany; beautifully fitted wardrobes and a bun foot chest of drawers, together with an elegant dressing table and stool, there were various other small pieces of furniture and two chairs upholstered in a pink chintz fabric. The oriel window was dressed in a burgundy velvet with rose pink tassel trims.

A light film of dust lay on all the wooden surfaces, this room had obviously belonged to Liz's mother and it looked as if the door had not been opened very often since the old lady had died.

Liz flung open one of the wardrobe doors and announced.

"Ladies have fun, I'm off to read a book, see you all later for a sherry."

And fun they had, firstly they took each item out slowly and carefully not quite convinced that a voice was not going to yell 'leave my things alone' but after a little while the oohs and ahhs became too much and they gave themselves up to the pure enjoyment of the moment.

Two hours later they came downstairs laden with their precious loot.

Not only had they found dresses to remodel but Liz's mother had taken the same size in shoes as Mary Johnstone and Catherine Coats, young Agnes took a size smaller but Jessie reckoned a bit of cotton wool would sort that problem out.

Not only were the three girls set to look lovely, after a lot of work on the part of Agnes, but Jessie and Agnes were also going to be beautifully attired. The outfits they had chosen were of a more recent vintage so very little in the way of alterations would be called for, Agnes could also use the cotton wool trick in her matching shoes. The only person who would need new shoes was going to be Jessie, with the best will in the world she could not manage to perform a Cinderella.

They tumbled downstairs laughing and carrying armfuls of dresses and accessories, hats, gloves, shoes, what a wonderful dream-like afternoon they had all enjoyed.

Liz got out of her armchair and put down her book. Their joy was infectious, and she entered into the spirit of the moment.

"Bride, pour the sherry. I'll just go into the kitchen and get some nibbles"

Liz brought out a silver tray holding little glass dishes, they contained, savory treats, everything from salted almonds to olives. None of the Gartsherrie ladies had ever seen, never mind tasted, olives. Mary put one in her mouth, thinking it was a grape; she screwed up her face and quickly disposed of the remains in her handkerchief.

Jessie, once again asked Liz if she was absolutely sure they could have all the beautifully tailored clothes and all the accessories.

Liz responded by saying.

"Jessie my dear, drink your sherry. Now tell me what have you decided to cannibalise for the wedding outfits?"

As chief dress designer Agnes spoke up.

"The sweet peas should be just coming into bloom in time for the wedding so I have suggested Catherine and Mary wear pink and lilac to complement the flowers. We found a beautiful nightwear set in ivory silk, trimmed with lace. I thought that would be ideal as the basis for young Agnes's gown, I will fashion an underdress. I have a few ideas but I can't say exactly what I am going to do at this stage."

Jessie piped up.

"Liz, we have also taken the liberty of taking an extra two outfits to remodel, one for each of Agnes's two girls, Mary and wee Jessie, my namesake. I know you really won't mind, but I just wanted you to know."

In return Liz just laughed saying.

Mary, for goodness sake please pour your mother another sherry.

The hilarity continued, probably because none of the Gartsherrie women ever drank alcohol, with the possible exception of a glass of sherry on Hogmanay. The drink, mixed with the excitement of being given access to wardrobes full of exquisite clothes was a potent combination.

Eventually Liz, who was not a natural cook or carer, thought. 'Even I can't be responsible for sending them back to Gartsherrie in that state, I've got to do something'.

Liz grabbed a book and hit the table several times shouting.

"I call this meeting to order. Let's all adjourn to the kitchen and make some tea or coffee or something. And, I challenge the good ladies of Gartsherrie to find something edible in my kitchen. Follow me, quick march, quick march."

Liz marched through the living room and along the hall with three young and two not so young women marching and laughing behind her.

Agnes and Jessie, being experts at making meals from nothing, were soon opening cupboard doors and checking the contents. They put together a little impromptu meal of tea with sardines and tomato on toast. Agnes managed to scrape together the ingredients for a batch of pancakes, which everyone enjoyed spread with blackcurrant jam, the remaining butter in the cupboard having been used in the pancake batter.

It was a joyful and thankfully reasonably sober group who headed back to Gartsherrie with their treasure trove of clothes and accessories.

Two young ladies who got a wonderful surprise that evening were Mary and Jessie Law. Agnes brought home a beautiful pale green outfit for Mary which looked wonderful with her fiery red hair and green eyes. Like the bride, Jessie's outfit was also going to be made from a lingerie set with a new underdress, Agnes had chosen blue for her younger daughter, a perfect choice as it complimented her blue eyes and fair hair.

Agnes and Jessie spent every spare moment over the following weeks sewing, they altered and remodeled the clothes donated by Liz. Every day saw the transformation of the discarded clothes into beautiful wedding outfits coming that bit closer.

Mary Law also used the cotton wool trick on a pair of fine cream leather shoes and Agnes somehow managed to find the money to buy Jessie a little pair of white sandals to complete her outfit.

The Law and Johnstone women, together with Catherine Coats, were set to become the best turned out ladies Gartsherrie Rows had ever produced.

Rab mumped and moaned about the goings on and all the frills and fripperies laying about his home, just because wee Agnes

Johnstone was going to marry a heed bummer from the Works.

However Agnes, knowing him of old, was astute enough to make sure that his, and the lodgers, meals were always ready on time in order to give him no cause for serious complaint.

Alex, on the other hand, was delighted that Jessie and her compatriots had managed to obtain all the beautiful clothes and were organising such a wonderful wedding for his wee lass.

About a fortnight before the big day, when Agnes and Jessie, were just starting to believe that all the outfits would be completed on time, an unexpected letter arrived at the Johnstone home in the Long Row.

Dear Jessie,

I remember hearing your friend Agnes say that she was finding it well neigh impossible to find all the dried fruit she would need to make a wedding cake for Agnes and Tom.

You will never believe it, but I, Liz, the most undomesticated woman on the entire planet, possibly the entire universe, has managed to acquire a supply of little dried out grapes.

Make sure you attend the meeting on Saturday morning and I will bring the objects of Agnes's lust with me.

Your friend
Liz

Jessie rushed round to Herriot Row to show Agnes the letter, they laughed like teenagers at the idea of the words Agnes and lust in the same sentence.

"That Liz really is a card, speaks as posh as can be, yet she is a really good egg." observed Agnes.

"Not only good," commented Jessie. Liz has a really incredible brain. Not just of the hard working and intelligent sort like my two girls. If she was a man she would probably be a General in the army or the Prime Minister, and I bet she would be better than that Lord Asquith.

Liz has all sorts of qualifications but being a woman holds her back from the kind of career she would like to have followed, that's why she is so involved in the Suffragette movement.

Actually, from a few things she has said recently I think she might also be flirting with another movement, Communism."

The days flew past, the dried fruits were collected and given to Agnes who added flour, hoarded sugar, farm eggs from Jean Shanks and some under the counter spices from the Works Store. Icing sugar and marzipan were proving impossible to procure so Agnes decided to simply dredge the cake with some finely ground sugar, and on the day tie some pretty pink and lilac ribbons around it and place a wee posy of sweet peas on top.

While Mrs Coats, Jessie and Agnes, together with their troops the two Marys' and wee Jessie spent their days organising the wedding, Agnes and Tom Coats seemed to float above the whole business.

One Saturday afternoon Tom called at the Long Row to take young Agnes out for the day.

"Let's go for a walk down to Coatbridge" he said, "Perhaps we could go for some tea or get something to eat."

They set off, holding hands, just happy to be in each other's company. Then Tom suggested they take a longer route. Eventually they came to a building site near the Drumpellier Estate where five bungalows were being built, in a little cul de sac. Tom pointed to the middle bungalow, saying.

"Well Agnes Johnstone, soon to be Coats, how do you like your new home?"

Agnes was astounded.

"Tom, I thought you said we were going to stay with your Maw and Paw until we found ourselves a home." Agnes stuttered.

"Yes, we are going to stay with my mother and father after the wedding. It will be another couple of months before we are able to move into our own home.

I chose the middle house because we will have the best garden, it will incorporate a couple of existing trees and it borders the woods, so we will have a lovely outlook. Agnes one day perhaps we can hang a swing on the old oak tree for our little boy."

"Or girl," laughed Agnes. "Oh Tom how on earth can we afford a house in Drumpellier. I have about four pounds in the Airdrie Savings Bank. How much have you saved?"

Tom smiled, "Agnes there is no need to worry I have enough money saved to buy the house, and furnish it with the absolute necessities. We can get everything else we want over time, we have a lifetime before us. My dearest girl I love you."

Agnes thought she was going to burst with happiness. Not only had she met and was about to marry the man she loved she was going to live in a beautiful bungalow, with a garden.

Jessie and Alex were thrilled when they heard about the bungalow. For them it represented one thing, and one thing only, security. They had spent a lifetime living in tied property, time and time again they had seen neighbours having to move on or take lodgings when there wasn't a family member capable of working at Gartsherrie Works.

It was a great joy for Alex and Jessie that their eldest daughter would enjoy a level of security that they could never hope to experience in their entire lifetime.

The end of May and into the first few days in June the weather was very showery, which gave the wedding planners many anxious moments wondering if the sweet peas would be ready in time. However, the weather turned on the fourth, the sun shone, and the sweet peas bloomed.

On the morning of the seventh the flowers had reached perfection, the weather was perfect and so was the bride, young Agnes Johnstone.

The Law children were all excited beyond words, the boys feigned disinterest, moaning about having to go to a sissy wedding and how all their pals would rag them but secretly they were all excited at the prospect of attending the wedding.

Wee Jessie made no secret of the fact that she had absolutely loved every minute of the preparation, even the sitting at night helping her mother to carefully unpick seams. Now the great day had arrived and she looked as pretty as a picture dressed in sky blue, as she walked to the church holding Mary's hand.

Mary too was delighted with her pale green outfit, complimented by cream accessories but she felt a certain sadness remembering how stark the recent wedding of her sister Charlotte to Charlie Fyfe had been, she wondered if she was the only one remembering poor Charlotte on this happy day.

Agnes had bought a wooden spoon which she bedecked with ribbons and a little piece of lace for young Jessie to present to Agnes and Tom as they came out of the church, which she did with much blushing and teasing from the boys.

After the marriage ceremony the wedding party made their way to the Co-operative Hall in Bank Street. As they arrived each guest was offered a drink, sherry for the ladies and a dram of whisky for the men.

The tables were set with snowy white table linen, the white crockery and stainless steel cutlery all bearing the Co-operative crest. On the tables were little silver vases each holding a posy of sweet peas in varying shades of pink, lilac, white and purple.

Everyone took to their seats, the Rev. Maxwell said the grace and the guests enjoyed a delicious meal of Scotch broth, steak pie, mashed potatoes, peas and carrots; followed by sherry trifle.

Finally the waiting staff in their black dresses and white frilly aprons brought out trays of tea and it was time for Agnes and Tom to cut the wedding cake, which Agnes Law had made with such loving care.

Everyone cheered as they cut Agnes's handiwork, the staff then quickly spirited the cake off into the kitchen to be cut into small pieces and served with the tea.

Tom made a speech thanking everyone, he made special mention of Agnes and her wonderful dressmaking and baking skills. He also made mention of his new mother-in-law's friend Liz, for her great generosity.

The speeches ended and the band arrived; it was time for the dancing to start, the first waltz commenced led by Tom and Agnes. Everyone followed onto the floor including Agnes and Rab, to the great astonishment of their children, and Agnes, who had absolutely no idea that Rab could dance.

Liz, who thought herself as somewhat brittle and self contained had been amazed, and secretly pleased, to be mentioned as generous by the bridegroom.

As the dancing got into full swing Liz decided to slip away quietly, she had just collected her coat when Mary Johnstone approached her.

"Liz, I just wanted to thank you for giving us the beautiful outfits. Don't you think my Ma and Aunt Agnes; particularly Aunt Agnes, who did all the clever needlework, have made a wonderful wedding for my sister Agnes and her Tom.

We could never have afforded to pay for a wedding like this and it has been so nice for my Ma to really feel she has contributed to the day and it's not just all due to the Coats money."

Liz, although seen as very confident within the Suffragette Movement, was something of a loner, so was not used to thanks and family gratitude.

Indicating to Mary some adjacent chairs, they sat down and Liz said.

"Mary, it's jolly nice of you to say I was helpful but honestly, the clothes were just lying in the wardrobe, I didn't really do anything.

However let's change the subject, tell me Mary, what do you do with yourself?"

Mary thought for a moment then replied.

"Not a lot really, when I left school I was lucky to get a job in the Post Office. I have had a couple of promotions, probably because of the War.

Weekends I usually go to the films with some of the girls from work and that is about it really, not very exciting I am afraid."

"Tell me" asked Liz, "have you never wanted to get involved in the movement with your mother."

"Ah that is a big question?" responded Mary. "Ma has been involved with the Suffragettes, in some capacity or other, for years and years. More so since the War started. Agnes and I have always supported her one hundred percent and tried to help as much as we could at home to give her time to attend meetings.

However, both Agnes and I have been really lucky in getting

office jobs, rather than having to work in service or in one of the factories.   But the price to be paid is that we could never get obviously involved in the Suffrage Movement, to do so would be instant dismissal.

We would love to have become involved in the movement but we talked it all through with Ma years ago, and we came to the conclusion that she would fight for our rights and we would fight her corner at home."

In her usual direct fashion Liz then asked Mary.

"What are you doing about continuing with your education?"

Mary somewhat taken aback, answered.

"Well I have taken Grade 4 and Grade 3 of the Post Office exams, I had to sit them in order to get my promotions."

Liz laughed,

"For heavens sake Mary, you are a bright girl, I said education, not exams."

"Well that is education." riposted Mary.

"I think not my dear girl." countered Liz. "Tell you what, you can borrow some of my books, I'll send a couple to you with your Ma, read them and perhaps we could meet sometime for a tea or coffee and discuss them, I'd value your opinions.

Now I'm off.   Give your Ma and Pa my thanks for inviting a crotchety old spinster to your family celebration."

The remainder of the evening went well, the celebration finishing up with a selection of Scottish Country Dances, including, Strip the Willow, the Dashing White Sergeant, and Eightsome Reels.

The night ended with the company all singing Auld Lang Syne before wending their way home.

After all the excitement of the wedding it was now time for the two families to get back to once again living an 'auld clothes and purridge' life.

The Law children spent the summer of 1916 back at Windy Hill Farm.   This time Jessie and Mary stayed with Charlie, Charlotte and their little baby, Robert.   Named after the man Charlotte had, and always would, consider to be her father.

The two boys insisted on sleeping in the barn with their pals, enjoying friendships renewed from the previous summer.

Mary took the children to Condorrat and collected them so she enjoyed two weeks away from the brickworks in Glenboig. Two weeks during which time she thoroughly enjoyed working with Mrs Baird, and gained huge respect for the work she accomplished and her organisational skills.

Sadly, all good things come to an end, the potato harvest was gathered and it was time for the children to return to school. Once again Charlie drove the four Law children to the railway station to catch the train home to Coatbridge.

They waved goodbye with Mary safely carrying their payment for the summer of work. This money was a really welcome addition to the Law finances and paid for school clothing and new shoes for all the children.

In some ways this was a measure of the Law's hard working spirit, what they didn't have they worked for, unlike so many families in the Rows they never had to resort to the shame of the Pawnbroker.

After they were settled in the train carriage Mary lifted a newspaper laying on the empty seat beside her. The reports made dismal reading the Battle of the Somme was a ghastly reality, the various battles now appeared to be leading towards a crescendo, how long the fighting would continue and how many lives would eventually be taken, it was impossible to guess.

Mary thought of Sam Johnstone and some of the other Gartsherrie lads fighting in France; also of the boys who had started to return with horrific injuries; and worse still, of the families who had received the dreaded telegram.

James, Robert and Jessie, still oblivious to the full horror of the War being fought in Europe, were playing snap with a packet of cards Charlie had given them and chatting about the previous year, when the Charlotte and Charlie drama had been enacted.
Mary hoped there innocence would last.

CHAPTER 12
December 1916

The romance and subsequent wedding between Agnes and Tom had provided the only bright spot in an otherwise depressing year in the Johnstone and Law households, and the country in general.

The Battle of the Somme had rumbled on all summer and ended in November with no clear winner, and enormous casualties on both sides.

The telegram deliveries increased and throughout the town the number of soldiers who returned from the front with horrific injuries spoke testament as to what was happening in France.

Shortages of food and other goods were now becoming more prevalent as the War continued to disrupt shipping and worldwide trade.

The Gartsherrie Works, like all heavy engineering plants, was running on full production helping to provide the wherewithal for the army in France to keep fighting.

A whole new list of characters began taking up many column inches in the newspapers. The Russian Tzar Nicholas and his wife Alexandra, together with their invalid son, and beautiful daughters; Rasputin; Kerensky; Lenin and the Bolsheviks; Karl Marx and Revolution.

The entire world seemed to have gone completely mad and yet the bigger political picture took second place, within the Rows, to worry and concern for family and friends involved in the bloody fighting.

Jessie dealt with her constant concern over the fate of Sam by throwing herself into the work of the Suffrage Movement.

Ofttimes she thought of her conversation at the beginning of the War with Ella Millar and the sagacity of her words.

As the War continued, women were taking on more and more of the jobs vacated by men serving abroad. Women were also serving their country in France as nurses and ambulance drivers. There was a groundswell of feeling, even from women who had no previous involvement in the Suffragette Movement, that the womenfolk would not be going back into their box after hostilities ceased.

As Hogmanay 1916 approached in Gartsherrie, the only wish for the New Year of 1917 was for peace. In all probability it was also the wish in every village, town, city and country involved in both sides of the bloody conflict.

Jessie was busy going through all the usual Hogmanay routines, washing, cleaning, cooking; making sure everything was as perfect as she could make it to see the auld year out and the new year in.

After the bells at midnight the Johnstone household intended to first foot the Law family in Herriot Row.

At around four o'clock in the afternoon there was a knock on the door. Jessie opened the door with a welcoming smile on her face; the smile instantly dissolved as she saw who was standing facing her. A young man in the navy uniform of a telegraph boy. He was holding in his hand the dreaded small brown envelope.

Jessie said nothing, she just took the thin missive from him, closed the door and walked back into her living room. Sitting down in the rocking chair she stared into the flames which were glowing brightly in the range. In her hand the unopened telegram, unopened Sam was safe, opened he could be dead.

Jessie did not cry, she did not move, she just sat quietly hypnotised by the colours and flames of the fire.

Somewhere in the furthest reaches of her mind she heard the works siren ending the shift. Ten minutes later Alex bounced into the house, ready to enjoy the New Year celebration.

Within seconds he absorbed the entire picture; Jessie, the telegram, the implication. Gently he put his arm around his beloved wife saying.

"Jessie my darl'n, we must open it; give it to me."
She was gripping the envelope so tightly he almost had to tear it from her hands.

With shaking fingers Alex opened the letter he had spent every day dreading, since Sam left for France, it read.

'Cpl Samuel Johnstone is presently in a field hospital in France.'

"What does that mean cried Jessie? Does it say anything else? How serious are his injuries? And, when did he become a Corporal?

Oh Alex, as every day, week and month has passed each day I've thanked God for keeping our Samuel safe and prayed for the day the madness would stop. What are we to do, what are we to do."

The tears now started to roll, not just tears from Jessie but tears from Alex.

Mary arrived home from work expecting to find the preparation for celebrating Hogmanay in full swing. Instead she found her parents crying in each other's arms, with a thin brown telegram laying on the floor beside them.

Hand shaking, Mary picked up the paper and read the ten words.

She tried her best to comfort her parents but no words or hugs would help their grief.

Mary realised that for the first time in her life she would have to take her mother's position as the practical member of the family.

"Listen Maw, please stop crying and listen." instructed Mary. "I am going to Drumpellier to tell Agnes and Tom the news, then I'll go and tell Aunt Agnes and the family."

With that she was gone and walking quickly through the dark cold night to pass on the worrying news.

Tom and Agnes together with the Law family gathered in the Long Row home of the Johnstone family and did their best to comfort and console.

The sirens sounded, the bells came and went, whisky and sherry were passed around, but the only solemn toast was for Sam and his safe return home.

1917 and no sign of the War ending. The weeks went past, each day longer than the last, following the old adage, that when you are happy the hours and days fly past but when you are sad they take on leaden feet

Jessie stopped attending meetings of the Suffrage Movement. Alex had no option but to go to work, although he did so like an automaton, the only thoughts going through his head each day were thoughts of Samuel, his boy Sam, his only son. Mary was a wonderful support to both her parents but at night, in the quiet of her bed, she too cried her salt tears.

The entire family prayed for a telegram and prayed not to get a telegram. News, no news, which was best?

One morning as Jessie was in the middle of doing some washing a knock came to the door, shaking she turned the handle. Friends in the Rows knocked then walked in, a knock without the door opening, probably meant a telegram.

It was not a telegram, it was a tall thin woman, with short hair and gold rimmed spectacles. Jessie threw her arms around her crying.

"Liz, oh Liz, it is so good to see you. You'll have heard about my boy Sam. Alex and I just don't know what to think or do. Every day we hope for word and every day we dread it."

Liz comforted her friend as best she could even though she did not have the natural warmth of the women in the Rows.

Liz had lived most of her life as a solitary soul. Although she had a good relationship with her mother they had little in common and since her mothers' death she had thrown herself more and more into her studies and the women's movement.

Her involvement with the Suffragettes was always more on an intellectual than a practical level and although she was invariably polite to all the women the only friendships she had forged at the Coatbridge branch were with Jennie Mathieson and Jessie, and even those were strictly on her own terms.

Liz and Jessie sat together all afternoon, fortified by cups of tea. They did not converse a great deal there were only so many times you could talk through the loop of possibilities.

Mary returned from work, her first words, as always, when she came through the door were.

"Any news Maw?   Oh, hello Liz, thank you so much for coming to spend some time with my Mammie.   Please stay on and have a bite of dinner with us, my Paw will be home soon."

"Thanks child, but I had better be off I have no wish to intrude." said Liz in her clipped voice.

Jessie seemed to come out of her reverie.

"Nonsense Liz, you are not intruding you are supporting.   Please stay, it's just soup, followed by the ham from the shank it was made with and a few potatoes but food shared with friends is the best of meat."

Alex returned from work, he too welcomed Liz and all four sat around the table, they ate Jessie's well cooked food and then drank cups of tea.

After the remains of the meal had been cleared away Liz said. "I really must go now, thank you all so much for your hospitality, and I hope you receive good news before long."

Mary returned to Liz a book she had borrowed some weeks previously, saying.

"Liz, thank you so much for lending me the biography of Elizabeth Fry.

I read it through carefully once and then dipped in again and again.

The Carnegie library is pretty good but I never realised before, reading is all in the choosing of books that open up doors of understanding and not just reading popular novels."

Liz smiled, "Mary, my dear, continue to open doors."

Jessie's unlikely friend, pulled on her coat and was gone.

Several weeks after Liz's visit a postcard arrived addressed to Mr and Mrs A. Johnstone, it read.

Recovering after gas attack.
Will write soon.   Love Sam

Jessie read the card once, twice, three times.   Then she grabbed her coat ran down to the bus stop and caught the first bus to Sunnyside Post Office in order to tell Mary the news.   After much hugging and crying Jessie walked as quick as she could the mile or so to the Co-operative offices in Coatbridge where her elder daughter Agnes was working.

Normally a married woman would have been expected to leave office employment but due to the War Agnes had been able to keep her job.

The poor girl at the Co-operative office reception was caught up in the Jessie whirlwind. Before she could argue, Jessie had demanded access to Mrs Coats, she opened the door into the corridor of offices, ran along it until she found one with the legend acid etched on the door. General Manager's, Secretary.

Jessie burst in grabbed her daughter and held her in her arms. More tears, the Johnstone women were both relieved beyond words to know that their Sam was in no immediate danger.

"I've got an idea" said Agnes. "Go down to the Works Office and ask for Tom, he might be able to arrange to have my Paw sent to the offices so that he can tell him the news. I can't bear to think of my daddy suffering another day."

"I'm on my way" said Jessie. "Bye bye my love, I am so glad I have three, no it's four now, wonderful children."

Back to the bus stop, sitting on the Baxter's bus Jessie felt every revolution of the wheels was too slow. She would have loved to just get out and push, such was her desperation to reach the Offices of Gartsherrie Works.

Briefed by Agnes, Jessie quickly found Tom's office and gave him the news. Although he did not know Sam personally he felt the relief on behalf of his new family.

"Don't worry Mrs Johnstone I'll get word to Alex as quickly as I can, not another hour will go past but his mind will be relieved." said Tom, with his hand on Jessie's shoulder.

"Thanks lad," said Jessie, "It was a good day when you became part of our family. I'm off up to Herriot Row now to tell the Laws. Agnes, Rab and their brood have been such a great support, I want them to know the good news first hand, now that the family have seen Sam's postcard. There is no way I want Agnes to hear the news on the grapevine."

In fact Agnes did hear on the grapevine.   Although it was strictly against Post Office rules, the postman told Agnes the good news.

"Mrs Law, don't say I telt you but knowing Jessie Johnstone is your best pal, I have to tell you, her boy is in hospital but he is on the road to recovery.   Great news ah?"

Agnes agreed it was great news then promptly made a batch of pancakes and put the kettle on in readiness for Jessie's visit.

Nothing further was heard regarding Sam's condition for a number of weeks but the postcard had given Jessie and Alex the hope they needed so somehow they got through the days until at last a letter arrived, Sam's letter read.

Dear Maw and Paw,
Goodness knows when you will receive this but I know you will be bursting for news.
I received a minor injury, not in battle, I slid in the mud, fell over and broke my ankle.   I had received first aid but I was still in the trenches when there was a gas attack.
I can't tell you how horrible it was but I was one of the lucky ones and made it behind the lines to a military hospital in XXX.
I am going to be repatriated, don't know when.
Will write when I have more news.
Miss you all - even Agnes and Mary
Sam

No more communications were received from Sam, winter turned into spring and it was almost time for the sweet peas to once again bloom, marking a year since Agnes and Tom's wedding.

One warm evening, with the front door open to the scullery, Jessie, Alex and Mary were sitting eating their evening meal around the kitchen table, when Mary looked up and saw her brother Sam standing in the doorway.

At least it looked like a shadow of her brother.   Sam was tall and favoured his father in looks, the man standing in the doorway

could have been Alex's older brother rather than his son.
Everyone rose from the table, speaking at once and sitting the tall,
gaunt, man down in a chair.

After hugging and kissing her boy, Jessie, being Jessie, started to
prepare some food for him, while all the time asking questions.

After everything had calmed down and Mary had left to tell
Agnes and Tom and the Law family the good news Sam at last
spoke to his parents.

"It was hell Paw, you can't imagine what it is like in the trenches.
But the day the mustard gas attack came went beyond hell. The
only reason I survived was because the day before the attack I broke
my ankle, I was sent to a field first aid unit for treatment, still in the
front line but well behind the front trenches.

The lads who copped the first wave of the attack all died within
minutes, I got a lung full, my eyes poured with water, my nose
poured with snot and I thought I was never going to breath again.

The medical staff realised they couldn't help the poor buggers in
the forward trenches so they just tried to put as much distance as
they could between the walking wounded and the gas which was
drifting through the air.

The next part is fairly vague, I can remember bits like the agony
of trying to walk on my broken ankle, staggering around blinded by
the pain and tears and then nothing, and then waking and the pain
was still there. Eventually we were put into ambulances and taken
to a Field Hospital behind the lines.

In their usual British Army fashion I was formally informed that
my injuries were such that I would be repatriated so after journeying
across France, then over the Channel and through umpteen camps
in England, here I am, half the man that left to fight the Hun."

Jessie put her arm around her son saying softly.

"My boy, you sitting in that chair is an answer to all my prayers.
Now you are home we will feed you, nurse you, you will be well and
have a good life before you."

Alex agreed.

"As usual your Mammie has said it all, you are home, you must
put the hell behind you and find a new life."

Mary returned with Agnes, Tom and the entire Law family in her wake, there was kisses, hand shaking and many good wishes but everyone who looked at Sam on the night of his return to Gartsherrie were devastated to see how the handsome lad who had left them had been aged and emaciated by his horrific experience of War.

Over the following days Jessie had an open door with friends and neighbours popping in for a cuppa and a word with Sam. Much as she was a sociable soul Jessie would have loved to close the door on the world for a little while and have Sam to herself but they lived in a community, and their friends and neighbours while having little money cared about and respected each other and Jessie would never have turned that caring away, so the kettle was never off the hob.

One morning after Alex and Mary had left for work and Jessie and Sam were enjoying a quiet cup of tea together Sam said.

"Mammie it's time I got back to work. I am going to take a bus up to Glenboig and see what chance I have of getting a job, I can't expect my old job back after nearly three years but surely they will offer me something."

The purpose of the journey to Glenboig was not only to try and get a job. Samuel was also going to see his secret sweetheart, Maria Riley.

While he was in the forces they had carried out a regular correspondence, he had even sent her little gifts, like a silk handkerchief sewn with his Regiment's insignia, and a number of beautiful silk embroidered cards.

When he got off the bus in Glenboig first off he visited the Brickworks, his former boss Ronnie Allen, gave him a warm welcome although he was really thinking 'My God, what has this bloody War done to that boy, he is thin, pale, aged at least ten years and with that dry cough, he sounds consumptive.'

After they had passed the pleasantries and caught up on each other's news Sam asked.

"Well Mr Allen, any chance of a job back in Glenboig Brickworks?"

The only work available at that time was on the production line and Mr Allen had no intention of offering Sam a job that he felt would kill him, just as sure as a bullet from a German sniper's rifle.

"Look lad" Mr Allen tried to answer the question that he knew would surely come, from the first moment of seeing Samuel Johnstone enter his office.

"This is very difficult for me, you know if I had anything suitable you would be my first choice. However, the truth is Sam I don't have a job for you."

Somehow Ronnie Allen's words came as a shock to Sam he had always believed that as soon as he came out of the army, if he survived that was, his old job would be sitting waiting for him. The last thing he expected to hear was that after serving his country for three years there was no job for him back in the work place.

Mr Allen continued.

"Look lad as soon as something comes up, either here or in one of the other works I'll let you know, I promise, I'll keep my ear to the ground for you."

Sam thanked his old boss and left the works as quickly as he could. He walked down into the village and bought himself a mutton pie and a bottle of ginger beer at the grocers and then walked out into the countryside. At last he found himself a place beside a stream where he felt he could sit and think.

And think he did, about Maria. His plan has been to get himself a job and then find Maria and propose marriage, he knew that it was never going to be easy, she was from a home of devout Catholics and he from staunch Presbyterians.

Three years in the trenches had taught Sam that life was precious. He had seen friends, of all religions, die, young lads like himself with hopes and dreams.

When he was gassed Sam had thought that his life had ended, but for whatever reason he had been given a second chance at living. That second chance he fully intended to spend with Maria, despite what their parents, and the society they lived in, would say.

As he munched his pie and drank his ginger beer Sam knew that he could hardly propose marriage until he had a job so the question was; should he contact Maria now or wait until he was earning again. His small army pension would not keep them and allow them to raise a family, no he had to get work, and soon.

He turned things around in his mind for several hours and at last reached a decision. He would walk back to the Brickworks and meet Maria as she finished her shift.

The siren sounded and the workers poured out the gates. Samuel saw friends and strangers leave the works but he approached nobody. He only wanted to see one lass, and that lass was Maria. Suddenly he caught sight of her unmistakable golden red hair as she pulled off her working turban.

He sidled up behind her and whispered,

"It's me dearest, I'm home."

Maria turned and she threw her arms around him, crying and laughing all at the same time.

He pulled her out of the melee and whispered.

"Maria we have to talk, let's just go for a walk, well away from everyone."

They rushed away from the workers, as they boarded the buses and carts to take them home. Five minutes of brisk walking, no talking, and they had passed through the village and were out into the open countryside.

They climbed a fence and walked through a field of sheep until they came to some woodland. Walking among the wild flowers and smelling the mossy earth, with the underlying smell of wild garlic, they at last started to talk.

Maria expressed all her concerns about how thin he had become and how pale he seemed.

"Don't worry about my being thin love" laughed Sam. "My mother is filling me with her good cooking; soups, stovies, rice pudding, you name it, I'm eating it.

He did not want to talk about his time in the trenches and the gas attack. The only person he had really confided in was his father. One night they had stayed up talking into the wee small hours, Samuel had opened up his soul about his War experiences, he had shed his tears, as had Alex. The War was now a taboo subject and he had no intention of discussing it with Maria.

"Maria the War is over for me now, I don't want to carry it into my future life.

The bad news is that there is no work for me at the Brickworks. I have a little repatriation money and the few pounds I've saved while I have been away, but that will soon disappear if I don't get work soon."

"I've managed to save a few pounds." said Maria. "The Brickwork has been on full production so I managed to get extra shifts and my Maw has been good about letting me save quite a bit of my extra money."

Samuel took her hand, saying.

Maria Riley we both know it won't be easy but will you marry me, you are the only girl I have ever loved and I want you to be my wife, just as soon as I can get a job and offer you a home."

Maria threw her arms around Sam. "Of course I'll marry you, I don't give a button what the auld yins say. This is our life, our future our children. Kiss me Sam Johnstone, because I love you."

The two young people talked, and talked, about their future and how they would break the news to their respective parents.
Sam decided that there was no time like the present and they should go straight to Maria's home in Glenboig and inform her mother and father.

As anticipated, the meeting did not go well. Maria's father was enraged at the idea of his daughter Maria with a Protestant. He shouted at the young couple.

"Nae dochter of mine will marry a bloody heathen proddy. Now get oot of my hoose boy and don't show your orange arse here again."

Both Sam and Maria knew that there was no use in arguing they both left the house with Mr Riley's boots flying after them and his parting words hanging in the air.

"Don't come back to this hoose Maria Veronica Riley until you get rid of that heathen, you're cut off from your family, from your religion and you are cut off from your God."

There was nothing else to do but take the bus back to

Gartsherrie and see how the Johnstone family would react.

As they walked up the Long Row hand in hand, Maria still sobbing at the cruelty of her father's words; they imagined every curtain was twitching and that the whole of Gartsherrie would be horrified at the idea that one of their Protestant own was going to marry a Roman Catholic.

Sam opened the door and ushered Maria into the kitchen. Jessie was in the house alone, Alex being out at an Orange Lodge meeting and Mary having gone straight to the Carnegie Library after she had finished work.

Jessie's natural hospitality came to the fore.

"Come away in lass, now Sam introduce me to your friend, you have kept quite about this pretty wee lassie, what's the matter pet, have you been crying?"

Sam strategy was to simply tell his mother the situation, as quickly as possible, using the minimum of words.

"Maw I have known Maria for years, we worked together in the Brickwork. While I was in France we wrote to each other as often as we could and today I proposed to her.

I know there are huge problems, Maria's family are devout Catholics, we told them our plans before coming here and they threw us out. Maw what are we going to do?"

Jessie took a deep breath thinking 'I didn't see that one sailing in from the Clyde'.

"Look you two, the first thing I am going to do is to give you both a plate of soup and we will talk this through quietly and sensibly before your Paw gets home."

In her heart of hearts Jessie too was not at all pleased about her only son marrying a Catholic.   However years of working with the women's movement enabled her to try and look at the bigger picture.

One thing was for sure these two youngsters were determined to marry, Jessie sensed she would have to watch her words very carefully indeed.

Mary returned home from the library, carrying three new books to read, no idea of the drama which would play out in her home that evening.

Seeing Sam and Maria sat at the table her initial thoughts were 'Our Sammy has been keeping secrets, he has had a girlfriend all these years on the quiet'.

Jessie did not waste time she immediately updated her daughter on what was happening, made her toast and scrambled eggs for her supper and then they all sat around the table drinking tea and awaiting Alex's return from the Lodge meeting.

As he came into the house he turned the key in the lock, knowing he would be the last person home.

His familiar voice rang out.

"Well me darl'n Jessie will you make a cup of tea for your... What in the name of heaven is going on here tonight? And, by the look of your glum faces it's not good."

Mary quickly rose and headed for the bedroom, saying.

"Maw, Paw, this is nothing to do with me, I'll leave you four to sort things out."

The smile had now well and truly left Alex's face. Jessie instructed her son.

"Sam tell your Paw everything you have told me, leave nothing out."

Sam took a deep breath and told his father all he had told his mother earlier.

Alex's face was like thunder as he burst out.

"Do you mean to say your mother and I brought you up decent, sacrificed for you, worried all during the years you were at the War and now you tell you that you are going to marry a Fenian, a wee red haired Fenian. Oh my God there are thousands of good Protestant girls in Lanarkshire and you find one of the other kind.

I don't blame her father for throwing her out I should do the same to you Samuel Johnstone bringing this terrible shame upon my house."

Jessie was in tears, she loved her mild mannered husband and couldn't stand the thought of him being hurt and feeling shamed by their son's behaviour.

Maria was once again in tears. Samuel rose from his chair and

The Laws of Gartsherrie

shouted in her defence.

"Paw, I am not shaming you or our family, Maria is a decent, hard working girl. I love her, and I have for years, if you want me to leave I will. We'll head off to Glasgow tonight, perhaps I can find work there, if not, when the War ends perhaps we can go to Canada or America.

Jessie now joined the fray.

"Look we will have no talk of rushing off to Glasgow tonight. Maria you can go ben the room and share with our Mary tonight. Tomorrow we will all talk calmly in the cold light of day.

Sam go down to your pal Calum's have a blether with him and spend the night at the Graham's house. But on no account tell him our private business until we have sorted everything out."

Having got rid of the young people Jessie put her arm around Alex who was now sobbing.

"What are we going to do Jessie lass, I don't want to lose my boy, not after the miracle of getting him back to us, but a Fenian in the family, and what of the weans. I could not live in a place where my grandchildren went to the Chapel with all they dirty priests and nuns. No Jessie, it canny be tholled."

Jessie decided that the usual tea remedy was not enough, she got out her supply of medicinal whisky and made them each a mug of hot toddy. As the hot liquid coursed through them bringing comfort there was a knock on the door. Alex got up and turned the lock, there stood Calum holding Sam, who was having great difficulty catching his breath. Calum explained.

"Mrs Johnstone, Sammy came down and knocked our door. I let him in and we were just away to have a game of cards and my Maw was pouring some of her home made ginger beer when he started to breath funny, it's as though he can't get his breath. We didn't know what to do so I brought him home."

Even as Calum was speaking Jessie sat Sam down in front of the fire and gave him a brown paper bag to blow into.
"Calm down son, blow into the bag, count to ten in your head, relax." Jessie tried to calm him and slow his breathing.

Hearing the commotion in the kitchen Maria ran through from

the bedroom to see what was happening. Jessie immediately grabbed her by the shoulders and propelled her straight back into the bedroom, saying.

"Leave him to me lass, he needs calm, not more upset. You just sit through in the room with our Mary."

Eventually Sam's breathing steadied and Calum left for home. There was no chance of keeping this a secret now. Calum would be speculating as to what was happening and speculation in the Rows usually meant two plus two making seven.

The following morning Alex left for his shift and Mary for the Post Office leaving Jessie in the house with Sam and Maria. They were eating breakfast around the family table when Maria said softly.

"Mrs Johnstone thank you for taking me in last night, I know it's not easy for you but Sam and I have tried to deny how we feel for each other many many times but we would always end up going back together.

What do you think we should do?"

Jessie had absolutely no idea what they should do but she was not going to say that first off. Instead she started to talk.

"Look Maria, it's not you personally we are against, you seem a very nice lass and you obviously make my lad happy. The real problem that arises from a mixed marriage is when the bairns arrive. How would you feel about having your children brought up as Protestants?"

"Mrs Johnstone I know that the usual course when there is a mixed marriage is that the girls follow the religion of the mother and the boys follow the religion of the father. I know it isn't perfect but what else can we do."

Jessie looked at them both, a pretty wee girl and a young man, aged beyond belief by the War, and from what she had seen last night, her Samuel's health was compromised for the rest of his life.

Jessie decided to take a firm stand.

"Maria, Sam, can you imagine a house where one half is constantly against the other, it would be a living hell. We have managed in this family to see our way through many hard times and the reason is we have all pulled together. You can't harness a cart with a

Clydesdale and a pony and expect them to walk in unison.

The answer for you both is that one or other of you change religion. I honestly think it is the only way. I will not lie to you it would break our hearts if Sam went your way Maria but I do understand that your folks would feel exactly the same if you joined our faith.

I know I have not said what you want to hear but you must understand there is no easy way forward. If you want to have a happy marriage one of you must change their religion.

Look I'm off up to the farm to buy some vegetables. I'll call in on your Auntie Agnes on the way back, you can have the house to yourselves for a few hours. Talk it all out but remember whatever you decide your decision is irrevocable. As far as I can see you have three choices. Separate, Maria accepts Presbyterianism or you Sam, you turn your coat.

I'll away now, you two think carefully."

Jessie bought her vegetables from Jean Shanks but didn't confide in her, a problem of this seriousness could only be discussed with one person, her friend from the Rows, Agnes.

Alexander was playing outside when Jessie arrived, he made a bee line for her.

"Auntie Jessie, Auntie Jessie, come and play with me, everyone else has gone to school."

Jessie took him by the hand, saying.

"Auntie Jessie is getting too auld to play my wee man. Now let's go and see if your Mammie has been baking, and we both know that your Mammie is the bestest baker in the whole of Gartsherrie, in fact she is probably the bestest baker in the whole of Scotland, the world even."

Agnes came outside to greet her pal.

"What is all this commotion going on outside my front door Jessie Johnstone? Come away in, I've just made some farls of tattie scones for the weans coming home from school, but they'll no miss three scones, one each for you and me, and do you think we should let wee Sannie here have one?"

"Perhaps we can spare one for Alexander, if he promises not to tell the others." laughed Jessie.

Jessie whispered to Agnes.

"Give Alexander his scone to take outside with him, I want to speak to you privately and 'small jugs have big ears' if you know what I mean."

Agnes handed Alexander his scone and told him to play outside and watch for the others coming home from school. Closing over the door her and Jessie settled down to their tea and scone.

"Well Jessie, what on earth is so secret you don't want wee Sannie to hear?" asked Agnes.

"Oh Agnes, I don't know where to start." bemoaned Jessie. "Remember we thought my Samuel had a shine on your Charlotte because they were always thick as thieves. Well it wasn't your lass he had a notion on. No, it was a wee Catholic lassie called Maria from Glenboig, can you believe it?

Well it's all come to a head, he has proposed marriage, her father has flung her out of the house, I had to have her stay at mine last night, sharing with our Mary.

As we sit here and eat our scones, they are discussing their future down at number 130. Do they separate, does she becomes a Protestant, or heaven forbid, does he becomes a Tim? There it is Agnes, the Johnstone family drama."

"Oh my God Jessie" exclaimed Agnes. "We thought we had trouble when our Charlotte got herself pregnant and married that cripple Charlie Fyfe, but at least he is one of us and they had a decent Protestant marriage at the Maxwell Manse.

Your Alex must be mindless, him being a member of the Masons and the Orange Lodge.

Honestly Jessie, I just don't know what to say. The best you can hope for is that she will turn, but with a name like Maria, well Catholicism will always be hanging aboot them like a bad smell."

Jessie smiled, saying.

"You know Agnes, I thought after all the years I have been involved in the women's movement, particularly my work with abused women, I honestly thought I was well over all this Catholic and Protestant nonsense. What we have in common is poverty and trying to better all our lives, that should come way before any religion, as my mother used to say, 'we are all Jock Tamson's bairns.'

But when I saw how pained Alex was last night and well, when push comes to shuve, I am just as prejudiced as ever I was. I want my lad to marry a Protestant girl."

Just then Alexander ran into the kitchen shouting.

"They are coming Maw, Jessie and James and Robert, they're coming up the Row. Can I have an extra tattie scone with them, please, please?"

"That's the peace and quiet finished." said Agnes. "I won't say a word to Rab, he will just wind your Alex up, you know what he is like."

Jessie finished her tea, then chatted with the children for a little while, Aunt Jessie was always a popular visitor in the Law household.

At last when she could not spin out the delays any longer Jessie said to her friend.

"Well Agnes, I had better get back to the Long Row, keep your fingers crossed."

Jessie walked down to her home, acknowledging greetings of friends and neighbours, they saw the usual friendly, pleasant Jessie. Inside she was in a turmoil as to what decision Sam and Maria would have reached.

Whatever decision she thought they would have made she did not expect what greeted her. An empty house and a letter laying on the kitchen table.

Dear Maw
We have talked and talked. The best idea seems to be that we leave here.
Maria is broken hearted at leaving her folks in Glenboig. Despite how they reacted I know they too are decent people. However, they would never accept a Billie just as my Paw and all his pals at the Orange Lodge will never accept a Tim.
Don't worry Ma, we will write and let you know where we are and what we are doing, we will also write to Maria's family.

This is the best way forward for everyone. Try and
explain to Paw and the girls.
I'll miss your cooking Ma.
I'll always be the son of Alex and Jessie Johnstone
Your Sam

Jessie fell into a chair and cried and cried. When she thought
Sam was lost in France she had cried bitter tears but to have to cry
them a second time for a lost son was unbearable.
As she cried, she had a moment of complete clarity, a moment of
revelation.

Religion, Lodges, orange and green, the priest the minister. It's
all a lot of damned nonsense. It's all control.
The Protestants are held in thrall by the Works Masters who bind
them to the Orange Lodge to get the Unionist votes and the church
colludes because the Works Masters support the Kirk. The Kirk's
job is to encourage a God fearing, disciplined workforce, the better
to serve the Work Masters.

As for the Priests, they hold the Catholics in their thrall by
indoctrinating them with fear, fear of the afterlife. They also
encourage large families which the poor cannot afford, simply to
have a larger flock to support the church in all its magnificence,
always bowing down to Rome and the Pope.

Jessie never felt the same way about religion again.

When Mary and Alex returned home they too read the letter and
in there heart of hearts all three knew that Sam and Maria had made
the right decision.

A week passed, it ran into two and at the end of the third week
the long awaited letter arrived.

Dear Paw and Maw
We decided not to write until we were settled. Maria is
also writing to her folks today.
We have been married by the Registrar in Glasgow, no
minister, no priest.
I have got a job working in the Furniture Department

of the Co-operative. You won't believe this but Maria
has got a job working as a Conductress on the tram cars.
We are renting a room and have decided to save every
penny we can and emigrate.
What will there be for us here after this War ends?
A life in a country full of cripples, and men made mad
by shell shock; no doubt there will also be a job short-
age when we stop making shells and bullets and all the
other rubbish of War.
We want better for our children, it's not just the
Catholic versus Protestant divide, it's more than that,
we want our bairns to feel free.
Please try and understand, I think I would have left
Gartsherrie, even if I had not been in love with Maria.
The War changed me, I need to live without being controlled by the Works.
Ma, I really understand now why you are so keen on
the Suffragettes. Incidentally, Maria is one hundred
percent with you on that one, so Pa, I too have married
a feisty girl.
I am still your son and respect your values. Maria
and I just need to have a life away from all the old
rules.
Love
Sam and Maria Johnstone

After Mary had gone to bed Alex and Jessie sat up and discussed the letter over a cup of cocoa.

"You know, I think the boy is right, so I do." said Alex. The wee lass, Maria, seems a decent enough girl. I am sure she will be a good wife to him, after all the Sam she welcomed home was not the Sam who left for the War.

Jessie, you and I got a big enough shock when we saw him, can you imagine how that wee slip of a girl felt.

I have been doing a lot of thinking since they left and that letter says it all. Do you really think Scotland will be a land fit for heroes when the lads eventually come home?   Because I, as sure as hell, don't."

Jessie reached out and took his hand.

"My big handsome Ulsterman, do you remember how we used to want to get on a boat and leave it all behind, start fresh in a land of pioneers.   Oh Alex, we couldn't get the fare together or we would have left Scotland.

We have around eight pounds in the Airdrie Savings Bank and I have a few pounds of emergency money in the house. Could we help them out with the fare?   I know it would take most of our savings but Agnes is well settled, and it is the best we can do for our boy.

Mary has a good job and we can try over the next few years to get back into a position to help her out when her time comes to marry.

Perhaps we could take in lodgers again or I could get a proper job instead of spending so much of my time working for free within the Movement, and just doing a bit of millinery work when I can fit it in.   What do you think?"

Alex took his wife's hand and said.

"I think you are the kindest, most generous woman in the whole of Scotland Jessie Johnstone, as well as the most beautiful.   That is what this daft big bruiser of an Ulsterman thinks."

Lass, write to Sam and Maria and tell them that we will give them the money as a wedding present.   I am sure they will appreciate it as much as our Agnes did all the lovely clothes you and Agnes Law made for her wedding gift."

Jessie wrote the letter and posted it first thing the following morning.   It had to be posted quickly as by helping them emigrate Jessie was well aware that she was saying goodbye to her son forever, and that her and Alex would never see grandchildren bearing the name of Johnstone.

Her words to the young couple read.

My dear Sam and Maria,
Your Paw and I have been doing a lot of thinking and
talking.   We have decided that you are probably quite

right in wanting to emigrate.
We do not say this because of the religious issues.
More because we want you two to have the start in life
we couldn't, because we could not raise the fare to start a
new life abroad.
We can let you have ten pounds.   Please keep us
informed of your plans and when the times comes let us
know and your Father and I will come into Glasgow,
give you the money, say our goodbyes and wish you both
well in your new life.
All my love, Maw

Jessie and Alex desperately needed some good cheer after the gloom and worry of the previous months. One Saturday morning their spirits were lifted when there was a knock on the door and a cheery voice called out.

"Hello Ma, Pa, any chance of a cuppa for two folks who have just walked all the way from Drumpellier to see you."

"Away with you, Agnes J...., sorry Coats, you two know the kettle is never off the hob in this house." laughed Jessie.

"Now is this a visit about something special or are you just here to cadge tea and scones?"

Tom couldn't keep quiet a minute longer.

"Jessie, Alex, we are over the moon. We are going to have a bairn. You are going to become grandparents, probably in February of next year.

Alex, I've brought you a dram to celebrate." Tom produced a bottle of Whyte & Mackay's finest whisky and the two men toasted 'the coming bairn'.

Jessie and Agnes settled for tea, and the inevitable wee girdle scone.

Mary returned home to find the foursome laughing and joking. The sound delighted her, as it was such a change from the sadness which had been felt at number 130 for so many months.

Agnes gave her sister the news that she was about to become an auntie. More hugs and kisses and feelings of pure joy.

The following week, hugging her secret that she was about to become a grandmother, Jessie made her regular visit to the Store. After buying her messages she intended to go and see her pal Agnes and tell her the good news they had received from Agnes and Tom.

Her happy mood abruptly ended when she found crowds of people buying newspapers, women crying, everyone seemingly in shock. She pushed her way forward and read the billboard.

Romanov Dynasty Dead

17th July in Yekaterinburg the Bolsheviks shot the entire Russian Royal family, Tzar NicholasII, his wife Alexandra, their five children, Olga, Tatiana, Maria, Anastasia and Alexei.

The newspaper headlines sent a wave of shock throughout the town, and throughout the world.

In Scotland there had been a small, and growing, groundswell of support for Communism, both within the working classes, particularly on Clydeside, and the educated middle classes.

The poor needed to look forward to something better than a life of constant toil and the middle classes while wanting a better, more equal life for all, were probably, consciously or unconsciously, wanting a classless society, but one where they would be at the top of the pecking order.

As further newspaper reports filtered through it was discovered that not only had the Royal family been murdered but their servants and other aristocrats who had accompanied them into exile had also suffered the same fate.

The Suffragette Movement, like all fair minded people were horrified by the brutality of the murders and for many within the movement, who were also Communists, this was one step too far.

Support for action against the Government was now growing by the day, hardly a week passed without a banner waving march, women chaining themselves to railings or some other militant action.

This was happening in Coatbridge and Airdrie, not only Glasgow or London, in Coatbridge. This was the town that until a few years previously had struggled to get enough members to fill Jennie Mathieson's drawing room.

CHAPTER 13
November 1917

Since Sam and Maria's marriage in the summer of 1917 there had been a regular correspondence between them and the Johnstone family in Gartsherrie. Jessie secretly hoped that they had decided to settle in Scotland and make a home for themselves in Glasgow.

Delighted with the announcement of her eldest daughter Agnes's pregnancy Jessie had written to Sam and Maria with the good news and gave them regular progress reports on how Agnes was keeping.

It was in the grip of a bitterly cold day in the bleak month of November 1917 when Jessie received the letter from her son in Glasgow, the letter that she had been secretly dreading.

Dear Maw and Paw,

The time has now come. Maria and I have been living as cheaply as we can and, making every penny a prisoner.

After much consideration and bearing in mind my chest condition we have decided to travel to Australia. Remember my old boss at Glenboig, Ronnie Allen, well he put my name forward to a Brickwork in a small place in the suburbs of Melbourne. I have secured a job as the day shift supervisor, but it is more like management than working on the floor. Who would have believed?

Both Maria and I are absolutely wasted, what an

opportunity.
Although we are both really sad at leaving our families
in Scotland.
Maria's mother has come around and accepted our mar-
riage but her father is absolutely adamant that she is dead
to him, as you can imagine she is very upset.
Especially since we have some good news, Maria has
just found out that you are going to be grandparents twice
over next year.
We still cannot believe that our son or daughter will be
born an Australian citizen.
The ship leaves Liverpool on the eighteenth of
December.
Can you and Paw come into Glasgow and see us
before we leave. If you could loan us five pounds that
would really help, the assisted passages cost five pounds
each, but we can find the rest of the money we need from
our savings.
Please give us your blessing.
Sam and Maria

As the months had passed Jessie had been lulled into a false
sense of security. With the New Year approaching she had decided
to start making overtures, possibly by going into Glasgow to meet
the young couple and encouraging them back fully into the family
fold.

The letter came as a bolt from the blue but in her heart of
hearts she knew the move to Australia was in Sam and Maria's
best long term interests.

All day she held her secret, as she chatted with the women at the
Store, as she walked the Row and acknowledged neighbours, she
couldn't even bring herself to tell Agnes when she popped in for a
quick cup of tea.

That evening Mary came home first, Jessie let her read the letter
from Sam and Maria, her reaction was.

"Hard on you Maw, and on Paw. A wee bairn arriving, your

grandchild, a lad or lass that you will probably never see. Unless they do really well and they can come back for a holiday.

I think it is bloody ridiculous that they have to run off like this because of religion but on the other hand I think it is probably a blessing in disguise. Sam is right, what have they got here in Gartsherrie. It must be really exciting to go to a new country and start life afresh.

You know what Ma, sometimes I think I'd love to run off to foreign parts and live a different life."

Just then Alex arrived home, cold and tired after a long day labouring at the Works. Jessie greeted her much loved husband.

"Alex, away and get washed, I'll fill the foot bath with hot water and add some mustard, you can soak your feet and that will heat you up. The meal is ready but before we start eating I have something I need to tell you."

Alex washed then settled himself in the chair before the fire with his feet in the mustard water to warm himself through. Jessie knelt at his feet, she took his hands in hers and quietly said.

"My darln' Alex, it's arrived, the letter from Sam. Maria is going to have a baby and they are off to Australia on the eighteenth of December. You can read the letter properly later but that is the jist of it.

We are about to be grandparents to a Johnstone baby and it will be born at the other side of the world."

Mary broke into their conversation.

"Maw, Paw, I think you two are forgetting something, our Agnes is also going to have a baby next year. What about equality, is not her bairn going to be a Johnstone baby.

Be positive about Sam and Maria going away, it's for the best, and you both know it's for the best. This place is full of bigotry, created to suit higher forces than you can imagine, and I don't mean God.

Do you really think there is a God up in heaven, sitting on his throne preferring his Billy supporters to his Tim supporters. For goodness sake, just wish our Sam well for the future and be done with it."

The normally quiet, thoughtful, nicely spoken Mary marched off to her room and left her parents dumfounded.

Alex looked at Jessie and smiled.

"Well that's telt us darling. It must be all they books that she is reading. I blame that pal of yours, Liz, so I do.

You know Jessie, Mary is quite right we should count our blessings. Agnes has made a good marriage and we are going to be able to see our wee baby Coats, who won't be one iota less special for not being called Johnstone."

Jessie decided to deal with this issue as she had dealt with so many others. Get on with life, and adopt the oft quoted Gartsherrie motto, 'get a grip of yourself' so Jessie got a grip and called to her youngest, Mary.

"Mary lass come through, your dinner is ready. Alex, it's your favourite, soup made with lamb shank and then the meat with some tatties. Good hearty fare for this cauld weather."

The family of three sat around the table and ate their food.

The following morning Jessie wrote to Sam and suggested a date when her and Alex would meet them in Glasgow to say goodbye. The letter safely posted, now it was time to tell Agnes and the Law clan.

A fortnight later, Alex dressed in his Sunday best and Jessie in the costume she had worn to Agnes and Tom's wedding, topped by her heavy winter coat and an elegant brown and beige felt hat which she had designed and fashioned, using her considerable millinery skills.

The two couples met under the Heilanman's Umbrella, Glasgow's nickname for where a section of Argyle Street is covered over by the railway bridge, leading into Glasgow Central Station.

The tunnel of shelter had traditionally offered protection and served as a meeting place for Highlanders travelling to Glasgow as far back as the Clearances. Today it's shelter from the cold of a Scottish December day, made it an ideal place for the Johnstone family to meet.

Jessie was first to see her son, and Maria's red blond hair glowing under her little blue hat. Jessie and Alex ran towards their Sam and his new wife and warmly embraced them both.

The four walked along Argyle Street to the Argyle Arcade and made there way into Sloans Pub and Restaurant for a drink and something to eat.

Settling themselves in the old Victorian hostelry with its beautiful stained glass windows and the all pervading smell of steak pie with an underlying aroma of tobacco and beer.

Alex and Sam ordered beer and the two ladies decided to celebrate with a wee glass of sherry.

After congratulations on their marriage and catching up on all the news Alex entered into the business of the day. He handed Sam an envelope saying.

"There is five pounds inside the envelope, and it's no a loan, it's a gift, so it is. There is also a letter from your Maw and me, together with a wee bible bound in white leather for your bairn. Don't read the letter until you have left the shores of Scotland. We have also brought with us some other mindings to send you on your way."

Tom and Agnes had sent a five pound note and a little knitted matinee coat for the baby, threaded with tartan ribbon.

Mary sent a pound note, together with handkerchiefs, embroidered with heather, for Maria and for Sam a little statue of Robert Burns, with a wee label saying: 'Remember when Ma and Auntie Agnes used to sing his songs'.

There was a parcel from Agnes and Rab containing a ten shilling note and a beautifully knitted baby outfit of pantaloons, jacket, and hat. Agnes had been knitting into the wee small hours to make sure the gift was finished in time.

The Law children had clubbed together and bought a white towel which Agnes had embroidered with a thistle.

Maria started to cry saying.

"Everyone has been so kind to us and our unborn babby. How on earth can I thank you Mr and Mrs Johnstone?"

Alex laughed.

"Well you can call us Maw and Paw, that would be a start."
Maria jumped up and kissed him on the cheek.

Jessie now decided to ask the burning question.

"Maria pet, how are things now with your family, I expect like us they have got over the shock and have all come around."

Maria answered in her quiet voice.

"My Ma has been in touch, by letter, but my Da is absolutely adamant I am dead as far as he is concerned. My Ma can't really go against him, besides she is terrified of the Priest, so she can't come to say goodbye.

I come from a big family, there were eight of us all told. One of my brothers was killed early on in the War, Ma still hasn't got over losing our Michael.

One of my older brothers, Dan, who has married and left home, is coming to Glasgow to see us in a few days time to say his good-byes. My sisters and our Paul, well I know I'll never see them ever again.

So there you have it Mrs, sorry Maw. You can see why we have decided to go to Australia."

"I can Maria, I truly can. I wish with all my heart it was different but in Gartsherrie, it is as it is, and I expect it is the same where you come from in Glenboig. We are all caught up in the stupidity. Let's just hope the wee babby you are carrying will grow up in a better and saner world than we have known.

Now, Alex, you said you were going to treat us all to a steak pie dinner, so get yourself treating."

They all enjoyed Sloan's famous steak pie and everyone tried to keep an air of jollity but at last the moment came and the goodbyes had to be said.

They said their farewells with hugs, kisses and many tears. Sam and Maria walked one way, into the future. Alex and Jessie went off to catch a train back into the past, and their life in the Rows of Gartsherrie.

CHAPTER 14
Hogmanay 1917

Thirty first of December 1917 was a reflective Hogmanay in the Johnstone household. The thought that Sam and his pregnant wife Maria would be bringing in the bells for 1918 on the high seas was never far away from their minds. Although, they still went through the usual traditions of cleaning, cooking and the ritual of first footing with the Law family.

Jessie was relieved when it was all over, the New Year was born and raw emotion could take second place to practicalities in her life.

It was the beginning of January, and the first meeting of the New Year for the Suffragettes was being held at the hall in Dunbeth Road.

Jessie was getting the chairs out ready for the commencement of the Meeting when Jennie Mathieson approached and, out of the blue, asked her.

"What age are you now Jessie?"

Jessie replied,

"I'm forty four this year, why do you ask Jennie?"

"I'm forty three, Jessie, do you honestly think we will live long enough to see women get the franchise never mind win some decent rights in this country?"

"Jennie, I truly don't know." sighed Jessie. "But I do know this we have worked all these years for our beliefs and women are working at every job you can imagine to keep the country going during this damned stupid War. We can't possibly give up now.

Liz joined them, enquiring.

"What are you pair conspiring about?"

"Just wondering if we will live long enough to see women getting the vote. Both Jessie and I are in our forties now and we seem to have given up our youthful years for a cause that isn't going anywhere." Jennie bemoaned.

Liz whispered. "Don't tell anyone but I passed the magic forty line last year so we are all three sailing in the same canoe.

However, never fear it's coming sooner than you think. I had a letter from a friend in London, which I can't read to the ladies because it is in confidence.   All I'm saying is, be of good cheer.

And Jessie, do you think I could have a word with you in private after the meeting is over, please?"

She didn't wait for a reply before waltzing off.

After the meeting Liz found Jessie speaking with a group of ladies. She tapped her shoulder saying.

"Can we have a little discussion please Jessie?   Let us adjourn to Wee Jean's Tearoom in Main Street and have a chat."

Liz had never done anything of this kind before and Jessie was intrigued to know what the reason behind the meeting was going to be.

They settled themselves comfortably in the warm steamy atmosphere of 'Wee Jean's' out of the winter cold, ordering tea and toasted muffins.

"This is all very nice, but we are not here for tea and muffins Liz, so for goodness sake tell me what this is all about?" asked Jessie.

Liz confided in her friend.

"You astute old thing you, I hinted in the meeting that exciting things were happening in London well they are and we need to be in a position to maximise gains and keep up the momentum.

Jessie I need a full time secretary, I can't do everything on my own. Besides, these beer bottle spectacles of mine tell their own story, do they not?

I know Mary has been demoted within the Post Office because several of the returning soldiers have come back to her district and demanded their jobs back, so bloody unfair.

Do you think Mary would like to do a course at the Pitman College in shorthand and typing, I need a well trained girl?"

Jessie responded. "I can't speak for my lass but I think she would love to attend College. However, it's the old old story, her Paw and I could never afford the fees."

Liz spoke in her usual clipped fashion.

"My dear Jessie I thought you understood. I will be responsible for all the fees including her train fares into Glasgow. I will also give her a small allowance while she is training. I know you can't possibly afford to lose her input into the family home while she is studying.

Here comes the tea, let us enjoy and you can ask Mary her opinion when you go home."

Mary's opinion was to dance round the kitchen with her mother. The opportunity was more than she could ever have hoped for. Agnes and Sam were facing the challenges of their new life in Australia, away from the Rows and the bigotry; Agnes and Tom were living in a lovely bungalow, and soon to be parents. This was her chance to move on in life, with her brother and sister. Pitmans College and a decent qualification was the key.

"Ma can I get a bus up to Airdrie and tell Liz tonight that I would love to take up her offer, it would be quicker than writing a letter."

Mary was so excited Jessie could not refuse her.

"Get your coat on pet and take yourself off to see Liz. I'll tell your Paw all about it when he gets home."

The Johnstone family had been very upset by Mary's demotion, after all her years of hard work in the Post Office; she was moved from her post solely due to the returning soldiers taking up their old jobs.

The fight that Jessie had been involved in through the Suffragette movement for so many years, to give women rights in their own country, had touched on her own family in a very personal way.

Jessie was immensely grateful for this offer from Liz, to be paid while receiving commercial training, would restore Mary's confidence in her own abilities, which had been so badly dented by her demotion.

Jessie told Alex the exciting news when he returned from a meeting at the Institute.

While he was pleased for his youngest lass he couldn't help but confide his fears in Jessie, as he tapped his pipe out and refilled the bowl with tobacco.

"They all seem to be leaving us lass, so they do. We will soon be sitting here like a couple of auld exhibits in a museum, so we will."

"What are you blethering about, Mary will still be living at home, and Agnes's home is just a few miles away. I will concede, our Sam has left us but at least him and Maria left on good terms, it could so very easily have been different. Although we are parted at least we can sleep at night, I pity that poor man Riley, Maria's Faither. Can you imagine his thoughts in the middle of the night, and all for the sake of damned pride."

"No my love" explained Alex. "I don't mean them leaving us by the distance of miles, I mean moving on by education and opportunity. Our wee Agnes is already living in a bungalow with an inside bathroom and fancy gas mantle lighting. Next it will be Mary who will move to something better than the Rows, and who can blame her."

To an extent Jessie shared her beloved Alex's fears but she would never admit to them. Holding his large work worn hands in hers she said gently.

"Alex Johnstone, you are a daft auld Ulsterman. Our three bairns will never be ashamed of us or where we come from. We have worked our socks off to give them all a decent respectable upbringing we can't be upset now if they surpass what we have achieved. Is that not how it should be, the next generation doing better than the last?"

Alex had no words he simply put his arms around his wife and they kissed with all the love and passion of young lovers.

Mary opened the door and bounced into the kitchen to find her parents wrapped in each other's arms.

"Honestly what are you two not like" Mary laughed. "Embarrassing your youngest daughter in such a thoroughly disgraceful fashion. And her about to train at Pitmans College, no less."

They all laughed together, and each member of the family knew how truly blessed they were.

At long last the end of the Suffragettes fight for the vote was in sight.

In February 1918 the many years of struggle were partially rewarded by the passing of the Representation of the People Act, giving the vote to women over thirty who met certain property requirements. This Act gave over eight million women in Great Britain the right to vote. It also enabled many more men over twenty one to vote, by removing property restrictions.

The struggle that had started in 1865 with the Liberal John Stuart Mill entered the beginning of the end in 1918, with an Act passed under another Liberal, David Lloyd George.

Suffrage had seen a partial triumph in the Representation of the Peoples Act but this was only a step to the final victory, and a long way from the real aim which was a universal franchise.

This partial victory towards the franchise was gained solely because of the War, and the part women were playing during the conflict. But, how could there be any true equality when men could vote at twenty one and women still had to wait until they were thirty. The movement was still a long way away from reaching its ultimate goal.

There was much rejoicing at the halls in Dunbeth Road. However the trio that was Jennie, Jessie and Liz, while delighted at the step forward, were afraid that this was simply a sop to ensure that women kept working until the end of the war and nothing more.

They met for tea in Jennie's home one afternoon, to discuss their private fears. Liz confided in her friends.

"I knew the way the wind was blowing some time ago, can't say more, you know how it is, other peoples secrets and all that. My dear friends, all the current rejoicing will be short lived. It will still take us years to get a universal franchise.

Jessie, that is one of the reasons I want your Mary as a Secretary, I intend to take the fight to Westminster and make sure that we are not going to allow them to pat us on the head and say, 'there there ladies, your hormones will have settled down by the time you are thirty, that will make you capable of putting a cross in a box'.

I don't know about you two but I'll be damned if I let this one go so easily, not after all our years of endeavour, I simply refuse to give up at half time, to use a sporting metaphor."

All three agreed and the general consensus was that many of their members would now move on to other things and as soon as the War ended it would be life as usual.

"I can see us giving up the lease on the hall and moving back to my Morning Room." said Jennie sadly.

Jessie, ever the optimist, was determined not to break up the gathering on such a sad note.

"Well if we do come back to meeting at your house Jennie, the tea will certainly be a lot better and does your cook still make that delicious shortbread?"

They all laughed and not for the first time Liz and Jennie were immensely grateful for Jessie's happy nature.

Much to their delight Agnes and Tom became the proud parents of a baby girl in the same month as the Act was passed, and for Jessie this seemed highly symbolic.

The baby was born in the Alexander Cottage Hospital, a first for the Johnstone family, who were more used to the idea of babies being born at home.

However, all went well and it was a proud Tom who chapped the door at 130 Long Row one chilly February morning.   He opened the door and found Jessie clearing up after the breakfast.

"Great news Ma, you are Granny Johnstone now, to a beautiful little girl, Agnes and I are absolutely thrilled, she is so wonderful. Honestly Jessie, she is the most beautiful wee thing ever born in Gartsherrie."

Jessie laughed as she hugged him.

Now questions; is my Agnes all right and what does the wee one weight and what are you going to call her?"

Tom simply could not lose his proud grin.

"Thankfully Agnes is fine, the labour lasted about four or five hours.   Baby Coats weighed in at six pounds, ten ounces.   And, naturally we will call her Jessie after you."

As quick as anything Jessie pronounced.

"I'd rather you didn't call her Jessie, I have always hated my name; then Agnes Law went and called her youngest girl Jessie, and I know for a fact she also hates her name.

Time to break with all this tradition nonsense. You and Agnes must have a talk and decide what name you would like your bairn to have, your bairn, your choice. Alex and I will be delighted with whatever you choose.

Now Tom Coats, have you told your parents the grand news yet?"

"No, I came to the Long Row first on my way back from the hospital." answered Tom.

"Well why are you still standing in my kitchen lad? Get yourself down to the Square this instant and put your poor mother out of her misery."

After much discussion Tom and Agnes decided to call their little darling, Emily. They knew that Jessie would be delighted that their baby girl bore the name of one of her great heroines, Emily Davidson.

Davidson was the Suffragette who had been killed trying to pin a Women's Suffrage rosette on the King's horse at the Epsom Derby in 1913. Another of her protests was that on Census night 1911 she hid in a cupboard in the crypt of the Houses of Parliament so that she would have to be recorded as being resident in the House on the Census night.

However, Agnes simply refused not to honour her mother by including her Christian name, so Tom and Agnes's longed for baby was christened at the the Maxwell Church, Emily Jessie Coats.

Many months after Emily's christening a battered letter arrived from Australia.

Dear Maw and Paw,

The Johnstone name will carry on through to the next generation. Maria has given birth to a grand wee boy. Well not so wee, he weighed in at over eight pounds. Mother and baby are both well and we have decided to call him Alexander, after you Paw.

We just hope he turns out as decent a man as you are,

and I hope to be as good a father to young Alexander
as you were to me and the girls.

The job is going well and although we both get a bit
homesick at times we think the move was definitely for
the best.

We are living in a little rented bungalow, one of the new
weatherboard ones, it is painted white, can you imagine a
white hoose in Gartsherrie? However, we are saving
every penny for a deposit to buy our own place.

As far as religion is concerned we have decided that we
will teach our wee lad, Alexander, right from wrong, a
belief in God and simple Christian prayers but he will
not be brought up as either a Billy or a Tim.

We have seen enough of religious bigotry to last a lifetime and we have no intention of bringing up our lad to
judge people by what church they attend.

Hope all went well for Agnes, and that her and Tom
have had a healthy bairn, the mail is dreadful, but we
hope to hear news from Scotland soon.

Hope you are both well and your last bairn, wee Mary,
is behaving herself.

With all our love

Sam and Maria, and wee Alexander

Correspondence between the branches of the Johnstone family
remained scrappy for a number of years, mainly due to the War and
it's after affects.   However, when a long anticipated letter did eventually arrive, either in Melbourne or Coatbridge, it was treasured,
read and re-read many times over.

CHAPTER 15
November 1918

A twelve year old Jessie was skipping home from school with no thought other than wondering what her Maw was making for the family dinner. Suddenly the Works siren started to bawl this was joined by another and another until every works siren in Coatbridge and the surrounding villages was blaring in a cacophony together with church bells ringing all over the town.

People were running out of their homes screaming, crying and laughing; neighbours were hugging each other, nothing like it had ever been seen in the Rows before.

Terrified Jessie ran as quickly as she could for the safety of home. There she found her mother sitting with her head on the table crying her eyes out. The little girl put her arm around her mother, saying.

"Maw, Maw, what is the matter? Why are you crying? And, why are all the sirens blaring at this time of the day?"

Agnes could scarcely say what was in her heart.

"Jessie my wee lamb, the War is ended and my boys have been spared. I was terrified it would go on and on and James would eventually have to go. Oh Jessie, we have been spared. When you say your prayers tonight, thank God that this house has been kept safe from the misery that has touched so many of our friends and neighbours."

The armistice was signed and hostilities ceased at eleven o'clock on the eleventh day of November 1918.

Nobody had as yet calculated the number of lives lost, or torn apart, in the bloodiest conflict the world had ever known.

Sadly, the misery was not yet ended. Over the following weeks and months the soldiers started to return home and the full cost of the War was apparent for all to see.

In the same month as the War ended the Eligibility of Women Act was passed at Westminster, this allowed women to become elected members of the British Parliament. Another step towards victory, one which Liz insisted was toasted in pre war champagne with her friends Jennie and Jessie.

Hogmanay 1918 the War was now over; women over thirty could vote, if they complied with certain conditions; a women could become a Member of Parliament and despite the fact that little Emily Jessie Coats was still a babe in arms, her father Tom, had erected a swing, in the branches of the old oak tree in the family garden.

The first few months of 1919 represented a strange time. There was relief that the War was at long last ended but the aftermath was almost equally frightening.

The unemployment that Samuel had predicted, and left for Australia to try and avoid, quickly materialised. Bringing with it a return to dire poverty for many families who had started to prosper a little during the industrial boom of the War years.

The trains, which had left bedecked with bunting and young men singing returned home carrying young men who had been crippled in France. Sometimes the injuries were all too evident, missing limbs, burns, blindness. However, many of the men carried scars internally that would last their entire lifetime.

There was also a generation of women in towns and villages throughout the land who were condemned to spinsterhood because their lover had been killed.

Some women simply never met an eligible young man because so many men of their generation had been wiped out during the four year visit to Hell.

Another visitor from Hell made an appearance at the end of the War, it was a pestilence which was given the name Spanish Flu. The influenza circled the entire world and when the final reckoning came it claimed more lives than the bullets.

The Spanish Flu, was named after the Spanish King Alfonso XIII, who suffered from the illness.   Because Spain was neutral during the War and there were no reporting restrictions it was assumed that the virus emanated in Spain.

The flu was unusual in that it often claimed the lives of young and healthy adults, rather than children and the elderly, as is the case with most epidemics, which normally target the most vulnerable of the population.

Jessie Johnstone read the newspaper articles chronicling the epidemic and she heard of friends of friends who had been affected but it touched her life for real when Liz contracted the Spanish influenza.

Prior to commencing her course at Pitmans Mary had started to take some French lessons from Liz, as she had never been taught a foreign language at school.   Two evenings a week after work Mary caught the bus up to Airdrie, shared a sandwich supper with Liz and then worked on her French for two hours before catching the bus home.

It was a biting chill day at the beginning of February Mary had worked hard all day, without a proper break.   She was tired and cold and a warm fire and tasty supper at home in the Long Row seemed like a very welcome idea.

However, it was Tuesday and she was due in Airdrie for a French lesson.   After much, will I, won't I, go tonight, Mary decided to take the bus to Airdrie but perhaps leave for home a bit earlier than usual.   In the bus she practiced her vocabulary lists, while thinking, 'Not long now until my course starts, I've got to keep up the work rate.   Can't believe I really contemplated not going for my lesson tonight.'

Mary rang the doorbell, no reply, another ring, no reply.   No lights on at the front of the house.   Mary walked round to the back of the house and saw a light in the kitchen, she knocked the back door, no reply.   Next she turned the door handle it was unlocked and the door opened into the kitchen.

Mary was now starting to get frightened that perhaps there had been a burglary.   There was no sign of life in the kitchen, Mary slowly went into the hall, as she did so she called out.

"Liz, are you at home, Liz, Liz" there was no reply.

Mary then opened the door into the library where she normally worked on her lessons.   Slumped on the leather Chesterfield sofa was Liz, barely conscious, sweating profusely and as white as a sheet.

Well aware of how rife the flu epidemic was, Mary immediately realised that Liz had caught the infection.

First off she lifted her legs fully on to the sofa and covered her with a woolen blanket, she then rushed into the bathroom and got a cold flannel to put on her head.

Mary wished with all her heart her mother was with her and Mrs Millar was within walking distance but she was not in the Gartsherrie Rows and she had no idea how to get the help she needed.

Telephone, that was what to do.   Mary went into the hall lifted the telephone and tentatively dialled the local exchange.   The operator answered and Mary asked.

"Can you put me through to the hospital please, my friend is very ill with the flu."

The operator answered.   "I will put you through to the hospital but I am afraid they are all completely full, there is not a hospital bed to be got in Airdrie or Coatbridge or any of the other towns locally.   They are all advising, either hire in a nurse or the family must look after the patient themselves.

Connecting you now madam."

The telephone rang out and was answered by an exhausted receptionist.

Mary quickly explained how she had found Liz and her condition.   The receptionist suggested she telephone Liz's own doctor and meantime try and make arrangements to have her nursed at home.   The woman apologised but explained that all the hospitals were full to overflowing and it was impossible to arrange another admission that night.

Mary quickly made another call, this time to the Telegraphic Office, she dictated a telegram to be taken immediately to her mother.

Ma, Liz desperately ill, please come.
Mary

Quickly Mary looked through Liz's telephone book, which was fortunately beside the telephone, and found the number of her doctor. His wife answered, the poor woman explained her husband had been run off his feet, however she took a note of the details, saying.

"I am afraid the doctor will probably not manage to get to Miss Wallis-Banks before the morning. The best you can do is make sure she has plenty of fluids and try to keep her temperature down."

With that advice she rang off and Mary knew that she was on her own and had better start dealing with the situation immediately.

Firstly she checked Liz and found she was now delirious and had thrown off the blanket. Mary headed for the kitchen and got some water which she gently helped Liz to drink.

After what seemed like forever but was in fact just over two hours Jessie arrived.

Mary had never been so glad to see her mother in her life. She put her arms around her Ma crying.

"I'm so glad to see you Mamie, Liz is really ill. I am sure it's the flu. I have tried to get liquids into her but I couldn't get her up to bed on my own.

Jessie went upstairs, prepared Liz's bed then lit the small fire in the bedroom. Once she was sure everything upstairs was organised she got Mary to help her and between the two of them they managed to carry Liz upstairs, get her into a nightdress and make her as comfortable as they could.

For the next three weeks Mary and Jessie stayed with Liz and brought her slowly back to health. Mary continued to go to work each day while Jessie carried out the nursing. In the evening Mary took over to give her mother a well deserved break.

Thankfully Liz had a housekeeper, Mrs Armstrong, who came in each day. There was also a young girl, Ellen who did the heavy housework and washed and ironed the enormous amounts of bedlinen.

Liz also had accounts at a number of shops in the town so Jessie was able to order food to be delivered and simply put it on Liz's account. Jessie did not skimp, she ordered best steak and made beef tea, chicken and made light broth. It wouldn't be Jessie's fault if Liz did not recover from her brush with the great epidemic.

Meantime, back in Gartsherrie, Alex fended for himself. Although Agnes Law was very kind and gave him dinner with her family every evening.

Agnes probably didn't even see it as kindness, it was just what you would do, Jessie had looked after her often enough, the least she could do was look after Alex while she was away nursing her friend in Airdrie.

In some ways the earlier days of Liz's influenza were easier for Jessie. As she started to recover Liz wanted to get up and work and it wasn't easy to make sure that she stayed in bed and rested.

Jessie had heard of many cases of the Spanish flu where the patient started to feel better, got up and went to work, and then there was a relapse, often fatal. Nurse Jessie was determined this was not going to happen to Liz.

Much bribing was necessary with Jessie bringing work up to the bedroom for a few hours each day.

When Jessie and Mary returned home they would only do so on the provision that Mrs Armstrong would come in every day, not just Monday to Friday, and Jessie would pop over a couple of afternoons a week and check that the erstwhile patient was eating properly.

Liz made a recovery but her health would never again be robust.

One afternoon a few weeks after Jessie had deemed it time to stop making regular visits to Airdrie there was a knock on the door of the Johnstone home. Jessie answered to find Liz standing on the doorstop, still looking very thin after her illness.

Jessie welcomed her in and immediately put on the kettle. As she was making the tea and opening her biscuit tin Liz said.

I have just came over to say thank you Jessie, I know I would be dead if it hadn't been for the swift thinking of Mary and your nursing skills. Don't quite know how to thank you properly so I have bought you and Mary a little gift. So saying she handed Jessie two small black leather boxes, each bearing the crest of Mappin & Webb.

Jessie opened one box it contained a beautiful pendent on a gold chain set with peridot, amethyst and pearls.

Before Jessie could say anything Liz blurted out.

"The other box also has a pendant, same stones, different design. Thought you and Mary could choose which you each prefer. But the stones tell their own story, Suffragette jewellery Jessie, our colours, green, purple and white. Couldn't possibly get anything else, now could I?"

Jessie started to offer her thanks but Liz cut her off in mid sentence, saying.

"When am I going to get a cup of tea in this house?"

Jessie knew Liz couldn't cope with gratitude easily so she just said.

"Patience, the tea is nearly ready and you know Elizabeth Agatha you are not nearly the crusty old academic you pretend to be. Now would you like a ginger nut with your tea or better still, one of Agnes Law's famous pancakes?"

Another family who were badly affected by the Spanish flu was Margaret Mathieson, now Mrs Smith, and her husband Martin.

Jennie had to rush down to Cambridge to look after the couple's two little girls, Jennifer and Margot, while their parents were seriously ill in hospital. At one point Jennie really thought she was going to lose them both, she even contemplated the possibility that she would have to bring up the girls by herself in Coatbridge.

Thankfully both Margaret and Martin eventually recovered but it took a long time for them regain their strength and Jennie had to stay in Cambridge the best part of three months to look after her family.

Mary started Pitman's College in the March of 1919.

After a year of hard work she qualified as a Pitman's Secretary in March 1920; first in year for Shorthand, first in Typing, second in Office Organisation and English, third in Arithmetic, and French, which was her additional subject, and second in book-keeping.

Overall she was Dux for the year, a proud moment for both the Johnstone family and Liz.

Jessie, wearing her wedding costume, accompanied by Liz, went to the graduation ceremony at Pitmans College in Glasgow.

Afterwards they all had a jolly high tea at Miss Cranston's Tea Rooms in Buchanan Street.

"Well my dear" Liz addressed Mary.

"That was the easy bit, now you are going to work for a thoroughly difficult, cantankerous employer, a real bitch of a woman. I feel incredibly sorry for you. There will be no summer holiday for you Miss Johnstone, you start work Monday morning at nine o'clock."

Jessie was well aware that her daughter would be kept extremely busy working with Liz, as she pursued her goals.

The day universal franchise was achieved Liz fully intended to celebrate for five minutes and then begin the fight to right the other inequalities which were presently written into law in the United Kingdom.

Using her new found skills the following weeks were the busiest of the young Secretary's life.

Mary relieved Liz of all the day to day responsibilities of life. This allowed Liz the luxury of being able to concentrate on her writing and correspondence with key members of the movement located all over the country.

Jessie and Alex were extremely proud of Mary, after all her hard work she was now doing a job that Jessie would love to have undertaken. Assisting Liz in her fight for equality for women, not just the vote, that was simply a cross in a box. Real equality was the goal.

Not only was Mary doing work of real value she was being paid a good salary, far more than she had ever earned in the Post Office.

CHAPTER 16
July 1921

After leaving school at fourteen Jessie Law found a job working in a Coatbridge sweet shop, owned by a Mr Cameron. The other children could not have been more pleased if she had got a job working in the Kingdom of Heaven. Robert particularly was delighted with his sister's employment.

After school he would often walk over to Coatbridge and stand outside the shop waiting an opportunity for Jessie to be alone. He would then enter the shop and hand over a farthing saying, with a perfectly straight face.

"Two caramels please Miss."

Knowing full well that Jessie would put six or seven in the paper poke.

One Saturday Jessie arrived home from her work at Cameron's Sweetie Shop around six thirty in the evening. Saturday were always the busiest day of the week so she was glad to take off her coat and shoes and look forward to enjoying a nice meal.

First things first, she handed her weekly wage packet over to her mother unopened. Agnes checked her payslip and then handed Jessie a florin as pocket money.

"Sorry Maw, no broken biscuits this week, there has been a bereavement in wee Edna's family, you know the Junior who started at the New Year. Mr Cameron has sent all the biscuits home to her mother, he thought they might be useful with people coming in and out and having tea.

Go and get my bag Robert it's through in the lassies room." said Jessie.

Robert did not need to be told twice, he was through into the bedroom like a shot. Returning brandishing Jessie's bag like a trophy.

"What have you got for us tonight Jessie?" he asked. "Any chance of puff candy this week?"

Saturdays were always popular days as Jessie was usually given a large bag of sweets to bring home for the family by Mr Cameron who owned the shop where she worked.

"I've no idea what is in the poke this week, you greedy wee carrot top. Just take what you get and think yourself jolly lucky. Now go and get some paper and cut it into squares and I'll divide up this weeks ration." said Jessie.

Robert ran to get a piece of paper and then cut it into seven squares which he laid out on the table.

Just then their father, Rab, arrived home with Alexander and James from the Miss Simpsons' house, up in Blairhill, where they had been gardening all afternoon.

Alexander was eager to check out his sweet ration but his mother snapped at him.

"Alexander, get yourself washed before you even think of sweets and none of you are having any until after we have finished the dinner. Mary should be back any minute and then we can get started. Now clear the table of all those bits of paper and get it set for the meal, you can worry about sweets later.

Jessie and Alex Johnstone are coming over this evening for a cup of tea and a blether so I want to get the food past and the place cleared up before they arrive."

Everyone was busy; getting washed, laying the table, checking the food, a normal Saturday night. Suddenly the door was pushed open and Mary Johnstone cried.

"Aunt Agnes quick give me a hand I've had to half carry your Mary home, she is not well at all."

Agnes sprung into action issuing instructions.

"Jessie turn down the bed and get out Mary's nightdress from the kist. James, Robert help me get her into the room and I'll get her undressed. Mary, can you make some tea for her and add two spoonfuls of sugar."

Within a few minutes Mary was undressed and in bed. Agnes tried to get her to drink the tea but it was hardly down until she was retching.

"Quick get the chanty pot my Mary is going to be sick." Agnes cried.

That sentence started a nightmare which lasted for weeks for the whole family and for the rest of Mary's life.

The evening wore on, whenever anyone tried to raise her from the bed Mary was again sick; she started to run a fever and complained of severe pains in her joints.

Mary Johnstone ran home to get her parents and by the time Jessie and Alex arrived Agnes was seriously worried about Mary's condition. Jessie examined her, then she whispered to Agnes.
"It looks bad to me. I don't think it is scarlet fever but I do think it is serious. Agnes, send one of the boys over for Mrs Millar, she will probably have a better idea as to what we should do for your Mary."

Agnes came out of the room and said to her husband.

"Mary is no better, Jessie here thinks we should send for Mrs Millar. Will I get our James to run over for her?"

Rab looked up from the bowl of soup he was eating and said.
"What! You want to send for that auld biddy, she is nothing but an auld witch, Ella Millar is not going to darken my door, so you and your pal Jessie can forget that idea, think on now Agnes. Nurse the lass yourselves."

Knowing Rab like she did Agnes did not argue she simply returned to the bedroom and shook her head.

For the next few hours Agnes and Jessie Johnstone did their best to bring the fever down and make Mary more comfortable. Their efforts were useless and Mary was now delirious.
Eventually Jessie Johnstone declared.

"I have had quite enough of this damned nonsense, we need Mrs Millar's advice. Does that daft auld bugger not realise his daughter's life is at stake here?"

Before Agnes could answer Jessie marched out of the room. Rab was leaning on the fence at the washing green, smoking a pipe with Alex. The normally easy going, good natured Jessie rounded on him.

"Look here Robert Law, I am going to get Mrs Millar this instant, regardless of what you say.   I will not see that girl die, and die she will if we don't get help for her.   Her illness is way beyond what Agnes and I can deal with."

With that she drew her shawl around her shoulders and ran off down the Herriot Row.

"Well Rab, that was you telt." said Alex.

"You know man, I think my Jessie is quite right you should let Mrs Millar come over and have a look at your Mary."

"You keep your family in check Alex, and I'll keep mine.   Jessie can bring back auld Ma Millar if she likes but I will decide whether or not she sees Mary." fumed Rab.

Jessie returned with Mrs Millar within ten minutes.

Robert barred the front door.   He didn't shout, he just spoke in a voice filled with menace.

"Jessie Johnstone, what do you think you are doing bringing that interfering auld crone to my door.   Agnes can nurse my lass, with help from my Jessie, the Laws' don't need your interference."

Jessie Johnstone was made of stern stuff, she fearlessly stood up to Rab.

"You can't frighten me Robert Law, that lass needs help and Agnes and I need somebody more experienced in medical matters than we are. So just move your bulk from the door and let us in to see your Mary."

Jessie pushed past him and Ella Millar followed in her wake.

In the bedroom they found Mary eaten up with fever, tossing and turning in the bed.   Agnes and young Jessie were fighting a losing battle.

Mrs Millar examined Mary thoroughly, saying.   "Get liquid into the lass, otherwise she is going to dehydrate, and keep bathing, we must try and abate the fever.   I've got a potion here which should help calm her."

They worked on Mary for some time.   Their efforts were all in vain and if anything Mary seemed worse than she had been earlier in the evening.

Mrs Millar left the bedroom and walked into the kitchen to get another jug of water. Rab and Alex were sitting by the fire drinking mugs of tea. "Well, you auld witch, how is my lass?" snarled Rab.

"You can insult me all you like you crabbit auld Ulsterman but your lass is seriously ill. I think she has a rheumatic fever. I have never nursed that kind of illness successfully, you need to send for the doctor. I know he will cost a pretty penny but it is your one and only chance to save Mary."

Robert roared.

"Agnes Law, you come here right now."

Agnes ran into the kitchen and faced Rab.

"Well Mistress Law" he said. "I know you hide past a penny or two, where is it. The auld woman can't help our lass so we are going to have to get the doctor to come, so we are."

Agnes went back into the bedroom and came out a few minutes later holding a piece of material tied with string. Carefully opening the pouch she spread the contents out over the table, it contained an assortment of small coins, threepenny bits, sixpences, pennies, far-things, half pennies, four florins, three half crowns and a ten shilling note.

"That is every penny I have in the house, together with Jessie's wages for the week, and some loose change, which is in my purse. I have already used James's dig money for this week to pay the Store bill. What do you have?"

Robert went into his pocket and emptied the contents, coins spilled on to the table. He shouted for James.

"Lad run as fast as ever your legs can carry you to Doctor Murphy's house in Blairhill. You know the one, his surgery is downstairs. Tell him that our lass is painfully ill and get him to come immediately, immediately mind."

Without answering James ran out of the house and headed for Blairhill.

Rab then rounded on Mrs Millar.

"I was right you are useless, away you go back to your hoose and leave me and mine to look after the lass."

Mrs Millar walked to the door but as she did she snapped at Rab.

"I'll be back you auld bugger."

Ella Millar returned a few minutes later bearing a pile of clean bedlinen. She walked straight through the kitchen and into the bedroom and gave the linen to Agnes, saying.

"You will need these, it's all I can do. Now, give me the wet bedclothes and I will get them washed and dried.

Jessie, it might help if you go home to the Long Row and get any clean linen you have, nursing is as important as the doctors' medicines. And, remember to get tepid liquids into her."

With her parting words she left the house glaring at Rab as she walked out through the kitchen.

By the time Doctor Murphy arrived it was gone midnight. He had insisted on finishing a meal and a bottle of fine malt with some of his cronies, from among the worthies of the Burgh, before he would leave the comfort of his home and walk down to the Gartsherrie Rows.

Dr Murphy examined Mary and confirmed Mrs Millar's diagnosis of rheumatic fever. He addressed Agnes.

"The girl will have a crisis sometime tonight or in the early hours of the morning. What happens then will determine if she will live or die. You can see for yourself, she is eaten up with the fever.

You must cut off all that rich red hair immediately, crop it close to her head, if she recovers it will grow again. You see the weight of it is not helping her beat the fever. Meantime I will give you a potion to help calm her into a deep sleep. Mrs Law I am afraid it is now down to the good Lord whether or not your lass pulls through."

Robert heard him speak from the doorway where he was standing. He spoke in his quiet measured way.

"You are as much a quack as auld Mrs Millar. The only thing you are both right about is that it is God's will whether my Mary lives or dies."

Agnes turned to Jessie. "Go and get my scissors from the work box and I'll cut her hair."

"No you don't my girl." Robert barred her way. "No scissors Jessie, you are not going to cut off that beautiful red hair. And, that is my very last word on the subject."

"Doctor, please" pleaded Agnes. "Please, please tell him we have to cut off her hair"

Rab snarled at the doctor.

"You might have the qualifications and the fine house but this is MY house, MY family. MY Mary will keep her bonny red hair. Is that clear to you all. Now tell me your price Doctor Murphy, I will pay you your due, then you will leave my house, so you will."

After a few minutes Rab returned to the room where Jessie and Agnes were quietly crying as they bathed Mary's fever.

He said "Do the best you can for her Agnes, but mind, leave her locks, they are not to be cut."

The rest of the night passed somehow. Agnes, Jessie, young Jessie and Mary Johnstone attending to Mary and trying to calm the fever.

In the kitchen the boys sat with Rab and Alex Johnstone. They drank tea, kept the fire burning and from time to time Alex and Robert tapped their pipes out on the range.

The crisis came around six o'clock. For a few minutes they were sure they had lost her and Agnes massaged her daughter's heart, she didn't know what else to do. At last Mary broke into a fitful sleep but the fever had broken and for the first time in the night of pure hell the women thought that she might just survive.

Jessie Johnstone exhausted, returned home with Alex and her daughter Mary. Young Jessie went into the boys bedroom, in order to get a few hours sleep; Agnes dozed off at the side of the bed holding Mary's hand.

When she awoke around nine o'clock the house was quiet and Mary was sleeping peacefully. Agnes started to rise but as she did she looked towards Mary and saw a sight that filled her with a horror she could not have imagined in her wildest dreams. Mary's beautiful red, wavy hair was laying across the bed, long thick skeins of beauty but poor Mary was laying, still mercifully sleeping, her face white and her head white. Doctor Murphy had been right, Mary's hair should have been shorn to her scalp, now it was too late.

Tears flowed from Agnes, tears for Mary, tears for her own weakness, tears of frustration, tears of anger, tears she did not know she had. They streamed down her face as she gently gathered up Mary's beautiful hair.

Panic now set into Agnes, she left the hair on the kitchen table and ran down Herriot Row to Ella Millar's home.

Agnes battered on the door crying. "Mrs Millar, Mrs Millar, something terrible has happened. Please come."

Ella Millar opened the door and was horrified to see the shock and fear on Agnes's face.

"What is the matter lass? Is your Mary having the crisis?" she asked.

"No," said Agnes in a breathless voice. The fever crisis is passed but there is another, an even worse, crisis. Her beautiful hair has all fallen out. I have gathered it up and I'll get rid of it, but how on earth will my poor Mary react when she wakes up."

Mrs Millar, always the voice of calm said, "Agnes come in off the step. Now first things first. Take one of my mutches to put on Mary's head to give the girl a bit of modesty. On no account destroy her locks. Here is a box and I have some tissue paper, wrap the locks in tissue and hide them away until everything settles and we find out if Mary's hair is going to grow back. Now I'll just get my shawl and we'll go and see your poor wee lassie."

Before Agnes had wakened, both Rab and James had left to work in the Miss Simpsons' garden, while young Robert and Alexander had left to play at an open air service for the Salvation Army. The boys would then attend the morning Holiness Service and Sunday School, before returning home after the three o'clock Praise Meeting.

During the day they were given soup with bread and generally biscuits or cake with big tin mugs of tea.

All of the menfolk would be safely out of the house for the entire day.

When Mrs Millar and Agnes arrived back at the Law home both young Jessie and Mary were still asleep.

Ella and Agnes looked at the mound of beautiful red hair laying on the kitchen table and even Ella Millar, who thought she had seen so much in her life that she was immune from tears, cried at the injustice of life. She then walked into the bedroom and gently placed the white mutch over Mary's bald head.

Shortly afterwards another visitor arrived, Doctor Murphy. When he saw the hair on the table he said.

"Just as I feared, I have occasionally seen this happening in the past. It was the sheer weight of Mary's hair that concerned me last night. But your husband is a powerful man, Mrs Law, his house, his family. You and I had no choice but to obey the auld bugger.

Now let me have a look at the young patient."

He examined Mary thoroughly, pronounced the crisis over but long term Mary would be left with a severely weakened heart.

"Your Mary will probably sleep for most of today, it is the way the body heals. When she wakes up give her a little tea with sugar and no milk or perhaps a little clear broth or beef tea. Start her on dry toast and build up her diet gradually. I will get my lad to hand in some heart pills, give her one every morning. And mind, Mrs Law if you want her to see the year out, no more working at the Brickwork for Mary. Light duties only for the rest of her life, mind now tell her father every word I have telt you."

Dr Murphy finished his report to Agnes and hurriedly left for his next home visit, relieved he he not encountered the erasable Robert Law.

Ella Millar put on the kettle and made some tea while Agnes wakened her daughter Jessie. They spent a long sad day tending to Mary.

Jessie Johnstone called in later, she too was shocked and upset, Jessie had known Mary since she was a tiny babe in arms and had always loved her as one of her family.

The younger boys arrived home from the Salvation Army around five o'clock. Rab and James were not far behind them, they walked into the kitchen carrying a sack full of vegetables and a tray of strawberries.

"Well Agnes, how is the lass now" her father asked. Agnes replied with a trembling voice.

"The doctor has been in to see her. Our Mary has been left with a permanently weak heart, she will never be able to do any long hours or heavy work again. But that is no the worst of her problems. Rab, her hair, her beautiful red hair."

At that Agnes had no more words, she burst into tears and couldn't finish speaking.

Young Jessie spoke up, with a courage that came from somewhere deep inside her, a courage that she did not know she even possessed.

"Paw, this tragedy, it's all your fault. Mary's hair has all fallen out and if you were not so pig headed, always having to be the boss, my sister would not be laying in that bedroom sleeping and not knowing the horror she is going to wake up to. If you had let Maw, or the doctor, cut her hair it would never have happened. You are a bully. Yes, you do it quietly, you never actually hit us, but you bully us all, particularly Maw. Well you are not going to bully me for the rest of my life."

With that she marched out of the kitchen and into the bedroom where her sister Mary lay, Jessie cried hot angry tears over her sister's bed.

All the boys and Agnes had listened with disbelief. No one in the Law household had ever questioned Rab's absolute authority and for it to come from Jessie, the gently one, was doubly shocking.

Rab turned to face Agnes. "Well wuman, is it true?"

"Aye Rab, it's all true." she replied through her tears.

Robert threw the sack of vegetables onto the table, turned tail and stomped out of the house.

CHAPTER 17
March 1924

It was the day of Mary's twenty fifth birthday. Since losing her hair to rheumatic fever, three years previously, she had been unable to carry out any full time work. Having to make some contribution to the household, Mary earned two shillings a time helping Mrs Millar to lay out bodies, she also helped at confinements but the money received depended on how much money the family could afford, sometimes she could spent several days at a home and only receive a shilling or two for all her skill and hard work.

Although the War was long over the fall out from the conflict was not. There was now a lot less work about and the brief prosperity that the War had brought, with full employment in the Iron and Steel Towns, was well and truly finished.

The Law family had been lucky in that Rab and his eldest son James had been kept on at the Works after the downturn. Also, young Robert had now started as an apprentice in the Engineering Shop, this good fortune was probably due to Rab's Orange Order and Masonic connections and perhaps a word from Tom Coats.

In the town generally the optimism and relief that had come with the end of the War had dissolved into a kind of acceptance that the lot of the working man was not going to greatly improve in the foreseeable future.

Men who had served their country with honour were now on the scrap heap. Men with no legs could be found begging; children ending up in the workhouse because their mothers could no longer cope with a husband who was off his head with shell shock; men having to take work at low, low, wages because it was all that was on offer and they had a family to feed.

Charlotte and her growing family had fared slightly better living in the countryside. Although Charlie did not earn a great wage they were never short of nutritious food and at Windy Hill Farm; far away from any industrial town, they did not experience first hand the new wave of discontent which was sweeping the country.

In the wake of the rheumatic fever Mary's life had changed beyond recognition. For the first few weeks nature had cushioned her, she spent her days in and out of sleep, totally unaware of the tragedy that had befallen her.

One evening Jessie was sitting with her, just talking about her day at the shop, when Mary said.

"When will I be able to stop wearing a mutch and see my hair grow properly again?"

In tears Jessie told her, as gently as she could of the happenings on the night of her fever crisis.

Even then Mary did not quite believe that her crowning glory, her beautiful red hair, had gone forever.

Jessie felt she had no option, she had to make her sister understand. There was no alternative, she went into the kitchen and asked her mother for Mary's locks. Agnes handed Jessie the carefully packed cardboard box containing Mary's hair wrapped in tissue paper.

Agnes knew that this day would eventually come, but when the moment arrived she could not stop her body shaking, nor the tears from blinding her eyes.

Jessie returned to the bedroom and carefully opened the box, removed the tissue and let Mary look upon her beauty.

The cries that rent the room were such as had never been heard in the Law home before, and never would be again.

Eventually Mary fell into the sleep of the exhausted with Jessie laying quietly crying beside her.

The following day Mary rose from her bed, thin and white and frail. With a shawl pulled around her shoulders over her nightgown she went into the kitchen. Her mother jumped when she heard her daughter say.

"I understand now Maw, I understand everything, everything, Jessie told me last night.

Mother I have got to find a way to live, I can't go out like this and I can't spent the rest of my days hiding in the house. What am I going to do?"

Relieved to be able to do something practical, Agnes said.

"I've been thinking lass and the best I can come up with is this. You take your locks, and wrap them around your head, I have managed to get some curling tongs, we heat the tongs on the fire and wave your hair at the front. I have bought you one of them new cloche hats, if you put it carefully on top you will look fine. At home you can wear a headscarf during the day, and just keep the mutch for night.

Mary my lass, I know it isn't a perfect answer but it is the best I can come up with, we just don't have the money for fancy wigs and suchlike."

And so began Mary's new life. Each day she dressed in her old working skirt and jersey in the morning, wearing a scarf tied in a turban style around her head. If she was going anywhere there was the hair tonging routine to give her the confidence to face the outside world.

One morning while Mary was helping her mother prepare the vegetables for soup and stovies Ella Millar knocked at the door. Turning the handle she came straight into the house, saying.

"Mary pet, can you give me some help for a few hours? Annie Houston is having yet another miscarriage, she lives down in the Square."

"Surely Mrs Millar" replied Mary.

Mary enjoyed working with Mrs Millar, she was perfectly aware that she would now never attain her ambition to be a nurse but at least helping Ella Millar gave her some fulfilment, away from cutting vegetables.

Mary pulled her coat around her and they set off at a pace.

On arriving at number 56 South Square they found Annie laying in bed crying her eyes out, sobbing.

"Six miscarriages, that's my sixth wee lost baby.   The other women can have them like shelling peas and here I am without a bairn to suckle once again."

Mary and Ella tried their best to comfort her after they had cleaned her up and Ella had burned the remains of what might have become a baby in the fire.

They stayed with Annie until her man Willie returned from his shift.   As soon as he came into the house Ella bristled, saying.

"Get your coat Mary, we have done all we can here."   In a sharp voice Mrs Millar then addressed the husband.

"Willie Houston, we have tidied Annie up and given her some tea and toast, it's up to you now to care for her, and, Willie Houston, here me now, I do not expect to be called to a seventh miscarriage. Do you fully understand me?"

With her parting shot she gathered up Mary and they set off back to the Herriot Row.

As they walked Mary questioned Ella.

"Mrs Millar why were you so nippy with Annie's husband? They have quite a nice clean house and he doesn't look the type who would be bad to her."

"Mary, there are many different ways of being bad." replied Ella.

"Look you are no longer a young girl Mary, you are well over twenty-one now so I am going to tell you something.   The reason Annie has lost all those bairns is Willie.

The dirty sod contracted a sexual disease from a prostitute, I am not sure what, probably syphilis, and he will have passed it on to her. That is why the poor woman miscarries and she thinks it is all her fault that she can't have a bairn.   If he had one ounce of decency he wouldn't touch her but you can bet your boots next year I will be cleaning up after her seventh loss, or she will die from either the disease or a broken heart.   Mary, see men, men's bastards."

The Law family were sitting down to dinner when Mary arrived home but Mary could hardly eat a bite she was so shocked, how could she have grown up totally unaware that depravity, such as Ella had explained to her existed, even in the Rows.

The following afternoon Ella Millar called and gave Mary two half crowns, informing her that Willie had called on her the previous evening and paid ten shillings for their nursing care of Annie.

"Nursing care be damned." Ella whispered to Mary. "It's money to keep my mouth shut."

Ella left and Agnes lifted the half crowns from the table, she then got out her purse and handed a shilling to Mary saying.

"There you are you can have a wee bit of pocket money to yourself this week."

As was to be expected Mary was very sensitive about the loss of her hair and for once the boys understood and there was never any teasing of Mary. Unfortunately they took this to excess and Mary missed out on a lot of the family banter, the boys now tended to treat her more as a second mother rather than a sister.

Shortly after the Annie Houston incident, Agnes asked Mary to go down to the Store one day for some shopping. After buying her messages Mary thought that she would pop in and see if her Auntie Jessie was in on the way home.

Walking up the Long Row she saw a group of children poking something with a stick. Mary went over to see what was happening and she found a tiny little black puppy laying on the ground, probably not far from death.

Mary's red temper had not entirely deserted her, she grappled the stick from the boy and threw it to the ground. Bending down she picked up the little scrap of humanity and found a flickering heartbeat.

As quickly as she could she reached the Johnstone home. Turning the door handle the rushed into the kitchen, calling. "Aunt Jessie, Aunt Jessie, I've just found this poor wee thing, do you think we can save it?"

Jessie, kind hearted as always said.

"If we can we will. Now lass you sit there and massage the wee thing's heart, I'll go and warm some milk and I have a wee taste whisky in the press, that might revive it."

Jessie gave Mary a little bowl with the whisky and milk and a clean rag. "Wet the rag lass, and drop it into the wee soul's mouth."

Mary sat the rest of the day nursing the little pup. Meantime

Jessie went up to the Herriot Row to tell Agnes what had happened and to tell her to expect a new addition to the family.

The pup survived the day and late that night Alex walked Mary home with her little surviver.

Over the following days Mary nursed the pup and the wee thing slowly thrived.

One day Alexander asked.

"Mary, I think that wee dog is here to stay, what are you going to call it? What about Albion or Rover, after the football, that would be good or maybe Bonzo? Have you any ideas?"

"I know what I intend to call her, it's Rags. If it hadn't been for the little rag Auntie Jessie gave me to feed her with she wouldn't be here, so Rags it is."

"Great name Mary, besides she looks like a wee bunch of black rags." said Alexander. "At least you are not going to give it a soppy name like Flossy or Bunty, that would be just too awful. Can you imagine me and our Robert shouting; 'Flossy, dear wee Flossy' we couldn't hold our heads up with the lads at the band practice.

Rags became Mary's constant companion, two souls who had been saved from the jaws of death, two souls who saved each other.

CHAPTER 18
April 1924

Jessie had worked for Mr and Mrs Cameron at Cameron's Sweetie Shop in Bank Street since leaving school at fourteen and she was now the Chargehand. At only eighteen she had an assistant, a plain, chubby girl called Edna and a young school leaver called Milly, who had recently taken her place as a Junior at the end of the pecking order, working under Edna.

Her Father, while glad that she had been promoted, and was now earning more money, was rather put out that she was doing so well at such an early age. He would often make barbed little comments like 'always a rise before a fall' or 'don't you go letting that Chargehand Badge go to your heed', 'just remember who you are and where you came from'.

With Mary's support and encouragement Jessie ignored his comments, but it would have been nice, just for once, to be praised, instead of being subjected to an undercurrent of snide comments which probably had their roots in a strange combination of jealousy and pride.

Rab's failing health had not helped his already prickly nature and being dependent on his children for the majority of the family income was difficult for him to accept.

It was a normal Monday morning at the shop. Mr Cameron had gone to the Airdrie Savings Bank from where he was going straight into Glasgow to buy supplies; Milly was cleaning the windows and brushing the pavement; Edna was renewing the stock in the jars and Jessie was filling the plates under the glass counter top with the high quality chocolates. There was absolutely nothing to indicate that Jessie's life was about to be caught into a whirlwind of change in the next few seconds.

The bell above the door rang and in walked a tall handsome man with a military bearing. Jessie looked up from what she was doing, saying "Yes sir, can I help you?" The gentleman spoke quietly.

"I wonder if I could have a word with you alone Miss Law?" He nodded his head towards Edna.

Jessie turned to her junior saying.

"Edna, please go out and give Milly a hand with the cleaning. I don't want Mr Cameron to return and find the outside of the shop not up to scratch. You know how he likes time spent on a Monday morning making the place absolutely spotless."

After Edna had gone outside muttering to herself, Jessie asked the mystery man.

"Why did you want to speak to me on my own?"

The man spoke with a beautiful, well educated Glasgow accent.

"I have recently taken a lease on a shop across the road, number eighteen Bank Street. I intend to open it in a few weeks time as a Drysalters, but also providing a wall-papering and decorating service. Would you like to come and work for me as the Manager?"

"What, me a Manager of a Drysalters, you must be mad." Was Jessie's immediate response.

"Tell me why I'm mad?" responded the man.

Hardly pausing for breath Jessie said. "For a start I don't know anything about Drysaltery; and you don't know me from, from, from a bar of soap and I have a perfectly good job working for Mr Cameron. Are those reasons good enough?"

The man laughed. "Miss Law I have heard excellent references about your work, if you can look after one shop you can look after another. Let me introduce myself; my name is Anderson McInnes. I have had a shop at the top of Main Street, 'McInnes Drysaltery' for a few years now, and another in Airdrie. Tell me Miss Law, how much does Mr Cameron pay you a week?"

"Do you not think that information is my personal business?"

replied Jessie.

"Yes it is, but it might be in your best financial interest to discuss wages with me. Tell you what, meet me in Lang's tea shop at one o'clock, we can have a sandwich and a cup of tea and finalise matters."

With that he walked out of the shop, leaving behind an astounded Jessie.

Jessie's lunch break was one until two o'clock so she decided to keep the appointment with the mysterious Mr McInnes. Try as she would she could not put Anderson McInnes out of her mind for the rest of the morning.

At five minutes to one Jessie went into the back shop, combed her hair and applied a rub of pale pink lipstick. With a last look in the mirror she took off her overall, put on her coat and headed off to Langs.

The mystery man had arrived before her and was seated at a table for two.

McInnes rose and smiled as she joined him, greeting her quite formally. "Good-day Miss Law, I am so glad you could join me. Now what would you like for lunch?"

"Just a tea, milk no sugar and perhaps a cheese sandwich." answered Jessie.

McInnes placed the order and one for tea and a ham sandwich with mustard for himself.

While they waited for the food they each waited for the other to speak in what became a long awkward silence.

Eventually McInnes said in an exasperated voice.

"Jessie do you have any idea why I have asked you to manage my shop?"

Jessie replied. "Absolutely none whatsoever, but I would love to know your reasoning."

"Well I shall tell you? Jessie you are like me, you understand how to sell to customers without them realising you have led the sale and how to maximise the profit from your sales. You understand your market Jessie."

"Well Mr ever so clever McInnes how did I manage to do all

that and not realise I had achieved so much. I must be pretty clever too." reposted Jessie.

"That is the key, my dear Miss Law, you do it instinctively. For example, did you or did you not suggest to Mr Cameron that he should buy in those nice round boxes to hold the special chocolates and finish the presentation with a gold ribbon, printed with the name Cameron? And, did you or did you not get him to buy in presentation boxes tied with pink ribbon for rose creams, and lilac ribbon for violet creams? And, did you or did you not come up with the idea of seasonal window displays? And, have these ideas, and many other ideas of yours, increased the sales in Mr Cameron's shop considerably? And finally, has Mr Cameron remunerated you for all the extra sales? Answer please Miss Law."

Jessie was saved from having to make an immediate answer by the waitress bringing their tea and sandwiches. She picked at her sandwich for a few moments before answering.

"Actually Mr McInnes you are absolutely right, I have increased the shop sales by a considerable amount, and made the shop more upmarket. My next suggestion to him was going to be that the staff should have the name Cameron's embroidered on our overalls.

In return for all my ideas and work I receive the correct wage for my age, not a penny more. The only extra I ever get is a bag of sweets, anything broken or poor sellers, to take home for my brothers on a Saturday night. But, I do know about sweeties. I don't know anything about wallpaper and paint."

"Miss Law you were not born knowing about sweeties, you had to learn, and if you can learn about sweets and you can easily learn about drysaltery. My guess is you are earning around one pound a week, if I offered you a starting wage of two pounds per week while you train at my Main Street shop. Then when we open in Bank Street in addition to your weekly wage we will set monthly targets and if you exceed them you will get a percentage of the profit. How does that sound?"

Jessie immediately made a decision. She thought, 'opportunities for a lass from the Gartsherrie Rows don't come that often, besides he looks and speaks like a real gent, I'm going to take a chance and I'm not going to ask Maw and Paw, they would never let me move from Camerons'.

"Mr McInnes, I would be pleased to accept your offer. When do you want me to start? And, by the way thanks for the lunch it was lovely."

"Excellent. But first things first, we are now colleagues, call me McInnes, everyone does, and can I call you Jessie?"

"Course you can call me Jessie, particularly since you are doubling my wages, if you want you can call me Princess Jessie of the 'Brig."

"Right, Princess Jessie of the 'Brig let's get down to business. Hand in your notice to Mr Cameron this very afternoon. Next Monday morning you start at the Main Street shop working for my Manager, Hugh Mason.

Hugh is a clever chap. Learn everything you can from him in four or five weeks. As soon as the Bank Street shop is ready Hugh will help you with the initial stocking and then, and then, my dear Princess Jessie you are on your own. You can take on an assistant and a trainee lad, if he is any good we will apprentice him as a painter and decorator. Initially the painters will work for Hugh but eventually I hope you will run your own team.

Now to business."

McInnes rose from his seat, paid the bill and together they left the tearoom.

Jessie worked the remainder of the week at Cameron's. On the Saturday evening she handed over her pay packet to her mother as usual, but still she couldn't find the right words to tell her mother that this was the last pay poke she would receive from Cameron's Sweet Shop.

Robert had spotted Jessie coming home and immediately came in from playing football with his pals.

"I guess that's the end of our Saturday sweeties." moaned Robert.

"What do you mean? 'An end to the sweeties' what are your talking about Robert?" questioned Agnes.

"Well Jessie isn'ae working at the Sweetie Shop any more, so she'll no get sweeties will she?" Robert explained.

By now Agnes was getting annoyed with him. "Speak clearly lad what are you on about?"

Robbie spoke slowly in a slightly exasperated voice.

"Maw, I go to school and play football with Robert Mackie, Edna's brother. Edna who works with Jessie. He told me that Jessie finishes today and Edna is going to be the new Chargehand so he will get the Saturday sweeties from now on."

Jessie listened to this exchange with a sinking heart.

"It's not what it seems Ma. I have another job," explained Jessie "and it is much better wages. I'll be able to increase my dig money from next week."

"Jessie Law, I want a full explanation as to what is going on. Don't you realise your Paw will go mad when he finds out you have given up a perfectly good job, without asking his permission. And, I'm none too pleased either. Speak up girl." demanded Agnes.

"Look Maw I've been offered an opportunity to train as a Manager for a drysaltery shop. I will be getting twice as much money and it is a really great chance to further my career."

"Since when did folk like us from the Rows have a career? We have a job and damned glad we are to have one. Have you taken leave of your senses girl?" snapped Agnes.

"I don't care what you and my Paw say. This is my opportunity to do something with my life and I am going to take the job that has been offered to me. Monday morning at eight thirty I will be starting work at the McInnes Drysalters shop in the Main Street.

Rab was furious when he arrived home and Agnes informed him of Jessie's decision to leave her job.

The expected row took place. On this occasion, both Agnes and Rab were in total agreement, neither of them could conceive as to why Jessie would want to give up a perfectly good job for another position, a position that seemed to both of them alien and 'above her station in life'.

Jessie held her ground, for all her gentleness and easy going ways she had a determined streak which was all the more effective as she seldom used it.

Eventually, she lifted her coat and said.

"Maw, Paw, enough.   If you want a wage from me next
Saturday I have to go and work for Mr McInnes, it's as simple as
that.   I'm going out for a wee while now, don't worry I'll be back
before nine o'clock."

Jessie headed down Herriot Row and towards the Long Row,
she barely acknowledged the greetings of neighbours as she
focused all her energy in getting to the safe haven of number 130.

On reaching the Johnstone household she found her sister
Mary having tea with Jessie and her daughter Mary Johnstone, Rags
laying on the rug in front of the fire.

Jessie welcomed young Jessie who was by now breathless and
flushed.

"Come in my wee namesake, what have you been up to to get
so red in the face?

Join us blethering gossips and I'll get you a wee cup of tea or
would you like a bit of dinner lass?"

"Thanks Aunt Jessie, I've just run down here from our house
because my Maw and Paw are fair mad at me.   We have just had
the row to end all rows."

"They are never mad at you Jessie lass, the boys; yes, but never
you."

Jessie took off her coat and told the entire story; from the
arrival of the mystery man at the shop, to lunch with McInnes,
keeping her secret all week and then her parents fury.

Jessie and the two girls listened, fascinated, at what seemed like
a story out of a magazine.

When Jessie had finished her tale Jessie Johnstone said.

"Well done Jessie lass, you are my namesake in more ways than
just one.

Sometimes in life you just have to do what feels right for you,
not what pleases others.

Your Maw is my best friend, we have been through thick and
thin together over the years but I think she is wrong this time, and
I'll tell her so.   I know what your Paw is like and I wouldn't have
expected any different from him but my God your mother should

realise that women must have rights over how they choose to live their lives.

Your mother was devastated when Charlotte went against her, I admit I was disappointed that her and my Sam did not make a couple, but I quickly came to my senses and realised that we all have to walk our own road.

Now you are striking out as an independent young woman. Your parents can see that they are losing their strict control over their children and they are not happy.

Do you know what? Jessie Law, I am real proud of your stance. If the women's movement taught me nothing else it taught me women have to take control of their lives, regardless of the feelings of their family and friends.

Both my girls have supported me in my involvement with the Suffragette Movement and in return I have supported them both in their life choices.

Now Jessie, you and Mary, finish up your tea and cake and get up the road to Herriot Row. The pair of you keep your heads down and try not get into an argument with your parents.

I'll come over tomorrow, when your Paw is out doing his gardening, and have a word with your Maw. Disappear and leave me on my own with her."

True to her word Jessie called into the Law home in Herriot Row the following morning. Agnes never mentioned the visit but she said no more about Jessie's change of job.

On Monday morning Jessie set out to work, not at Cameron's Sweets, but at McInnes Drysaltery, Wallpapering & Painting Shop.

After years of working with chocolates and an assortment of sweets and biscuits Jessie's first reaction on entering the shop was the heady aroma. A combination of paraffin, firelighters, cleaning materials, varnishes and turpentine, a unique heady perfume of a smell to be found in every Drysalters in the country.

Jessie arrived at the shop in Main Street at quarter past eight, she knew opening time was eight thirty but she wanted to show willing.

As she arrived two boys were taking down the shutters and she could see a older man writing at the polished wooden counter.

"Hello," said one of the boys, "you must be Jessie Law. Mr Mason has been expecting you, I'll let you into the shop."

The butterflies in Jessie's stomach were doing a Charleston, but on the outside she was doing her best to appear calm and collected.

"Good morning Mr Mason my name is Jessie Law, Mr McInnes has employed me to work in his new shop. I'm reporting this morning for training."

Hugh Mason was a widower in his late fifties. The War had not treated him kindly; he had lost one son in France; his younger son had served in the navy, after the War he married a girl from Portsmouth and was now settled hundreds of miles away on the south coast. Tragically his wife Ethel and daughter Grace had both died in the Spanish flu epidemic.

Hugh was alone, lonely, and in order to survive his pain he worked every hour he could in the shop. His loyalty to McInnes was absolute, the elder Mason boy, Fergus, had served in the same regiment as Major McInnes and it was McInnes who had written the condolence letter to Hugh and his wife Ethel. There are some kindnesses that can never be forgotten, or fully repaid.

Hugh looked at this little slip of a girl from the Gartsherrie Rows, who new absolutely nothing about drysaltery, and thought to himself. 'The boy has gone mad, what on earth is McInnes thinking about putting a wee lassie in charge of his new shop.'

Putting his thoughts aside what Hugh actually said was.

"Good morning lass, we are going to be working together between the two shops, my job is to teach you the trade. The lads all call me Mr Mason, and you will be known as Miss Law to all the staff. It's all right to call me Hugh in private but in front of the others, always Mr Mason and I will address you as Miss Law. That is your first lesson, make sure the staff know who the boss is, you don't have to be a dictator, just set yourself a little apart.

Now Miss Law you have a terrible lot to learn in a few short weeks, I'll have to show you all the basics before we can even look at the book work and estimating.

You know McInnes has set you a real formidable task, are you aware of how hard it's going to be to garner enough knowledge to move down to Bank Street in a few weeks time?"

Jessie, trying to sound more confident than she actually felt said.

"Mr Mason, I'm not in the least afraid of hard work. I will do my very best not to let you and Mr McInnes down."

"Ah" said Hugh, "McInnes is a law unto himself, he expects everyone from the King to the midden man to address him as McInnes, second lesson, drop the Mr as far as the boss is concerned.

Now lass come into the storeroom with me and we'll start to get on with teaching you the job proper."

Hugh Mason had decided that there was only one way to deal with McInnes's daft idea of putting a wee lassie in charge of a shop, he was going to work her hard. Harder than she could possibly imagine and he was also going to set her work to do at home in the evenings. For the next few weeks Miss Jessie Law would only have time to sleep.

If she couldn't stand the pace she was not going to get the shop, he would see to that. McInnes would be saved from himself, whether he liked it or not.

However, Hugh had not allowed for Jessie's streak of determination or her lifetime spent in the Rows with Rab and Agnes Law as parents.

Jessie was given a brown overall and the training started. Soft soap, soap flakes, soda, baking powder, vinegar, bleach, what to recommend for removing a stain. How to differentiate between grades of chamois leather; the importance of the Poison Register; how to measure out oils into small bottles from the gallon containers; who to re-order from when stock was becoming low.

Hugh was obsessive that all his staff knew the price of each and every item in the shop. Even as he was instructing Jessie on other matters he would suddenly ask 'how much is a full bar of carbolic soap? and 'how much a half bar?'

While she was eating her sandwich and drinking a cup of tea at lunch time Jessie was still absorbing information, listening to every nugget of conversation.

Each day when the shop closed Hugh would hand Jessie pages of arithmetic to work on at home. He also gave her paint charts and expected her to know the names of each colour produced by each manufacturer.

Drysaltery skills were far removed from working in a Sweetie Shop and to a large extent more masculine. Jessie was an exceptionally pretty girl and she knew if she was to succeed in a man's world she would have to be not just as good as, but better than, her male colleagues.

As each day passed Hugh had to reluctantly admit that Miss Jessie Law was not just a pretty face, she knew how to work hard and she was accurate. If he gave her a formula, eighth of a gill of this, two eighths of that five of the other, he could be sure that her measurements would be reliable.

Hugh also found that a pretty face in the shop was not necessarily a bad thing. Jessie's skill in serving customers sweets and biscuits transferred easily to selling lavender furniture polish and Sunlight soap.

On Saturday night, after the boys and painters had all finished for the day, Jessie was helping Hugh count the takings and prepare the weekly summary for McInnes.

Hugh surprised her by saying.

"Jessie I have your pay poke for the week and I have to be fair and say you have certainly earned your money. I own I had grave doubts about you but if you keep up the work rate you have set this week I think you might, you just might, make a go of the Bank Street shop.

Mind you, you have a long way to travel yet, but a good start lass, a good start. Now I think you need a wee break from arithmetic and paint charts."

He handed Jessie a pile of house design magazines and publicity blurbs from the big wallpaper and paint companies, saying.

"Read these lass. You must have a handle on what is, and what is not, fashionable. In our game there is no point in stocking up with brown paint when cream is the 'in' colour. Also the customers need your advice on how to make their homes look good, get it right and it's big business, get it wrong and you will be the laughing stock of Coatbridge.

Now away with you lass, have a night out at the dancing or the films and start your studies again tomorrow."

Jessie couldn't put the magazines down, it was like a door opening in her head, she had found where she wanted to do in life, her path was making homes look beautiful.

When Jessie arrived back at the Herriot Row her father and the boys were out, only her mother and Mary were at home.

Agnes accepted her enhanced wage packet, she checked the payslip and then handed Jessie her usual two shillings.

Jessie took a deep breath and said.

"Maw, I am working a great deal harder now than I was at Cameron's and earning a lot more money so I think I should get more pocket money."

Agnes reacted like Mr Bumble shouting at Oliver Twist. "More, More, why would you need more girl, are you not well fed and I bought you a winter coat two years ago, and it's only weeks since you got a new pair of shoes.   How dare you ask for more."

"Ma think about it." reasoned Jessie. "James is earning less than me and he gets five shillings a week pocket money.   It's not fair."

"Fair is it" stormed Agnes.   "James is a lad, you are a girl. Now I have heard enough of this nonsense."

A week of working like a slave had given Jessie courage, once again she challenged her mother.

"Maw what was my Aunt Jessie fighting for on the votes for women issue if it wasn't for equality.   Surely you above anybody should want women to get a fair deal, now can I have the same as our James."

"No you can't and that the end of it." thundered Agnes.

On no account was she going to allow Jessie to change the strict order of things in the Law household, besides Rab would be mindless if he thought for one moment that one of the girls was financially equal to one of his lads.

"Look I'll tell you what I'll do, you can have three and six a week from now on and if you get any more increases we might bring it up a wee bit. Jessie that is my final word on the subject, now take your three and six and let's have done with it."

Jessie knew when she was beat but at least she had made a stand and three and six a week was better than two shillings.

Jessie's second and third weeks working with Hugh followed the same pattern as the first, work all day and study all night.

There was no sign of McInnes and sometimes Jessie wondered if he was in fact a real person or was he merely a figure of her and Hugh's imaginations.

By the start of week four Jessie was starting to feel much more confident. First job in the morning was setting up the till for the day; then, checking the stock and preparing the re-order book; giving the painters their dockets with instructions and materials; phoning the wholesalers with any orders required, not a job she relished as the new fangled candlestick telephone terrified her; preparing the invoicing from the previous day's jobs and placing them in the post dookit.

While carrying out all these jobs she had to constantly stop and serve customers.

"Quarter a pun of saft soap hen and give us a cake oh yer pipe clay." Or "I'm jist here to collect my paraffin, I left the can with your laddie last night." Or "Would you be so good as to request Mr Mason to call at my home and give me an estimate for painting and papering my dining room."

Jessie joked, was respectful or efficient, in fact, she adopted whatever attitude was called for in order to ensure a contented customer left the McInnes shop in Main Street, Coatbridge.

On Wednesday morning Hugh called Jessie into the inner sanctum, his office in the back shop. It was located in the far right hand corner, two wooden partitions and a door had been added to form an office, both partitions had glass windows to enable Hugh to keep an eye on the goings on in the shop at all times, even when he was sat at his desk.

Hugh addressed her quietly.

"Right Jessie lass you have worked well in the shop but today I intend to take you out estimating with me. You have a lot to learn and I can't teach you overnight, part of it is simply accuracy in taking measurements but a lot is instinct on how you sell an idea to a client, sometimes you have to save them from themselves. I have three estimating jobs to go to today, just stay quiet, look, listen and learn."

By the time they had returned, just before lunchtime, Jessie had developed a whole new respect for how Hugh operated. His measuring and pricing skills were extremely efficient but Hugh's real skill was in how he advised the client, by turn he was respectful, agreeable, amusing, however by the time he left the premises the client's ideas had been transferred to paper in an entirely do-able format and any peculiar ideas had been severely censored.

When he returned to the shop he transferred the information he had gleaned into detailed estimates and included proposed dates for carrying out the work. These were written up into an official estimate and put into the post dookit so that the clients would receive the estimates without any undue delay.

For the remainder of the week Hugh took Jessie out each day on his estimating forays. By Friday he was allowing her to do the measuring and on the Saturday morning he even allowed her some input into the discussions.

Saturday night in the Herriot Row and Jessie once again handed over her wages and received three and six pocket money.

After eating her dinner she said to Mary.

"Let's go out for a couple of hours to the pictures, I've heard there is a new Rudolph Valentino film on at the Cinema in Bank Street."

Within fifteen minutes they were at Sunnyside Road waiting for the Baxter's bus to take them into Coatbridge.

Once settled in the bus Jessie said to Mary.

"I'm not that bothered about the pictures, I just wanted to get out of the house and tell you how things were going at the shop this week.

Hugh Mason took me out estimating Mary, I absolutely loved it.

On Monday he is going to show me how to turn the notes into accurate estimates. Not only did we go to houses, we also went to shops and offices, it was wonderful. I can't wait to get into Bank Street and head up my own team, my head is simply buzzing with all kinds of ideas.

For the first few months Hugh will control the painters but if I get everything else right he will train me to operate my own painting team and I will truly be the boss in Bank Street.

I am so excited but I just can't say too much at home, you know what Maw and Paw are like. 'We mustn't get above ourselves' and the idea of me in a qualified job before any of the boys well, it simply doesn't bear thinking about."

Mary agreed with her sister's caution.

"You know what Jessie, you are absolutely right, best say as little as possible. It's not fair, but neither is life fair, once you get established they will have to accept you are on the upward ladder. It you are seen to be climbing too soon and too fast they will push you off.

You must be earning near as much as Paw, I'd keep well quiet on that subject."

"That's easy" laughed Jessie. "Me with my three and six to splash about, what a joke."

Week five started on a positive note. Monday morning about eleven Hugh addressed Jessie.

"Make us both a wee cup of tea and then come into my office." Hugh didn't preamble. He came straight to the point.

"Jessie this is your last week in Main Street, the shop fitters are almost finished in Bank Street. This afternoon we will prepare the initial stocking lists and you can telephone in the orders. Arrange for deliveries on Friday or Saturday and you can open the doors of your new shop next Monday.

I have also set up a number of staff interviews for you this afternoon, my suggested questions are written on this piece of paper. Take notes but remember instinct counts for a lot. McInnes had an instinct about you. I must own I was not at all convinced at the outset that you could do the job, in fact I was dead against the idea of a slip of a girl managing one of McInnes's shops but I think you might, you just might, make a go of it.

I reckon we will work together over the next few months on the painting side but I promise you lass as soon as I think you can go it alone you can start to build up your own team of painters.

Now I am off out on a job, you sit yourself down behind my desk and get your head around how you are going to tackle the interviewing.

Tomorrow I'll take you down to see the shop and we'll spend Wednesday, Thursday, Friday and Saturday getting everything ready."

Jessie was so happy she thought her heart would burst. Approval from a man like Hugh was, in her eyes, worth everything. So far, so good, rung one on her new career ladder.

The following days did not seem to contain enough hours. Wednesday morning Jessie and her mentor met at the new shop and set to work.

Jessie had managed to get one of the new lads, Stanley, to start immediately.   He was a veteran from the War who had lost most of his right leg.   Hugh had not been convinced about his employment, aware of how physically hard drysaltery shop work could be. However, Jessie in her quite way insisted on her choice so Stanley joined the McInnes family.

Hugh, Jessie and Stanley hardly stopped working, together with the tradesmen and delivery men who constantly came and went.

Hugh insisted that they stop every day at one o'clock and have a half hour break to eat lunch and Jessie kept them fortified with cups of tea throughout the day.

Hugh would often give Stanley money and ask him to go to the City Bakeries for Paris buns or crumpets to have with their tea, noticing how little food he brought with him for his lunch break.

Around four o'clock on Saturday afternoon Hugh said.

"I need to get away up to the Main Street Shop now and cash up the money. Jessie there isn't much left to do, you and Stanley finish up now, then you can lock the door and get away home. Monday is going to be a big day, now lass, enjoy your weekend."

They checked everything was spit spot then Jessie sent Stanley proudly home with his wage poke, the first the ex-soldier had seen in a great many years.

With the shop all to herself Jessie walked around and looked at the results of all their hard work, everything was indeed 'tickety boo'. The window display was eye catching; all the shelves were fully stocked and everything priced; the wooden counter was gleaming; the paraffin tank was full; fresh roll of craft paper at the ready with scissors on a long string; yes all was well for the grand opening on Monday morning.

Jessie started to do a little jig around the shop, singing her happiness.

Her singing was interrupted by the bell ringing as the door opened, in walked a tall handsome man.

His first words were.

"Well Princess Jessie of the Brig, I hear from my Lieutenant Mason that you have passed muster and you are ready to accept Monday's challenge."

He then presented her with a bunch of spring flowers, offering his gift with a theatrical flourish.

"For you, Jessie Law to celebrate the opening of our Bank Street shop and the further expansion of the McInnes empire."

Jessie was dumbstruck, she had not seen McInnes since he had offered her the job all those weeks ago. Now on the brink of the shop opening he turns up, not only turns up, but turns up with a beautiful bunch of flowers.

"I was beginning to think you were a figment of my overactive imagination" said Jessie.

"I've been busy in Glasgow." McInnes informed her. "As well as the shops I have a real job in shipping. Unfortunately the last few weeks have been hectic so I have had to depend on my man Hugh to keep me up to date on what was happening in the Coatbridge outpost of my empire.

Tell me Miss Law, how have you enjoyed the past few weeks under the tutorage of Lieutenant Hugh?"

"Enjoyed isn't exactly the right word Mr McInnes, sorry

McInnes, Hugh told me on no account to call you Mr. Why? And, don't you have a Christian name like other people?"

"Of course I have a Christian name Miss Law. I sign all my correspondence T. Anderson McInnes."

"T isn't a proper name and Anderson is another surname. What does T stand for Mr, err McInnes?"

"Ah ha Miss Law that is for me to know and you to find out.

Now Jessie Law tell me all about your training from Hugh and what you intend to do with the shop, because I am pretty sure you have plans."

Jessie spent the next hour telling him all about the work she had been doing over the past weeks; her fears, her triumphs, her disasters; her excitement, the staff she had engaged and best of all her ideas for Bank Street Shop.

He interrupted her recitation mid flow.

"Let's lock up the shop and go for something to eat. We can talk more comfortably over a bite of supper."

Jessie suddenly realised what time it was.

"I would love to come out for some supper but I have to get home now. My family will be expecting me."

"No problem" said McInnes. "I have my car parked outside, I'll give you a run home, you can freshen up or whatever ladies do, and then we can head out somewhere nice for supper."

Jessie was horrified at the idea of driving up the Herriot Row in a motor car, although she was thrilled at the idea of riding beside McInnes.

"I'd love a ride in your car but honestly McInnes, you can't possibly drive up the Herriot Row, firstly it's all cobbles and secondly you, well you just can't. My father would go mad if he saw me riding in a motor car. We are not the kind of family who ride about in motor cars."

"Well, Miss Law" said McInnes, "I beg to differ, you are exactly the kind of person who rides in a motor car and I fully intend to take you home, before your parents start sending out search parties.

Now Miss Law, let's get this shop locked up, pick up your flowers and we are off."

True to his word McInnes drove to Gartsherrie and Jessie directed him to the Herriot Row. Neighbours from the length of the Row came out to see the incredible sight of wee Jessie Law sitting in the front of one of them new fangled motor cars beside a real toff, clutching a large bunch of flowers.

McInnes parked outside the Law home. As Jessie got out of the car Robert and Alexander ran out of the house to take in the sight of their sister being brought home, not just in a motor car, but in a bull nosed Morris Cowley, wow.

Jessie hurried into the house, fortunately her father was having a rest in the bedroom so had not heard the commotion.

"Maw, Mr McInnes has just given me a lift home" Jessie explained to her mother.

"I just wanted to give you my pay packet and put my flowers in water, then I am going out with him for something to eat so we can discuss the opening of his new shop on Monday."

Agnes spoke quietly, so as not to disturb Rab.

"You are, are you, Jessie Law. Going out with the gentry for something to eat. Well let me tell you, no good will come of it, so just get out there and tell him you are not going out anywhere with him."

Jessie spoke equally softly, but with equal determination.

"Maw, you have enjoyed my new wages for the past few weeks, haven't you, well Mr McInnes is my boss, I am going out with him to discuss the shop, because that is what I have to do to keep my job. Now if you want to keep enjoying my wages let me get a quick wash and change of clothes. I won't be late back. I'll be home by around ten o'clock, same time as Mary will be back from the films with Ina."

Without any further discussion Jessie quickly got changed and was outside and ready to leave within fifteen minutes.

What she found was McInnes in deep conversation with her two younger brothers discussing the finer points of his bull nosed Morris Cowley.

Seeing Jessie come out of the house he said.

"Right lads, got to get off now, but the next time I call I promise to give you both a ride in my pride and joy."

He held the door open for Jessie and helped her into the car, much to the delight of the boys. There would be weeks worth of teasing from this encounter, as well as the prospect of a ride in the Morris.

McInnes drove to the Royal Hotel. He then opened the car door and helped Jessie out, escorting her into the restaurant.

Jessie was initially horrified at the complicated French menu but she was smart enough to put it down and say to McInnes.

"I like most things, I am sure whatever you order will be lovely. Actually I have had nothing to eat since a sandwich at about one o'clock so I would probably enjoy anything."

They ate a chicken consommé, followed by poached chicken with a light cream sauce, vegetables and sauté potatoes.

During the meal they spoke of Jessie's learning experience with Hugh and her ideas for the shop.

After they had finished the main course McInnes asked Jessie what she would like for a pudding.

"The food was lovely, however I am absolutely full" said Jessie. "Do you think I could just finish with a cup of tea."

"Of course you can" agreed McInnes "but wouldn't you like to try coffee for a change? We could go into the lounge and enjoy our coffee with a few petit fours, that's just fancy words for wee sweeties."

McInnes placed the order for the coffee, together with a glass of Glenmorangie for himself.

"My dear Jessie, I am not going to give you whisky, your mother would be mindless and probably forbid you from working at the McInnes Empire."

Jessie laughed. "Oh I don't think so McInnes, my mother likes the idea of my enhanced pay poke too much. Maw probably hasn't told my Paw how much I am earning so it's all extra money for her."

"How much do you pay her in housekeeping?" asked McInnes"

Are you kidding" replied Jessie. "I give her my entire wage packet and she gives me three and six pocket money. I had to stand my ground for that, she didn't want to give me an increase from the two shillings I was getting when I worked at Cameron's Sweet Shop."

"Jessie Law, this is your first lesson in tactics." explained McInnes. "I intend to set sales targets for the shop. If you exceed your target you will receive fifty percent of the excess profit. This is a generous deal but I want to incentivise you to work hard.

Now this is where the tactics come in, you must ask me to pay you your monthly bonus, and I am confident there will be one, separately from your normal weekly pay packet. You, my dear Jessie, will open a bank account at the Airdrie Savings Bank and you will put your bonus money straight into your account. The passbook you will keep well hidden in the shop, and watch your savings grow. Having your own money will make you an independent woman. Now, does that sound like a good idea?"

Jessie laughed so much she thought she would get a stitch in her side.

"Oh McInnes, what an idea, I can't imagine pulling one over on my Maw, she is all seeing."

"Jessie, 'what the eye doesn't see the heart doesn't grieve for' and if she hasn't seen the money she won't grieve for it, now will she?

Ah here comes the coffee, let us talk of something other than business."

They adjourned to comfortable easy chairs in the lounge and McInnes poured the coffee.

Jessie looked at the petit fours and thought 'Robert and Alexander would soon make short work of these sweeties'. What she actually said was.

"This all looks delicious, I've never drank coffee before but I am looking forward to giving it a try."

They sat quietly for a few minutes drinking their coffee and eating a few sweetmeats.

At last McInnes reopened the conversation.

"Now a question Princess Jessie. Before today what was the happiest and the saddest day you have known in your young life."

"Happiest, that's easy" replied Jessie. "It was Agnes Johnstone's wedding. My family used to lodge with the Johnstone family years ago, we were all brought up together, we call them Aunt Jessie and Uncle Alex, actually I was called after Jessie Johnstone. I just wish she had been called something else, like Anne or Louise or even Susan, anything but Jessie, I hate being called Jessie.

Sorry, I'm going off my story, The Johnstone's have three children, Agnes, Samuel and Mary, Agnes being the eldest. During the War Agnes got married to a chap called Tom Coats, he is a Manager at the Gartsherrie Works, and the family are very comfortably off.

Jessie was at her wits end as to how she would dress Agnes and the bridesmaids, when this rich pal of hers gives her free access to her dead mother's wardrobes.

Well my Maw and Aunt Jessie had a field day. We were all decked out in the finest. I had the most beautiful sky blue dress, trimmed in lace, made of the finest material. My mother even bought me a wee pair of white shoes and socks, what a luxury that was. My older sister, Mary, put my hair into cloths the night before the wedding so I had beautiful ringlets, instead of my usual straight hair.

Mind you my Mammie and Jessie are a wily pair, they chose for themselves beautifully tailor made costumes from the wardrobe and top quality accessories. The pair of them are set up with Sunday best outfits for the rest of their days.

We ate delicious food, there was dancing and everyone was so happy, they really made a lovely couple.

But the absolute highlight for me was being given the most wonderful present. Tom Coats bought the bridesmaids little seed pearl necklaces as a thank you. Someone must have told him I was giving them a good luck favour outside the church. He presented me with a lovely single strand blue crystal necklace at the reception and gave me a kiss. I still have it and sometimes when I feel down I open the box and touch it and remember how gloriously happy we all were that day. Mind you, Robert and the other boys teased me dreadfully about the kiss.

Another bonus was my Maw brought home so many ribbons

from Aunt Jessie's friend that I had beautiful ribbons in my hair for years afterwards, sometimes my sister Mary would put my hair into rags, to give me curls, like she did at the wedding, and with the lovely ribbons I used to really feel really special.

I can't really tell you about my saddest day, perhaps sometime in the future but not yet, because it involves my sister. However, I'll tell you about my most frightening.

I was very small, in fact this is my earliest memory. Someone living near us must have been quite well off. It was wintertime and there was a very elaborate funeral, with a fancy black hearse, and a mahogany coffin covered in a big wreath of white lilies. The undertaker was dressed in a black suit with a shiny top hat. The hearse was pulled by two big, well they seemed enormous to me, black horses, with great black feather plumes attached to their harness.

One of the horses started to hit its hoof against the cobbles, which were quite icy, this made the other horse get skittish and the undertaker was having real difficulty keeping them under control.

I must have wandered through the crowd and I can just remember the huge horses rearing up and I was underneath them. Somebody, I've no idea who, caught me up in their arms and the next thing I can remember was being handed over to my Ma. I was terrified, I couldn't even cry I was so frightened. My mother took me into the house, gave me a cup of milk, then Ma being Ma proceeded to give me a strict lecture and forbid me to go wandering off on my own ever again.

Well there you have it, life on the Rows. Now McInnes, I think it is time you took me home, I don't want to be late. Besides Hugh says I must have a restful weekend before the big day on Monday."

"If my man Hugh gives an instruction, who are we not to obey." pronounced McInnes. "I'll settle the bill and drive you home."

Once again McInnes opened the motor car door with great courtesy, and settled Jessie in, before driving her home to the Herriot Row.

On the journey back they chatted companionably but in her

head Jessie simply could not quite believe that she was sitting in a Morris Cowley being driven to the Gartsherrie Rows by an incredibly handsome gentleman.

McInnes dropped Jessie outside her home. His parting shot before he drove back to Glasgow being.

"Jess, I'll come through to Coatbridge next Saturday to see how your first full week goes. Perhaps we could go out for a meal again. Would you mind going out for dinner with an old man like me?"

Jessie did not hesitate.

"I would love to go out with you again McInnes, auld man or not." Jessie laughed as she waved him goodbye.

And so began the whirlwind romance between wee Jessie Law from the Rows and the sophisticated Glasgow businessman T Anderson McInnes.

CHAPTER 19
January 1925

Mary Johnstone had just finished typing another chapter in Liz's latest book, 'The Internationalist Woman'. It had been a long day and she was feeling rather tired.

Walking through into Liz's office Mary thought how much she had grown to love this house, with it's fine furniture, well proportioned rooms with beautiful cornicing and above all the peace and serenity. Liz's home provided a quiet haven away from the Rows, the Rows where privacy and silence were always in such short supply.

"Liz, I've finished typing your latest Chapter and I've prepared the cheques for the monthly accounts ready for you to sign. Do you want me to get you anything else before I leave?" asked Mary.

"Actually there is something I'd like to discuss with you before you head off on this cold winter night, Mary.

Fancy making a pot of tea and we can go through to the sitting room and make ourselves comfortable?"

Mary prepared the tea tray and Liz stoked up the fire in the front room.

They sat down companionably in front of the fire with the low tea table between them.

Liz opened the conversation. "Mary I want to discuss something with you but I don't want you to go all silly and sympathetic on me.

As you know I never had wonderful eye sight, made worse by the Spanish flu episode, and a life spent reading too many books. Well, not to put too fine a point on it I am going blind. Another year, perhaps slightly more, and the curtain will have fallen."

Mary immediately rose and knelt in front of Liz, gently taking her hands.

"Oh my dear, how will you cope, how will we cope? Reading and campaigning through writing articles has always been your lifeblood. Liz, oh Liz, how long have your known?"

"Not long my dear" responded Liz. "I have known for some time now that I had problems but I suppose I just kept thinking, 'reading too many books you old trout' cut back, listen to damned music, buy a gramophone or something, why don't you.

Anyway, remember I made a trip down to London last month, well it was at the instigation of my Doctor in Glasgow. As you know I have been attending Marion Gilchrist in Buckingham Terrace for years. We are sisters in the movement as well as the fact that she is an eminent eye specialist. Marion suggested that I pay a visit to Moorfields, the famous eye hospital in London. On her recommendation I had a consultation with a fine chappie who put me through umpteen tests. The results, well I have just told you, a year to eighteen months and then, blackness.

But before you start going all weepy I want to ask you something my dear girl. I would like to visit Europe once more, before the blackness finally envelopes me. I want to see the azure Mediterranean Sea; the Acropolis; Paris, beautiful beautiful Paris; to eat the food of Italy and Greece, sardines cooked on white beaches; olives eaten in the Tuscan hills; delicious home made pasta.

Oh Mary my dear, remember the first time you tried an olive, you thought it thoroughly disgusting, then hid it inside your handkerchief.

That was the day when the Gartsherrie ladies raided Mama's wardrobe, what a time that was. My only worry was sobering up your Ma after three glasses of sherry."

They both laughed but Mary's laughter threatened to turn into tears at any moment.

Liz was having none of it, she rounded on Mary.

"Mary stop that blubbing right this minute, I want to put a plan in front of you and I can't possibly talk sensibly to someone who is blubbing.

Even I realise it is completely unrealistic for me to go off gallivanting around Europe on my own. Mary would you accompany
me and let me see it all through your eyes, and when we get home
and my days are dark we can relive it all together?

I know it's asking a lot to ask a bright young thing of twenty
eight to accompany a woman old enough to be her mother on her
final jolly around Europe but would you Mary, would you?"

Mary didn't hesitate for a moment.

"How could I possibly say no Liz? You have educated me,
been my mentor, friend, everything. Of course we'll go jollying
together around Europe. We will have the trip of a lifetime and I
will be your eyes and look after you every step of the way.

Now I know you too well to give you sympathy, what I will give
you is hope. Tomorrow we will start to plan the trip. When do
you want to leave?"

"Springtime I think, around the beginning of April, and I plan
to be back before the autumn. I would love one last chance to see
the autumn in Scotland. Perhaps we could end our jolly by going
North for a week or so and then by winter, well that will probably
be my winter.

Go home Mary, tell your mother and father all we have spoken off.
I want their agreement before we take the plans to the next stage.

Now get your hat and coat on, the sooner you go home to
Gartsherrie and ask their leave for our adventure the sooner we can
start planning."

On the bus home Mary didn't know whether to be happy or sad.
The diagnosis from Moorfields for Liz was devastating but for her
to be given the opportunity to spend months travelling around
Europe was a dream come true.

Since Agnes's wedding, when she was barely seventeen, Liz had
been educating her, the books she had read had shown her a life and
a world far away from the confined atmosphere of the Rows and
now she was being given an opportunity not only to read about life
on the outside, she was being given the opportunity to experience it
all first hand.

Mary arrived at 130 with her head full to bursting with confused emotions.

Jessie was busy laying the table for the family meal, after having cleared away all her millinery paraphernalia for the day. She greeted her daughter.

"You are a bit later tonight pet, it's been bitterly cold today, was the bus delayed?"

"No Ma, that's not why I am late. Liz wanted to talk to me tonight before I left, and I am afraid it's very bad news. Mamie, she is going blind. You know her eyesight has never been wonderful, well apparently she has had tests at the best eye hospital in the country and she will be lucky if she has another year or so before she loses her sight completely."

Mary broke down and the tears that had been threatening since hearing the news poured down her face.

"It's so not fair, Liz is such a good person. I know she can seem a bit sharp to people who don't know her but behind that 'nippy sweetie' front she puts on, she has a heart of gold.

And Ma, there is more, Liz want's to go to Europe for one last trip and she wants me to accompany her, to help her see her favourite places one last time.

Please Mammie can I go?"

Jessie held her weeping daughter.

"Mary, of course you can go, you are well over twenty one, you can make your own decisions in life.

What is it with this family that they want to go travelling, first Sam and Maria gallivanting off to Australia and now you off to Europe. How are we going to tell your Paw?"

The door opened and a familiar voice said.

"How are we going to tell your Paw what? Whit in the name of God are you pair of scallywags up to now?"

Jessie and Mary by turns told him the news from Airdrie. After listening carefully to all they had to say Alex gave his considered opinion.

"Mary I think you should go with Liz, for a wheen of reasons. The poor woman is about to lose her sight, if it is in your power to do anything to give her comfort it would be a kindness to do so.

Liz has been right good to you, so she has; sending you to Pitmans College, giving you an education and a real opportunity to better yourself.

More than that, she had been a true friend to your mother over the years, through the Suffragette Movement.   Nor will we ever be able to repay how she was there to comfort your Maw when we did-n't know if our Sam was dead or alive.

And, Mary lass, I'll never forget those stories of you and your Ma with the other lassies and your Auntie Agnes plundering her poor dead mother's wardrobes, what a laugh we all had about that nonsense, so we did.

Mary, your Ma and I will miss you to madness but you must go, tell Liz you go with our blessing."

The following morning Mary willed the bus to go faster and faster the sooner to reach Airdrie and allow her to tell Liz to 'get out the atlas'.

The remainder of January, February and March were spent plan-ning routes, organising travel and accommodation, purchasing travel cheques.   The house was a hive of activity, on top of all the admin-istration such a long trip entailed, Liz continued to work on her book.

Mary Law was engaged to travel to Airdrie and check the house twice a week, she would also forward any mail to the two travellers. For this commission she was paid the generous sum of one pound ten shillings a week.

After her mother received her share and she had paid her bus fares, Mary managed to buy a beautifully cut dark blue winter coat, together with smart accessories, matching cloche hat, black patent shoes and handbag, leather gloves and as a finishing touch silk stock-ings with the remainder of the money.

Into all this activity Liz had to fit in another trip to London to visit Moorfields Eye Hospital but also to have meetings with several political groups who were still working hard for the evasive equal franchise.

Liz decided that Mary should accompanied her on the journey. This was the first time Mary had left Scotland, in fact other than the time spent at Glasgow studying this was Mary's first time away from Coatbridge and Airdrie.

Travelling first class from Glasgow Central to London Euston. Mary found a new talent as an actress pretending she always travelled in such luxury, when she really wanted to cry out 'would you look at that', 'I just don't believe people live like this', 'what would my Mamie say'.

There was one other passengers in their carriage, an elegantly dressed gentleman in his 50's, who after wishing his fellow passengers a polite 'good morning' swiftly removed a copy of Punch from his briefcase and settled down to read.

Mary opened the latest copy of Vogue. Liz had expressed a desire that as well as dealing with medical and Suffragette business, that they would use the time in the Capital to buy some new clothes and accessories for the forthcoming trip. Mary intended to be fully up to date on the latest fashions.

Luncheon in the Dining Car was another revelation for the Johnston lass from the Rows. Cream of mushroom soup, garnished with cream and chopped chives, followed by lamb chops with mint sauce and all the trimmings. Exquisite food served on tables laid with spotless white napery, crystal glassware, monogrammed cutlery and little posies of pretty flowers.

Not only was she amazed at how the staff managed to cook and serve such delicious food in a moving train but the surroundings were nothing short of magnificent, polished mahogany, mirrors in ornate frames, plush upholstery, Mary thought the First Class Dining Car looked fit for the King and Queen.

On arriving in London a porter helped them with their luggage and hailed a taxi. As she had made the booking Mary confidently directed the driver, "Savoy Hotel please."

Nothing could have prepared Mary for the grandeur of the ultra modern Art Deco hotel on the banks of the River Thames. They were booked into a suite, two bedrooms and a large lounge with a desk which Mary could use for any correspondence her employer required.

Mary managed to stay silent until the hotel porter had taken their luggage into the bedrooms and left with a two shilling tip from Liz. Then she positively let her feelings go.

"Liz, I never for one minute imagined we would be staying somewhere as luxurious as this, heavens above, it's like a palace. You have been staying here on your trips to London for years and then you come and visit us in the Long Row. Doesn't it strike you as so unfair that some people can come to stay in a place like this and people like my parents work all the hours God sends and they will never experience luxury on this scale in their entire lifetime."

Liz was not naive, she understood the class divide very well but somehow, probably rather naively she had not expected Mary to have such confused feelings of class difference.

Removing her hat and gloves, Liz lifted the telephone and ordered coffee and biscuits. "We need to talk Mary. Let's freshen up, change out of our travelling clothes, and we can have a chat over coffee."

Fifteen minutes later the tray of coffee was delivered and they sat down on the comfortable sofas.

Liz opened the conversation. "Firstly, Mary I want to apologies for being so insensitive as not to realise that The Savoy is a million miles from The Long Row, it was truly unforgivable.

There are some other things I think you should know since we are going to be travelling together. My name is actually The Right Honorable Lady Elizabeth Agatha, not only have I inherited a title I have inherited a great deal of money and property.

I have to be honest the wealth does not sit entirely easily on my shoulders, never has. However, over the years I have rationalised my situation. The money has allowed me the freedom to study and travel. I have my independence, I'm beholden to nobody and I can sometimes, anonymously, do a little bit of good.

Mary, all I can say is please just enjoy the luxury, who knows what the future holds for any of us. This London visit is not going to be particularly easy for me, as well as a visit to Moorfields I intend to meet up with a few close friends and tell them about my condition. Probably, literally the last time I will see them.

Mary we have a busy few days ahead of us. Let's not waste a

minute, tomorrow morning while I am at the hospital you must organize a wardrobe for yourself for our European trip. Take a taxi to Harrods and Selfridges, purchase a selection of outfits, don't skimp, tell the staff the countries you are visiting and take their advice.   I am having luncheon with friends at the Ritz.   We can meet back here for tea around fourish.

Liz had reverted back into her businesslike manner, Mary would have to deal with her emotional reaction to the wide gap between the haves and have nots by herself.   This was a new side of Liz that Mary was seeing, although she had being doing her household accounts for some time she had no notion that Liz was wealthy rather than merely comfortable.

Mary quickly realized that she had two clear options; she could enter into enjoying a life experience that nobody else living in Gartsherrie could imagine.   Alternatively she could let the gap between rich and poor embitter her.

Lying in bed on her first night in the Capital Mary was pondering the whole morality of enjoying staying at The Savoy when she felt her mother's presence as conflicting thoughts ran through her head.   Her Ma had spent her life trying to improve the lives of her family and other women through the Suffragette Movement, of course she would want to see her youngest daughter enjoy a fulfilling life.   Mary thought of Jessie's pride the day she was awarded the Dux at Pitmans College.   Her joy at Agnes's marriage to Tom.   Her excitement at each letter received from Australia with news of Sam and Maria's achievements. 'My Ma would approve of me moving on to new horizons, as long as I don't forget my past'.   With that comforting thought Mary fell into the deepest of sleeps.

The following morning Mary carried out her employers instructions, after a delicious breakfast they both went off in different directions.

Liz had accounts at both Harrods and Selfridges, all Mary had to do was show her letter of authority and whatever she chose was charged to the Wallis-Banks account.

Agnes favored her mother in looks and build, Mary favored her father's Irish heritage.   Tall for a woman, she had thick, wavy, almost black, hair. Handsome rather than pretty, she could look serious but when she smiled or laughed she had the look of her father, Alex, with his twinkling blue eyes. Mary's elegant figure and looks perfectly complimented the fashions of the 1920's, she looked stunning in almost every outfit she tried on. A sales assistant's dream customer.

Returning to The Savoy laden with boxes and carriers Mary threw off her shoes as soon as she reached her suite, picked up the telephone and ordered tea and sandwiches, totally focused on the shopping she hadn't even stopped for a bite of lunch.

On her return Liz joined Mary in a cup of tea. Although Liz was completely disinterested in fashion she got enormous pleasure from watching Mary's delight at the new outfits she had insisted on her buying for their European tour.

So caught up were they in the shopping conversation that Liz was able to avoid discussing her hospital appointment and luncheon.

The remaining few days flew past. Liz had discussions with several famous politicians as well as meetings with her Lawyer, Accountant and Stock Broker. These meetings she attended alone and Mary, as well as more clothes shopping was kept busy with other commissions.

The return journey did not seem quite so formidable to Mary, she was quickly accustoming herself to the better things in life.

Mary left the train at Sunnyside Station and took a taxi home with some of her new possessions. Liz had taken the new cases and the remainder of the clothes back to Airdrie. Part of Mary just could not bring herself to let her parents see the full extent of her new wardrobe.

Jessie welcomed her daughter home and exclaimed over her daughter's new summer dresses and wonder of wonders a beautiful cream trouser suit, the very latest fashion for women. Jessie laughed. "You had better not let your Uncle Rab see you wearing that, can you imagine, women in trousers. Poor auld bigot, he would have a heart attack, so he would."

They were still laughing when Alex came home, he too admired the new clothes, and wished her 'well to wear them'. This came as a relief to Mary, she sensed she had been right and her parents would not be annoyed or angry at her enjoying life's luxuries, on the contrary they were proud of her and her employment as a Secretary.

After supper Alex, Jessie and their youngest wean enjoyed a box of exquisite Fortnum & Mason handmade chocolates with their cup of tea. Not many families in the Rows would ever do that.

The following week it was back to work in Airdrie for Mary, the London adventure over but with the promise of Europe still to come.

They intended to leave Airdrie on the 8th of April, their travel route being; London, Paris, Berlin, through Switzerland to the Italian lakes then down Italy, spending time in Tuscany visiting Pisa and Florence. From Italy they intended to visit Greece, on departing Athens they had booked a cruise around the Greek Islands, returning home via Marseilles and the South of France.

Liz had decided to include Berlin in the itinerary at the last moment as she wanted to see what was really happening inside Germany's Weimar Republic, and what was the state of play with the Fascists and Communists vying for control of the country, Liz ever the seeker of truth.

Returning from work one evening in early April Jessie Law saw Mary Johnstone walking up the Row, she ran to catch up with her.

"Well Mary, I hear it's all change for you, off to Europe soon. What an adventure, I bet you are really excited."

"Yes I'm certainly really excited." replied Mary. "However, I am also a bit apprehensive. I have a feeling it's going to change my life completely. I'll never again be Mary Johnstone, the Johnstone's youngest wean, and I'm not sure if I will be able to come back and settle into life in the Rows again.

I am sure you understand Jessie, in fact you are probably the only one who does around here. Now that you are managing your own shop, don't you find it really hard coming home and being treated like wee Jessie Law, the youngest Law lassie?"

"Don't I just" agreed Jessie. For me the hardest part is my Maw and Paw just won't accept McInnes. They think because he has a motor car, speaks beautifully and was an officer during the War he is out of my class. According to them I should 'know my place and station in life' I should just be content to spend my life as Wee Jessie from the Rows, that is their attitude. So much for the emancipation of women, that concept certainly hasn't reached Gartsherrie.

Mary, are we so very wrong to want more from life?"

"I don't think we are" answered Mary. "I am really lucky my Ma is happy for me to get on in life but I also know fine well she doesn't want to lose her youngest, especially with our Sam having emigrated to Australia. The real truth is I don't want to make her and my Pa unhappy."

"No easy answer then." concluded Jessie. "Nearly at your door Mary, look if I don't see you before you go have a wonderful adventure and remember to send me a card from time to time. Our Mary and I would love to share in your discoveries and find out if all the exciting place names are as wonderful as we all imagine them to be.

You know Mary, it's not easy having a bit of ambition and living in the Rows. But as your Mammie would say, 'you must follow your path'. Lucky lass, your path is taking you off to Europe in a few days time. Bye Mary, our Mary and I wish you the best of luck."

CHAPTER 20
MAY 1925

The relationship between McInnes and Jessie had been strength-ening as the months passed. No longer was the emphasis purely on business, they spent every spare minute in each other's company and McInnes opened up windows on a life far removed from the Rows for wee Jessie Law.

Visits to the theatre, concerts, good restaurants, walks around the Botanic Gardens and museums in Glasgow, day trips to the Clyde coast or Edinburgh. McInnes was taking his Princess by the hand and slowly leading her into a new and exciting world.

It was Easter Monday. McInnes drove them down to Gourock in the Morris, and from there they caught the ferry over to Dunoon. McInnes had packed a picnic basket and the weather was blue sky perfect. As the ship sailed across the Clyde Estuary they stood at the rail enjoying the soft breeze and the perfection of the Scottish scenery looking out towards the Cowal Peninsula.

Jessie decided to ask McInnes a question she had often pon-dered on but something had always held her back from asking.

"McInnes, you are always wanting to know about my family and the mischief we got up to as children but you never speak about your own family or childhood, why?"

"That's easy it was boring, really, really boring. I have two older sisters, they are spinsters and still live in the old family home. They have a private income but Alice also teaches piano, actually she is not all that good but she has passed the exams so I can only sup-pose that the Mamas who send their little brats to her are all tone deaf. They are called Alice and Effy, I know, I know, Euphemia, what chance did the old duck have? They live firmly in the past, when they talk about 'the dear old queen' they don't mean Queen Alexandra, they mean Queen Victoria. I go to visit them for tea about once a month, I am ashamed to say it's duty rather than love.

My elder brother Fraser, now there is a pompous chappie. He is married to a permanently anxious wee woman called Francis. He is always saying 'Fanny do this, Fanny do that,' honestly if I was Fanny I'd probably murder him.

He is a Director of quite a successful business but I try and avoid him and Fanny if humanly possible. I suppose he is all right really it's just that he is so full of himself. He thinks the sun revolves around the planet Fraser Harold McInnes.

I was, as they say, one of life's little surprises. My parents both died when I was in my teen years and I am happy to say I was packed off to boarding school when I was fourteen. The next few years were the best I had ever enjoyed, sport, rough and tumble with the other lads, a jolly decent education.

I never returned to the family home. When I left school, I decided not to go to university, instead I rented a room in a flat in Byres Road, not far from where I live now. Got myself a job in a major shipping company and worked my way up through the ranks.

Then came the War, I one of the lucky ones, I survived, came home and took up my career again.

Then came the best bit, I met my Princess Jess of the Brig. Want a sandwich?"

Jessie held his hand tightly in hers. "So that's why you love listening to all the tales of when we were bairns. I suppose we were poor but we still managed to have quite a lot of fun. Especially Robert and me, we were always a great team. But the two biggest mischiefs by far were Sammy Johnstone and our Charlotte, they were much older than us but we used to love to hear the tales.

Did I ever tell you about the sardines?" Jessie asked.

"No, I've never heard a tale about sardines. Go on tell me before the boat docks" laughed McInnes.

"Well, Sam and Charlotte had been out catching minnows in a

jam jar, they had loads and didn't know what to do with them. It was Sunday night and Maw had bought my Paw a tin of sardines for his tea as a treat, he loved sardines on toast. Didn't the mad pair not get some of the minnows and mix them in with the sardines. Maw made his tea and as he was saying 'tasty wee bite lass, so it was, right tasty' they were doubled up laughing. If he had ever found out he would have roasted them."

They both dissolved into a fit of giggles.

"Can you wonder I love to hear your stories?" asked McInnes My siblings were all so much older and I didn't even have any cousins near my own age. My sisters were prim and proper and Fraser was a boring swot. Haven't a clue who I take after but I think I have some Highland blood, reckon I come from the cattle thieving branch of the McInnes clan.

Look Jessie, we are nearly at the harbour. First stop I'll show you the statue of Highland Mary on Castle Hill, one of Robert Burns girlfriends. Very pretty lass, but not a patch on you my darling."

They spent yet another happy day together but as they drove home Jessie thought about McInnes's childhood, living in a mausoleum of a home. He had plenty of good food and comforts but without any fun. Perhaps she had enjoyed the happiest upbringing after all.

One Friday, just before closing time McInnes arrived at the Bank Street Shop. As usual he entered like a whirlwind.

"Good evening my beautiful Princess Jess. What film are we going to go and see this evening?"

"Oh, you startled me there" said Jessie. "I don't know, there are a few choices, we could go and see that American Western, I think it is called Tumbleweeds, alternatively there is a Charlie Chaplin, called The Gold Rush on at the Bank Street Cinema which everyone seems to be raving about."

"Before we decide" said McInnes "I am just away out to the motor, I have a surprise."

He went out to the Morris and returned with a his trusty wicker picnic basket.

"Lock up the McInnes Empire's latest Emporium Miss Law, we

are going to sit in the back shop and have a delicious picnic. I have visited Coopers in Howard Street and have bought some lovely treats. Ham carved off the bone, cold chicken, pate, potato salad, bread, grapes, and knowing you, some delicious chocolates. I was going to bring a bottle of wine but I am quite sure your parents would disapprove, in fact I think I disapprove of plying young ladies with wine, in the stockroom of a respectable emporium.

So, my dear, get the kettle on and we will wash our food down with a nice cup of tea. After we have eaten we can choose which film to go and see."

The food was delicious and they chatted companionably about this and that while they ate. Jessie made him laugh telling him about the tricks played on various apprentices during week, by their foremen.

"Honestly, we have had them coming in wanting to buy 'tartan paint', 'a long stand' all the usual but Hugh had a new one. 'A pound of rusty nails please'. Mind you what made it funny was that his lad William, went into the back shop and said to Hugh, 'Mr Mason can you tell me where you keep the rusty nails?' Hugh said he didn't know whether to laugh or give him a rollicking for being so stupid.

Stanley is doing well. He really appreciates having a job with us. Do you know McInnes, he has had nothing since leaving the army, no work at all, poor soul he has just been managing from hand to mouth. You would think after what the lads went through in the War the Government would have organised more retraining programs, the only one I have heard of is the one for men blinded by the mustard gas, getting training as masseurs."

"I know" agreed McInnes. "It's bloody disgraceful but the way things are just now in Scotland able bodied men are lucky to get work, never mind the disabled.

Jess, enough talk of the shops.

A little bird has told me that your birthday is next week, did the wee bird chirp correctly?"

Jessie laughed. "If it chirped the 25th, it was correct. I will be nineteen this month, getting quite old really."

"Well before you get any older, and me not wanting to spend my life with an old woman.

Will you marry me, my Princess Jess of the Brig?"

Jessie kissed him and answered.

"Yes, my McInnes, yes, yes, a hundred times over. I would be honoured to be your wife. Mind you I can't see my Paw and Maw giving their permission. We will probably have to wait until I am twenty one before we can wed."

"First things first" said McInnes. "Next Saturday put Stanley in charge for the day. I'll meet you in Glasgow and we will pay a visit to the Argyle Arcade. We can choose an engagement ring that you like and then there will be no going back, if you change your mind I'll sue you for breach of promise.

We'll catch the early program at the pictures tonight and then it's a visit to the Herriot Row and I'll ask your father formally for your hand in marriage."

The film, the latest Charlie Chaplin, was most enjoyable. Unlike the visit to ask Rab for his youngest daughter's hand in marriage. The problem for Rab and Agnes was they could not actually find a good reason to object to a marriage between Jessie and McInnes, but that did not stop them trying.

The outcome was that Rab eventually agreed to the engagement, however there would be no wedding before Jessie was twenty one and had reached the age of consent, and on that point he was absolutely adamant.

While seeing McInnes out to his car Jessie whispered to him.

"I think we got off fairly lightly, knowing my Paw. Will you be coming through to Coatbridge tomorrow?"

"No darling, but I'll come through on Sunday and we can go a run somewhere into the countryside. I'll bring my picnic hamper with some sandwiches and a thermos flask. See you around eleven o'clock."

When McInnes called to collect her on the Sunday morning Jessie asked him if they could go for a ride out to Condorrat so that she could introduce him to Charlotte, Charlie and their bairns.

McInnes readily agreed so they headed off in the Morris to

Windy Hill Farm.   As they were driving Jessie told him all about the
War years when the family worked at the farm during the school
holidays and the saga of Charlotte and Charlie's romance.

"I had the easiest time, Mrs Baird had a bit of a soft spot for me
so I got all the good jobs, like shelling peas or picking berries.   We
had some great times at the farm and the barn dances were always
wonderful fun."

They arrived at the farm unannounced but Charlotte gave them
both a warm welcome.   A fifth pregnancy and years of hard work
had robbed Charlotte of some of her youthful beauty and slim figure but she had lost none of her happy go lucky nature.

Charlie and the children were also delighted to welcome their
unexpected visitors.   Robert, Jim, Willie and wee May were over
the moon when their new Uncle McInnes took them out for a ride
in his Morris.   That adventure would ensure boasting rights at
school for many weeks to come.

McInnes produced the picnic basket and suggested they all sit
outside on the travel rug and share the sandwiches and cake.
Charlotte produced some scones with butter and jam and mugs of
milk for the children, as usual, the adults drank tea.

McInnes was delighted to meet Charlotte and put a face to the
girl whose childhood adventures he had so avidly followed.

Charlotte addressed McInnes.   "You know McInnes, don't be
fooled by Jessie's angelic expression she could be a right wee devil
when she was young.   Has she told you about 'knock door, run
fast'?"

McInnes laughed.   "No Charlotte I don't think she has told me
that one.   Come on Jess, tell us about 'knock door, run fast'."

"You are a horror Charlotte Law, everything Robbie and I knew
about knocking doors we learnt from you and Sammy Johnstone.   I
can see I am not going to get any peace until I tell you."

Jessie regaled everyone on how her and Robert played their
game.

"You know how two doors face each other in the Gartsherrie
Rows, well we would get a bit of clothes line from Maw, telling her it
was for a skipping rope.   Or quite often we would cut a bit from

the line of one of the other women's washing ropes.   Then we would tie an end to the handle of each door, knock the two doors loudly and hide, usually behind the toilet blocks.   Naturally the people in the houses would try to open the doors, one would get it a bit open, then the opposite house would pull it shut.   They could go on like that for ages, and the swearing, sometimes it was choice, particularly at the Irish houses.   Best laugh was the Poles because they would lapse into a mixed up version of Polish and Scottish.   All you would hear was shuksa muksa tooska lookie BUGGERS moiksa toiska doiska WEE SHITS...

If we ever felt hard done by or we thought anyone in our family had been, they would get 'knock door' but sometimes Robert and I just did it because we were a couple of wee middens, so there, that was the tale of 'knock door, run fast'."

Charlotte, Charlie and McInnes were in fits of laughter, fortunately the children were playing chases in the grass so didn't hear just how how naughty their mother and Aunt Jessie had been as children.

Before leaving to return to Coatbridge Jessie took McInnes to meet Farmer and Mrs Baird.   They both gave him a warm welcome and Alice Baird in particular was delighted to see that her favourite Law girl, Jessie, was gloriously happy and had found herself a good man.

The following working week, Monday through to Friday, Jessie didn't know how she managed to get through the days until Saturday and her rendezvous with McInnes at Glasgow's Argyle Arcade at the appointed hour of eleven o'clock.

Another person who was happy to see Saturday was Stanley, as this was the first time he had been left in charge of the shop. After so many years of feeling worthless and unemployable the idea of holding the keys to an up and coming shop, and having responsibilities, made him feel a real man once more.

Time stands still for no man, or girl, excited at the thought of getting engaged. At last the appointed day arrived and Jessie made her way into Glasgow by train.

The young couple met outside the Argyle Arcade, one of the earliest covered shopping arcades in Europe, dating back to 1827, a place where so many Glasgow couples had paid a visit to one of the numerous elegant jewellery shops to buy their wedding and engagement rings.

The Argyle Arcade was something of an institution in Glasgow, and young girls dreamed of the day they would visit this great Cathedral to jewellery.

The choice was stupendous, Jessie and McInnes spent ages window shopping before eventually going into James Porter & Son, a well established jewellers, to make their purchase.

Jessie tried on a number of rings but when McInnes slipped a beautiful three diamond ring on her finger, they both knew, this was the one.

The assistant said.

"Excellent choice, a really exquisite ring, with a simple setting to show off the beauty of the diamonds. Do you know what a ring made up of three diamond in a straight line means?"

Neither of them had a clue.

The jeweller enlightened them.

"It means, 'I Love You', lovely isn't it. I hope you will both be very happy together. Now I'll just away and give your ring a polish and find a nice wee box to hold it safely."

He returned with the ring box which he handed to McInnes, to Jessie he handed a long black leather box with the name and crest of Porter & Son Jewellers emblazoned on it. Inside was a silver jam spoon.

"Just a wee gift from us to wish you both a sweet life." he said.

The happy couple celebrated with a lunch of smoked salmon sandwiches at Miss Cranston's tearoom in Buchanan Street and then McInnes insisted on buying Jessie a new outfit in Fraser & Sons Department Store, one of Glasgow's most prestigious and elegant shops.

Jessie was extremely unsure about allowing McInnes to buy her anything to wear, she could hear her mother's disapproving voice in the back of her head. However, McInnes reassured her that it was all perfectly proper now that she was his fiancée, besides she was now wearing his ring and she was just one short step away from being Mrs Anderson McInnes.

They had a wonderful spending spree and McInnes eventually bought Jessie several stylish outfits, complete with matching accessories, together with a bottle of the latest Rimmell perfume in a smart Art Deco style bottle, called 'Mon Yvonnette'. They left Fraser's Store laughing and laden down with smart carrier bags and boxes.

Next it was off to see Will Fyffe, of 'I Belong to Glasgow' fame, at the Empire Theatre up in Sauchiehall Street.

A delicious light supper at the Ca'Doro Restaurant in Union Street rounded off their Engagement Day.

When McInnes dropped Jessie off at the Heriot Row she was floating on air. As she was about to get out of the car she kissed him and whispered.

"Darling, today beats Agnes Johnstone's wedding by a mile."

The remainder of the summer saw McInnes and Jessie on a roller coaster of happiness.

With the three diamond engagement ring firmly on Jessie's finger the couple started to make plans in ernest for the expansion of the drysaltery business.

McInnes also had other ideas in mind, he wanted to set up a reasonably priced home interior design company.

One Sunday as they were driving down to Loch Lomand McInnes put the idea of the home design company to Jessie. He explained.

"I would love to take the wallpapering and painting side of the business to the next level. This is my idea Jess, people who have pots of money can get in a designer to compensate for their bad taste, they charge the earth and then they sub contract the decorating work, getting a commission from the contractors.

We already have trained painters who can produce first class work using all the latest techniques. My idea is that after we are married you could offer a customised design service. Our prices would be moderate, making it affordable for people who could previously never have aspired to having their own interior designer. We don't have to contract out the work, we have our own team of workers, so can guarantee quality work on the painting and decorating side, other things like carpets and furniture we can supply on commission. What do you think Jess?"

"I think it is a brilliant idea but I have never had any formal training at Art College, granted I know what goes with what, but would that be enough do you think?"

"Actually in your case I think it would be enough, you have a wonderful innate sense of style, but my idea is we start this part of the business after we get married. When you are living in Glasgow you could go on a design course at the new Mackintosh College of Art in Renfrew Street. A formal qualification would give you more confidence and at the same time we could be planning how we would sell the idea to the aspiring middle classes.

I think it would be good fun, when it is up and running I can then start to disengage myself from the shipping industry and concentrate on our own business full time.

Enough blethering about work, come on Jess, tell me some more of your stories about when you and your brothers and sisters were children."

"Not again" laughed Jessie. "You can't get enough of my childhood stories, I think you are going to use them as blackmail material after we have bairns of our own."

Jessie launched on another tale.

"Well, you know my mother was a widow when she married Paw so Charlotte is really my half sister. Although he is only her step father my Paw always had a soft spot for her, I think it was because she enjoyed the whole Orange Order thing and she had a reckless streak that Mary and I certainly didn't have.

Charlotte would go down to the Store for his jug of porter or baccy, wearing orange ribbons in her hair and she was always at the front of the crowd watching the Orange Marches, 'Proddie and Proud', that was our Charlotte.

There was a family called Docherty who lived near us. The auld grandfather was Catholic through and through, a real Hibernian Lodge man. The old fellow used to sit on a chair outside the house with a green plaid over his legs, smoking his clay pipe and watching the world go past.

Whenever Charlotte, and her accomplice Sam Johnstone, saw he was on his own they would sing, to the tune of the Sash my Father Wore.

> *'Oh the Pope he had a pimple on his bum*
> *and, it nipped, nipped, nipped so sore*
> *that they sent for King Billie*
> *and, he rubbed it with a Lily*
> *So it nipped, nipped, nipped no more'*

Naturally poor Mr Docherty was ropeable, the old man used to complain to his family, my Maw, Auntie Jessie, anyone who would listen, about their behaviour.   Charlotte and Sam would just look innocent and pretend that the old man was senile, but the poor old soul wasn't in the least bit senile, they were just a right pair of scallywags.

I'll tell you how daft they are about religion in Gartsherrie, you can tell a man's religion by the flowers he grows in his garden"

McInnes burst out laughing.   "Don't be silly Jess, you can't possibly do a mad thing like that."

"Oh yes you can," retorted Jessie.   "If you grow Sweet William and Orange Lilies, Protestant.   White Lilies Catholic.   Honestly, you couldn't make it up, could you!

Anyway, that's your ration of stories for today, we must be nearly at Balloch by now.   Can we go to that really good fish and chip shop at the harbour for a fish tea?"

"Anything you want sweetheart, anything you want.   But it will take us another fifteen minutes or so to reach Balloch, time for another story."

McInnes did not give up easily.

"All right, I'll tell you the naughtiest thing I ever did, and it was really naughty, even I am thoroughly ashamed of doing such a terrible thing.   Before I tell you, you must promise never to repeat this particular tale to any of my family, they still suspect Robert."

"I'm bursting to hear this one" laughed McInnes.   "What on earth did you do?"

"There was this old black cat who had kind of adopted us, you know the way cats do, it never had a proper name, we just called it Cat. Well this thing liked it's comforts and it was always seated on the fender getting the best heat during the winter. Cat always had a smug look on its face as though it was getting one over on us all.

One cold winter day it was sitting there looking at me ever so smugly and preening itself. I though 'I'll sort you out', so I got out my mother's scissors from her work box and cut off it's whiskers.

I didn't realise that cats measure things by using their whiskers so the poor creature was completely disorientated.

When my Paw came home from work he went on the rampage. shouting 'Which of you buggers cut the Cat's whiskers, I'll murder youse, so I will.' Cat wasn't looking so smug now, it kept falling over, as though it was drunk.

Because he was such a wee devil, everyone suspected Robert. All I did was stay quiet and nobody ever thought it was me."

"Jessie Law you are a wee besom, I don't know if I want to marry a cat murderer." laughed McInnes.

"Away with you, you daft thing, Cat didn't die, the whiskers grew back eventually, but it never looked quite as smug again.

Nearly at Balloch now. Walk and then fish and chips? And, remember, you promised, Cat's whiskers is our secret."

While Jessie and McInnes were out enjoying themselves, back in Gartsherrie Agnes started to quiz Mary.

"I'm sure I don't know what has got into our Jessie's head over this McInnes carry on. Since they have got engaged we hardly ever see her. I think she has got above herself, trying to be what she is no. What do you think, our Mary?"

"I think we should all mind our own business." answered Mary. Jessie loves the man, she is happy and she is giving you good dig money. What more do you want Maw?"

"She won't be giving me good money for much longer, neither she will. They intend to get married as soon as she is twenty one in May of 1927. No doubt he will pay for a fancy wedding, how will we look compared to his upper crust family?"

Mary had no intention of letting her mother have all her own way in this particular conversation.

"Look mother we are decent, respectable folks why should we worry about his folks being toffs. I like McInnes and he is always kind to Robert and Alexander, taking them for runs in his car.

If you don't stop being so difficult about Jessie and McInnes you will end up losing her, is that what you and my Paw really want?"

Mary stood up and called for Rags, the two of them headed down to the Johnstone home, where she knew her Aunt Jessie would be liberal with tea, sympathy and good sense.

CHAPTER 21
Early August 1925

James and Robert were walking down Sunnyside Road after the Sunday night meeting at the Salvation Army.

Robert, always the joker started to bait his elder brother.

"I see that skinny lass, Margaret Smith has her eye on you Jimmy my boy, if you aren't careful she'll have you up the aisle before you can say Jack Robinson. I'll grant you she is quite pretty but she has a bit of a mean look aboot her. You would be much safer with that wee red haired lassie Mamie Buchanan, the one our Mary is pally with, or that other wee smasher that fancies you from the Whifflet.

Tell me Jimmy, why do all the girls fancy you, what do you have that the rest of the lads in the band don't, apart from an amazing ability to play off key?"

James answered laughing.

"I don't know really, other than my incredible good looks and wavy black hair. I am just playing the field, I don't want to settle down too soon. Besides it's no really fair on Maw and Paw if I up and leave the house the minute my apprenticeship finishes and I get my papers. Mine will be the first qualified wage coming into the house."

James followed up the banter from Robbie.

"Anyway, who are you to be giving great advice on romance, a wee brother who hasn't even had a kiss yet. You sound mair like my sister than my brother. I think I'll call you Roberta from now on. Come on Roberta, race you as far as the Institute." called James, as he started to run.

They arrived home breathless and laughing.

The following morning James was told to go to the Work's Office and report to the General Manager. He had no idea why he had received this unexpected order but as always he obeyed.

James sat on a bench in a waiting room from where he could see the typists working in a large general office, James being James was eying them all up wondering who he would like to take out on a date.

Eventually a middle aged lady with steel grey hair set in tight waves came out of the office and showed James along the corridor to the office of The General Manager, Mr George Watson.

Mr Watson was immaculately dressed in his tail coat, spotless white shirt and sober tie. On the hat stand was a well brushed bowler hat and a top quality black woollen coat.

Sitting behind his polished mahogany desk he addressed James in a formal voice.

"Good morning to you Law. Well I am sure you will have guessed why you have been summonsed here. You have completed your apprenticeship satisfactorily as a Joiner so it is my pleasure to present you with your Journeyman's papers, signed by the Directors.

"Law, in addition to giving you your trade papers it is also my pleasure to inform you that you have been awarded the great honour of being chosen as the Apprentice of the Year.

On Saturday night at the dance in the Work's Institute you will be formally presented with the award. Well done Law, my wife and I will be present on Saturday for the ceremony. Now I expect you would like to get back to the Joinery Shop and tell the other lads of your good fortune."

James stammered his thanks and left the office. The entire interview had lasted less then five minutes.

James's heart was beating a tattoo as he hurried back to the Joinery Shop. He couldn't believe that out of hundreds of apprentices he had been chosen as the Best Apprentice for the year of 1925.

As well as this unexpected honour his twenty first would bring many changes. He would soon be given the traditional key of the door, a symbolic key to prove that he was now a man. Not an actual key, the houses in Gartsherrie all had one huge iron key which was permanently kept in the lock on the front door. The key was turned twice each day, when the first person rose in the morning and when the last person went to bed at night.

Financially James was also going to see changes. His weekly wage would now be more than doubled after successfully completing his time. He had come through the ranks; firstly serving a year as a Goffer, running errands and making tea. The following five as an Apprentice and a further final year to get his papers. All that to receive recognition as a Time Served Journeyman.

When he got back to the Joinery Shop he was greeted by loud cheers from the other Apprentices and Joiners.

"How on earth did you lot know I had received the award?" shouted James above the din.

"We know because any news goes round this place like wildfire, and because Willie Kennedy's wee sister works in the office and she telt the new Goffer Sandy, who was down at the Offices handing in some keys for Mr McCosh. Sandy ran back here like the wind, so we all know" said John Clark, as he put his arm around James's shoulder.

Mr McAllister, the Manager of the Joinery Shop came out of his office and into the workshop, saying.

"Lads, enough celebrating for now. You can all do that on your own time on Saturday night at the dance, meantime Law, a word, come into my office."

Mr McAllister sat James down saying.

"We are all very proud of you lad, I have sat with the secret for a couple of weeks, but the news is out now, so I think you should run home and tell your parents.

I know your Paw has not been well and I would not like him to hear the news from someone else, it should come from you lad.

You know your family have always been highly respected in the Rows. Your Pa is a grafter and your Ma has always kept you all decent and well fed, which is more than can be said for some of the families in Gartsherrie.

Now run home, it's twenty minutes until the two o'clock siren, after that goes off the news will be out. Go on your way, I want to see a clean pair of heels mind."

James didn't need any second bidding, he ran out of the workshop and was home in five minutes.

He ran into the kitchen, lifted up his mother, swung her around, and cried breathlessly.

"Maw, you really have something to be proud of now, I have been awarded Apprentice of the Year."

Agnes, pretended to be annoyed.

"Come on you mad boy, put me down, put me down this instant, what will the neighbours think."

But he was right, it was one of her proudest moments. At long last the Laws were something in the Rows, not just illiterate Irish from the bogs.

As he put her down she said.

"Away through to the room and tell your Paw. He hasn't even been able to rise himself out of bed today, maybe your news will buck him up a bit."

James pushed open the bedroom door. He saw his father lying in bed with his eyes closed. James paused unsure whether to waken his Paw and deliver his news.

Rab opened his eyes, saying.

"I'm not asleep lad, I heard you tell your mother about your award, so I did. Well done James my boy, but remember don't you be going and getting yourself a big head now."

James accepted a quick cup of tea and a girdle scone from his mother before hurrying back to the work to finish his shift for the day.

The evening meal around the big scrubbed wooden table was noisy and full of fun. Robert, as usual, started the teasing.

"My my, Apprentice of the Year, what a line that will be with the lasses. Can you no just hear him in his wee romantic voice. 'Oh Daphne, Margaret, Ellen, Mary, Molly, or whatever your name happens to be. Will you no come to the moving pictures with me, the chosen one, not only the handsomest lad in the whole of Gartsherrie but The Apprentice of the Year."

"Leave him alone" said Mary. He has done well, let's see if you get Apprentice of the Year when it is your turn Robbie."

"Nae chance" laughed Robert. I'm not handsome enough, besides I don't crawl to the Managers like our Sir. Yes sir, no sir, three bags full sir."

Jessie laughed. "Well maybe his nickname Sir, has helped him get the award. But seriously it won't do him any harm job wise. You are on the promotion ladder now, Sir James, we your humble servants salute you."

The banter continued as they ate and then came the knocks on the door. As the word had got around, friends and neighbours called in to congratulate and say, 'well done' to the eldest Law lad.

Saturday morning dawned, James collected his pay packet from the Works Office. He proudly brought home his first full pay poke, the first journeyman's wage packet that any of the Law boys had brought home. Agnes accepted the brown packet, smiled, then handed it back to James unopened, saying.

We will follow with tradition in this house lad, you keep your first full pay poke to yourself. Go down into the 'Brig and get yourself something smart to wear for your presentation the night, and mind you get yourself something of decent quality so that it will last.

Mary handed him a little parcel, it contained three snow white handkerchiefs and a smart tie from her and Jessie. While she had no intention of taking the shine from James's day she couldn't help but think, 'Jessie never got all that fuss and she has been handing in a full wage for ages, and she never got an unopened wage packet to spend on clothes.'

Robbie and Alexander had bought socks, which they left with Mary to give to him, the idea of giving your brother a present being just too cissy for words.

When he got off the Baxter's bus at the Whitelaw Fountain, his first port of call, was a visit to Bryson's the tailor where he bought himself a smart dark blue lounge suite and a white shirt with one of the new attached collars. Thinking the present from his sisters of a maroon and blue striped tie would look well with his choice of suit. James then paid a visit to the shoe department in the Co-operative Emporium, where he bought a pair of shiny black leather shoes.

Delighted with his purchases James returned home so that he would have some time to practice his acceptance speech before the dance at the Gartsherrie Institute.

Rab had not been able to work for many months now. The winter of 1924 - 25 had finished him. His auld bones could no longer take the cold and the hard manual work.

Rab's attitude epitomised the expression, 'the spirit is willing but the flesh is weak'. All his life he had been a worker, a provider, and he was taking it very hard not to be able to contribute to the family income.

James, his eldest boy by Agnes, was now a Journeyman Joiner and had been honoured as Apprentice of the Year; Robert was working as an Apprentice Engineer; Jessie was earning a good income working for McInnes and Mary was earning her keep by working as a maid two days a week and helping Mrs Millar or Granny Fraser at confinements or to lay out bodies. Even his youngest, Alexander was due to leave school shortly and start his apprenticeship, by working his year as a Goffer. Meantime, Alexander did most of the gardening for the Miss Simpsons, and provided the vegetables and some fruit for the family.

Collectively Rab's children were well able to keep the household solvent, that was no consolation to a proud Ulsterman.
Without contributing a working income, he no longer felt the head of the household.

He was now over seventy years of age and in receipt of the state old age pension of ten shillings each week, this simply added insult to injury as far as Rab was concerned.

Now almost completely bedridden due to the severity of his rheumatism. Agnes and Mary nursed him and did their best to make him feel comfortable. Their kindly efforts simply added to his woes and the guilt he felt.

Whenever Mary did him a kindness, arranged his pillows, read him a newspaper, or gave him a meal, feelings of guilt overwhelmed him.

All his life he had been a man of few words and now he simply could not articulate an apology to Mary for refusing Agnes his permission to cut off her hair when the doctor diagnosed rheumatic fever.

It was like an itchy scab, a constant irritation, that would not leave him. No matter how he tried to justify his decision on that fateful night he could not rid himself of the niggling pain caused by the knowledge that he had wronged his lass.

On Saturday night while the youngsters were at the Institute for James's presentation, Alex and Jessie Johnstone, although they too enjoyed a celebration, decided to visit the Laws home as they were concerned about Rab's condition.

Alex wanted to talk with his auld pal from Ulster, more than a shared country, they shared memories of a farming childhood in the green, green County of Fermanagh.

Mary took Alex through to the bedroom where her father was laying on clean white bed linen and kept warm by grey woollen blankets. As always the room was spotlessly clean but stark and comfortless. Even at the last Rab had no time for frills or fancies.

"Good to see you Rab" said Alex.

"Good, good, Alex Johnstone you tell me whit the hell is good aboot a working man laying in bed while his weans pay for his meat?" growled Robert.

"Rab, the years pass, eventually Jessie and I will depend of our two girls for help, that is the cycle of life." Alex tried to comfort his friend.

"Cycle of life my arse, you know Alex, laying here in bed and being waited on by the women folk gives me too much time to think. To consider my life, the good the bad and the mistakes. And, Alex auld pal, when you are lying on what will be your death bed, the mistakes bloody hurt.

The best and the worst cards that fate dealt me was being born in Lugarstown. The best, because I loved the green County of Fermanagh, the loughs and the farming life. I came from a good decent family, you know. I had a happy childhood with my brothers and sisters, and my auld Maw made sure none of the Law bairns ever went to bed with a hungry belly, even in the poor years.

The worst, not having the opportunity to learn to read and write and get an education. Not having that knowledge has made me what I am, an ignorant Billy from the bogs."

Alex started to speak but Rab stopped him.

"Naw Alex wheesht, it's true and we both know it. If I had

been an educated man I would have been able to get a decent job and provide well for my family, without both my wives having to take in lodgers and work like slaves to keep the home together.

Alex, I can say this to you and I know you will ever repeat it to a living soul.

I am bloody terrified about meeting my maker, so I am, after the sin I committed on my Mary.

That poor lass has to go through life as bald as a coote because I had to be Rab, the man of the hoose. Lord and Master of a wee hoose in the Herriot Row. God man, I must have been mad, but at the time I felt I had to assert my authority on the educated doctor, and the wife who could read and write, I wanted them to know that I was boss, the master, inside these four walls."

Alex had no words, he just held Rab's hand tightly, as the tears flowed down the old mans lined face.

While this sad scene was being enacted in the Herriot Row the young folks, with the exception of Mary, were all out enjoying the celebration and dance at the Gartsherrie Institute.

Jessie, accompanied by McInnes, had got permission from her parents, to take Alexander with them to the dance. Robert had brought a young lass called Molly Smith, who was a neighbour's daughter, a pretty girl, but she looked as if she could be Robbie's twin as she too had the Irish green eyes and red hair.

The Johnstone family were represented by Agnes and her husband Tom. Mary, Samuel and Maria all being in distant lands.

The young, and not so young, of Gartsherrie were all enjoying a wonderful evening, and a welcome break from work, at the weekly Institute dance.

At last the band took a break and the dancers paused for breath. Mr Watson took over the microphone to make his announcement.

"Ladies and Gentleman may I have your attention please. Tonight I would like to present the prestigious award of Apprentice of the Year to a young man who has not only worked very hard for the entire duration of his apprenticeship but has shown great respect to his superiors."

Robert sniggered and whispered to Jessie.

"He did that all right, oor Sir."

"Shut up and behave yourself." whispered Jessie.

Mr Watson completed his speech, ending up by eulogising on how lucky the population of Gartsherrie were to have such a wonderful employer as Wm Baird & Sons.

At last he asked his wife to come forward and present the Silver Trophy, with the name of William James Law inscribed in elaborate lettering. James was also given a small replica trophy which would be his to keep permanently and an envelope, which unthinking he put into his pocket.

James's acceptance speech was much shorter than the one he had been practicing for days, nerves having taken over. However, he did not discredit himself and he left the platform to spirited applause.

The dancing started again and Margaret Smith made a bee line towards James, she grabbed his hand and pulled him into a foxtrot, the dance which was presently all the rage.

Robert pulled Jessie's sleeve and pointed out James's dancing partner, saying.

"See that one dancing with our James, I wouldn't trust her an inch. Her name is Margaret and she has mean eyes and a bit of a reputation as a right money grubber."

Jessie, ever one to see the best in people tried to find something good to say about Margaret.

"Well she is quite pretty and well turned out, who knows perhaps this is the one."

Alexander piped up.

"Actually for once our Robbie is absolutely right, he is not exaggerating. At the Salvation Army word has got around among the lads to give her a miss, she is only interested in them to get the money from their wallet. Now that our James has his papers she will be trying to sink her teeth into him."

Jessie was astounded that both boys were united in their dislike of James's latest girl, if in fact she was, James always seemed to have a lass in every port, or being a Salvationist, at every Corps. His love life made for much joking and teasing in the family, particularly among the boys.

The three boys were all very close and their involvement in the Salvation Army, where they all played together in the band, made the brothers even more of a united force.

After dancing the foxtrot James brought Margaret back to where the family were standing.

Jessie was first to speak.

"James, who is this young lass you are dancing with?   Come on speak up and tell us all her name."

James introduced McInnes, Jessie, Tom and Agnes together with young Molly to Margaret, then said.

"The boys both know Margaret from the Salvation Army.
Now can I treat you all to a glass of lemonade or ginger beer?"

Margaret took his arm saying.

"That would be lovely Jimmy, I'll come and help you carry the drinks back."

As they walked over to the bar Robert and Alexander glared after her.

Jessie spoke first.

"I know she only said a few words but I get a feeling about her, and can you imagine what my Maw would say if she heard Margaret calling her beloved eldest son 'Jimmy'.   And you know what Robert, I think you are right she has got mean eyes."

The evening wore on with James receiving congratulations and pats on the back for his achievement from his friends and work mates.   Margaret never left his side, basking in his reflected glory.

At ten o'clock McInnes and Jessie left the Institute, as he had a long drive back into Glasgow. They took Alexander with them and Robert promised to walk Molly to her house and to be home himself by eleven o'clock.

The following morning after breakfast James was hanging up his new, much treasured, suit when he went into the pocket and found the envelope given to him by Mr Watson.   To his astonishment when he opened the slim white envelope it contained four crisp five pound notes.

James had never seen money like it in his life, his first reaction was to rush into the kitchen and show the family.   Then he sat down on the bed for a few moments to take his find in, his fingers were shaking as he touched the notes.

He thought, just for a little while, I'll keep them in my pocket and pretend I'm a millionaire. Yes, I'll pretend my name is Baird and I always have twenty pounds in my pocket, just for spending money.

His thoughts and dreams were interrupted by Mary shouting.

"James, can you come through to the kitchen please, you have a visitor."

As he walked through the door who was standing in the kitchen but Margaret Smith, looking very smart in her Salvation Army uniform.

Before James could speak she said.

"I was in the area and I just thought that perhaps we could go to the Holiness Meeting together this morning."

James, although surprised to see her, said.

"Just give me a minute and I'll get into my uniform and we can get going. My younger brothers Robbie and Alexander left earlier, they wanted to practice a new piece of music together.

The women of the house eyed up Margaret. Agnes spoke first.

"Tell me lass, how long have you known my lad?"

Margaret answered politely.

"I have known all your lads for some time now Mrs Law, we all worship in the Salvation Army Corps at Sunnyside, you know. However, it is only recently that Jimmy, err James and I have become special friends."

Neither Agnes nor Mary failed to notice the 'Jimmy' slip up, Agnes stored it away for future use. No way was her son going to get inveigled into a relationship with a woman who called her boy 'Jimmy'.

As they walked to Sunnyside Citadel Hall Margaret took his arm and James felt very special. Apprentice of the Year, a man on a Journeyman's wage and twenty pounds in his pocket, he couldn't help a little secret smile to himself.

"Why are you looking so incredibly pleased with yourself Jimmy Law?" asked Margaret.

"I suppose because I am holding a little secret." James replied teasingly.

"Go on tell Margaret your little secret.   We had such a wonderful evening last night we shouldn't have little secrets from each
other." teased Margaret.

James fingered the money in his pocket. The excitement of the
last few days took over from his normally deeply cautious nature.

"All right, I'll tell you my secret, but you mustn't tell anyone,
especially not my two brothers.   I must tell my Maw and Paw before
they hear it from one of the others." explained James.

Margaret was now beside herself, crying.

"Tell me now handsome, come on tell, Margaret wants to share
your special secret."

James put his hand into his pocket and pulled out the notes.
Margaret's small eyes opened wide in astonishment.

"Jimmy Law, have you robbed a bank?" she said breathlessly.
Never taking her eye of the four bank notes for a single moment.

"No indeed I haven't you silly lassie, it's my prize for becoming
the Apprentice of the Year. I can scarcely believe it myself. I was
given the envelope last night but I didn't open it until this morning.
Maw is going to be thrilled, she could do with a bit of money after
years of always scrimping and scraping and making do."

"Don't be too hasty now" said Margaret in a soft voice.
"Twenty pounds would see you set up in marriage. If you give the
money to your old Maw it will take you years to save that kind of
cash again. Especially since she will take the bulk of your wages
and only give you back pocket money. Think on, you worked hard
for that money Jimmy, you keep it safe."

Over the following weeks every time James turned around
Margaret was there beside him. Even Robert and Alexander found
it difficult to spend time with their elder brother.

Despite Margaret's frequent offers to look after his money, ever
cautious James had put his notes away in an envelope inside the back
pocket of his new suit trousers and there his secret stayed.

Sadly there was something happening in Herriot Row that was
of greater concern than James's hidden cash, and beyond the power
of anyone to alter.

Everyone in the house knew that their father was seriously ill and each sibling had his or her own feelings, feelings they each kept to themselves, although every member of the Law clan wondered what changes would happen within the family when their father passed away, as it was obvious he shortly would.

CHAPTER 22
Late August 1925

In the Law home in Herriot Row the blinds were drawn and the mirrors covered, not only in the Law household were the blinds drawn but also at the homes of their neighbours in the Herriot Row, both Catholic and Protestant, as a mark of respect for both Rab and the entire Law family.

Family and friends all gathered together in the wee house in Herriot Row, Gartsherrie, for the funeral of Robert Law.

Charlotte, who was pregnant with her fifth child, her husband Charlie and their four children, Robert, Jim, May and Willie had made the long journey from Condorrat.

Rab's son, also called Robert, by his marriage to Mary Ann had arrived from Glasgow with his wife Mary and their young family to represent his first family.

His children by Agnes were all assembled, James with his latest girlfriend, Margaret, Jessie with her fiancé, Anderson McInnes and the unattached, Robert, Alexander and Mary.

Supporting the family, as always, were Alex and Jessie Johnstone, together with; Agnes and Tom, Mary not yet having returned from Europe with Liz. Although Agnes Law was more of an acquaintance than a friend Jennie Mathieson was also there in the background. Earlier in the day she had handed in a pound of tea, knowing the kettle would never be off the hob.

As the funeral was being held late on a Saturday afternoon many of his workmates, neighbours and members of the Orange Order and Masonic Lodge had also gathered.

In the packed living room the chattering ceased as the Reverend Maxwell arrived. He formally paid his condolences to Agnes and the family, before going into the bedroom to say a prayer over the body of Rab.

Robert Law's earthly body lay in a plain pine coffin, sitting on wooden trestles in the boys' bedroom. He was dressed in his Sunday suit, which had been bought for his wedding to Mary Ann McGuire, and over his hands was the black bowler hat and orange sash which he wore, with such pride, when marching with his Lodge.

As each person had arrived at the Law home they were offered a drink and something to eat, they then went through to the bedroom to pay their last respects. Saying his final farewell to his auld pal Alex dropped a few coins into the coffin.

"There you are you auld bugger, payment for the ferryman. May the good Lord forgive you for whit you couldn'a forgive yerself for."

Alex's final act for his friend was to screw down the coffin lid to allow the funeral to commence.

Rev Maxwell gave his eulogy; the mourners recited the Lords Prayer and then they all sang the hymn The Lords My Shepherd to the tune of Crimmond.

Tears came for Jessie as they sang the words:
Yea, though I walk in death's dark veil
Yet will I fear none ill
For though art with me and they rod
And staff me comfort still

Reverend Maxwell closed the service with a prayer. The coffin was then carried out to the waiting handcart bier. As the male mourners formed a procession behind the cart young Robert carried out his father's last wish and sang Macushla, in his haunting tenor voice.

Macushla, Macushla
Your sweet voice is calling
Calling me softly
Again and again...

As the final words of the Irish song rang out Robert Law's earthly remains started their journey to Old Monkland Cemetery. The men took turns pushing the bier and the number of mourners testified to the respect in which Robert was held by his workmates, neighbours and lodge brethren.

None of the assembled company would ever have guessed Agnes's thoughts as she said farewell to her husband.

'Mary Ann McGuire you have got him at the last. May he bring you more happiness than he ever brought me and mine'.

The Monday after the funeral James, Robert and Jessie left for work, Alexander set out for school and Mary and her mother started the usual daily round of housework and cooking. They stopped around noon for a sandwich and a cup of tea.

As they ate Agnes completely knocked the wind out of Mary's sails by saying.

"Mary, I want you to go down to the Work's Office, after we finish our bite to eat, and speak to Mr McCosh. You know that nice corner house in the Long Row, number twelve. Well Mrs Murphy's man died a few weeks ago and there is only her and her eldest son living there now. I've heard she is flitting to number 27; a one bedroom is fine for them and it will be a bit less rent. Ask Mr McCosh if we can get a move into the Long Row."

"What!" exclaimed Mary. "We only buried my father on Saturday and you want to flit to another house immediately, what on earth will people think?"

"Actually Mary, I don't care what they think. I've never liked Herriot Row and this house is cold and without creature comfort. I want the Laws' to move to a nicer place and get some new things to enjoy. The first improvements are going to be linoleum and a few rugs.

Now don't argue girl. Run down and get our name on number twelve before anyone else beats us to it."

Mary did as she was bid, she rushed down to the Work's Office, and made the application.

Although somewhat surprised by the request, so soon after Rab's death, Mr McCosh agreed, and they completed the paperwork there and then.

The following Saturday, one week after the funeral, the Law family, after some twenty years in Herriot Row, moved back to the Long Row.

The next few weeks were full of activity with the family settling into their new home. On Rab's death Agnes had received some money from the penny insurance; she had also managed to save a little money now that three of the family were working and contributing wages to the household.

Rab would not tolerate her spending money on the comforts of life but now she was in charge Agnes had every intention of bringing the Law family up in the world.

Jessie brought home paint and wallpaper and decorated the kitchen and two bedrooms, she even whitewashed the scullery and stencilled a pretty border of leaves just under the ceiling.

Agnes went to the Store Emporium and ordered linoleum that imitated parquet flooring, for all the rooms. Her next plan was a good quality carpet. Meantime, her and the girls made rag rugs while Agnes fashioned curtains to add to the homeliness. Rab would have turned mindless had he seen the Morris design materials in the kitchen and boys room and the chintz in the girls. Agnes slept in the recess bed in the kitchen, now she could enjoy the residual warmth from the fire on cold nights.

Another of Agnes's ploys was to join a ménage where a number of ladies would meet one evening a week to make quilts. They each took it in turn to receive one of the completed bedspreads. Agnes was delighted when her name came first out of the hat meaning that she would acquire her first quilt within a month or so.

One morning shortly after the move Agnes said to Mary.

"When you are down at the Store today do you think you could post this letter for me Mary, it's to my Mother. Your Paw and my Ma and Pa did not see eye to eye, to put it mildly. Occasionally my mother has sent word to me through Jessie Johnstone or Ella Millar letting me know about what was happening in Glasgow and how my two older brothers were doing. Now I can invite her to Gartsherrie and you, Jessie and the boys can meet your grandmother."

That evening when the whole family were seated around the dinner table Agnes made an announcement.

"I have today written to my mother, your Granny Neilson. I hope she will come out to Gartsherrie and meet you all very soon. I haven't seen my Maw since wee Martha died and I think it will be good for you all to get to know my family."

There was much whispering between the siblings about this latest chapter in the goings on of their mother. While they were doing the dishes Jessie said to Mary.

"Honestly Mary, since Paw died we just don't seem to know what Maw will get up to next. Mind you it will be interesting to meet Granny Neilson."

The following Saturday the mysterious Granny Neilson arrived for a visit. Agnes had also invited Mrs Millar and Jessie and Alex Johnstone over to join the family for tea.

Agnes put on a good spread, tinned salmon and boiled ham sandwiches, sausage rolls, home made pancakes, fruit loaf and an apple pie.

Martha Neilson was now a widow, her husband having died about five years previously, although Agnes had known of her father's death, through Ella Millar, she had not mentioned it to her husband or children, knowing any mention of her family would inevitably irritate Rab and lead to a row.

The visit went well, Granny Neilson turned out to be quite a vivacious wee body. They conversation steered towards happy times and how well the family were doing, no mention was made of the long time without any contact, or the events around Martha's birth and subsequent death.

Granny Neilson and Ella Millar had been corresponding for years so were happy to have the opportunity to renew their friendship. Although both were now well into their seventies they were both still very bright and active.

When it was time for Martha to take her leave Robert and Alexander walked their grandmother to the railway station at Blairhill and saw her safely on the train, back to Carnarvon Street in Glasgow.

Comfortably settled for her journey home Martha Neilson wiped a tear from her eye, and pretended it was soot, as she thought about all the wasted years when she had not been able to enjoy contact with Agnes, her grandchildren and friends in Gartsherrie. 'Damn that bloody Ulsterman' she thought 'damn him to hell'.

Out of all his children Jessie probably missed her father the most. He had always been very strict with the three boys and even before Mary's rheumatic fever they had endured a somewhat strained relationship.

Rab's soft spot was for Jessie, the prettiest of all his girls. Particularly after Charlotte had married Charlie Fyfe and moved away to Condorrat.

One Friday evening, just after closing time, McInnes arrived at the shop in Bank Street. He found Jessie leaning over the counter-top reading some letters.

"Jess sweetheart why are you looking to solemn reading that mail?" asked McInnes.

"They are letters of condolence the family received after my Paw died. Some of them are from half brothers and sisters I never really knew I had, they all live in and around Glasgow and are married with families. It seems really strange that my father had two lives and they never really touched.

The only son from his first marriage we ever heard mentioned was Robert, he was at the funeral with his wife Mary and their children. You know my Paw had seven bairns with his first wife, four boys and three girls.

I think one of the reasons he lost touch with some of his children was because he couldn't read or write. It must be a terrible thing to have to depend on someone else to read your post, nothing would be private.

My father was not a particularly easy man but over the last few months I have started to feel a great wave of sympathy towards him, life didn't offer him up much happiness.

McInnes, I am so happy with you and we have such fun together, I can never remember my parents ever laughing, joking and having fun together. It was nothing to do with not having much money, Alex and Jessie Johnstone were every bit as hard up as us but they were always happy, he used to tease her something terrible, and you could tell just from the way they looked at each other that they were in love."

McInnes put his arms around his fiancé, saying.

"Jess put the letters away, what is past is past. We have our future to think about. I have a surprise for you, Sunday we are leaving early and going down to Rothesay for the day. When we are there I have a truly gigantic surprise lined up for you.

Can you get an early train into Glasgow and meet me at the Shell in the Central Station, then we will catch the train down to Wemyss Bay and get the ferry across to Rothesay.

As arranged on Sunday morning they met at the Shell, Glasgow's favourite meeting place for courting couples. McInnes swept his fiancé up into his arms and swung her around, saying.

"Just in time my darling we will just about make the ten twenty train. They caught the steam train with moments to spare. During the train ride down to the Clyde Coast and on the ferry over to Rothesay, McInnes steadfastly refused to tell his Jess what the great surprise was going to be.

As they sailed into Rothesay harbour they could see the new Winter Garden which had become the Mecca for entertainment on the Clyde. However, the Winter Gardens was not McInnes's secret. As they left the boat he guided Jessie towards the trams going towards Mount Stuart, home of the Marquess of Bute.

Much of the money to built this opulent mansion came from profit derived from the labour of the Welsh coal miners. Another instance of the poor workers being kept in abject poverty for the betterment of the few.

However, a beautiful sunny day in early autumn was not one where the young lovers intended to discuss, or even think about, politics or social inequalities.

After three stops McInnes and Jessie alighted from the tram. Before them was a field full of people and at the centre of the crowd was a small, blue painted, bi-plane.

McInnes's big surprise was that he had booked a flight for him and Jessie over Rothesay Bay, with the famous air aces, Jim Mollison

and Amy Johnstone.   They walked across the field to the plane,
Jessie's high heel shoes getting caught up in the soft earth.

The pilot, a tall man wearing a fur lined leather jacket and brown
leather helmet, snug to his head called out to them.

"You must be Mr McInnes and Miss Law, are you ready for your
spin? I'm your pilot, my name is Jim."

Before she had time to feel fear Jessie and McInnes had donned
leathers and were sitting in the plane.

Jim engaged the engine it made putt putt noises which gradually
grew louder and louder as the pilot revved up the engine.

The crowd were all waving and cheering as the plane taxied and
slowly lifted from the ground.   It rose steadily until it reached it's
cruising height and then they headed over towards the harbour and
the new Winter Gardens.

Jessie had never felt so terrified, or so exhilarated, in her entire life.

The people, the buildings, so far below them, all looked like children's toys.   The Firth of Clyde, the vast expanse of blue water,
between the coast of Ayrshire and the Isle of Bute, was dotted with
boats and ships of varying sizes and types, from the working puffers
that plied their trade with the Western Isles to the Caledonian
MacBrayne Ferries purposely sailing back and forth from port to
port.   Small fishing craft and pleasure boats also added interest to
the absorbing scene.

McInnes tried to talk to Jessie but his words were carried far
away into the air.

The flight lasted less than an hour, then the little plane descend-
ed with a bumpy landing back into the field, to the roaring cheers of
the admiring bystanders.

After they were safely landed on terra firma Jessie, and for that
matter McInnes, couldn't quite believe that they had been soaring
like birds over the Firth of Clyde, the great estate of Mount Stuart,
the ruin of Rothesay Castle and the exciting new Winter Gardens.

They shook hands with Jim Mollison, their young pilot, and
thanked him for the most amazing, memorable, experience.

Walking back to the road to catch a tram back to the Winter
Gardens, once again Jessie's heels sank into the soft ground.   Did

she care? she cared not a jot. As long as she lived Jessie would never forget flying with McInnes over beautiful Rothesay on the Isle of Bute, that glorious gem set in the Firth of Clyde.

The remainder of the day was also wonderful, a lovely meal followed by a variety show at the Winter Gardens, before catching the ferry back to the mainland.

Travelling back alone on the train from Glasgow to Coatbridge, Jessie pondered on whether or not to tell her mother all about her day. Certainly she could talk about her visit to the Winter Gardens and the sail over to Rothesay, but the flight, her flying in an airplane, would that only alienate McInnes even further from her Maw?

Whatever else, she would tell Mary, her wise sister, all about the flight. Mary could always be relied on as a repository of secrets.

CHAPTER 23
September 1925

Liz and Mary Johnstone returned home from Europe in early September. When their train steamed into Coatbridge Central, they said a fond goodbye, Liz got into a taxi heading for her home in Airdrie where her housekeeper was waiting for her and Mary piled her cases into another taxi.

"130 Long Row, Gartsherrie please." Mary instructed the driver.

Not a lot of taxis travelled to the Long Row, a beautiful young woman with good quality cases going to Gartsherrie, this was definitely an unusual fare for the driver.

Mary paid off the taxi, added a generous tip for the cabbie and then positively bounced into her family home, she rushed towards her mother cuddling her and lifting her up into her arms, saying.

"Ma, oh Ma, I am so glad to see you. I have had such an wonderful, sparkling, eye opening, incredible trip. I've brought you and Pa home some presents and I've brought home a lifetime full of memories, I just can't begin to tell you."

Jessie was simply over the moon to have her lass home and to see her looking so radiant, dressed in a fashionable Nile green calf length dress and short coat, with pale grey accessories and topped with a co-ordinating cloche hat.

"Take your cases through to your bedroom pet, I'll put the kettle on and we can have a lovely blether and you can tell me all about your adventures in Europe."

A few weeks before Mary's arrival home a crate had been delivered containing a beautiful pair of Venetian glass vases, these were now sitting in pride of place on either side of the Johnstone mantelpiece.

"I see the vases arrived safely Ma" observed Mary. "Did our Agnes and my Aunt Agnes also receive the glassware we sent to them?"

"Indeed they did pet." answered Jessie. "They were both absolutely delighted. You got it just right, a pair of vases for the mantelpiece in beautiful autumn colours for your Aunt Agnes, honestly she was all wasted; and our Agnes absolutely loved that dish you sent her, all varying shades of blues and greens, just like the sea. It is in the middle of the table in her dining room, well out of wee Emily's way. Mary, can you believe what I just said, my wee daughter Agnes has a Dining Room, I would never in a million years have thought it possible."

"The world is changing Ma, not quickly enough for Liz, but it is going to change." Responded Mary as she went into her bedroom and opened her cases.

By the time her mother had made the tea she returned with some presents wrapped in tissue paper. For her mother there was a beautiful silk scarf and an Art Deco style rhinestone necklace, earrings and brooch set, in a velvet lined leather case bearing the name of a famous Paris jeweller.

Jessie exclaimed at the beauty of the gift and then almost immediately said.

"Mary lass what a lovely present but it is far too much, you have already sent me those lovely vases from Italy. You can't afford to spend all that amount of money on gifts."

"Yes I can" laughed Mary. "Just wait until you see what we have bought for my Pa. It's a Meerschaum pipe, apparently it is the finest of pipes. We just thought, the finest Pa in the world must have the finest pipe. Actually we have bought him two, a fancy one in a lined case, that he can keep for special occasions and a plainer one for everyday use.

We didn't want to carry anything heavy so we have brought back silk scarfs for our Agnes, my Aunt Agnes, all the Law girls and Jennie. Silk handkerchiefs for Tom and the Law lads and for darling Emily, we bought the most beautiful dress you could imagine also a little silver pendant, set with turquoises, and a matching bracelet. We even posted gifts to Sam, Maria and their brood from Berlin, goodness knows when they will receive them but at least they will know we have been thinking of them.

Liz wanted everyone to have a little reminder from our travels. The only heavy thing we have bought back is a box of Swiss chocolates for you and Paw, but I certainly won't object if you choose to share them with your youngest daughter."

Over the next few days Mary distributed her gifts, even posting a scarf and handkerchief to Charlotte and Charlie in Condorrat.

Jessie had been so looking forward to Mary's return home but as the days passed she realised that the Mary who had left for Europe was not the Mary who had returned. It wasn't the descriptions of the different countries. It wasn't stories of delicious foods to be found at the markets, or wonderful meals they had eaten in bistros and restaurants. It wasn't the thrill of speaking French in France. It wasn't the beautiful clothes she was wearing. It wasn't the first class travel nor the staying in famous hotels.

It was the constant references to Liz. Every sentence seemed to start; We bought, We visited, We ate, Liz said, Liz gave me, Liz introduced me to.

Jessie understood human nature, she knew that people in love want to talk about their loved one. And, her daughter Mary was clearly in love, Jessie hoped that everyone else would assume that her glow of happiness and excited talk was simply the result of having experienced a trip that nobody else in Gartsherrie could possibly imagine, even in their wildest dreams.

For days Jessie had been trying to act normally and convince herself that she had no need to worry about Mary. She desperately needed to talk but this was certainly not a conversation she could have with Alex, Agnes Law or for that matter her daughter Agnes, on the other hand she was wise enough to know that her suspicions definitely needed an airing.

There was only one person Jessie could talk to openly about her concerns and that person was her friend and campaigning sister,

Jennie Mathieson.

Jessie headed to Blairhill, to the haven that was Jennie's home. A place where over the years she had often felt the hand of genuine friendship.

The door was opened by Jennie herself who warmly welcomed her friend.

"Jessie, always lovely to see you. Come through to the kitchen with me and I'll make us a cup of coffee, today isn't one of Mrs Alan's days. Remember in the old days when we used to have Sally to serve tea in the morning room? She left when the War started, went to work in the munition factory in Dundyvan Road for a time and then got married after the hostilities. Three children she has now, doesn't time pass quickly?"

As Jennie prepared the pot of coffee Jessie got out the tray and set it, in the companionable way you can only do in a real friend's house.

They took the tray through to the morning room and settled themselves down. Jennie looked at her friend and said.

"By the look on your face Jessie Johnstone you could do with something a wee bit stronger than coffee. I'll pour us both a sherry."

As she was taking the decanter out of the sideboard she reminisced.

"Do you know every time I have a glass of sherry I think of your story about raiding the wardrobe at Liz's house, then you and Agnes Law getting seriously tiddly on sherry. It must have been an absolute hoot."

"It certainly was, in fact it's Liz I want to talk to you about." said Jessie as she accepted the sherry. After taking a sip she started to tell Jennie about her concerns.

"Jennie, this isn't just a social call, I haven't popped in just for coffee. I need to talk about something and I just don't know where to start and you are the only person I can possibly confide in."

"Oh Jessie, you know I will always be a listening ear for you, how many times over the years have we told each other our concerns about things that seemed important at the time but have now vanished into oblivion. Now come on Jessie, tell your Auntie Jennie."

It took Jessie a few minutes to gather her thoughts before she could express her fears to Jennie.

"The trouble is Jennie, I just don't know where to start or what I can do or say to make things right.

My Mary came home from Europe with Liz on Tuesday afternoon. A week on Saturday Liz and Mary are off again, this time to Perthshire and then up north as far as Inverness for a few weeks. Apparently Liz's sight has deteriorated quite a bit since they have been away travelling, so this will definitely be the last autumn she will see. It doesn't look as though poor Liz will enjoy the daffodils next spring."

"How desperately sad." sympathised Jennie. "It was very kind of your Mary to escort her on her last sighted trip, although I am sure it was also good for Mary to see Paris and Berlin and all those other lovely places they visited.

In fact Mary called the other day and left me a beautiful silk scarf with a card from her and Liz, unfortunately I was out at the time."

"The problem is I think Mary was a good deal more than just an escort." At last Jessie had managed to articulate her fears, she continued.

"Jennie, how long have we known Liz?"

"Actually I remember exactly the first time we met her, it was the first time you came to a Suffragette meeting in this very room. Margaret and I had arranged an informal gathering as both you and Liz were new to our group."

"Yes," agreed Jessie, "and that was around nineteen hundred, we were all in our twenties, since then we have lived a lifetime, what with the War and our partial success by winning a limited franchise. I have become a grandmother, your Margaret's girls are getting to be young ladies now. And, my poor Jennie, you lost your great love in the War.

Do you see what I mean, we all know about each other, we have been involved in each other's lives. What do any of us know about

Liz?   Nothing.   Over the years she has breezed into and out of our group.   Other than you and me, I wouldn't say she has made any real friends in quarter of a century with us.

I think we would both agree Liz is not the most feminine of women, well I think she has corrupted our Mary.

Honestly, when she came home my Mary looked like a woman in love.   I tried to find out if she met any gentlemen on her travels but I seem to be hitting my head against a brick wall.   It's Liz this, Liz that, and wait to you hear the best bit, it's Countess this and Lady that, and did you know Liz is really the Right Honourable Lady Elizabeth Agatha Wallis-Banks?"

"What!" exclaimed Jennie, "Right Honourable Lady, she kept that well hidden."

"Exactly" said Jessie, "What else has she kept hidden.   I think she is a lesbian, and all that sending Mary to College and giving her books to read was all part of her long term plan.   Mary is now her girlfriend, at least that is what I suspect, it's just all too horrible to contemplate."

Jennie stood up and refilled the sherry glasses, the coffee was left to grow cold.   They both sat quietly sipping their drinks for few moments before Jennie said.

"You know Jessie, thinking about it all coldly and logically it makes a kind of sense.   However, Mary is not a child any more, she is an adult and a jolly sensible one at that.   If she wants Liz as a life partner I suppose it is her decision, however tempted we are to interfere.

Look at my sister Margaret and Father Martin, against all the odds that relationship has worked out wonderfully, they have two beautiful daughters and are a really happy family.   Remember the gossip and all the horrible things that were said on both sides of the Catholic Protestant divide, Gartsherrie had a field day on that one.

Tell me Jessie, did Mary ever have any boyfriends?"

"Actually, not really.   When she was young her and Agnes would sometimes go dancing with the Law girls, I suppose she met lads then but she never brought any of them home."

Jennie questioned Jessie further.

"Have you thought perhaps Mary was always inclined towards her own sex and Liz spotted it and tried to make life better for her. Can't be easy to be different in a place like the Gartsherrie Rows."

"Jennie, over the years I have had to learn to lose my prejudices. Look at that business with Sam and Maria, they are now well settled in Australia, two wee boys and another baby on the way. Reading their letters I can tell they are happy and strong as a couple. It's this daft place that's wrong, with all it's wee petty rules and conventions on how everyone should live their lives.

My problem is that I just do not want Alex to know my suspicions, which I am sure are fact. My darling man would be broken hearted, I can't begin to tell you Jennie how upset he would be.

He loves all his bairns but I know he feels that both Agnes and Sam have found the kind of love that we have and he longs for Mary to do the same. I think he is frightened that she will be left on the shelf with nobody special in her life."

"Like me," said Jennie. "I am well and truly on the shelf. I had my opportunity, I should have taken my chance of happiness when I could.

As you know, the first time I went down to Cambridge to visit Margaret and Martin I met John Armstrong. We got on so well you can't imagine how happy we were in each other's company. Over the years we had some wonderful times together with Margaret and Martin in Cambridge.

What you didn't know Jessie, we also used to meet in York or London, once we even went to Paris. Now don't be shocked Jessie, we holidayed as Mr and Mrs Armstrong, and I don't regret it for an instant.

John had his career at the University, I had my life here, neither of us could quite organise ourselves to get together and marry. We thought we had a lifetime ahead of us, but the War knew better. My one real love died at Ypres, we lost our chance to marry, and I lost the chance to become a mother.

As you say Jessie the years have changed us. Now I am inclined to think if Liz and Mary are happy together, just accept, let them enjoy the moment for who knows what the future may bring."

"Thank you so much Jennie, my dear dear friend. I just had to talk this through and ask your advice, as always you have got straight to the heart of the matter. I will speak to Mary on her own and if she confirms that she is in a relationship with Liz or one of the other Ladyships, well I will let her know that I accept her life choice. After all I have accepted both Agnes and Sam's paths in life, my Mary must not be treated any differently.

However, I think it would be best that it's all kept hidden from my Alex, he would be so hurt and probably horrified if he ever knew the truth."

"You are probably right there, but I think you should discuss with Mary whether or not she wants to tell her father and her sister." advised Jennie.

"Now I am going to make us a fresh pot of coffee and a bit of scrambled eggs and toast for our lunch. We need something to soak up the sherry, two glasses before noon, we are decadent Mrs Johnstone, terribly, terribly decadent."

They both eased the tension by laughing and headed for the kitchen.

Later that evening when Alex was out at a Masonic Meeting Jessie had an opportunity to speak to Mary on her own. She had already decided that no good would come from beating around the bush, no she would come straight out with her fears and give Mary the opportunity to explain her feelings.

"Mary lass, I know you had a wonderful trip to Europe with Liz but I want to ask you something about your travels. Did you meet someone special and enter into a relationship? Since you returned home you have had the look of a woman who is in love? Are you? And if so, with whom?"

Mary knew full well her mother was no fool and in her heart of hearts she knew that sooner or later this conversation was going to take place.

"You are not daft are you Ma, I guessed I would have to tell you. Yes, Liz and I are both Sapphic. I have always known I was different from our Agnes and Charlotte Law. I never wanted to have boyfriends, marry, or have babies, I couldn't explain why I felt as I did, I just knew that what they wanted was not what I wanted from life.

At Agnes's wedding when I spoke with Liz and she promised to give me books to read I knew I wanted to be her friend and learn from her life experience.

I used to live for the times we met in one of the tea rooms in Coatbridge for a cup of tea and a chat about what I had been reading, everything from the poems of Owen and Sassoon to Bernard Shaw and Ruskin to George Eliot.

When Liz paid to send me to Pitman's College you simply can't believe how wonderful it was for me to attain a formal qualification and then work closely with such a very special person, it was as though all the reading and studying had prepared me for working as Liz's Secretary.

Ma, there was no question of her ever trying to seduce me in any way, it was me who first kissed her. I think I knew for a long time that she loved me, and I certainly loved her.

It was being away from Gartsherrie, far away from all the old taboos and small-mindedness that allowed us to express how we really felt about each other.

After the trip up north I intend to move into Liz's home in Airdrie. Don't worry I will be known as her Live in Companion and as she is almost blind now nobody will see my moving in with her as in any way odd."

While processing all this information and getting to grips with her daughters lifestyle change Jessie knew she had to ask the question.

"Mary, you are my daughter, I love you and if living with Liz is going to make you happy, so be it. But I have to ask you, what do you intend to tell your father, also Agnes and Tom. Do you want them to know the truth, that Liz is your life partner, not just your employer?

If I am being honest I would rather your Paw thinks you are simply a Companion. However, the decision must be yours and yours alone. Mary pet, why don't you get ready and go to bed before he comes home, give yourself time to think. You can speak to him tomorrow."

Mary did think, she thought very carefully. Her instinct, after the freedom she had enjoyed while on her European tour had made her want to be completely above board, to tell her father, together with Agnes and Tom the truth. Also to write to Sam and Maria letting the entire family know that she too had found love and happiness.

However, the reality was she was not in Europe, she was in Gartsherrie, where prejudice could reach epic levels. After much thought Mary decided against telling the rest of the family about her true relationship with Liz. The more people who knew the more chance that word would spread and while she did not mind for herself the thought that any of her beloved family would suffer from cruel gossip was unbearable.

The following morning, after the breakfast had been cleared away Mary made her feelings clear to her mother.

"Ma, I've thought and thought and I realise the only way forward is for me to become known as Liz's Companion Secretary. Everyone will accept it as a respectable job. I won't tell my Pa or Agnes and Sam, better they think I am a spinster with a career which I love, rather than them knowing I have a person to love.

We will be heading north shortly, I will move back to Airdrie tomorrow to prepare for our journey, we will leave the following Saturday. After we return from the Highlands I will come home for a few days and announce to everyone I have a new post, Live in Companion Secretary to Liz.

Don't worry Ma, I'll come and visit you and Pa every week, besides I have a grand wee niece and her parents living in Drumpellier. You don't think I would ever lose touch with our Agnes do you?

Only you will know the truth, can you cope with holding our secret, play pretend for years and years. Can you Ma, can you?"

Jessie took her youngest daughter's hand, saying.

"Of course I'll keep my council. After a time I will come to believe that you are a Companion Secretary, and no more. Your mother has been the repository of many secrets over the years you know, some that would surprise even you Mary.

Now go and start to get your things sorted out, then pop over and see our Agnes and Tom and tell them your plans. This evening you can tell your Paw the travel arrangements for the Scottish trip. Also tell him that you have discussed with Liz the possibility of becoming her permanent Companion because of her impending blindness.

I really hate having to deceive your father but I think a wee fib now is the best option all round.

Mary I am so very sorry it has to be like this, perhaps one day far far in the future two women will be able to be open about their feelings, but at this time and in this place, it is far better for everyone concerned to simply play the game."

That night in bed Alex whispered to his wife.

"Jessie my love, our Mary has changed, so she has. This trip away has made her grow away from us, it's like she has become educated and living in a society well beyond our reach.

Our Agnes made a marriage above us but she is still our Agnes and her Tom is like another son to us now. Even Sam and Maria and their bairns, all them miles away, still seem like part of us when they write and send photographs. But my wee Mary, hard as she tries to be part of us, she is moving away, so she is.

Jessie lass I don't want to lose my Mary."

Jessie held his hand tightly and whispered.

"My Alex, we have to let her go, that way she will come back to us. If we try to stop her moving into more educated circles, than we can ever imagine, she will only get bitter and unhappy.

Mary is happy travelling and working for Liz, she gets to meet all sorts of interesting people and hopefully she can take my place in the struggle for an equal franchise.

I am proud of my Mary and all she has achieved but now is the time to let her take flight.

Cuddle down now my Alex and get some sleep, another hard day of work tomorrow."

Mary and Liz travelled north as planned, they reveled in the majestic autumn scenery, the trees losing their green mantel and turning to shades of yellow and burnished gold, the moorland alive

with purple and lilac heather, the salt tang of the sea and the sun
bursting through after the early morning haar. Liz filed each scene
in her mind, memories that could never be taken from her, unlike
her sight, which was rapidly diminishing.

As well as staying at comfortable hotels they visited friends of
Liz who lived in a Scottish Baronial Castle. They enjoyed Highland
hospitality, visited a distillery, Mary even tried fishing and croquet.
A lifestyle as far removed from Gartsherrie as could possibly be
imagined.

Liz refused to let her impending blindness spoil the magic of
their tour. Although the real magic was her blossoming relationship
with Mary, whom she had loved from afar for so many years.

On returning from their Highland sojourn Mary settled into her
new life with her beloved, enjoying a love that could never be spoken of within her family, or the community she had grown up in.

To the folks of the Gartsherrie Rows Mary Johnstone was, and
always would be, a spinster, an unclaimed treasure, an auld maid.
Only her mother and Jennie Mathieson knew different.

CHAPTER 24
October 1925

"What on earth's the matter Maw?" asked Mary. "You haven't seemed yourself since yesterday. Do you feel ill? Will I get one of the boys to fetch the doctor?"

"No Mary, there is nothing any doctor on God's good earth can do to make me feel any better."

"Come on Mother, tell me what is really wrong with you, are you in any pain?" asked Mary, while secretly thinking that her mother was simply being a bit of a drama queen, recently she had been perfecting that particular role.

"Aye, I'm certainly in pain Mary, a pain of the heart."

"Maw, will you please tell me what is wrong, stop being so melodramatic, nothing can be that bad."

"Look Mary is some ways you have suffered the most from my sins. I have got to tell you the honest truth, but you must promise me, on the Bible, that you will NEVER repeat to anyone what I have to tell you."

"Look Ma, have you ever known me to gossip, it's not Robert or James you are telling. I am going to mask us a pot of tea and there is a wee drop of whisky left from the funeral, I'll put a taste in your cup."

Mary hurried off to the scullery. As Agnes listened to the homely sounds of Mary busy making the tea, she looked into the heart of the fire and took herself back down the years.

Mary brought the tea tray into the kitchen, she gave her mother a cup and sat down opposite her with her own cup in hand. They sat in silence for a few minutes sipping their tea. Eventually Agnes started to speak.

"Mary, I received a letter yesterday, it came while you were down at the Store getting the messages. It was from my son, my firstborn."

Mary's jaw dropped in astonishment. She started to blurt out questions, Agnes held up her hand to stop her from speaking.

"Look Mary, don't say anything or I'll lose the courage to tell you. Please don't interrupt me, just listen to all I have to say. The letter was from my son, who I haven't seen since he was a year old, he is a grown man now and wants to meet me.

When I was young my life took a lot of twists and turns and I fully acknowledge that I gave my parents more than their share of worry.

I think it would be better if I go to the beginning of the story and explain how it all happened, thinking about my past, it seems like a story that happened to someone else and not Agnes Neilson from Glasgow.

I left school at fourteen and got a live in job as a scullery maid to an important family who lived in a lovely house out along Great Western Road in Glasgow. The cook, Mrs Hunter, kept me busy, scrubbing pots, washing the floors and generally making myself useful, but she was quite a kind auld biddy really, she taught me a lot about cooking and on my day off she would always give me a nice cake or savoury to take back home to my mother.

There were quite a lot of servants. The butler, Mr Strang, who was in charge of the household. Miss Amelia, the Ladies Maid. Then there was Johnny, who was known as the Boot Boy but he was well over 50 if he was a day. Norah, she was the Parlour Maid, and, several other women came in as day workers to clean, or help if we had a big dinner on for the gentry.

There was also a lady who was Governess to the two little girls. We didn't see much of her as she had all her meals either with the girls or on her own in her room. Mrs Hunter used to call her 'a distressed gentlewoman', whatever that may mean.

Now you must remember I was a young maid, I had long black hair, black like Charlotte's, and a peaches and cream complexion like Jessie, I was slim and even if I say so myself, quite a good looker.

I was also ambitious and wanted to become a Ladies Maid and

wear a black gown with a little white lace apron and a lace cap. I used to dream of getting a place in a grand house and travelling abroad with my Mistress. Perhaps meeting a handsome butler or valet and getting married, we would have a lovely little cottage on an estate. How I would dream my life away, while I was cleaning or peeling the potatoes. You know Mary, it's not only the gentry that have ambition.

As Agnes continued her story, Mary thought. 'How dare she talk of ambition, her and my father ruined my ambition and she has done her best to ruin Jessie's chance of making a go of her life.'

Agnes carried on with her tale impervious to the statement she had made or to Mary's feelings.

My mother had taught me how to sew, which was an essential skill for a Ladies Maid. I used to help Amelia in the evening with plain sewing. She appreciated that I worked neatly so she taught me how to do embroidery and lacework. One winter she gave me a piece of fine lawn linen and I worked a beautiful handkerchief for my mother. It was edged in lace I had made myself and each corner had a little posy of daisies, which I embroidered with silk threads.

Do you know I think that was my happiest moment when I took that wee handkerchief, all wrapped up in tissue paper and tied with a ribbon, to my mother on Boxing Day. Maw was so proud of me, so was my Paw for that matter.

As well as the handkerchief I brought other treats home; some boiled ham with a jar of Mrs Hunter's extra special Cumberland sauce, and a dozen mincemeat pies. I gave Paw ten shillings saved from my wages. We had a wonderful day, my last memory of when I was truly happy with all the freedom and promise of youth.

All was going according to my plan. Norah left to nurse her mother, I was made Parlour Maid and we got a new Scullery Maid, Emmy. As well as the sewing Amelia taught me how to use a goffering iron and launder the Mistress's good clothes. It was lovely handling the soft silk and fine cotton. Can you believe, she even taught me how to manicure nails and dress hair. I was getting nearer my ambition with every month that passed.

Then one day the son of the house, Albert, came home from

school in England.   Although I had been at the house nearly three
years I had never seen him before.

We were of an age and he would pay me little compliments and
make me blush.   Then he started to give me a little cuddle and so it
went on.   Oh Mary, I was only human, a pretty girl, and a handsome lad.   Well to cut the story short we were caught in my room
doing what we should not have been doing.   The worst of it was, it
was Amelia who found us.   My mentor was angry, hurt and disappointed all at the same time, after all the time and trouble she had
taken to train me.   I was marched in front of the Mistress, given a
weeks wages in lieu of notice and immediately sent packing.   Worst
of all, I was not given a reference.   The Mistress sent a letter to my
father explaining exactly why I had been fired.

Everything seemed black.   My parents were furious with me,
and it was obvious I would not be able to get a good job in service
without a decent reference.   The only option left open to me was to
take a job in a factory and live at home.   I got a job sewing gar-
ments on piece work in a little factory in the Gorbals, called
Salmonds.

But youth has a short memory, and I started to walk out with one
of the lads who worked in the factory.   Ben was the owner's nephew,
again, the same old story; handsome lad, pretty girl, recipe for disas-
ter.   But this time it was oh so different, we fell madly in love.

Ben was the only man I have ever loved, and he loved me,
deeply and truly.   However he was Jewish and Jewish families, even
poor Jewish families, do not want their sons to marry a shiksa.
That is the word they use if the girl is not Jewish, and it is not a very
nice word.

I missed my monthly and realised I must be pregnant.   I was
terrified to tell Ben but when I did he immediately promised to
stand by me.   He took me to his folk's house and told his parents
that we were going to get married.   Well I can't tell you the stooshie
that caused.   He was the youngest son, and the favourite.   His
mother was crying,

"Oy my Benjamin, my consolation for old age, my beautiful boy,
giving his precious seed to a shiksa."

The auld mother went on and on.   His father started to talk in a funny language, it was called Yiddish, but it was obvious he was also furious. I knew they wouldn't be pleased but I never imagined they would be so full of venom.

The tears were running down Ben's face as he pleaded with his parents.   I found out much later that the reason they were so angry was that to be a Jew comes down through the mother, therefore as I was a gentile any children we had would be gentiles and not Jews.

Ben's sister Ruth was also in the room.   Eventually she screamed at them all to shut up.   She grabbed her shawl and shouted.   'Enough, I am going to get David, he'll be a voice of reason in this family.' Then she ran out of the house.

Mary, truthfully, I had not spoken a word I was so shocked. After Ruth left there was just tears, the auld couple crying like they had been told their son was dead, not that they were about to be grandparents.   Ben sitting with his head in his hands crying, and me in complete shock.

Eventually Ruth returned with her elder brother, who was a Rabbi. He took Ben by the shoulders and sat him upright in the chair.

As soon as he had appeared on the scene the shouting started all over again. David's voice boomed out above the rammy.

'Please, Mama, Papa, harsh voices are not helping this situation one little bit.'

Then he more or less said, 'what's done is done' all in a mixture of Scottish and Yiddish.

They all seemed to take notice of David, it was like he was the boss. He turned to me and said.

'Are you going to have my brother's child?'

I said, 'Yes'. He then said.

'Well I have a question to ask you.   Now think carefully before you answer me. Will you take instruction, convert to our religion, and be a good Jewish wife to my younger brother?'

I was so frightened, and I so wanted to make it right for Ben, that I just said 'yes'.

David then seemed to take over.   He issued the orders and we all obeyed.

I started instructions on Judaism at David's home, where I met his wife Miriam, and a right snotty stuck up cow she was too.

A wedding was arranged at the Gorbals Synagogue. Meantime I was living at home and going to work, pretending everything was normal.

I knew my Maw and Paw would be every bit as angry as Ben's folks. I had been brought up in the Church of Scotland, with occasional nights going to lantern shows at the Christian Mission. Paw was in the Masons, we were a family of staunch Protestants. I just did not have Ben's courage.

I told my parents that I had got another job in service, which meant I had to live in. I then packed my portmanteau with my few belongings and moved into the tenement flat in the Gorbals, sharing a bedroom with Ruth.

Ben's mother never really liked me and she did all she could to make life difficult. The auld man always spoke in Yiddish but I knew full well he could understand Scottish, and speak a bit.

David was all right in a schoolteacher kind of way, he certainly made me work hard learning all about their history, festivals, food rules, on and on the instructions seemed never ending.

That wife of his, Miriam, never as much as offered me a cup of tea, in her eyes I was not good enough to sit with the Rabbi's wife. All this after a long day working at Salmonds factory.

Ben and I hardly saw each other, because he was sent to live with his uncle, Isaac Salmond, until I completed instruction and we could be married. The only one in the family who was halfway decent to me was Ruth. She taught me how to cook the Jewish way, some of the food was really lovely, but my God the rules, you can eat this with that and not with the other and certain foods go with certain festivals. You can't imagine how complicated cooking can be when you have to use two sets of pots and crockery, one for flesh and one for dairy.

We eventually got married in the synagogue, me with my big bump, his family looking like they were at a funeral, and my family thinking I was safely working in service.

After the wedding under the canopy at the synagogue, we went back to the flat in the Gorbals and had a toast with a wee glass of sweet wine, muzzeltof!   The only good thing about the reception was the apple strudel cake Ruth had made, now that was delicious.

Actually there was something else good, Uncle Isaac gave Ben a promotion, with a bit more money, and it was agreed I would now do finishing work in the flat, so I did not have to go to work at the factory every day.

Ruth moved into a hurley bed in the living room and Ben and I pushed the two single beds together in the bedroom. Come to think about it, if anyone should have had a down on me it should have been Ruth, she had to leave her bedroom, but she was always very kind to me.

When my son was born the initial labour was fairly easy and Ruth and the old mother helped me through the confinement. He was born a grand wee lad, we called him Samuel after the auld man, apparently his name was Samuel but it was a funny spelling, S.H.M.U.E.L. Just as the afterbirth was coming away the auld woman started to panic and speak in Yiddish. There was another baby, a wee tiny girl. We thought she was going to die, she was so small compared to Samuel, it was as though he had taken all the goodness. But she was a game wee babby. To everyone's surprise my wee fighter lived. We called her Sarah, after the auld mother, I had asked them to call her Ruth. But tradition is all with the Jewish folks so my little girl was named Sarah. I just hoped that she would grow up to be as decent and compassionate a person as her aunt, no matter what her given name.

We rubbed along for a year or so, happy to be together with our wee family. I did my best to be a good Jewish wife to Ben, mother to his bairns and earn some extra money sewing.

One winter morning Ben was running late for work, so he jumped on a horse drawn tram. The horse must have slipped in the snow, I don't really know what happened but the horse fell and the tram was jolted forward. Everyone on the tram was thrown about and there were lots of minor injuries. Ben was brought home with cracked ribs. The auld woman bound them up and he had a couple of days off work. He seemed to be perfectly fine for the next few weeks.

One day there was a chap on the door. It was Uncle Isaac, he brought the worst news possible. Apparently Ben had been standing in the office talking to Isaac about an order, he bent forward to hand him some paperwork and my husband, my Ben, dropped dead on the floor.

It turned out he had a broken neck, the damage was done in the tram crash and it just took him to move a certain way and he was dead. My decent, handsome, husband; father to our twins Samuel and Sarah, and him not yet twenty-five, dead.

The funeral happened really quickly and then they all sat crying and praying for days on end, it's called sitting shiva. At the end of the crying there was a family meeting. David, as usual, was the spokesman. He announced that in view of my youth it would be better if I returned home to my own people. The family would provide for the twins and ensure they were brought up as good Jews. I will never forget the look of pure triumph on that bitch Miriam's face.

So there I was, returning home after two years, with only my portmanteau. I had made no contact with my Ma and Pa because I thought it was better to sever links rather than constantly spinning more and more lies.

Can you imagine my parents' reaction? At first they were pleased to see me safe, if not sound. Then came the questions, my Paw was like a lawyer the way he questioned me. He went on and on trying to wear me down, but I never told them the whole story, just that I had eloped with a boy called Ben Fisher and he had been killed in an accident. But his name wasn't Fisher; it was Fischer, with an c.

As a widow I managed to find a job in service as an Assistant Cook. The work was in a big household up in the Park Circus area in Glasgow and I was kept very busy, as well as the normal meals they were always having fancy dinner parties.

I visited my family on my day off and, all credit to my parents, the missing two years were never spoken off, it was as though they had never happened.

At the start of 1896 I felt I was slowly getting back on my feet. I was heart sore for my bairns but my one consolation was that I knew they would be loved and well cared for.

Ruth and I kept in touch, well once every few months or so she would send me a postcard to my parents address, as if she was an old school pal. Just a few words, but written in such a way that I could tell the bairns were thriving.

Men are always trouble, so then I met Bertie Coyle, he was an Irish Catholic from County Mayo who got a job working in the garden at the fancy house. He was good looking, had the gift of the gab and flirted with all the girls, even the cook, Mrs Wilson. He would come in with some vegetables and usually go out with a slice of her pie or cake.

We all knew he was a ladies man but he made us laugh with his jokes and well, I hadn't laughed in a long time.

Same old story, laughter then the tears. Charlotte was conceived in the potting shed at the bottom of the garden and I was soon back with my Ma and Pa in Garscube Road.

Charlotte was born in the December of '96 and my Ma had just about had enough of me by that time. Thankfully she looked after Charlotte while I worked at a Manse up in Springburn. I think she thought I wouldn't be able to get into any more trouble in a guid Church of Scotland household.

Honestly, what do you think the Minister would have thought if he had known that his lunch was being served by a Jewess with a bastard Catholic child. Poor Protestant man, him and his wee wife would have been mortified if they had known.

Then my Ma and Pa moved to Carnarvon Street. The flat was further away from work but what luxury we had an inside lavatory with a proper bath, I've told you before the Neilson family were not only respectable folks they were quite comfortable.

One hot summer evening I went for a walk with a girl called Rose, who stayed on he same landing. We met two young men, who were sharing a lodging with some other Irishmen on the other side of St George's Road, in Shamrock Street, they were all working as labourers or on the railways.

My Paw saw us chatting to the fellows, well did I get hell when I went home? Another stern lecture, but youth does not heed wis-

dom, and Rose and I met the lads a few times more on the quiet.
Nothing happened with them, I was too frightened of Paw and I
knew there would be no more chances for me. If I had ever got
pregnant again, I would have ended up in the Workhouse.

One night we went back to their flat. Eight men were sharing
the two room flat and several of them were quite old. One of the
men masked a pot of tea and we all just sat around drinking the tea
and blethering. The men were all Ulster Protestants who had come
to Scotland looking for work and were just getting a living any way
they could. The oldest of the men seemed to watch me all night
and when we left he walked us back across St George's Road to
Carnarvon Street.

Yes, it was your father, Robert Law. He took to meeting me
from the tram at night. He told me he was a widower with grown
up children. I told him I was a widow and had a little girl called
Charlotte, he assumed that she was Ben's daughter and I told him no
different. Besides that was the story my Ma had given to the new
neighbours, nothing if not respectable were the Neilson clan.

We had barely been acquaintances for a few months, just the
walk from the tram a few nights a week and an occasional meeting
in the street, when out of the blue he upped and asked me to marry
him. I said 'yes', why, I honestly don't know, even to this day.

After church the following Sunday your Paw came to our house,
dressed in his best suit, and asked my Father and Mother if he could
marry me.

I hadn't warned them that he was coming to ask for my hand,
for in truth, deep down I did not believe that it was going to happen. All hell broke loose, my Pa called him an illiterate waster from
the bogs, and told him to get out.

I'll never forget his response, he just said with great dignity.
Agnes is a widow woman, with a child, so she is. I don't need to
ask your permission to wed her, the choice is hers and hers alone.
Then he walked out.

The next night he met me from the tram and he asked me again
if I would marry him and the sooner the better.

We wed in the February of '98 and you were born in the March of the following year. It was no shotgun wedding but in some ways that made it even harder on my parents as it was my free choice.

Your Father wanted me to go to live with him in the lodgings in Shamrock Street but my Ma really drew the line at that. Eight men and me, there was no way on God's earth that was ever going to happen.

After the wedding he was allowed to live with our family. He was as welcome with my kith and kin as I had been with Ben's family. Religion was not the reason this time; they just did not want an illiterate Irishman, who did not have a trade, in their family. I suppose even within the poor there is snobbery. My Paw was a Master Bricklayer and my two brothers, who were both married, were time served tradesmen.

We lived in a nice flat, Ma kept the black grate shining with Zebo, and the metal burnished like silver. We had rugs, some of them made by Ma, and a mahogany sideboard, table and chairs. My mother is a great dressmaker so she made curtains, soft covers, fancy bedspreads, all the things you and your sisters were never able to enjoy when you were growing up in the Rows. The Neilson family even had horsehair easy chairs and gas mantle lights. Yes Mary, we were respectable, very respectable, good heavens, my Pa was an elder in the Church of Scotland.

After a few months of marriage I found out I was pregnant and Rab was very pleased, I think it proved to him that he might not have much status in the workplace, or in the home, but in the bed he was still fertile.

I will say this for him, he was good to Charlotte, and he would play with her and bring her home sweets on a Friday after work.

As I got fatter I eventually left my job at the Manse and I spent time at home with my mother. I managed to get some sewing work so I was still earning a bit of money.

The tensions in the house got worse and worse. One night during a row my Paw said 'after Agnes's man died we took her back in '94'. Well Robert couldn't read or write but he could work out if I was a widow in '94 and Charlotte was born in '96, her father was certainly not Ben Fisher.

He went berserk, accusing me of being a slut and worse, it was the row to end all rows. I collapsed and went into labour. You were born in the early hours of a cold snowy morning in March of 1899.

After he came home from work he walked into the room where I was laying in bed feeding you. He looked at you, such a bonny wee bairn, with your soft red hair and said.

'The bairn has the look of the Irish. I want her called Mary Ann McGuire Law. Now listen to me Agnes, and you listen good. I want that bairn registered Mary Ann McGuire Law and don't you to go changing a single word.'

He then stormed out of the house and we did not see him for a few days. I secretly hoped he would not come back and that I could raise my wee girls with my Maw and Paw.

To my surprise he did came back, early one morning, he was brandishing a piece of paper with Mary Ann McGuire Law clearly written on it.

'Right my girl', he said. 'you'll get yourself down to the Registration Office and register the bairn now, so you will. Then, pack your bags, we're moving.'

My mother tried to talk to him, saying I had just given birth and needed time to recover. He just ignored her and said.

'Get your shawl wrapped around you now, Mistress Law, you'll do as I tell you, so you will.'

I was too frightened of him to do anything else. I just went to the Registrar's Office, registered you as Mary Ann McGuire Law and returned home as quickly as I could.

When I got back to the flat he was gathering up our few possessions and putting them into a sheet, which he then pulled up at the corners and knotted, for we had no suitcase. I tied a woollen shawl around Charlotte and we left. Him holding the sheet and Charlotte and me carrying you and my portmanteau.

My Maw was crying as we left, she put her arms around me and slipped a ten-shilling note in my hand. Her eyes said, 'don't you dare tell him'.

We travelled on the train to Sunnyside Station and then walked to the Long Row and became lodgers of Alex and Jessie Johnstone. Alex had also come over to Scotland from County Fermanagh, and at one time had been Rab's lodger. That was the connection between Alex and your father.

The rest you know Mary. Mary lass, what should I do about the letter from Samuel?"

Mary was completely lost for words. Over the years all the children had laughed at Agnes's secretive ways and hatched plots to open the portmanteau. Robert used to say it was full of gold or five pound notes. Now Mary knew, it contained evidence of her mother's secret life.

Just then the spell was broken by Mrs Crawford, a near neighbour, giving a loud chap and then opening the door.

"Hello Mary, Mrs Law, I just knocked to let you know I'm away down to the Store. Do you want me to get you any messages?"

The diversion gave Mary a chance to pull herself together.

"No messages today thanks Mrs Crawford. My Maw is feeling a wee bit tired this morning so we were just sitting here having a cup of tea. Would you like me to get you a cup?"

"No thanks Mary lass, another time, I need to buy the sausages for the stovies or they'll no be ready in time. My man likes them cooked nice and long and slow, for when him and the boys get home from their shift at the Work."

Mary cleared away the cold tea things went into the scullery and put the kettle on for a fresh pot.

As she busied her shaking hands with washing cups and saucers, boiling the kettle, setting a tea tray with milk and sugar, her mind was birling. Tough question still needed to be asked and decisions would have to be made.

Mary brought in the tea tray and poured them both a fresh cup. For a few minutes all was quiet, with unspoken words and thoughts choking the atmosphere.

Mary spoke first.

"Maw, if you converted and became Jewish, does that mean all six of us are Jewish?"

Agnes looked up from her cup.

"God Mary, I've never given it a thought, I expect you are all Jewish. But it's all right, Jesus was Jewish and it never did him any harm."

Mary was shocked at her mother's flippant attitude but she let it pass and asked the question to which she desperately needed to have an answer.

"Look Maw before we go any further I want to know why did my Paw give me that horrible Catholic name. I thought it was just Mary Ann Law, that was bad enough but Mary Ann McGuire Law."

"That was to hurt me, as deep as you can hurt any woman," said Agnes. "Mary Ann McGuire was your Paw's first wife. Apparently she was Irish and had beautiful red hair like you. But she wasn't a Catholic, she was a Methodist. Apparently the Catholics spell their name MAGUIRE and the Protestants Capital M, small c.

The Irish are a right funny lot, they march to their own tune in more ways than one."

"Maw, you seem to forget," said Mary, her voice trembling. "I no longer have beautiful red hair. I have the locks that fell out wrapped around a naked head. When I was ill with the rheumatic fever did he stop you cutting my hair short because of memories of her, Mary Ann McGuire?"

"Probably, I don't really know. All I do know is your father's word was Law as well as his name. I would never have had the courage to disobey him. Even the doctor obeyed him.
Auld Doctor Murphy could easily have got out his scissors and just cut off your heavy locks but he would not go against your father, after all he was the man of the house, his name on the rent book, he had to be obeyed."

This was Agnes's sad reply.

Although she was still seething inside Mary tried her best to appear calm on the surface. After listening to her mother's story, one part of her registered it was the truth but another part still could not believe Agnes's confession.

"Maw, the past is the past, but we have to think now of the future. Can I read this letter that could well blow your whole family apart?"

Agnes reached into her apron pocket and handed over the missive that had caused her such a trauma and forced her to confess her past life to Mary.

Dear Mrs Law,
My Aunt Ruth has given me your address, as given to
her by your mother, Mrs Neilson.
Aunt Ruth has kept track of you over the years as she
felt it was important that my sister Sarah and I should
one day have access to your place in our history.
My grandfather has passed away after suffering ill
health for many years. I understand you too have suf-
fered bereavement recently with the loss of your husband.
Aunt Ruth had a meaningful talk with Sarah and
myself some time ago. I think she wanted to "tidy mat-
ters" before finally closing the family home in the
Gorbals.
I would like to meet with you, at your convenience, to
discuss your place in our lives.
You can reach me at the above address. Should you
not wish to do so rest assured I will not pursue the mat-
ter.
Yours sincerely
Samuel Fischer

Mary read the letter several times.

"Well Maw, he sounds, polite, well educated and if anything rather cold. The question is, what do you want to do about his letter? You can burn it in the fire here and now, the end. Or, you can meet him in Glasgow. You can't possibly have him come out here to Gartsherrie. You know as well as I do, everyone lives in everyone's pocket in the Rows, your secret past would soon be out for all the world to hear."

"I know what you say is right Mary, but I have never been back to Glasgow since the day I came here with you and Charlotte. Goodness, I have only been into Coatbridge to Register births, and deaths and on a few other occasions. How can I possibly go to Glasgow? I would be too scared, and that's the God's honest truth of the matter.

Besides, what story could I possibly make up for going into Glasgow, everyone would think I had lost my mind."

Mary's voice took on a stern note.

"Just answer the question Maw. Do you want to end it all now in the flames or do you want to meet your son?"

Agnes's answer was six words. "I want to see my son."

"Well Maw if you really want to meet your son Samuel then you had better write to him." said Mary.

"Oh Mary, I'm too shaken to write, can you no put pen to paper for me?"

Mary went into the cupboard and brought out paper, ink and a nib pen. Just in case any ink spilled she put some newspaper over the table, took a deep breath and started to write.

> *Dear Mr Fischer,*
> *My name is Mary Law and I am writing this letter on behalf of my mother, Agnes. As you can imagine she was very shaken by your letter and she feels unable to write personally.*
> *My mother has not travelled from Gartsherrie since she arrived here in 1899. The idea of finding her way to Glasgow is very frightening for her.*
> *Can I suggest that I will meet you in the city. We could then discuss a way in which you and your sister could perhaps arrange to meet my mother.*
> *I look forward to receiving your reply.*
> *Yours sincerely*
> *Mary Law*

The following days were like walking on eggs for the Law household. Agnes was by turns weepy or grumpy. The family knew something was wrong but did not dare ask what. Apart from Mary they all assumed Agnes's mood swings were some sort of delayed reaction to their father's death.

Worst affected was young Alexander who had to stay at home in the evenings and do his homework. The others were all able to find ways to escape the home for a few hours after work and supper.

Poor Mary, as usual, bore the brunt of the worry. At last the postman bought a second letter from Samuel, it read.

Dear Miss Law,
Thank you for your letter. I understand your mother's
position.
I would be pleased to meet you as follows:
On Sunday first around twelve noon at The Samovar, a
Russian Tea Room in King Street, near the
Trongate, Glasgow.
If this is convenient, no need to acknowledge. I will
await you Sunday first.
Yours sincerely
Samuel Fischer

Mary read the letter and passed it to her mother.

"Well it looks like I have to find an excuse to go to Glasgow on Sunday afternoon."

"He will have chosen Sunday because it is the end of the Sabbath. The Jewish Sabbath is Friday sunset to Saturday sunset." said Agnes.

Mary thought for a moment.

"What if I say I am going into Glasgow to hear some preacher. I could go to one of the churches afterwards and come home with details of the service so I don't have to tell lies.

I can get a train from Blairhill to Queen Street and I am sure someone can direct me to Argyle Street and then on to King Street. Maw, I'm going to need a bit of money for train fares and something to eat."

"That's the least of our worries Mary." said Agnes.

"Our real worry is what are you going to say to him? He must think his mother deserted him and Sarah all those years ago. But,

as God is my witness, I had no option in the matter. My love for
him and Sarah never ended. I used to lie in bed at night and think
of them both, imagine what they looked like, wonder if they were
good at school. I always felt incomplete without my first two
bairns."

For Mary the next few days passed too slowly and too fast all at
the same time. One part of her was furious with her mother for
having led such a colourful past, a past that she was going to have to
deal with. Another part was jealous, she felt hurt to hear her mother talk of two strangers with such sincere love.

As a mother, although always deferring to her father, Agnes had
been kind, made sure they were all well fed and kept clean but
expressions of love, cuddles and kisses never formed a part of their
upbringing.

The worst part of the whole situation was having to keep the
whole sorry saga a secret from Jessie. If it hadn't been for her
beloved dog Rags, to whom she confided all her troubles, Mary
wouldn't have been able to keep up the deception.

At last Sunday morning dawned, and with it a knot in Mary's
stomach that she felt would never be unravelled.

In a top floor flat in the Garnethill area of Glasgow another
young man had a knot in his stomach. After saying a swift prayer
on rising, he carefully washed and dressed in his black suit with a
clean white shirt. His black hair was cut short; although an
Orthodox Jew by upbringing he felt strongly that as immigrants to
Scotland it was better not to wear traditional ringlets and
Ashkenazim dress, in any case it was not essential according to the
Torah.

Standing out did not help Jews prosper in their adopted country,
especially since the war with Germany. Yiddish language, European
clothes and customs. Too many reminders of an old life that was
past. Samuel knew that the Jew, like everyone else, has to move on,
but without losing the essence of what makes him a Jew.

He said a blessing and then smeared his bread with some chick-
en fat, called schmaltz, and made a cup of Russian tea, with a slice
of lemon. Breakfast over he tried to read a Kafka short story, in

the original German, until it was time to leave for King Street.
Samuel could not concentrate and he seemed to have read the same
page ten times over. It was a crisp dry autumn morning; perhaps a
walk down to the Clyde would help calm him down for the ordeal
ahead.

The Law's home in Gartsherrie was noisy and bustling. The
boys were getting ready to attend the Salvation Army meeting.
While Mary was cooking the breakfast with the help of Jessie.

"Would you like me to come into Glasgow and go to the meeting with you?" enquired Jessie. "I don't particularly fancy the long
sermon but it would be company for you and we could have a good
look in the shop windows."

"No, its fine," replied Mary. "I will probably meet Ina and
Mamie Buchanan anyway. Besides I know you would rather meet
McInnes, I expect he will be coming through from Glasgow to see
you. Or are you meeting Sadie and the crowd and going for a
walk?"

"Meeting Sadie. McInnes is working today, he has to get the
books ready for the accountant." replied Jessie.

"One thing you can do for me," said Mary. "Please will you
make sure Maw has something to eat. You know what she is like,
tea and toast, tea and toast; she would live on it if I would let her."

The next two hours passed in a blur of activity before Mary
donned her good navy blue coat and matching navy cloche hat.
Around her neck she was wearing a lovely silk scarf in the latest
colour of Nile green that she had borrowed from Jessie.

Before leaving Mary bent over to kiss her mother goodbye and
whispered. "Try not to worry, we'll talk it all through tomorrow.
The house will be too busy when I get home."

"Bye Maw, Bye Jessie. You can have some peace at last, now
the boys are off to the Salvation Army at Sunnyside. Let's just
hope James doesn't get into another pickle over some girl, especially
that Margaret one from Coatdyke. See you both tonight."

After her sister left for the railway station Jessie said to her
mother.

"Maw, did you not think Mary was kind of tense and secretive this morning. And, why is she leaving at 10.00 to go to a Church Meeting? Do you think she has a secret boyfriend that she is not telling us about?" guessed Jessie.

"Enough of that nonsense" replied Agnes. "If you want to go out with your pals today you can give me a hand to get tidied up and don't dare say anything stupid like that to the boys. You know what they are like, especially our Robert. That is all those boys need, a stupid remark from you in order to encourage them to make the poor girl's life even more miserable than it is, thanks to her bastard father."

Jessie was astonished. Her mother never swore and she certainly didn't ever criticise her late father, no matter how difficult he had made all their lives.

Jessie thought, 'I'm getting out of this house as soon as I can, Maw is in a right mood this morning.' However, in order to keep the peace, what she actually said was.

"I'll away and get the dishes finished and peel the tatties and carrots for the dinner Maw."

Mary walked to Blairhill Railway Station and caught the train into Glasgow. She used an old hankie to open the door and carefully placed it in her bag, she did not want to arrive for the meeting covered with soot marks. Alighting at Queen Street Station in a cloud of sulphur steam, again she used the hankie to open the door and then walked briskly through the station.

Mary, and Charlotte had only ever been to Glasgow on a few special occasions so Mary was not really familiar with the city. Although all the shops were closed, it being a Sunday, there were still a lot of people about, some of them heading towards the new Barras Market in the East End, or the Jewish shops in the South Side, which were allowed to open on a Sunday, the Christian Sabbath.

The streets were busy with horse drawn vehicles as well as the exciting electric trams in their Glasgow Corporation livery, there were also a number of motorcars, that only the very rich could afford.

With great care Mary left the station and crossed George Street

and into George Square. Although feeling nervous about the
impending meeting, she was still filled with awe at the impressive
Glasgow City Chambers building. Also, the magnificent statues in
George Square, including her mother's hero, Robert Burns.

Mary was not so keen on Burns, excellent writer and poet he
certainly was, but what a philanderer, pity his poor wife, Jean
Armour, that was Mary's considered view. The flowerbeds were just
at the end of their season and the trees were taking on their autumn
hues. All in all it was a wonderful sight and well worthy of the
Second City in the Empire.

Walking through the square Mary wished Jessie was with her and
they were just enjoying a day out in the city. Perhaps they could
have gone to one of Miss Cranston's tearooms, apparently she had
some designer called Mackintosh and his wife carry out the decor
and they are now the last word in style. Imagine drinking tea from
a silver pot with a wee jug of extra hot water and what to eat, mmm,
toasted teacake or perhaps a scone with butter and strawberry jam
or an Empire biscuit.

Mary pulled herself out her reverie, thinking. 'Right girl, give
yourself a shake, this isn't a jolly outing with Jessie. I can't believe I
am doing this, going to see a half-brother I didn't know existed a
few days ago. Honestly I could fair murder my Maw for landing me
with yet another problem.'

Mary walked through the Square and down to Ingram Street,
where she saw two respectable looking, middle aged ladies, walking
towards her. Mary stopped them and asked for directions to King
Street. They were kind and helpful, even drawing a little map.

Right, thought Mary, fight or flee, she took a deep breath and
marched down towards King Street and The Samovar Tearoom.

Samuel had arrived early and settled himself into a discrete corner, where he could read his book. A tall handsome man with black
hair and blue eyes, which he had inherited from Agnes. He was
plainly but smartly dressed, wearing an unadorned black yarmulka.
He looked what he was, a prosperous, serious, young Jewish man.
Outside work he was most likely to be found reading, not necessarily
the Talmud or the Torah, his taste ranged from philosophy to poli-

tics, he was also interested in art and history. His friends had given up on trying to get him to accompany them to the Moving Pictures or Music Halls; he preferred the Art Galleries and Museums. Even the famous Glasgow Hengler's Circus had held no real attraction for him as a small boy.

Mary took a deep breath and entered The Samovar. Samuel was seated in a corner table, pouring over a black bound book, one look at him and Mary knew without a trace of doubt that they shared the same blood.

"Good day" said Mary. "Are you Mr Samuel Fischer?"

"Yes, Miss Law. I am he. Would you like some tea, or would you prefer coffee?"

"Tea please." answered Mary.

"Would you like a slice of apple strudel, or honey cake? Or perhaps you would prefer something savoury, a bagel with lox, that's smoked salmon, and cream cheese or some barley broth. They also do a very nice beetroot soup with sour cream."

Samuel seemed unable to stop himself from speaking inconsequential rubbish. He thought. 'What is the correct conversation to have with your hitherto unknown half sister? How and where do I begin?'

"Please, Mr Fischer." Mary interrupted the flow of menu. "Tea will be fine, although the honey cake sounds very nice."

Samuel placed the order and for a few moments they sat in silence. Samuel heard himself speak in a voice that sounded diffident, certainly not his normal confident self.

"Miss Law I know I asked to see you but I just don't know how to begin this conversation. There are so many questions I want to ask you but now that we are face to face I feel completely tongue tied."

Mary answered by saying. "I feel exactly the same way. You must admit this isn't exactly a normal Sunday afternoon outing for tea is it? Please ask anything you wish but I can't promise to have all the answers. Perhaps we could start with you calling me Mary, Miss Law seems very formal under the circumstances."

The waitress brought their order and a few minutes were passed organising the tea and honey cake on the table. At last Samuel spoke.

"You are absolutely right Mary, please call me Samuel. To start with just tell me about your family, your brothers and sisters, what do they look like, what kind of personalities do they have."

Unsure exactly where to begin, Mary thought, in for a penny, in for a pound; just jump in and tell the truth, or as much as you know.

"I have two sisters. One is my half sister Charlotte, she is the eldest, or I thought she was. Charlotte has married a farm worker called Charles Fyfe and moved to Condorrat, they met during the War when James, Robert and Jessie all went to the countryside to work, during the summer holidays. Even after the War, the children kept going every summer to see Charlotte and help with the harvest.

Charlotte has black hair and blue eyes like you and she is very jolly and very hard working. Her and Charlie have four children; and another baby due in a few weeks time. Charlotte is an excellent mother and farm wife, money is always tight with six, soon to be seven, to feed, but she never complains.

Then there is my other sister Jessie, before she was working Jessie used to love going out to the farm during the school holidays, feeding the poultry and helping in the kitchen, always the best jobs for Jessie as she was a favourite with the Farmer's wife, a Mrs Baird.

When he was old enough our youngest, Alexander, also went tattie howkin for Farmer Baird during school holidays, but he starts work as an apprentice joiner in the New Year so that will be the end of the Law family visits to Condorrat for summer work.

Jessie is my younger sister; she is the beauty of the family, again she has the blue eyes of my mother but her hair is a light brown, she was very fair when she was a bairn and she has the most beautiful peaches and cream complexion imaginable. Not only does Jessie have good looks she has a good heart. Not in a Goody Two Shoes kind of way, she can be extremely funny and she is great company, you would like Jessie.

My sister is quite ambitious, she manages a drysaltery and painters shop, owned by her fiancé, and she also has quite an artistic talent. Jessie has excellent taste and would love to spend her days furnishing and decorating houses.

I know she is my sister and I would never actually say this to her face but Jessie is really and truly the kindest person I know.

In May of this year she became engaged to her boss, a man called Anderson McInnes. He was a Major in the War and he is much older than Jessie. My mother doesn't approve, neither did my late father; I think Maw is just frightened of Jessie leaving and going to Glasgow to live; there is nothing actually wrong with McInnes he is very good looking and hard working, a really decent man.

I have three brothers. The boys all play in the band of the Salvation Army.

James is the eldest; he is extremely handsome and is usually involved with some girl or another, often more than one at any given time. At the moment he is keen on a girl called Margaret but whether they will marry I really don't know, the family are fairly united in their disapproval of Margaret and for once I think we are right to disapprove.

James has the same black hair and blue eyes as you and Charlotte. He has now finished his apprenticeship as a joiner. In fact he was awarded Apprentice of the Year by Bairds of Gartsherrie. In his quiet careful way James is quite ambitious and I think he will do all right for himself.

Robert, the middle boy, is called after my father, he has the Irish red hair and green eyes. He is smaller than James and thick set. Although not as handsome as the other boys he has a great personality and sense of fun, everyone loves being in his company. Robbie is a real joker and always up to some trick or other.

All the boys are very musical but Robert has a real talent for playing the cornet and he has a wonderful tenor voice.

Robert also works at the Gartsherrie Works, as an apprentice engineer. He has a few years to go before his time is out so he is still on quite a low wage.

Alexander is the youngest, born shortly before the War. He is tall for his age, certainly the tallest in the family, good looking with a shock of wavy fair hair. When he finishes school, guess what, he has a job lined up at Gartsherrie as an apprentice joiner. Actually I think Alexander would really like to continue his education rather than start an apprenticeship, his nose is never out of a book. But needs must, if he gets a trade at least he will always be able to support a family.

I have to say I recognised you immediately, you are the image of young Alexander but with James's shock of black hair and you all share the same shade of blue eyes as my mother.

Well Samuel, there it is, a thumb nail sketches of all my family."

Samuel had listened intently to every word as Mary described an entire family with whom he shared blood. "Mary" he responded. "You haven't told me about you yet."

Mary looked uncomfortable, quickly saying. "Nothing to tell really, I look most like Robert and I take care of my mother and the family. I have a heart condition, which makes it difficult for me to have a proper job."

"I suspect there is a lot more to you than looking after the family but don't worry Mary I respect your privacy and I won't try and draw you any more." responded Samuel.

"But Mary you know I have got to ask you the difficult question. What is my mother like and why do you think she left Sarah and me all those years ago and had another new family and another new life?"

"That is a lot of question." Mary took a deep breath and then started to speak.

"Well to understand what my mother is like first of all I have to tell you about my father, Robert Law. My mother used to say, 'Law by name Law by nature' His word was always Law, my Maw had to abide by his will, even when it was to the detriment of her or one of her children.

Father wasn't completely bad he never laid a finger on any of us, sometimes he would sing. He had a lovely voice; the boys inherit their musical talent from him. He worked very hard all his life for very little money. He was a Protestant Ulsterman, a countryman, from the County of Fermanagh who lived his life in the Iron Work Rows of Gartsherrie. He toiled in the black tar pit, bombarded by constant noise when all he wanted was to have his hands in the soil and see the sun.

My mother was always in his shadow; his needs came first. Dinner was always on the table, as soon as he had washed. The children well mannered and well behaved; 'children should be seen and not heard' was a favourite saying in our house. If we needed to be chastised Maw wouldn't hesitate to give us a skite. We would just never have got into a situation where Paw needed to reprimand any of us. And, then there was always her threat that if we did not behave we would go to the 'bad fire', when you live in a town where furnaces are constantly glowing, images of hell and the bad fire are tightly woven together.

Maw had very dark hair, it is going a bit grey now but it is still very thick; she is small and still neat and thin; her eyes are blue like you, and all of the others, except Robert and me. I guess you would say she is still a fine looking woman. My Maw loves Burns songs and poems and she too has a fine voice. When we were little we used to love when her friend Jessie came over to our house and they would sometimes sing songs together.

I would say she is quite a calm person, at least on the surface. Although she can be sharp when she is thwarted. Always organised: house spotlessly clean; good food well cooked on the table; laundry starched, ironed and mended. Considering how little money the family had, as children we were always well fed and decently turned out.

Maw is great with a needle; she is also good at knitting and darning. I suppose you could just say she is an excellent housewife. Some of her expressions come to mind; 'We might be poor but we are respectable'; 'I might be strict but I'm always fair'; 'Waste not, want not'. Does that sum her up for you?"

Actually there is something else. My father died in August this year, Jessie and I thought she would go to pieces but in fact she has shown a lot of strength. We have moved house at her instigation and she is making decisions about things like buying new furnishings for the house.

Maw has also made contact with her mother, my grandmother, actually, thinking about it, she is your grandmother too. Old

Grandmother Neilson has been out to visit us in Gartsherrie, she
never came when Paw was alive, apparently they absolutely hated
each other.

I can hardly say this out loud but I think my Ma is really rather
enjoying the independence of life without my father.

Samuel, my mother is the most respectable person on the planet.
You can't possibly imagine what it was like for me the day your letter
came and Maw told me all about her past. Honestly it was like a
story about some other person. Even now sitting here opposite
you I still find it all difficult to believe. If Charlotte, Jessie or
myself had behaved a fraction as badly as she did she would have
murdered us. To be perfectly honest I am furious with her for putting me in this awkward position, particularly since she has made me
promise not to tell my sister Jessie."

"Would you like some more tea Mary?" Samuel asked.

"No thanks, perhaps we could go outside and walk. I feel I
need some fresh air." Mary replied.

Samuel paid the bill and they left the Teashop and started to
walk south towards the River Clyde. "Lets walk to Glasgow
Green." he suggested. "We can have a look at the Museum and Art
Gallery in the Peoples Palace and it will be nice and warm in the
Winter Gardens."

Mary had never heard of the Peoples Palace but after the
strangeness of the day so far nothing would surprise her. "Yes, that
would be fine." she responded.

As they walked they continued to talk.

"Samuel I have told you about my family will you talk to me
about you and yours?" asked Mary.

"Not much to tell. My Uncle David, who is a Rabbi, wanted
me to train for the rabbinate. I was schooled in Hebrew and
encouraged to follow in his footsteps. However, my Great Uncle
Isaac had other ideas. He never married and he had been training
my father, Ben, to eventually take over his business. When my
father died naturally he set his sights on me as his future heir.

When I wasn't studying the Torah under the influence of Uncle
David I was learning how the factory worked under Great Uncle

Isaac. As a good Jewish boy I didn't really have much of a say in what I wanted to do, I just obeyed.

When the War came everything changed, it was no longer family first. I really did not have a choice, although I am inclined to be a pacifist by nature, I knew I had to go up to Maryhill Barracks and enrol in the Highland Light Infantry.

As a Jewish boy living in the Gorbals, with grandparents who spoke mainly Yiddish, which sounds an awful lot like German, I really had no option but to show my patriotism, after all Scotland had been good to our family. If my grandparents had stayed in Russia there would probably have been no Samuel Fischer, we would have been wiped out in the pogroms. So I joined the Highland Light Infantry, you know the H.L.I. After spending two ghastly weeks at Maryhill Barracks on basic training my Great Uncle Isaac died of a massive stroke.

God forgive me, but it was a massive stroke of luck for me. The War Office had issued the business with a lot of army contracts for uniforms. Before I knew what had happened the War Office had me out of uniform back into civilian clothes and running the factory. I was now performing essential war work, so I was safe from the army.

Even my Uncle David conceded that since I had inherited Salmonds from Uncle Isaac, Factory Owner should now be my path in life so there was no more talk of me becoming a Rabbi, thank goodness.

After the war the initial transition to peacetime work was very hard. Fortunately I had laid down plans for life after the conflict, so Salmond Clothing Manufacturers came out better than a lot of the other military supply companies, many of whom spent unwisely during the prosperous years of the War."

"I see you not only know your Bible but apply it" said Mary. "You remembered the 'The Seven Fertile Years and the Seven Lean Years in Egypt', well done."

Samuel laughed, "Mary, Mary we'll make a good Jewish sister of you yet."

The walked on companionably. Mary had never been to

Glasgow Green and was amazed to see a park with dozens of clothes poles ready to take washing lines.

Samuel explained there was a Steamie nearby and during the week the Green was full of the tenement women hanging out washing, with their children playing nearby. Then he went on to explain.

"There is a Bandstand at the other end of the Green near the river and there will probably be a concert there later this afternoon. If we walked over to the Clyde now we would probably see the students and rowing clubs practicing. Well Mary what do you think of The Peoples Palace and Glasgow Green?"

"Beautiful, absolutely beautiful. Mary replied in an awestruck voice.

"Come on then," said Samuel. "Let's walk in the Winter Gardens first and get heated up, then we can explore the main building, it contains some really interesting exhibits and artwork."

Mary was thrilled with the exotic palms, sansevieria, orchids, and huge ficus plants. They walked along the wooden slatted path, enjoying the heat after the cold outside, and wondering how such a marvel could exist in the cold, grey city of Glasgow.

Samuel explained to her how the radiator system worked and kept the temperature constant for the orchids and other tropical plants.

Eventually they left the warm humid atmosphere of the Winter Gardens and walked up the grand staircase to the top floor and the Picture Gallery. They walked around for about half an hour looking at the works of art which the Victorian City Fathers had invested in for the benefit of the city. It was pleasant to just relax and talk about the paintings, after what had been a tense and emotional few hours. Suddenly, their conversation was cut short by a uniformed attendant.

"Right ladies and gentlemen the gallery closes in fifteen minutes. Please be making your way to the exit."

The spell broken Mary realised she would be sorry to leave Glasgow, and Samuel. When she left Blairhill on the 10.35 train she could not have envisaged meeting a highly intelligent older half brother that she would actually like.

They both new that there was still a lot unsaid but neither of them wanted to push the relationship of two families and two cultures too quickly.

On the walk back to Queen Street Station they kept the conversation general   The new Agatha Christie thriller;   Mussolini's fascist takeover in Italy;   what musical instruments Mary's brothers played. Samuel told Mary that he had heard of an odd book published in Germany called Mein Kamf by a political reactionary called Adolph Hitler.

"I haven't actually read it yet but some of my friends have and apparently the man and his political party are quite mad but Germany is a breeding ground for dangerous ideas since they lost the War, what with Facism and Communism.   You know Mary ISM are the three most dangerous letters in the alphabet."

As they crossed George Square Mary interrupted him.

"Before I go back to Coatbridge Samuel can you please tell me how your Aunt Ruth is keeping.   My mother was extremely fond of Ruth and she particularly asked for news of her.   And, what of Sarah, what is happening in her life?"

They settled themselves on a bench and Samuel began.   "I'm pleased to say that Aunt Ruth is well.   Dan Jakobson has been her friend for many years but Aunt Ruth always seemed to be taking care of someone, she always put the rest of the family before her own happiness.

First Sarah and me then Bubbe and Zayde, that is our names for grandmother and grandfather.   Aunt Ruth also used to babysit David's children when their mother was working.

My Aunt Miriam is involved in all sorts of charity work, to be honest she likes to be a bit of a Queen Bee on Committees, she is very much 'I'm the Rabbi's wife' don't you know.   Poor Aunt Ruth was left to look after her brood while she played Madam Rabbi.   I shouldn't really talk like that about her but she has never endeared herself to me.

Anyway, at last old Dan has persuaded Ruth to marry him and she has gone off to a lovely house in the South Side of the city. Bubbe is with them, although she is very old now, she is much easier to look after than Zayde ever was, so all is well within the Jakobson household.

Sarah my sister, well where to begin. Sarah is very bright but as a little girl she was always kept in my shadow. I would never be expected to help with housework or prepare food. But poor Sarah hardly got time to do her homework from school never mind other reading or hobbies. Her childhood was a constant round of 'Sarah run down to the shops and get,' or, 'Sarah can you peel the vegetables,' or, 'Sarah can you do the ironing.'

The War also gave Sarah an opportunity to find her path in life, she joined the Territorial Force Nursing Service. Initially as a very lowly trainee, however it wasn't long before she moved up the ranks. By the end of the War Sarah was a Sister in Stobhill Hospital, treating soldiers who had suffered terrible injuries at the front. My twin sister is now working as a Nursing Lecturer at Glasgow Royal Infirmary, I am extremely proud of her achievements.

Actually, Sarah is one of the main reasons I wrote to your mother. Sarah has a friend, a fine doctor called Alan DeSilva. He is a very decent chap and I would certainly welcome him as a brother. However, his family belong to an old Sephardic Jewish family. They are very keen to know all the in's and out's of Sarah's background.

It is a bit complicated to explain but you know what it is like when a Catholic and Protestant marry, they are two different branches of the one Christian faith but their values and traditions are different. Well the Fischers and Salmonds are Ashkenazi Jews, my grandparents originally came from a shtetl in the Pale, so we are Russian Jews.

Sephardic Jews, like Alan's family, come from Spain or Portugal they have different traditions, food and language; for example we use Yiddish and they speak Ladino, although we both understand Hebrew. There are also other branches of the Jewish family, Yemenite, Ethiopian and there are a number of different Jewish communities in India. The Jews who have settled in Great Britain are mainly Ashkenazi, and to a lesser extent Sephardic. Although the Sephardic Jews have a thriving community of very long standing in London."

While Samuel was explaining Jewish emigration traditions all Mary could think was. 'Sarah has had the career I wanted, she was better off being fatherless and abandoned by her mother. I wish to God I had had her opportunity to have a career in nursing. Just like Sarah I would also have grasped it with both hands, instead of being an unpaid slave.'

Mary interrupted him. "Samuel can I meet Sarah? I would have loved a career in nursing, Jessie would have loved to go to Art College and study design but in Gartsherrie the tradition is obviously the same as with the Jewish families in Glasgow. One of 'Golden sons and tin daughters'.

Some women might have the vote now but they have got little else. In the Law household it was, and still is, always the boys first and the women are expected to look after the menfolk."

"Yes" responded Samuel. "Women have a long way to go on the equality road. But Mary, there can never be true equality while women bare children. A woman has to sacrifice the comfort of marriage and children if she is to have a career. Only a single woman can pursue truly meaningful work.

If Sarah does enter into marriage with Alan that will be the end of her professional life. Everything she has worked for, all those years studying to no avail.

Married women can work in a non-professional capacity, which is essentially saying poor married women can work. However, since the end of the War it's almost impossible for middle class married ladies to work. They are expected to transfer their skills to charity work and look after their family."

Although not a sentiment she wanted to hear, Mary knew Samuel spoke the truth. Mary also knew it was time to take her leave.

"Samuel, I have so enjoyed today, seeing the People's Palace and talking with you about all sorts of things, not just our secretive mother.

Tell me where do we go from here?" asked Mary. "Do you really want to meet my, or should I say our, mother? Would it be possible for me to meet Sarah? What information do the DeSilva family need to know? I honestly think today has beggared more questions than it has provided answers to, for both of us."

"Mary, you are so right." Samuel replied. "I also feel confused and I can quite understand why you too are angry with our mother. Mary, I have got to ask you the question I am sure you must be anticipating. Why did my mother desert her twins?"

There was such a sadness in Samuel's voice, on the surface a successful, sophisticated man and one sentence made him sound like a young boy. Mary tried to answer but she knew only her mother could tell him the whole truth.

"Samuel to be perfectly honest, and this is just my opinion, I think my mother was weak. After your father, Ben, passed away she just did not have the courage to stand up for her rights. When your family said, 'We will look after the children and bring them up to be Jewish, you are young, return to your parents.' My mother simply did as she was told. That did not mean she did not love you both, she has told me how much she loved you and spent many sleepless nights thinking about you. However, Ma sometimes takes the line of least resistance, it's just her nature. My father ordered, mother obeyed.

Now if it had been me, I would have fought your family tooth and nail to bring up my children, I think that must be the Irish blood in me.

Samuel, to be perfectly honest I don't know where we go from here but I do know this, I am very glad I have met you. I think we should both go home now, think things over, and I will write to you in a few days time."

They walked across the road to Queen Street Railway Station. Samuel escorted Mary to the platform and insisted on waiting with her until it was time for the next train to Coatbridge to depart from the station.

They waved goodbye in a haze of steam, Mary to report back to her mother and Samuel to return to the quiet of his flat in Garnethill to do a lot of serious thinking.

When Mary returned to Gartsherrie, after her meeting with Samuel, she was fortunate in that only her mother and Alexander were home.

Mary quietly whispered to her mother.

"Look just don't ask me anything now. I am going to bed, we will talk tomorrow when everyone is out at work."

Mary went into the room she shared with Jessie and got ready for bed. Sleep was impossible, as the hours passed she heard the others all come home and was aware of the normality of family life, happening in the kitchen and scullery, a life that she no longer seemed to be a part of. The smell of toast being made; water running to make tea; the boys laughing and joking; Robert singing Sweet Georgia Brown; Agnes asking Alexander if he had finished his homework and packed his satchel for school.

All the activities and conversations that were happening in normal homes throughout the Rows of Gartsherrie but Mary no longer felt normal, she was no longer part of a normal family, her mother had plunged her into a nightmare of doubt and she had absolutely no idea as to what her next step should be.

When Jessie came to bed Mary pretended to be sound asleep in order to avoid any questions about her day or having to listen to Jessie telling her of the wonderful Sunday she had spent with her friends catching up on all the latest gossip of the Rows.

Back in Glasgow Samuel was struggling with the same emotions as Mary. He too lay awake into the wee small hours pondering his next move.

The following morning in Gartsherrie everyone prepared for school or work and by half past eight Mary and her mother were alone in the house.

"Well" asked Agnes, at the first opportunity. "What happened yesterday in Glasgow?"

"What happened, what happened. My life came tumbling down, that's what happened." snapped Mary. "Mother you don't seem to have any idea of the enormity of what you asked me to do yesterday. As it happens Samuel is a very nice person, you are the mother of a decent, hardworking, and very successful, son.

Sarah too has done well in her life, and guess what, she has trained as a nurse and has a good job Lecturing at the Royal

Infirmary no less. Her good luck was losing her parents, my bad luck was having two parents. A father who cared more about being obeyed and his curious Irish love that embraced my red hair, rather than me. And, a mother who had a background that sounds like a trashy penny novel, but who has always placed a morality on her family that she herself did not adhere to in her own youth.

Mother, what on earth do you think can come of all this? We can never join together the Law and the Fischer families, sadly, because I would be very proud to call Samuel my brother, but it is not going to happen. Now I am going out. I will be home this evening but I need some time away from you and away from this house."

With that she put on her coat and hat and walked out of number twelve and down the Long Row to the bus stop, opposite the Gartsherrie Institute, where she caught a Baxter's bus into Coatbridge. Mary had absolutely no idea what she was going to do in Coatbridge, she just knew that she had to get away from her Mother and the Rows.

Meantime in Glasgow Samuel was sitting at his desk in the factory, by seven thirty, on Monday morning. Around nine o'clock Ralph Lewis, his Manager, came into his office with some figures requiring his attention.

"Good weekend Mr Fischer?" enquired Ralph.
"Interesting, let's just say interesting." Samuel replied.
Ralph I have a few letters to write which I want sent immediately they are completed.

Please make sure no one disturbs me for the next hour or so and then I want one of the Juniors to go to George Square Post Office and make sure my mail is sent post haste."

Using his business headed paper Samuel proceeded to write two extremely difficult letters.

Dearest Sarah,
My dear sister, as you know I wrote to our mother and
as a result of the correspondence I have met with our
half sister Mary.

I have today written to her and informed her that I will not pursue contact with our mother and the Law family, I am convinced this is for the best.

Please come to my flat this week for Shabbat dinner we will discuss how much information should be given to the DeSilva family, regarding your background. I am sure we can find a way to tell them what they want to hear.

Mary is a very fine person and I have the very highest regard for her. Our half sister would have liked to follow a career in nursing and she has expressed a wish to meet with you. I would recommend that you comply with her wish. I am sure that such a meeting would be useful for both of you. We can discuss such a meeting on Friday.

However, after you meet Mary it would probably be best if the Fischer and the Law families do not have any further contact.

Your ever loving brother
Samuel

He then wrote a second letter to Mary.

My dear Mary,
Firstly, I would like to say that it was my great pleasure to have met you yesterday, albeit in a set of circumstances that neither of us could ever have envisaged. Mary, you have impressed me greatly with your bearing and your sensitive handling of what must be a fairly unique situation.

I have thought deeply as to what path we should now follow and I think it would probably be best for your brothers and sisters to know nothing of your mother's indiscretions. I have reached this conclusion mainly because I could see how hurt and disillusioned you feel by our mother's actions. It would not be helpful for

your siblings to suffer similarly.
Therefore with much sadness I think it would be better
if I did not meet with our mother. It therefore follows
that it will not be possible for us to develop our relation-
ship as brother and sister.
I have written to my sister and asked her if she will
meet with you. I am sure Sarah will agree to see you
and she will be in touch shortly regarding arrangements.
Mary, I wish you well in your life and if there is ever
anything I can do for you please contact me. I will
always think of you as a sister.
With my kindest regards
Samuel

As he finished writing Samuel felt a tear in his eye. He wished he had never written to his mother because now he was left mourning the fact that he could not have a friendship with Mary. He had not expected to feel a bond with this woman, they came from different backgrounds; different religions; different fathers. But they shared blood, and Samuel knew that if ever Mary needed a friend, a brother, he would always be her kin.

The letters were given to Ralph to arrange postage and Samuel then got on with the job of running the Salmond factory.

Agnes, although she should not have been surprised by Mary's outburst, was. She was so used to Mary being the rock, the sensible one, the dependable daughter, that she failed to fully realise just how much hurt she had caused.

At times like this there was nothing else for her to do. Agnes put on her coat and hat and headed up the Long Row to visit her friend Jessie, where she knew she would always receive a warm welcome and a cup of tea.

Mary returned to the family home around five o'clock' before the others came home from work, and Alexander from football practice. Agnes had prepared mince for the family dinner and the potatoes and turnip were also peeled and ready. Always a good cook she had made a suet pudding with syrup and it was simmering away on the range. Even the custard was made ready to be gently re-heated.

"Well, are you going to talk to me?" asked Agnes.

"Mother, I just don't want to discuss yesterday in any detail. It is enough that I tell you Samuel is a very fine man. Sarah has a career in nursing and she might be getting married. Ruth is well and has recently married her long term suitor. Ruth's father is dead but she is still looking after her mother. That is as much as I can tell you. Samuel will write soon, then you can see what he has to say for yourself."

The others started to return from work, the house took on its busy, gossipy face. Everyone was looking forward to dinner. Jessie set the table, and Mary finished off making the meal. They all sat around the table enjoying the food and talking about the events of the day. All was well with the Laws' at number 12 Long Row. Nobody seemed to notice that Mary was quieter than usual.

The following morning the letter arrived from Samuel. Mary read it then passed it to her mother.

"Now you know Maw, you are not going to meet your son. I think Samuel is absolutely right. I am sure you don't want the others to know about your sordid little secrets. Especially our Charlotte, after the truly despicable way you treated her and Charlie. Best to close your portmanteau, and we will all go on with our lives as usual."

A few days later a telegraph arrived. Mary assumed it was from Samuel and tore it open. It read.

'CHARLOTTE NEEDS MARY.' *Mrs Alice Baird*

There was nothing else for Mary to do but pack her mother's portmanteau and head to the railway station at Sunnyside.

By the time Mary arrived in Condorrat Charlotte had given birth to a beautiful wee lass, whom she named Irene. The confinement had been a difficult one, even with the help of the Farmer's wife, Alice Baird.

Alice greeted Mary in Charlotte and Charlie's little tied cottage.

The farmer's wife was very fond of Mary and remembered with much affection the summers when the Law children came to work on the farm.

"Am I glad to see you lass. Your sister has had a bad time with this wee bairn. The others all popped out like peas from a pod, but there were complications this time. Charlie had to get the Doctor for her and the auld quack says that this will be the last bairn that she will have. I say, thank God for that.
Five bairns is more than enough for any woman. Mary you are going to have your hands full with four weans, a bairn, Charlotte to nurse and Charlie to feed."

I had to send for you, Charlotte needs a wheen mair care than I can give her. I'll need to take on her dairy work as well as all my other jobs. Good luck to you lass, we have a busy few weeks ahead of us."

The following days were lost in a haze of work for Mary, interspersed with an occasional welcome cup of tea and blether with Alice Baird.

Wee Willie in particular clung to her. He kept saying, "Auntie Mary I want to go and live with you and my Granny in Gartsherrie."

Initially Mary thought that this was just his way of looking for attention but eventually she was concerned enough to talk to Charlotte about his obsession with wanting to live with the Law family in Gartsherrie.

"Even before you came to stay he was always going on about wanting to live in Gartsherrie." said Charlotte. "I've no idea why he doesn't seem settled. The other weans love living on a farm and while we are hardly rich we are never short of good food, they can play in the woods and they have plenty of animals running around, dogs and cats as well as the farm stock.

Charlie is a good father, he never lifts a hand to any of the weans. In fact if anything he is a bit too soft on them, they can birl him around their fingers, particularly our May. Our Willie is a complete mystery to me."

"It might me a mystery." replied Mary "But you and Charlie

have to sort this one out. You need to speak to the lad and find out what is wrong."

The following evening Mary waited until the children were in bed before tackling Charlie and Charlotte again on the subject of Willie.

"You two really must speak to that child, he is obviously unhappy. He plagues me constantly, wanting to go back to Gartsherrie with me when I leave next Saturday morning. What do you two feel about his desire to leave his home?"

Charlie didn't miss and hit the wall.

"Mary, he just does not like life on a farm. He doesn't like being around the animals. He hates having to walk miles to and from school every day. And, he is always fighting with Robert, Jim and May. Actually Mary the honest truth is, Willie is a little shite. I sometimes wonder if he really belongs to Charlotte and me, it's as if the stork dropped him at the wrong cottage. That is exactly how I see the Willie problem." said Charlie. "What do you think Charlotte, do you not agree?"

"I know he is my flesh and blood but you are right Charlie, he is a wee shite. I have had more bother with him than the other three and baby Irene put together.

Mary, could you no take him back to Gartsherrie just for a few weeks to stay with you and my Maw? Maybe if he spent some time away he would see the advantages of living on a farm."

The last thing Mary wanted was to take Willie back to Gartsherrie. What with the Fischer saga and the recent move to the Long Row. Then there was the family romances; wondering who, among his many girlfriends, James was going to eventually marry; Jessie's forthcoming marriage to McInnes and her impending move to Glasgow; even Robert at nearly eighteen was showing an interest in some of the girls at the Salvation Army. Alexander was now grown up and ready to leave school. Adding a seven year old into the mix was positively unthinkable.

"How can I possibly take Willie back with me." asked Mary. "Maw would have a fit. We are a household of adults now, our youngest, Alexander, leaves school in a few weeks at Christmas time, he has got a job lined up as an apprentice at the Joiners Shop in the Works.

We are simply not equipped to take on another bairn. You must sit down and talk to Willie and try and sort it out as a family. Now I mean it, Willie stays on the farm and tomorrow after school we will all have a serious talk with him."

Charlotte did not have much faith in Mary's talk but she said nothing.

The following day Mary was dreading the confrontation with Willie. Privately she agreed with Charlie, he was a wee shite, but he was still a child and she had to find out what was going on in his head.

Charlie finished work early in the dark winter nights so he was home before the children arrived back from school. Mary had baked some shortbread for the three boys when they arrived back from school, May was not yet at school, she enjoyed playing big sister to baby Irene during the day. Mary gave all the children hot milk and shortbread and then sent Robert, Jim and May through to the bedroom to play.

Mary knew she had to take charge of the situation. Charlotte and Charlie would always be happy to jolly along and follow the line of least resistance.

"Willie since I have been here helping your mother you have constantly asked me to take you back to Gartsherrie. Now I want you to tell your Ma and Pa why you want to leave them and your brothers and sister and wee baby Irene to go and visit your Granny in Gartsherrie?"

Willie immediately piped up.

"Aunt Mary, I don't want to visit Granny in Gartsherrie. I want to live there for always and always."

Mary responded sternly. "Yes, I think we have got that, you want to go to Gartsherrie. But Willie the question is WHY do you want to live in Gartsherrie? There must be a good reason, seven year old boys don't want to leave their parents and brothers and sisters in a home where they are well cared for. Now Willie you are a bright boy so I want a sensible answer."

"Aunt Mary, that is the answer I am bright, all the teachers say I am clever. I am usually top of the class and I would always be top if I could do my reading instead of having to work in the garden after school or show May her letters. I want to be an Engineer and if I stay here all I can be is a farmer and I don't want to be a farmer. Besides, my Ma is so busy now with wee Irene that she has no time to help me with my reading and school work. Please Aunt Mary take me back with you to Granny in Gartsherrie."

Mary listened to the boy in amazement.

"Willie take your milk and biscuit through to the room, I want to talk with your Ma and Pa."

All three adults were astounded at Willie's articulate outburst,

"What on earth are you going to do about that child's behaviour?" Mary asked. "You are the parents, you need to take control."

"I don't think we can do anything with him." said Charlie. "I can't turn the farm into an engineering works. Besides what would he be here but a farmer without land. I will always be a farm worker, and if he stays here he will end up a labourer. The likes of us can never afford to buy land."

"I completely agree with Charlie" said Charlotte. "The best thing would be if you take him home to stay with you and my Maw. He would get on so much better with you and my mother."

Mary suspected that Charlie and Charlotte really just wanted rid of a problem child; rather than looking for the best opportunities in life for Willie. Mary could feel herself being drawn into a corner and she had no idea how to escape.

"I'll think about it tonight." said Mary "We will decide in the morning before Charlie runs me to the station in the trap." Mary saw the look that passed between Charlotte and Charlie and in her heart she knew that she had lost.

Sitting in the train watching Willie munching a sandwich, seemingly without a care in the world, Mary could happily have slapped him. She knew she had been manipulated, not just by Willie but by Charlotte and Charlie and for the life of her she could not see how she could have avoided the inevitable.

"Aunt Mary, how long will it take us to get to Gartsherrie?" Willie asked.

"It'll take as long as it takes Willie." replied Mary. And while we are about it young William, listen to me and listen good, If you are troublesome in any way, smart talk, or annoy your Granny you are going home on the first train. I will personally take you to Kilsyth and put you on the Condorrat train and your father can meet you. Now do we understand each other?"

"Yes Aunt Mary" replied Willie in a subdued voice. Mary was not so easily fooled.

When Mary arrived home trailing Willie behind her, the family were all eating dinner.

Jessie was first to speak up at the astonishing sight of her sister with Willie in tow behind her.

"Mary, why on earth have you brought Willie home with you?"

Mary shrugged her shoulders saying, "Willie has been giving Charlotte and Charlie a really difficult time. He just doesn't want to live on a farm and poor Charlotte really has her hands full, what with the new baby. Incidentally Irene is a lovely wee thing." responded Mary.

Agnes interrupted, snapping.

"Never you mind about how nice baby Irene is Mary. What's all this, Willie wants, Willie wants. My God Mary when did a wee lad of seven dictate what he wants.

My family are all up and working, even Alexander leaves Gartsherrie School in a few short weeks and you are bringing yet another bairn home."

"It wasn't choice Maw, besides he is just here for a fortnight to give Charlotte a bit of peace. The wee blighter has been warned to within an inch of his life that he must behave himself, no impertinence."

"Well Mary lass, I suppose, under the circumstances, we have no alternative but to feed him." Agnes sighed, saying.

"Jessie, lay another two places and I'll dish out more plates of stovies and I've made a nice rice pudding with stewed apples for afters."

CHAPTER 25
NOVEMBER 1925

The following morning Mary accompanied Alexander and Willie to Gartsherrie Primary School. Mary arranged with the Headmaster to allow young William Fyfe to attend the local Gartsherrie School for the next two weeks.

Relieved to be rid of Willie, if only for a few hours, Mary returned home to her mother, looking forward to a short rest and a cup of tea before carrying out her work for the day. Soon as she entered the house Agnes handed her a letter, saying.

"Postie delivered this for you when you were at Condorrat, getting inveigled into bringing that Mr Mischief to Gartsherrie."

The letter was addressed from: The Department of Nursing Studies, Glasgow Royal infirmary. It read.

> Dear Miss Law,
> My brother Samuel has spoken very warmly to me about you, and asked that I make contact.
> I would be very pleased to meet you. Perhaps we could go to one of Miss Cranston's tea rooms for lunch or a high tea.
> Saturday and Sundays are the best days for me.
> Could you please write and suggest a date and time?
> Wishing you and all your family well.
> Yours sincerely
> Sarah Fischer

Mary handed the letter to her mother to read, saying.

"I intend to go Maw. I am going to write to her today and make an arrangement. Everyone else in this family has a life bar me. Looking after others, without any career or payment, that is my lot in life, thanks to you and my father. Well I'm going to meet Sarah and find out how she escaped."

Mary got out her writing box and wrote.

12 Long Row, Gartsherrie, Coatbridge
Dear Miss Fischer,
Thank you for your kind letter.
Apologies for taking so long to reply. However, my sister Charlotte has recently given birth to a baby girl and I had to go to Condorrat, for a few weeks, to assist her.
I would be delighted to meet with you as suggested. Would Sunday first be suitable? If so, perhaps we could meet outside Queen Street Railway Station (facing George Square) at around twelve noon. If this arrangement meets with your approval there is no need to acknowledge. Looking forward to meeting with you.
Yours sincerely
Mary Law

Mary put the letter in an envelope, put on her hat and coat and headed down to the Store to buy the messages for the day and post her letter.

Willie was on his very best behaviour for the next few days, to the point where it felt downright unnatural. He would meet Jessie coming home from work and offer to carry her bag; as soon as he came home from school he would go out to the coal house and fill the pail, to top up the coal box beside the fireside range; he accompanied the boys to the Salvation Army meetings; homework was always done on time; any wee errands or jobs Granny and Mary wanted doing, were done as if by magic. Yes, Willie was the

ideal house guest.   However, at the back of her mind Mary was
still extremely suspicious as to his motives.

One evening when Mary was making sure Willie's satchel was
correctly packed for school the following morning, she found an
empty shoe polish tin containing some farthings, half pennies and
a few pennies, two threepenny bits and even a sixpence.

"Willie" shouted Mary

"Come here this instant and tell me what this tin containing
money is all about?"

Never short for an answer Willie launched into a tale.

"Well Aunt Mary, the Airdrie Savings Bank have got this
scheme so that we can save our pennies at school, we get a wee
blue bank book and everything, when we reach ten shillings in the
wee book the money gets transferred to a real Savings Account at
the Bank in Coatbridge and we get interest.   I have been saving all
the money I make doing wee errands for the neighbours and
Auntie Jessie gives me pocket money, it's supposed to be for sweeties, but I am saving all my money."

Mary's eyes reached heavenward.

"And tell me this Master Fyfe, why exactly are you saving your
money?"

Willie looked at her with a face totally free from all guile.

"Well, Auntie Mary, I could be sneaky and say I was saving up
to buy a present for Granny, but that would be a lie and I don't
want to go to the bad fire when I die.   I am really saving up to be
a millionaire like Mr Carnegie, we have been learning all aboot him
at school, so all my money goes in the Carnegie Tin."

Jessie dissolved into gales of laughter and even Mary had difficulty in keeping a straight face.

Later than night when the wee pest was safely in bed Mary and
Jessie had a blether about him and his tricks.

"I'll tell you this he goes back to Condorrat when the school
finishes for Christmas, him and his Carnegie Tin.   I have quite
enough to deal with without having to look after a bairn, and not a
normal bairn, a Willie." complained Mary

"I know what you mean," laughed Jessie.   "When you and I

were bairns we used tins to play at peever outside the house, marking out the beds with a bit of pipe clay we begged from Maw.
Never in a million years would we have dreamt up a Carnegie Tin.

Good luck to Charlie and Charlotte with Willie as a Christmas
present. I think I'll bring home some wallpaper and we'll send
him home gift wrapped."

By an unspoken tacit agreement Agnes and Mary did not speak
of the proposed meeting with Sarah. Sunday came around, and
once again Mary dressed in her best blue coat and hat and set off
to Blairhill Station to catch the train into Glasgow.

Leaving Queen Street Station and taking up her position to
await Sarah, Mary looked at all the people going about their business and wondered if any of them had a stranger meeting arranged
for a Sunday afternoon.

For a few minutes Mary thought Sarah would not arrive. Then
she saw a woman, dressed similarly to herself crossing George
Square. Mary instantly felt a connection, the woman crossed the
road and walked straight towards Mary.

"Mary?"

"Sarah?"

"Well we recognised each other immediately." said Sarah.
"Fancy going to the Willow Tea rooms in Sauchiehall Street. Kate
Cranston has well retired now but the Cranston Tea Rooms are still
pretty good."

They walked together the short distance along Sauchiehall
Street, past all the department stores with their enticing window
displays; Pettigrew & Stephens, Copeland & Lye, and the creme de
la creme Dalys; these cathedrals to shopping were interspersed
with specialist shops like Boots the Chemist, and Birrell's Sweet
Shop. Being Sunday all the shops were closed, only the hotels and
restaurants remained open.

"Let's have a treat and go to the Room de Luxe for Ladies
upstairs." said Sarah.

They climbed the elegant Mackintosh staircase and asked for a
table for two. They were lucky as there was a table available in the
curved bay window, so they could look down on Sauchiehall Street

as they ate lunch.

They both removed their gloves and coats, leaving on their cloche hats. Mary was wearing a cream satin blouse fastened with little pearl type buttons. Sarah a white cotton blouse trimmed with broderie anglaise.

Sarah and Mary examined the menu, all of which sounded delicious. They both eventually settled on poached eggs on top off toasted muffins with a selection of cakes and scones to follow; all accompanied by pots of tea.

Mary did not feel nearly as nervous with Sarah as she had with Samuel when they first met, she asked.

"Is it all right for you to eat in a regular tea shop? I thought you might follow the Kosher rules on food."

"Goodness no." Sarah replied. "I don't eat any pork or shellfish but I don't keep strictly to the Laws of Kashrut. It would have been well nigh impossible when I was training but in any case the only part of our family who are really strict is my Uncle David, the rabbi, and his family. The rest of us eat a lot of Jewish food and we keep the main holidays like Chanukah and obviously Yom Kippur but we are not strictly, strictly, orthodox.

Isn't it funny meeting like this. We are half sisters but we don't know anything much about each other. One thing I do know is you have made a great impression on Samuel, he is the clever serious one of us twins. I have to work hard to learn what he seems to know just by breathing. So Mary Law if Samuel likes and respects you, you must be all right.

I know you want to ask me about the nursing but I am dying to know so many other things. Why did you have to rush off and look after your, or is it our, sister?"

"That wasn't the worst of it." answered Mary.

"In the first place I had to go because Charlotte had just given birth to her fifth child, a pretty wee girl called Irene. Charlotte had a really bad time at the birth, so that's the end of the babies now, thank goodness.

Charlotte is actually my half sister but I always thought she was my full sister until her and Charlie got married. They live in a farm cottage out in Condorrat.   Charlie is the farm Charge-hand and Charlotte helps in the dairy and she also does work in the farmhouse for Mrs Baird, the farmer's wife.

Charlotte is keeping much better now, although she won't be back working in the dairy for another few weeks.   As I said, looking after the family and nursing Charlotte back to health wasn't the problem; the problem was wee Willie."

"Wee Willie, who is wee Willie?" asked Sarah avidly, sensing a story.

"Wee Willie is the sneakiest child in Scotland, that's who wee Willie is.   He is just six, almost seven years old but he wants to leave Condorrat and come and live permanently with his Granny. He hates life on the farm and wants to enjoy the comforts of living with us in Gartsherrie."

Sarah was then regaled with the Carnegie tin story.   They both laughed until the tears fell.   Eventually Mary tried to give Sarah an explanation, or as good a one as she could find, as to why Willie had decamped to Gartsherrie.

"How can I best explain, Charlotte is well, a bit rough and ready. I'll give you an example.   If my mother wanted to make an economical dinner for all the family she might get some potatoes, two or three onions and a pound and a half of liver and then she would peel wash the potatoes carefully and leave them in water ready to cook at dinner time; she would soak the liver in milk to tenderise it and the would slowly cook the onions in beef dripping until they were meltingly soft.   At dinner time she would put on the potatoes, coat the liver in flour and gently fry the pieces, keeping them warm in a covered dish in the bottom oven until every piece was cooked; she would then return the onions to the pan and crisp them up; the drained potatoes would get a sprinkling of parsley, everything served nicely at the table.   Result the family get a delicious and inexpensive dinner.

Charlotte would take the same ingredients, rinse the worst of the soil off the potatoes then boil them; chop the liver and onions roughly and stick the lot straight into the frying pan.   The results of her efforts would be tipped out on a large plate and they would all dive in.

The other children are all very healthy and as happy as sand boys living on the farm. Charlie and Charlotte are not big on discipline, but they are a devoted couple and they do care for the bairns. Although, they are not adverse to keeping them off school for a few days if they are needed for work on the farm.

Now wee Willie, likes his comforts and even at seven he knows that he needs a good education to get on in life. My staying for a few weeks was just the opportunity he needed. He manipulated his way home with me, supposedly for a fortnight, but I can tell he is working on making it a permanent arrangement."

"What about Charlotte and Charlie are they not upset at losing wee Willie" asked Sarah.

"Upset?" laughed Mary. "Charlotte and Charlie are absolutely delighted to get rid of him, he is more bother to them than all the other weans put together. I can just imagine them crossing their fingers and hoping that he gets round my mother. Mind you it's me who is going to have to look after him."

"I know just how you feel" sympathised Sarah. "If it hadn't been for the War that was going to be my lot. Staying home, looking after everyone and doing finishing work from the Salmond's Factory to earn a bit of money.

Soon as the War started, I suppose I was like little Willie, I seized the opportunity and started training as a nurse. I won't say the following years were easy, because they certainly were not. I worked long hours, saw some terrible sights for hardly any money. I would certainly have been a lot better off financially doing work for the factory."

The waitress bought their order and they settled down to enjoy their eggs.

"That was delicious." Sarah announced. "Now for the sweet things. I love the selection on these three tiered cake stands, the only problem is what to choose?"

They decided to share a scone with butter and jam and then have room for a little cake each.

"Samuel seemed concerned that your fiancé wanted to know a

great deal about your background and I guess he might not approve if he found out that your mother wasn't Jewish. What is happening now? Have you told him the saga?" asked Mary.

"Well for a start Alan isn't my fiancé." laughed Sarah. "He has asked me to marry him but I'm over thirty and I have a good career now at the Royal Infirmary. If I was to become Mrs Doctor De Silva there goes everything I have worked for. I am back at home, having babies, looking after the house and financially dependent on Alan. Besides I've just gone and got the vote, how much more independent can I be?

You are wrong about one thing Mary my dear, your, our, mother IS Jewish. Trust me, my Uncle David will have made sure, i's dotted and t's crossed that the conversion is acceptable. And, that means technically you and your brothers and sisters are all Jewish. What an absolute hoot, would they be horrified do you think?" Sarah asked Mary.

"Actually I only told Samuel part of the story. It is all so much worse than, you could possibly imagine. I don't know whether to laugh or cry." said Mary.

"Laugh, it's the only way" said Sarah. "Now start at the very beginning and tell me the whole story, don't miss out anything. I'll listen while I eat my cake, will I have a French Fancy or a Japp Cake? French Fancy I think, now Mary you must tell me all."

Mary narrated the whole story as Agnes had told her that fateful morning in number twelve. She also related how strictly and respectably Agnes had brought up the family which only emphasised the unreal aspect of the entire saga.

When she had finished, Mary poured herself another cup of tea and said. "Phew my turn for the tea and cake now, I think I'll have a slice of Dundee cake."

"How can you calmly say 'Dundee Cake' after that story?" asked Sarah.

"And you are having to keep all this secret at home while pretending your, our, mother is Mrs Ohso Respectable. You must be an incredible actress, Gloria Swanson has nothing on you Mary Law. Drink your tea, I want to talk.

I have an idea which I want to discuss with you Mary, it might just be your route to independence. I can't promise anything yet but it's an idea I have been trying to get off the ground with the hospital management for some time.

We can't sit here much longer, it's after three o'clock. Look let's go back to my flat and we can talk some more."

Sarah insisted on paying the bill.

"Your turn next time Mary." she said. "We have to meet again, I refuse to let my new sister go out of my life, so there."

Sarah took Mary's arm and they headed out into Sauchiehall Street.

We need to get a tramcar over to Shawlands on the south side of the city. Sarah explained.

"When my Auntie Ruth decided to get married and move to Newlands her and Dan wanted me to go with them, but I decided I wanted my own place. I had been used to staying in nursing quarters and Samuel had bought his own flat in Garnethill during the War years. I suppose I wanted my independence with my own home, it was the final proof a woman could survive in a male dominated world.

I had saved a bit of money and Auntie Ruth's husband, Uncle Dan gave me a loan to help buy furniture and decorate. I have been paying him back ever since, not much left to go now and then Flat 2/3, and everything in it, will be all mine. You can see why after such a gigantic struggle to succeed in a male world I am finding it difficult to say, 'yes', to Alan."

"Yes, I can see it must be difficult but I suppose the real question you have to ask yourself is, 'do you love him?'" responded Mary.

"Wow, you don't miss and hit the wall do you Mary Law? Here comes the tram car, reprieve, I'll tell you when we get to the flat."

They arrived at the second floor flat laughing after a pleasant journey where they had gossiped about the latest film stars, flapper dresses and popular songs.

"Can you imagine, " said Sarah. "Thousands of little girls are going to be called Suzie, after that song of Eddie Cantors. 'If you knew Suzie'. Can't you just imagine Samuel saying. 'Ladies, you should listen to some beautiful classical music on the gramophone, not that American rubbish.'"

They reached Sarah's close. It wasn't quite the Wally Close, like those to be found in the more salubrious parts of the West End of the city but it was very clean and smart, with a dark mahogany bannister which had recently been polished. The half stair windows were set with sparkling coloured glass in the Victorian fashion and the walls painted a pale green and cream with a neat pipe clay border down each side of the stairs.

Mary thought she had never seen anything so tasteful as the high ceilinged flat, with the original Victorian cornice, where Sarah lived.

There was a living room boasting a Templeton's carpet in blues and greens, with a wood surround that had been well polished with lavender floor polish. The furniture was plain oak, with a leather chair at either side of the fireplace; the wallpaper was a simple pale green stripe. What made the room so memorable for Mary was the two large vases of cream colored chrysanthemums.

Directly off the living room was a neat little scullery.

The bedroom was decorated in shades of cream and pale blue, with a beautiful silk bedspread and eiderdown.

There was a stylish front room with a three piece suite in a shade of warm cream; the wooden furniture was also oak and in the arts and crafts style; while the floor was parquet with a large Chinese rug. The winter afternoon light was now starting to fade so Sarah drew the heavy velvet curtains around the oriel window.

Even the bathroom was stylish, all black and white tiles with thick white Turkish towels.

"What a truly beautiful home you have." Mary said. "Jessie would just love your style, she studies all the latest decorating trends. I suppose she has to, what with managing a painting and decorating shop."

"Never mind the flat Mary. Do you like coffee?" Sarah asked.

"I've no idea, I've never tasted coffee." replied Mary.

"Well you have a treat in store, hang up your coat in the hall cupboard and I'll get the percolator on. I've also got some strudel biscuits; and before you ask, I didn't make them, they are courtesy of my Aunt Ruth.

Sarah lit the fire and they settled down with their coffee and biscuits on the two leather chairs in front of the fire with its brass log box and companion set.

Mary concentrated on the coffee for a few minutes, it was certainly unusual but she liked the flavour, and Sarah's Aunt Ruth certainly could bake, the biscuits were delicious, and exactly like the jam'n raisin biscuits her mother made.

Sarah launched into her project.

"Firstly, I'm going to tell you the idea which I am working on and intend asking the hospital board to agree to trial.

There are lots of women who work as nannies or housekeepers and have no idea whatsoever of either first aid or basic nursing. Mary a little knowledge can save lives. My idea is that ladies who intend to be anything from school teachers to nannies can come along to a short course, say one week or a month and learn the basic skills.

If it works out well within a year or two we could offer more extensive training with certificates to say that the ladies who had attended had reached a certain level of competence. I am not trying to create nurses, just ladies who know what to do in an emergency and when they should call for professional help.

The hospital could charge for the courses so they would be self funding, in fact they could probably raise money for the hospital. And, the end result would be better home nursing.
What do you think Mary? If I can get 'the powers that be' to agree, would you be interested in training as one of the instructors?"

Mary felt a catch in her voice as she replied.

"Would I, would I, I would jump through flames for the opportunity. Oh Sarah, do you really think there is a chance?"

"I've been working on the details for ages and I have a paper almost prepared. I hope to put my formal proposal to the Nursing Board within the next month or so. Well Mary Law, are you with me?"

"Sarah it's a wonderful idea, and if there is any possibility I can get involved it would really turn my life around.

There is only one problem you know I have a heart condition, due to rheumatic fever would that weakness stop me working at the hospital?"

"I don't think so Mary but I am a nurse and a woman, I know your illness has not just damaged your heart." said Sarah gently while taking Mary's hand. "Do you want to talk about it?"
Mary had tears in her eyes as she said.

"So it is that obvious, I thought I managed to hide it quite well."

"You do hide it well, especially with the current fashions, which work in your favour. I have nursed cases of rheumatic fever Mary, I know the potential side effects. I am sorry if I have upset you but I thought we should get everything out in the open, no secrets from your sister Sarah."

Mary smiled. "Actually Sarah I am glad you brought it up I've been wondering how to tell you. The shortened version is when the fever reached it's crisis my father refused to let my mother, or for that matter the doctor, cut my hair. The next morning it had all fallen out. No going back, fortunately my mother kept my hair and I have managed to work out a way of winding it around my head and then waving it at the front, on goes the cloche hat and I can face the world.

Sarah, I'll have to leave soon to make sure I get a train back to Coatbridge at a respectable time, the family think I am at a church meeting."

Sarah laughed her ready laugh.

"Come on you brave girl off home with you, but what a hoot if the family only knew the truth about where you have been today, and it certainly wasn't a prayer meeting.

Mary my girl, keep up the act and we can arrange to meet soon and I'll give you the latest progress report. Meantime, I'll give you a manual on basic home nursing and first aid. You can start studying on the train as you go home."

Sarah walked Mary to the tram stop and they agreed to meet

same time, same place, in a few weeks time, between Christmas and New Year.

Sarah's last words as she waved to Mary were. "A lot can happen in three weeks, keep your fingers crossed my lovely new found sister."

CHAPTER 26
December 1925

After her meeting with Sarah, Mary spent every spare minute reading the First Aid and Home Nursing Manuals. The Carnegie Library in Coatbridge also provided a good source of reference books for her to study.

Although she said nothing about the possibility of working at the Royal Infirmary to the family, every waking moment she dreamed of Sarah's plans coming to fruition.

Willie's stay had extended over the agreed two weeks. However, Mary also had a plan for Willie. In a few days time the schools would break for the Christmas holidays. Alexander was due to finish school at Christmas and start work as an apprentice joiner on 2nd January. What would be more natural than Willie would finish school in Gartsherrie on the same day as Alexander and go straight home to his family in Condorrat for Christmas. This time there would be nobody to bring him back to Gartsherrie.

For some weeks Mary had been getting pains in her side, not every day, but the time between the bouts of pain seemed to be getting less and less.

Mary being Mary had not mentioned the discomfort she was feeling, in fact she wondered if it might have been brought on by the stress of the Fischer saga, and this being the case didn't want to bring the subject up with her mother.

It was Christmas Eve, the boys were all at the Salvation Army Christmas Concert; Willie had been packed off to Condorrat, albeit under protest; Jessie was out with McInnes. Only Mary and her

mother were at home, the house was peaceful and everything prepared for a family steak pie dinner the following day. Agnes looked
up from the newspaper she was reading and said.

"Mary lass, let's just have an easy tea, what about a wee bite of
scrambled egg and toast?"

Even as the words fell from her lips she saw Mary fall to the
floor clutching her side.

As she tried to pull her on to a chair Mary screamed in agony.
Agnes left her where she lay and ran out of the house to her neigh-
bour, Mrs Hamilton. Without ceremony she ran straight into the
Hamilton house shouting.

"Our Mary has been taken real bad. Can you get your Joe to
run up the Row and knock Jessie Johnstone's door, ask her to come
immediately, and then go straight up to Blairhill and get auld Dr
Murphy."

Agnes then turned on her heel and ran back into number twelve.
Mary was now unconscious but still groaning in pain.

Within a few minutes Jessie and her daughter Mary, who had
been visiting with Christmas presents, arrived. They managed to
undress Mary and get her into a nightdress but they were not successful in getting her into bed, every time they tried Mary screamed
in agony.

After what seemed like hours, but was in fact less than half an
hour, Dr Murphy arrived in his pony and trap. He gave young Joe
Hamilton a few pennies to mind his pony as he rushed into the
house.

Waving the women away and got down onto the floor to examine Mary. In his strong Irish accent he then gave his diagnosis and
issued his orders.

"The lass has a badly ruptured appendix it's too late to try and
get her to hospital. Mrs Law there is only one chance, I'll have to
operate on the kitchen table. You must all do exactly as I say. Mrs
Johnstone send your lass to bring Mrs Millar down here. I know in
the Rows you all think that we are enemies, daggers drawn, but I
admire the women's pluck.

Mrs Johnstone you and Mrs Law scrub the kitchen table thoroughly with carbolic soap and prepare the lass's bed with clean linen for after the operation. Also get me a spotless tray or better still a little table so that I can lay out my instruments.

Agnes once again ran next door to her neighbour to borrow a small table they kept in front of the window, displaying an aspidistra plant.

By the time Mary Johnstone returned with Ella Millar the scene was set.

Dr Murphy had boiled his instruments in the kitchen and laid them out on the aspidistra table, which was now covered in a clean towel. The gas mantles were turned up to high and a paraffin lamp had also been lit.

"Right ladies, we must get her on the table, I've given her something to kill the pain. Mrs Millar and Mrs Johnstone take a leg each, the lass you and I will take her shoulders. Mrs Law hold the lamp, I need as good a light as I can possibly get."

This time Mary moaned but she did not scream when she was lifted on to the kitchen table.

The doctor lifted his bottle of chloroform from the table and placed a gauze pad over Mary's face. He slowly dripped the liquid onto the pad until he was sure she was under the influence of the drug.

He stood back and took a long look at Mary. Under his breath he said.

"Jesus, if we are going to do this we need to do it now. Mrs Millar, hand me the instruments as I dictate. Mrs Law, you be holding that lamp steady. Mrs Johnstone keep an eye on Mary's breathing, the slightest change you be telling me. And you lass, guard the front door, on no account let anyone into this room until the operation is over and Mary is safely back in her bed.

Privately he thought, 'if she ever sees her bed again it will be a bloody miracle, so it will'.

With shaking hands he made the first incision. As the operation progressed he groaned.

"Jesus, Mary and Joseph, what a rupture, while issuing instructions to Ella. Mair swabs, give me the forceps, the big ones, now the scalpel, no that one, the broad one woman. And so it went on for well over an hour, during which time Jessie dripped more chloroform onto the gauze over Mary's face.

As the old doctor put in the final stitches he said.

"Well tonight as I sat drinking my Christmas tot of whisky I never dreamed I would be here operating with the assistance of four lasses before the night was oot.

Right, now the difficult part. We have to get her off the table and into bed now. Get a blanket and cover it in a clean sheet, we'll use that as a stretcher."

As gently as they could the four women and the doctor got Mary into bed.

Dr Murphy addressed all four of the women.

"Mind you've got a very sick girl there, I've done what I can. It's all down to nursing now. I'll call in tomorrow and see how things are. I won't be wishing you a merry Christmas, there will be no mirth in the Law household this year, so there won't."

The first snow of the year was starting to fall as Dr Murphy went out into the cold night. He thanked young Joe for looking after his pony and gave him another penny.

As he drove home he thought, 'come tomorrow, if that lass is still alive, I'll need to give that family mair bad news, so I will'.

Grim thoughts haunted him and he wondered if the numerous drams he had consumed that evening had made any difference to his surgery skills as he carried out the operation.

The family started to return home to the shocking news of the kitchen table operation and that, once again in her short life, Mary was lying in bed at death's door.

Jessie Johnstone became the chief organiser. The three boys moved in with Jessie and Alex, to allow Agnes and Ella Millar to concentrate on nursing Mary, with young Jessie helping when she returned home each day from work.

On hearing of Mary's illness Liz at once offered to pay for all the linen to be laundered and someone to come in and help with the cleaning. Mary Johnstone gently explained to her that money wasn't the issue it was the support, so over the following weeks, whenever she could, Mary came to Gartsherrie, she ironed, cooked, dusted, whatever was necessary to help and support her family.

Mary's loving support of Mary Law was also a great comfort to both Jessie and Alex, they now both realised that Mary still remembered her roots, regardless of the lifestyle she now enjoyed with Liz in the Victorian mansion in Airdrie.

Christmas passed unnoticed, apart from a short visit from Dr Murphy who was genuinely surprised to see that Mary was still alive.

On Boxing Day the doctor returned. He told Agnes he wanted to speak to her in private and took her into the boys bedroom which was empty.

"I am afraid Mrs Law I have some very bad news. When I was operating on Mary the rupture was such that I had to take some drastic action. Mrs Law, to put it simply, Mary's womanly organs have been severed, she can never have children."

Agnes who up to this point had just been relieved that Mary was still breathing burst into tears.

"How do I give that lass mair bad news doctor?" asked Agnes. "Last time she woke up bald, this time she will awaken to find she is barren. It's too much for any lass to have to suffer, how could God do this to a good girl like my Mary?"

Mrs Law I truly sympathise but I had to make you aware of the situation, although perhaps the extent of the scaring might have warned you that the operation had been somewhat drastic." explained the doctor.

Dr Murphy left and Agnes returned to Mary's sick bed. She sat at Mary's bedside for a few minutes holding her hand before saying to Ella Millar.

"The auld quack has told me he has butchered her, she will never have a bairn."

Putting her arm around Agnes's shoulders Ella said.

"Agnes I guessed as much during the operation but I said nothing, we didn't even know if Mary would pull through.

I am afraid you are going to have to break the news to the lass, but not yet, she needs a bit of time to gain her strength before she is hit with this blow. Don't tell anyone, even your own Jessie and Jessie Johnstone until Mary is told, it wouldn't be fair on the lass."

Over the following days Mary gradually regained a little strength, although she suffered a great deal of pain from the jagged scars over her stomach and side.

When the bells rang out 1925 and welcomed in 1926 there was no real celebration within the Law and Johnstone families.

However, life moves on and changes were taking place. Alexander had started his year as a Goffer at Gartsherrie works before beginning his Apprenticeship proper; Jessie was working long hours at the shop and then spending most of her free time in the company of McInnes, and consequently less and less time in the family home.

James was now engaged to Margaret Smith, much to the chagrin of the entire family.

What made matters worse was that Margaret constantly tried to ingratiate herself with the Laws, while at the same time Robert and Alexander were bringing home lurid stories about her behaviour.

Stories which included words like; debts, expensive clothing, bad reputation, pawn shop, stealing, brother involved with the police.

Without her daughters Mary and Jessie to talk the James and Margaret saga through with Agnes felt very isolated. Thankfully she had the kindly ear of Jessie Johnstone, who was always a great source of comfort.

Agnes had also been nursing another worry. During the weeks of Mary's slow recovery several letters had arrived from Sarah. Firstly Agnes hid them in her portmanteau, kept under the bed. However, when the third letter arrived Agnes decided she had no option but to open it.

Putting on her spectacles she read.

> *Dear Mary,*
> *Please explain, why didn't you meet me in Glasgow*
> *and why have you not answered by letters? It is now*
> *well over a month since I have heard from you.*
> *I really thought you would like to have been part of my*
> *home nursing and first aid project and I am so sad that*
> *you have not been in touch with me.*
> *Please, please Mary, let me know what is happening.*

Samuel thinks it very unlikely you would suddenly desert us.
Looking forward to a reply very soon.
Your sister
Sarah

Agnes put the letter back in the envelope with trembling hands. This time she knew she had to reply or face the real possibility of Sarah or Samuel turning up in Gartsherrie and with them the exposure of her past life.

Agnes got out her writing paper, and wrote.

Dear Sarah,
I am sorry to have to be the bearer of bad news.
Mary had a ruptured appendix on Christmas Eve.
The doctor had to carry out an emergency operation at our home.
My lass is still in a bad way, requiring constant nursing care.
I will give her your letters when she is feeling better.
If there is any change in her condition I will write again.
Meantime, I hope you and your brother are well.

Agnes then sat and looked at the letter, what words could she possibly use to sign off. Agnes Law? Your mother? Mary's mother, Agnes? She was still sitting pondering the problem when Jessie Johnstone called in, carrying some messages.

Not wanting to draw attention to her letter writing she quickly scribbled, "Your mother, Agnes", folded the letter, put it into its envelope and placed it in the pocket of her floral overall.

Later that afternoon Agnes kept an anxious lookout for young Joe from next door returning from school. As soon as she saw him coming up the Row she hurried out to meet him, gave him a half penny for a few sweets, and asked him to run to the postbox and post her letter in time for the five o'clock collection.

The following morning Sarah was surprised to find a letter from Gartsherrie, addressed to her, and written in an unknown hand.

After reading the letter Sarah's first reaction was to rush out to Gartsherrie, armed with flowers and fruit, and visit her half sister.

However, by the time she had reached her office in the Royal Infirmary she had decided that it would be best to phone Samuel and ask his advice.

Samuel's initial reaction was similar to that of Sarah's on opening the letter, take the first train to Gartsherrie.
But Samuel, being Samuel, said.

"Sarah we mustn't rush into anything and stir up a hornets nest. Let's think this through carefully and I'll telephone you later this afternoon."

Samuel telephoned his sister as promised.

"Sarah, my dear, why don't we meet for a high tea and discuss the news of Mary illness face to face. I don't want to discuss this matter over the telephone."

"Agreed" said Sarah. Let's meet at Reid's Tearoom, say about six o'clock.

The brother and sister met up at Reid's on the cold, sleety January evening. Shaking out their umbrellas, they removed their coats and found a table for two.

They each ordered haddock and chips, with bread and butter and a pot of tea.

Without any preamble Sarah asked Samuel.

"What on earth are we going to do? Poor Mary is laying seriously ill for the second time in her life and our hands are tied."

"What do you mean second time?" asked Samuel.

"Goodness, I don't suspect you know the full story. You do know that Mary has a heart condition?" enquired Sarah,

"Yes, but not the details."

"Well I'll give you them. Mary had rheumatic fever about five years ago, hence the heart condition, but her father would not let the women bring down the fever by cutting her hair, so she lost her entire head of beautiful thick red hair.

Every day she carefully winds her own hair, which luckily was preserved by one of the women, around her head, and then waves it with crimping irons. Fortunately the fashion for cloche hats works well for her, so she can go about her business without anyone knowing.

Samuel was horrified at this further piece of desperately sad news about Mary.

"Sarah, let me read the letter for myself."

Sarah handed Samuel the letter which he read several times. The waitress in her black uniform with spotless white frilly apron and cap, brought them their meal.

"Would you like anything else, tomato sauce, tartar sauce or beetroot." asked the waitress.

"No thank you, just the tea." replied Sarah.

They ate their meal without conversation. Eventually Samuel broke the silence.

"I think you should write a short letter to Agnes, our mother, enclosing a postal order for ten pounds. Ask her to buy anything necessary to help with Mary's recovery. Also request her to write and let us know if we can be of further help.

Perhaps you could also enclose another sealed letter for Mary, promising we will do all we can to help with her recovery.

I think support from a distance is the only thing to be done. We can't rush out to Gartsherrie and disrupt goodness knows how many lives. I particularly don't want Mary upset and exposure of her mother's past would not help her recovery one little bit."

"Reluctantly I have to agree with you" said Sarah. "I'll write tonight when I get home and post the letters first thing tomorrow morning."

They finished their food and Samuel took out the money to pay the bill, he then handed Sarah two five pound notes, saying.

"Sarah, please use this money to buy the postal order, and remember to let me know immediately if we can be of any further help."

They left the warmth of the restaurant and headed out into the dreich grey Glasgow night to catch their respective trams the bleakness perfectly matching their mood.

Agnes opened the letter from Glasgow, frightened at what she

would read.   Firstly, out fell the postal order for ten whole pounds.
The letter read.

> *Dear Mrs Law,*
> *Please find enclosed some money which we would like*
> *you to use to assist with Mary's recovery.*
> *We thank you for your letter and are greatly saddened by*
> *the news of Mary's illness.*
> *Please give her the enclosed letter when you think she is*
> *well enough.*
> *Yours sincerely*
> *Samuel and Sarah Fischer*

Agnes put the letter for Mary into her portmanteau to join the
others.   The letter addressed to her she burned in the flames of the
fire.

Staring at the postal order for some time she wondered what
excuse she could possibly make to go into Coatbridge and visit the
Post Office.

Alice Hamilton, next door's oldest lass, was working on the Post
Office counter at nearby Sunnyside so there was no possibility of
going there to cash an order for ten whole pounds, the Laws would
have been the talk of the Rows.

The excuse arrived from an unexpected quarter.   Later that day
Ella Millar called round to visit Mary.   After checking on her patient
she was having a cup of tea with Agnes when there was a loud
knock on the door.

'What next,' thought Agnes as she rose to answer the summons.
On the doorstep stood a Telegraph Boy in his blue uniform.
He handed over the thin brown envelope, saying.

"Telegraph for Law, any reply Mam?"

Agnes opened the telegram with shaking fingers.   It read.

> *Maw, Willie impossible, sending him to you.*
> *Arrives Coatbridge Central at 4.00pm. - Charlotte.*

It was now two o'clock, and too late to telegraph Charlotte, Willie would already be on his way from Condorrat.

Agnes sent the Telegraph Boy away and returned to the kitchen where she handed Ella the telegram to read.

"That is all I need, Willie arriving." exclaimed Agnes. "Mrs Millar can I ask you a huge favour, will you stay with Mary until I go over to Coatbridge and meet the wee bugger?"

"What are friends for?" said Ella. "Of course I'll stay with your lass. Now get yourself ready and get down to the bus stop. Poor Agnes, you have certainly had your troubles recently."

Agnes caught the Baxter's bus but she did not get off at Coatbridge Central she carried on another two stops to the Post Office in Bank Street, where in the busy office, she anonymously cashed the postal order.

Ten whole pounds in her worn leather purse, Agnes could scarcely believe she was carrying such a sum of money.

Before walking back to meet Willie from the train station she stopped off at the Fishmongers and bought herrings for the family dinner, together with a nice piece of lemon sole, which she intended to steam, between two plates, with the top of the milk, for Mary.

Willie came off the train carrying his school satchel, together with a brown paper parcel. Even Willie quaked in his shoes at the sight of Agnes striding towards him.

"Well, you wee bugger what have you been up to now? And, what does your daft mother and father think they are about sending you to me, with your poor Aunt Mary still in her sick bed?" stormed his grandmother."

Willie kept his head down and handed her an envelope. Agnes took the envelope and put it in her pocket. Giving him a piercing look that would have turned milk sour, his grandmother snapped.

"Right you wee scunner, follow me to the bus stop and I'll take you home to Gartsherrie. But mind this, I intend to get to the bottom of your nonsense once and for all. You will be heading back to Condorrat sooner than you think my lad."

Willie had the good sense to stay silent on both the bus ride and then the walk back to number twelve the Long Row.

By the time they arrived home Robert and Alexander had
returned from their shifts and Ella Millar was in the scullery peeling
potatoes.

The boys greeted Agnes with a chorus of questions and just
when she thought the day could not worsen James's fiancé Margaret
came strolling in, saying.

"Mrs Law can I stay for my tea, Jimmy and I are going to the
pictures tonight so I thought it would be more convenient."

Agnes was in no mood for this nonsense.
Drawing herself up to her full height of five foot two she rounded
on Margaret.

"Don't you dare call my lad Jimmy, his name is James. Besides
the whole house has had enough of you and your kind, Margaret
Smith. You are nothing but a gold digger, get out of my home and
leave a respectable lad alone. Don't darken my door again."

Margaret, not to be outdone, shouted.

"You bossy auld crone. Don't think you can come between me
and your precious lad Jimmy. I'll make sure we wed before the
spring comes you auld bitch."

This was too much for Robert, he didn't have red hair for nothing, and he would not stand by and hear his mother called an 'auld
bitch'.

Alexander had to physically restrain him from attacking
Margaret.

Mary was shouting from the bedroom asking what was going on
when James arrived home to join the melee.

Mrs Millar called for calm but Margaret was having none of it,
she grabbed James by the arm and propelled him out of the house
to Robert's cry of.

"Good riddance to bad rubbish." ringing in their ears.
Agnes burst into tears, a sight seldom seen but the dam of her self
control had broken.

In walked Jessie from work to find her mother crying; Mrs
Millar making tea; Robert bright red with rage; Alexander sporting a
shocked expression and trying to calm Robert; Mary's voice coming
from the bedroom, asking what on earth was happening; and there

in the centre of the chaos was Willie, standing in the corner, still in his navy trench coat, clutching his satchel and a parcel, wrapped in brown paper.

"Maw, have I walked into a mad house. What on earth is going on and why is Willie back here again?" enquired the astounded Jessie.

Agnes could not answer for crying, so it was left up to Ella Millar to enlighten Jessie as to the goings on of the day.

Agnes pulled herself together and suddenly remembered the letter. Removing it from her coat pocket she opened the envelope took out the missive, carefully put on her spectacles, and slowly read it aloud.

> Dear Maw,
> I am so sorry to have to send Willie to you again but he has gotten himself expelled from school.
> The wee blighter was on his last warning when he cheeked one of the teachers. The teacher said "attention boy, give me your eyes." He rolled two marbles down the classroom floor and shouted, "I canny take oot my eyes, but will these do for you miss?"
> He was packed home and suspended until after the Easter holidays.
> Please Maw can you send him to school in Gartsherrie until Easter and then I promise, I really do promise, to take him home.
> Please give Mary our best wishes and tell her Charlie and I hope she is better soon.
> Your daughter
> Charlotte

Jessie couldn't help herself, she burst out laughing, saying.

"Oh Maw he really is a wee blighter, he must take after Charlie Fyfe, none of us would have dared behave like that wee menace.

I'm going to have a chat to Mary now. I'll give you a hand with the meal later."

Jessie sat on the edge of the bed while she enlightened Mary as to the goings on of the afternoon. After discussing the latest drama in the James and Margaret romance they relaxed and had a good laugh when Jessie told her sister the story of Willie's antics and why he had been expelled.

The household slowly returned to normal over the next few days but James remained quiet and sullen. Robert and Alexander tried to get him to talk about the Margaret situation but he would not be drawn.

With Mary still recuperating in bed, on this occasion Agnes had to take Willie to Gartsherrie school and enrol him for a term. During the interview with the Headmaster she was somewhat economical with the truth regarding the reason for him moving to Gartsherrie again, but she succeeded in her mission and Willie was duly enrolled at Gartsherrie Primary school until the Easter holidays.

After she returned home Agnes decided that as Mary was now out of danger and starting to make a recovery from the operation, that it was now time to give her the letters from Sarah in Glasgow.

Mary read the three letters without comment and asked Agnes if she would give her a pen, ink and paper.

Mary wrote.

> Dear Sarah,
> Thank you so very much for your concern. It is only today that I have received your three letters.
> As you will now know from my mother I have been very ill with a ruptured appendix, which necessitated an emergency operation.
> My recovery seems to be very slow but I am sure I will eventually come good.
> Everyone has been very kind and my mother has been plying me with all sorts of nourishing foods, thanks to the kind gift from you and Samuel. Please thank him from me.
> When I am feeling better I will be in touch and per-
> haps we can arrange another tea at Miss Cranston's in

Sauchiehall Street.
With my very best wishes
Your sister
Mary

Agnes posted the letter on her way to the Store for messages and for the first time felt guilty about all the subterfuge within the family, caused by her secret past.   Perhaps all the other disruptions in the household were her punishment; what with Willie's escapades and the continuing tensions with James over Margaret Smith, nothing seemed to be going well.

However, Willie and James were the least of her worries. Agnes knew she could no longer delay telling Mary the details of the kitchen table operation which had left her sterile.

Walking home with her shopping she knew there was no putting off the inevitable.   What must be done, must be done.

Knowing that she couldn't let her courage fail Agnes simply left her bag with the messages in the scullery, removed her coat and hat and went straight through to the bedroom where Mary was lying reading a book.

Agnes sat on the bed and said.

"Mary lass, put down that book I have something to tell you and it isn't good news."

Agnes described the operation and as gently as she could told Mary that the surgery had butchered her so that she would never be able to have children.

Agnes had anticipated all sorts of reactions and dreaded each one but she was astounded at Mary's calm words.

"Well mother, isn't it a good job my father had made me unlovable to any man before another man left me barren.

Your news isn't that great a surprise, look at my belly, look at the vicious ugly red scars.

Mary Law, bald, barren and deformed and with a name given for hate that about sums me up.

Well Mother, I suggest you do what we always do, go into the kitchen make a cup of tea and then we all get on with life. I can't turn the clock back and neither can you."

Mary spoke her words in a flat steady voice. There were no tears, no hysterics, simply a bitter resignation that in five years she had changed from a beautiful healthy girl with a bright future to an old maid with a heart problem.

Over the following weeks and months Mary recovered physically but she had changed, changed in ways that were not obviously apparent to the rest of the family.

What happened on the kitchen table in the Long Row on Christmas Eve 1925 would live with Mary each and every day until the day she died.

CHAPTER 27
April 1926

Samuel pulled the brass doorbell outside Sarah's flat.   He was carrying a pretty bunch of spring flowers and wondering why his sister had telephoned him and all but summonsed him to come for supper.

Sarah greeted him in her normal carefree manner.

"Come in, come in, dear brother.   Take your coat off.   Wow, what lovely flowers and for your sister.   Samuel Fischer you should be buying beautiful flowers for a nice girl who would give you babies and carry on our family name."

"Shut up you silly girl.   You know you are the only woman in my life, well you and Aunt Ruth and Bubbe and actually Mary.   You know I had a lot of misgivings after I wrote that letter to our mother but I don't regret getting to know Mary, she is a very decent human being is our half sister."

They went through to the living room where Ruth had set the table for an easy supper of a cheese and egg pudding served with a baked potato and salad.

Before they settled down to eat Sarah addressed Samuel.

"Samuel it'd like you to read a letter I received a few days ago from Mary.   I have cried many tears and I am sure in your heart you will also cry when you read it.

You cannot imagine the debate I had with myself as to whether I should share it with you but for reasons I will explain later I thought you had to read it in order to fully understand my feelings and the action I am about to take."

The letter read.

My Dear Sarah,

Firstly I want to thank you and Samuel for all your
kindness when I was ill.   I really appreciated knowing that you both cared and wanted to help.

My apologies for not being in touch all these weeks but
I simply could not bring myself to put pen to paper.
To put it simply, my mother told me that the doctor
'butchered' me during the operation, apparently he had
been drinking.   So not only am I bald I am now also
barren.

Although on the surface I am putting on a brave face
for the family inside I feel devastated.

The main reason for my writing to you Sarah is to say,
grab your happiness.   Don't end up an old maid for the
sake of a career.

If you truly love Alan, and it was the one subject we
avoided in your flat, make a life together.

It would be lovely to meet up again for lunch.

Unfortunately I am still not strong enough to travel on
my own.   I will write to you again when I feel well
enough.

With every good wish.

Your Sister

Mary

Samuel returned the letter to Sarah, saying.

"Sarah, I honestly don't know what to say.   I so wish we could
do more for Mary.   I know we can't do anything for her conditions
but we at least could be supportive to her if everything was out in
the open.   It's at moments like this I actually hate our mysterious
mother."

Sarah put her arm around his shoulder, saying.
"Samuel, hate is never the answer, please don't use that horrible
word in this house.

I will dish the supper and we can talk as we eat."
They sat down to eat, the meal looked delicious but Samuel had lost

his appetite. However, he tried to eat a little since Sarah had made the effort to prepare a meal after a long day at work.

Sarah opened the conversation.

"I've thought and thought about the contents of Mary's letter and I think she is right.

Alan and I have known each other for years, I love him and we also enjoy a deep friendship and shared interests. I suppose I thought I could have it all ways, Alan and a career, without losing either.

Mary's letter has prompted some self analysis and I have decided to accept Alan's offer to make me a respectable woman.

Before the year is out I intend to be Mrs DeSilva."

Samuel rose and kissed his sister on the cheek.

"My dear, dear, sister. I am so very pleased for you both, have you told Aunt Ruth yet?" asked Samuel.

"No" laughed Sarah. "Actually I haven't told Alan yet, but I will, promise."

They both burst out laughing. Samuel recovered first.

"You really are totally incorrigible Sarah.

When are you going to tell Alan that he is marrying into a mad dysfunctional family?"

"Later tonight." answered Sarah. "He is coming round for coffee.

I know it might seem a bit unconventional but I'd like to tell him when you are here because I think he has every right to know about our history.

There have been too many secrets and I have no intention of carrying on the subterfuge."

Samuel was frightened that Sarah's scheme would blow up in her face and that Alan would simply not accept the skeletons in the Fischer cupboard but he hid his thoughts from Sarah.

"Come on big brother finish up your meal and I'll get the dishes cleared and prepare the coffee, I bought some Nestles Walnut Vanilla Cream chocolates to have with the coffee. What a treat, besides I thought poor Alan would need some sugar after he hears what we have to say to him."

Sarah started to clear the table and Samuel was busy laying out the coffee things when he heard the brass door pull ring.

Samuel welcomed Alan into the flat, hanging up his coat and showing him into the living room. He knew he was blethering a diatribe of complete rubbish to his friend but he could not imagine how Sarah had came up with this madcap idea, to propose to Alan and with her twin brother present.

They all settled themselves down while Sarah brought out the tray of coffee and sweets from the little kitchen.

Before the men could say anything Sarah launched into her speech.

"Alan, you are going to find the next hour or so very odd indeed but knowing me as you do, odd is fairly near normal, so I'll start."

Firstly she told him about Agnes, her conversion to Judaism and subsequent marriage to their father. She explained how shortly after the birth of Samuel and herself their father had died and the family had rejected Agnes.

Sarah then reiterated an outline of Agnes's life story and her widowhood giving Alan details of her half brothers and sisters in Gartsherrie.

Then came the explanation that the Gartsherrie family were Protestants, although technically Jewish. Nothing important was left out, this was a conversation that Sarah never intended to have with Alan again.

The whole truth once, was her intention.

"Alan, I know this is all a huge shock for you but I think perhaps Samuel should tell you a little bit about Mary, she is the sister that we have met and both of us hold her in the highest regard. Over to you brother." Sarah handed the floor to her brother.

Samuel then explained how he had got in touch with the Law family and about his meeting with Mary.

As he tailed off he looked up at Alan, with his high clever forehead and dark brown eyes. Laughter lines were appearing around his eyes, and a smile started to waver around his lips. He could hold it back no longer. Alan burst out laughing, as did Sarah and Samuel. The three of them laughed until the tears came.

"An invite for coffee, I don't think, Sarah Fischer. If you have set out to shock me, it's not possible. I am totally unshockable as far as you are concerned, you are a law unto yourself.

Now why have you really set up this charade, it's not just a lesson in the weird and wonderful world of Fischer Family History, is it?" asked Alan.

At this point Samuel got up from his chair, muttering.

"Well I think everything I need to be here for has been said. I'm off to get the tram back to Garnethill. Goodnight you two."

As Samuel made his way to the front door he heard a little voice whispering.

"Keep July free Samuel."

He was out of the door and down the stairs as fast as his legs could carry him.

Left to their own devices Alan put his arms around Sarah and said.

"Is this it my darling, are you at long last going to agree to make me the proudest man in Glasgow and become my wife?"

In reply Sarah gave him a long kiss.

"Yes, yes, my wonderful Alan. Let's get married as soon as possible, how does July sound?"

"Tomorrow sounds better." said Alan "However, if you say July, July it shall be my beautiful Sarah.

They spent the rest of the evening cuddled in each other's arms, making plans for their future life together.

CHAPTER 28
May 1926

Mary and Jessie were in the kitchen washing and drying the dishes after the evening meal. Their brothers were off out to band practice at the Salvation Army and their Mother was sitting in front of the fire reading the Airdrie & Coatbridge Advertiser.

"Thank goodness the general strike is over" said Jessie. "I know it sounds terribly selfish but McInnes promised to take me out somewhere special for my birthday and we couldn't possibly go out in the midst of a serious strike.

My birthday is the anniversary of our engagement and all being well next May 25th, when I am twenty one, we will celebrate our wedding, I'm so excited and I know I am so incredibly lucky to have met such a wonderful man.

McInnes has given me money for my birthday and told me to go to Miss Aitken's Shop in Academy Street and buy a stylish outfit. I've seen a lovely pale blue crepe de chine dress and jacket, it would look lovely with my cream shoes and handbag. Oh Mary, can you believe, your wee Jessie wearing a crepe de chine outfit and leather shoes.

It seems a terrible thing to say but, apart from your operation, since Paw died this family has been getting on ten to the dozen.

We have moved to the Long Row; the boys are earning and contributing more; I've got a good job and I'm able to give Maw far more than ever I did when I was working at the Sweetie Shop. You and Maw have organised the house with linoleum, rugs, new curtains better furniture, the boys have even saved up and bought a gramophone.

And, Maw is back in touch with her mother. That's about two or three times Granny Neilson has been out here to visit and her and Maw write to each other every week.

Things are even going well for Charlotte, Charlie is very much Farmer Baird's right hand man at the farm, they have a better cottage now and if she can't have any more bairns, well that is good news. Five bairns is more than enough for anyone."

Mary interrupted her.

"It might be going well for Charlotte but we have that wee scunner Willie back staying here again. It's me who gets all the extra work and worry with him. Between him and the other children that I look after from time to time for a bit of money. I get all the work of parenthood without any of the joy."

"Never mind" said Jessie. "Maybe some day you will meet someone nice who will look after you and see you for the special person you really are."

Mary nodded, but in her head she thought. 'What man would settle for a bald, barren wife, besides I have had enough of men, I would rather have had a career any day. I'm better off with pals of my own sex, what did men ever do for me but ruin my life.'

Jessie's twentieth birthday fell on a Sunday. The whole family were gathered for breakfast. Agnes and Mary made bacon and scrambled eggs with buttermilk pancakes, a real treat.

After breakfast Jessie washed and dressed carefully. Leaving to catch the train into Glasgow she looked absolutely beautiful. A stylish cream hat, with a blue trim completed the blue crepe de chine outfit and with her peaches and cream complexion the only makeup she needed was a little pale pink lipstick.

Jessie walked to Blairhill Station with a glad heart excitedly looking forward to a whole day spent with McInnes. Treating herself to a first class ticket she enjoyed the journey relishing the excitement of having a delicious lunch with the man she loved; the man who had taught her so much and broadened her horizons and given her ambitions far beyond the confines of the Gartsherrie Rows.

From Glasgow Queen Street Jessie walked to George Square, where McInnes was waiting for her beside the statue of Robert Burns.

"You look absolutely breathtaking." said McInnes as soon as he saw her. "You are indeed my Beautiful Princess Jess of the 'Brig."

"Thank you my handsome prince," Jessie riposted. "I have been so looking forward to my twentieth birthday. Do you like the outfit I chose? Where are we going for lunch? Incidentally, the shop has had its best week so far. I knew we had been busy but the accounts prove just how busy, you are going to be really pleased when you prepare the monthly figures."

"Enough Jess" said McInnes, "We are not going to talk about business today."

He took her hand and they walked along St Vincent Street to Buchanan Street then walked down Buchanan until they came to Gordon Street.

"Where are we going?" asked Jessie.

"My secret, wait and see Princess," replied McInnes."

They walked along Gordon Street and then they turned left, their destination the Central Hotel, that magnificent edifice where all the famous film stars, politicians, theatricals and anybody who was anybody visiting Glasgow stayed.

McInnes guided Jessie into the beautiful entrance with its Italian marble floors. It was every palace, castle, elegant hotel, Jessie had ever imagined rolled into one. The staff in their monogrammed uniforms; the women guests dressed in the latest fashions; the sparkling chandeliers; the exciting buzz in the air as friends, lovers, families, business associate, met for a hundred different reasons.

Jessie was so busy taking everything in that she completely failed to notice the admiring glances turned on her and her handsome escort.

The Maître 'D showed them to their table set with crisp white linen, crystal glasses, monogrammed crockery, silver cutlery and a silver vase containing a little posy of a pink carnations and white gypsophilas.

Jessie had never seen such a magnificent dining room and she was completely awe struck as the waiter pulled out her chair and then with a flourish placed the snowy white napkin on her lap.

The waiter liked to look at his customers and weave a little story around them, while at the same time guessing who the best tippers would be.

This couple were difficult to pigeonhole. He was tall, distinguished, well dressed and entirely comfortable with his surrounding. The girl on the other hand was obviously overawed by the grandeur of the hotel, but she was certainly not the tarty type. On the contrary she was very nicely, if not hugely expensively, dressed. And attractive, in her simple but elegant outfit, with very little make up she was by far the most beautiful woman in the entire room. Quietly and nicely spoken but without the cut glass accent that spoke money. Interesting pair.

They enjoyed a wonderful meal together; a smoked salmon starter with champagne, followed by roast beef with all the trimmings and finally an ice cream bombe. Jessie had let McInnes choose from the daunting French menu and she certainly was not disappointed by both the food and being served by attentive waiters. While in the background there was music from a trio of musicians, dressed in bow ties and tails.

Jessie had a fleeting thought. 'What a story I am going to have for Mary and Maw tonight' when McInnes broke into her happy mood.

"Darling Jess. There is something I must tell you, I am sorry my Jess but I cannot put off this conversation any longer. I have not been feeling too well recently so I went to the doctor, he referred me to a specialist and well, and he thinks I might have a fairly serious problem."

Jessie's heart reached her boots. One moment at the pinnacle of happiness and then without warning being told that McInnes, her tall, handsome, strong, fiancé was ill. Impossible to believe.

Jessie's voice rose barely above a whisper. "What exactly does the doctor think is wrong with you?"

"It is not a very nice subject to discuss over lunch. But I had to share the knowledge of my illness with you my darling. The doctors hope, because I am young and strong, that they may be able to cure me.

Darling Jess, don't let us wait until your birthday next year. Let's

plan an autumn wedding.   We may not have years, and years together, like we planned, but we can make the most of the time we do
have.   If we are lucky we will have our children and you will certainly have security for the rest of your life.

CHAPTER 29
June 1926

Outwardly Mary had recovered from her appendix operation but inside she was still silently fighting a deep depression.

Jessie's news that McInnes was seriously ill had done nothing to dispel her gloom nor her conviction that everything in the Law household was starting to fall apart.

There was James's forthcoming wedding to Margaret Smith which was scheduled for the end of June. This was a worry on a number of levels; no one in the family liked or trusted the girl and although she had never actually verbalised the thought, Mary was worried about the drop in the household income when James left the family home.

There was also the problem of Wee Willie. He had managed to survive the Easter deadline. Charlotte had written to say that May and baby Irene had both contracted measles. The boys were sleeping at the farmhouse and she did not think she could cope with Willie's arrival home.

Although it was now nearing the summer holidays and another opportunity to send him packing Mary was sure either the little pest himself or Charlotte and Charlie were plotting yet another delay.

Hearing the morning mail falling through the letterbox onto the floor Mary went into the scullery to see what had arrived. Amongst the family post she had received two handwritten letters, one postmarked Glasgow the other local.

Recognising Sarah's handwriting Mary quickly opened the letter from Glasgow, it read.

Dearest Mary,

Well my dear sister I took your advice and Alan and I are going to get married in six weeks time at the Gorbals Synagogue. My uncle David will marry us, then we are going off to London for a few days to meet Alan's extended family. Thereafter we are having a fortnight in Cornwall before we return to Glasgow and I become Mrs Doctor DeSilva.

We intend to sell both our flats and buy a house in Whitecraigs. That should keep me out of mischief for a while but hopefully I will find something useful to do in the longer term.

Mary, I am so very sorry but as a married woman I will not be able to keep my position at the Royal Infirmary. Therefore my idea on first aid and home nursing training courses will not come to fruition.

I am so terribly sorry, I know you would have loved to have become an Instructor and it would have been wonderful for us to have worked together but alas it is not to be.

Alan knows all about our peculiar family dynamics and we would both love it if you could attend the wedding.

I have enclosed a formal invitation card, not at all me, but Aunt Ruth and Alan's mother are in cahoots and they are arranging the festivities.

Please come and see us wed under the chuppah and wish us muzzeltof. It would mean so very much not only to me but also to Samuel.

With love

Sarah

Mary handed the letter to Agnes to read while she opened the second letter. It was from a Mrs Watson who lived in Drumpellier Estate. Mary had worked for her as a part time maid before the operation. It read.

Dear Miss Law,
I understand that you are now recovered from your
illness.
Would you care to once again work for me a few
afternoons a week?
Perhaps you could call around to see me tomorrow,
Wednesday, at around two o'clock to discuss.
Yours sincerely
Ethel Watson (Mrs)

Mary looked at the two letters, one telling her a career in lecturing home nursing and first aid, her chosen vocation, had ended before it had even begun. The other contained a job offer to be a skivvy in someone else's home.

Mary passed the second letter to Agnes, saying.

"Well Maw I guess that is my future sorted, working as a servant and looking after you and dear little Willie.

I'll walk over to Drumpellier and see Mrs Watson tomorrow."

The following afternoon Mary arrived at Mrs Watson's home at the designated hour.

Her future employer answered the door and showed Mary into the kitchen where she wasted no time launching into a list of her future requirements. Ethel Watson made no offer of hospitality, she didn't even ask Mary how well she was recovering from her illness.

"Mary, I would like you to come three afternoons a week, Tuesday, Thursday and Friday from around one thirty until four thirty.

Your duties will be to prepare a little light snack for my friends who call for tea, you know the kind of thing, a few pancakes and sandwiches, or some other savoury, perhaps a cake. You can serve them around three o'clock and then clear away and wash the dishes before your leave.

The extra time available you can use gainfully, perhaps polish the silver or prepare the evening meal, do the ironing, whatever else comes to my mind on the day.

I will organise a uniform for you. In future I would like you to wear a black dress with a white frilled apron and a little matching mob cap.

Now let me think, that will be nine hours a week you will be working, one and sixpence an hour, total weekly wage, thirteen shillings and sixpence.   Is that agreeable?

Mary did not waste words.

"Agreeable Mrs Watson, I'll start Tuesday first"

Mary arose from the kitchen chair and Mrs Watson showed her out, through the back door.

As she was leaving the house, Mrs Watson said.

"Incidentally Mary, I would prefer it if you would address me as Mam or Madam in future."

Mary smiled sweetly and replied politely.

"Right Madam"

The sarcasm was completely lost on Mrs Watson who was totally absorbed in her own importance, but at least it gave Mary a feeling of satisfaction and a rye smile.

Mary thought long and hard about whether or not she should attend the wedding of Sarah and Alan.   When she could put a decision off no longer she wrote to Sarah.

My Dear Sarah,

Firstly my congratulations on your forthcoming wedding. I am sure you will both have a wonderful, joyous, day. I have struggled very hard with the decision as to whether or not to attend.   I am sure I will stand out and I would hate any awkward questions to be asked. Perhaps a compromise would be best, I could sit at the back of the synagogue and watch your marriage, afterwards I would just drift away and get the train back to Coatbridge.

To attend a meal and the evening festivities would be impossible, as we both know lies are never the answer and I am afraid I would have to tell as many as 'Tam Pepper' if I were to be a guest at your reception. When you return to Glasgow and are settled in your new home I would love to hear from you.

*With all my love and good wishes for your future
happiness.
Your sister Mary*

The lead up to the Fischer and DeSilva wedding in Glasgow was less fraught that the Law and Smith nuptials which were booked for the following week at the Salvation Army Citadel in Sunnyside, Coatbridge.

James had acquired a house to rent at the top of the Long Row, just a few doors away from the Johnstone family.

Margaret had been using what was left of James's prize money for fitting out the house in the latest of fashions.

When James's money ran out Margaret organised hire purchase agreements to cover the the cost of a new bed; also an oak dining table and chairs with a sideboard to match, two easy chairs covered in brown moquette a square Axminster carpet, and a roll of linoleum, which completed the living room furnishings.

James had talked Jessie into decorating the bedroom, kitchen and scullery for them. This had been a real dilemma for Jessie, on the one hand Jessie, like the rest of the Laws, heartily disapproved of Margaret but on the other hand she loved her brother and felt she had to help him.

Jessie made a lovely professional job of the wallpapering and painting, paying for all the materials as a wedding present.

When the house was completed to her satisfaction Margaret called into number twelve one afternoon to see Mary and her future mother-in-law, Agnes.

"Good afternoon Mrs Law, Mary. Now that Jessie has finished the decorating and the furniture has been delivered, I just thought I would invite you both up to see the lovely house where Jimmy, err James and I will start our married life.

Agnes's initial reaction was to tell Margaret that she was not in the least interested in her house and that her and Mary had better things to do than encourage her prospective daughter-in-law's show-ing off.

Mary however, felt it was better to know what exactly was going on at number 140 Long Row.

"Come on Maw, get your coat, we are going for a walk to see James's new home." said Mary, while looking at her mother with an expression that said. 'I think we had better'.

As they walked up the Row Margaret chatted on about how her wedding was going to be a full Salvation Army ceremony, with everyone wearing uniform, although she would be carrying a bouquet of flowers, freesia and roses. After the wedding all the guests would have a meal in the Salvation Army hall; steak pie and a pudding, naturally, purveyed by the Co-operative. When the festivities were over her and James were going off on their honeymoon to the Ayrshire coast, a boarding house in Largs called Cumbrae View.

Mary and Agnes said nothing but they drew each other plenty of looks.

The three women arrived at number 140. Margaret opened the door with great pride, saying.

"Well Mrs Law, Mary, what do you think, isn't it the finest house in all the Rows? Jimmy and I are so very pleased. Jessie has papered it quite nicely but I chose the paper and the paint colours, beautiful aren't they?"

Mother and daughter were open mouthed with shock at all the opulence displayed by the soon to be bride.

Agnes wasted no time in making her opinion felt.

"Margaret Smith, in the name of God and all that's holy what have you done. My boy never had the money to buy all this nonsense. Where did you get the money, did you steal it? We have heard the rumours you know, rumours about the kind of people you come from."

Margaret burst out sobbing then snapped at Agnes.

"You evil auld woman, have you never heard of hire purchase. We have bought all we need now and we will pay for everything over the next year or so. We will use my wages to pay the furniture shop and live from Jimmy's money. Better that than living in some kind of make-do and mend hovel."

Agnes turned to Mary saying.

"Take me home lass. Me and mine have never had a penny of

debt in our lives. I refuse to look at what that hussy has landed my boy with, the black burning shame of it all."

With that she took Mary's arm and walked out like a Duchess. On the way home they called in to see Jessie Johnstone and enlighten her on the goings on just a few doors away.

Jessie confirmed that she had seen furniture vans arriving but had no idea that Margaret had furnished the house so grandly, and all on the never never.

They were all horrified at the idea of debt, these were women who all their lives had seen their neighbours pawning clothes and household items to put food on the table until the following pay day. The Law and the Johnstone families had always been proud of the fact that they might have been poor but they had always lived untouched by any debts.

In the middle of the exclamations of horror and tales of the terrible ends other debtors had came to Mary suddenly burst out laughing. Agnes and Jessie looked at her as if she had gone mad. Mary could hardly get the words out for giggling.

"Have you two ever heard the like 'going on honeymoon to Largs, Cumbrae View no less' since when did the likes of our James go on honeymoon. The pair of them must have gone stark raving mad. The next thing they will be employing a maid."

They all saw the funny side and Jessie laughed as she put on the kettle and they all sat down for a good blether over tea and a wee home made scone.

At last the wedding day arrived. The three Law boys were wearing their Salvation Army uniforms, with a carnation pinned on their tunics to mark the occasion. Robert was going to be Best Man and Alexander an Usher. Robert had railed against being involved in any capacity but after a number of arguments he had at last agreed, in the end it came down to 'blood being thicker than water'.

Truth be told James was also starting to have doubts as to the wisdom of getting married to Margaret but he felt he was in too deep and he just could not work out how to get out of the whole ghastly proceedings.

Besides, him and Margaret had tried out the new bed at number 140 so there was no chance of backing out now.

With McInnes getting more poorly by the day Jessie was in no mood to attend a wedding, likewise Mary had no wish to go as she felt it was hypocritical to pretend to approve simply by her presence.

Agnes had categorically refused to attend, saying she was now too old to undertake a journey to Coatbridge. Everyone knew that if she had wanted to Agnes could have journeyed to London, but nobody dared say so.

The family gathered with many friends, mainly Salvationists, at the Citadel, the organist played Trumpet Voluntary and Margaret marched down the aisle like the cat who has just licked the cream.

The Salvation Army Major married them, the registration documents were signed and Margaret Smith ate her steak pie and trifle as Margaret Law.

After eating the traditional steak pie purvey, and toasting the newlyweds in lemonade. There was no wee dram at this wedding, being Salvationist it was a strictly teetotal affair, the Laws returned to Gartsherrie.

James and his new bride set out for Glasgow in time to catch the 4.15pm train to Glasgow, from where they would travel to their Ayrshire love nest.

Over a cup of tea the family, minus James, but including the Johnstone's clan discussed the whole sorry mess.

Eventually young Jessie said.

"Look I know how we all feel, the first of Maw's lads to marry and we all disapprove. However, what's done is done. I think it would be better if we all just shut up about James and Margaret and let them get on with their lives. None of us know what the future holds, they may make a go of it and be very happy together, who knows."

Everyone quietened down, knowing full well the situation with McInnes, and suddenly realising how hard it must have been for Jessie to even attend the wedding.

"I think I'll just go for a wee walk now." said Jessie, as she pulled her cardigan around her shoulders and went out into the summer night.

CHAPTER 30
August 1926

As the day neared to the wedding between Sarah and Alan, Mary constantly questioned herself as to whether or not she should attend the celebration, even in a limited way, by sitting at the back of the synagogue. Having no desire to elicit any questions or speculation by her presence she constantly worried that she would stand out like a sore thumb, a Protestant at a big Jewish family gathering.

Meantime, James and Margaret had returned from their honeymoon on the Ayrshire Coast and were settling into their new life at number 140.

From time to time they called in for a meal and Mary fed them with as much good grace as she could muster. No invitations were ever forthcoming to visit the newlyweds home, nor did the family expect any.

Mary also found the loss of James's wages hard to bear, she had to shop more carefully and Agnes was no longer able to save money to buy household luxuries, once again the Laws had to tighten the family belt.

Sending Willie, under protest, back to Condorrat at the start of the summer holidays was one less mouth to feed but Mary had a sneaking feeling that she had not seen the last of the wee blighter.

The additional income from her job as a maid to Mrs Watson certainly helped but it was hard work for someone with Mary's medical conditions, particularly since she was now effectively running the home, life for her seemed to be just one long round of hard work.

However, complaint was not in Mary's nature, she just made the best of things and enjoyed the rare moments she spent in the company of her friends Ina and Mamie or walking her beloved dog Rags.

It was the day before the Fischer DeSilva wedding. Mary had sponged her best blue coat and matching cloche hat, her black patent shoes were buffed with Vaseline and she had bought a new pair of silk stocking. The pretty silk scarf Mary Johnstone had given her, in shades of pinks, purples and blues was taken out of its tissue lined box ready for the occasion. Mary loved it and always thought it looked like a beautiful sunset, it was draped in readiness around her coat, just in case she decided to attend the wedding service.

The wedding clothes were hanging in the cupboard but to go or not, even at this late hour Mary was still swithering as to what decision would be best for all concerned.

Mary and her mother had not discussed the wedding since the day the invitation had arrived. It therefore came as a complete surprise to Mary when out of the blue Agnes said.

"I know I haven't mentioned Sarah's wedding but after that travesty between my James and that, that, floosy Margaret, I just could not bear to think about another family wedding. A wedding that I will not be welcome to attend.

Mary lass, what have you decided, will you go?"

Mary was taken aback by her mother's question but she suddenly had a strong feeling that she should attend the wedding, she should show Sarah and Samuel that their Law family did care.

"Actually Maw I have been trying to make a decision on whether or not to go to the synagogue for weeks now. One moment it's yes, the next no. However, I think perhaps I really should make the effort and attend the ceremony.

After everyone has left for work tomorrow I'll get ready then head up to Blairhill and catch a train to Glasgow. I will only stay for the service so I'll be home, and changed out of my good clothes, long before the family return.

What do you think Maw, am I doing the right thing?" Mary asked her mother.

Agnes rose from her chair and went into the bedroom, she returned a few minutes later with a small package wrapped in brown paper and tied with fine string. As she handed the little parcel to Mary, she said in a gentle reflective voice.

"Mary lass I would like you to give this to Sarah, it's all I can give her, tell her it was a gift to me from her father Ben. I have held on to his last present to me through all the hard years, there have been so many moments when I have been tempted to sell it but somehow I always managed to keep it hidden in the lining of my portmanteau. Now is the time when I feel I must part with his gift and I am sure Ben would want me to pass it on to our darling daughter Sarah."

Mary accepted the package, taking it into the bedroom and putting it carefully into her handbag. In her head one word was ringing, darling, darling. When had her mother ever called her or any of her brothers or sisters 'darling'.

The morrow dawned and Mary travelled into Glasgow by train, then took a tram car over to the Gorbals. Arriving early she headed into a little cafe near the synagogue, from where she could drink a cup of tea and observe the wedding guests as they started to congregate.

When she saw the taxi arrive with the groom and his best man Mary decided that the time was right to find a seat for herself in a quiet corner of the Jewish house of worship.

Following the elegantly dressed women upstairs Mary settled herself in a pew, half hidden by a pillar.

This was Mary's first visit to a synagogue, she had been very unsure as to what to expect but surprisingly it reminded her very much of many Protestant churches with its upstairs balcony and beautiful stained glass windows and smell of polish from the fine mahogany woodwork. There was no excessive ornamentation and to her it felt peaceful, even allowing for the excitement she was feeling.

Sarah entered the synagogue on Samuel's arm, she looked breathtaking in her low waisted, ivory silk dress, Alan's mother had given her a wedding present of a pearl tiara which held her exquisite Honiton lace veil in place, her shoes had shaped heels with the straps held in place with little diamanté and pearl studs.

The current wedding fashion was for enormous bouquets of lilies, Sarah, never one to follow the crowd, carried a small posy of white bud roses and blue muscari which perfectly matched the blue of her eyes.

Mary almost forgot to breath as she watched enthralled at the marriage ceremony taking place under the chuppa, the glass was smashed underfoot and Sarah Fischer was Sarah DeSilva.

As the happy couple signed the Register, Mary quietly walked downstairs and left the synagogue, standing outside on the fringe of a group of opportunistic children, who as soon as they saw a wedding taking place were hoping for a traditional scramble. The children were prepared to risk life and limb scuffling for the coins thrown by the senior gentlemen attending the wedding celebration.

Mary watched Sarah and Alan pose for photographs outside the synagogue together with their families and friends who then boarded the bus that had been hired to take the guests to the reception in the West End.

Samuel was standing alone when Mary saw her opportunity. Walking up behind him, she slipped him the little package from Agnes together with a short note she had written and said quietly.

"Please give this to Sarah, it's from my mother."

Mary quickly disappeared and was on the train home to Coatbridge within the hour.

Samuel was then caught up in the moment and it wasn't until later that evening when the dancing was in full swing that he opened the note from Mary.

Dear Samuel,
Please be good enough to give this little package to
Sarah with my mother's love.
I have no idea what is inside but apparently it was the
last present from your father Ben to my mother.
My mother has cherished the gift and although times
were often hard for her she managed to keep it hidden, and
treasured.
Samuel, please wish Sarah and Alan muzzeltof from
me.
Mary

Sarah had disappeared into a bedroom at the Grosvenor Hotel to get changed into her going away outfit, it was a soft blue dress and jacket which had been specially made for her at Salmonds, her accessories and hat were all of a delicate shade of dove grey and had been purchased at Daly's in Sauchiehall Street.

Samuel took the opportunity to attract Alan's attention. He gave him the package Mary had handed him outside the synagogue, together with the accompanying note. Samuel asked his new brother in law to give it to Sarah, at a time he thought appropriate.

After spending the night in the Honeymoon Suite of the Central Hotel, the following morning Alan and Sarah were sitting comfortably in a first class compartment of the Flying Scotsman on their way down to London.

They were discussing the wedding and what a wonderful day they had enjoyed. All the little fun moments, 'did you see your Auntie Anna's hat? how many birds gave their lives for that' 'I can't believe your dad didn't know about the scramble and ended up throwing out silver, the weans of the Gorbals will never have known a weddings like it, sixpences, shillings and even half crowns' 'poor little beggars, probably a few got killed in the scuffle' 'didn't your Aunt Ruth look so proud of you standing there as the bride's mother.'

And so it went on as the wheels turned and the train chugged towards England. Sarah seemed to sink into a quiet reverie for a few moments and then she observed.

"Wasn't Samuel looking handsome in his morning suit, he certainly looked the part. You know I really wish he would meet a nice girl and get married."

"Wait just a tiny wee minute" laughed Alan

"How many hours have you been married and you are already trying to push your brother into matrimony. How many years did I try go get you to walk up the aisle? And then, you decide the time is right, and before I could draw breath I was standing under the chuppa. Sarah DeSilva, nee Fischer, you really are a law unto yourself."

"Shall I tell you something?" asked Sarah

"The only woman I have ever known him to really talk about

with respect and affection is the one woman he can't have, and that is our half sister, Mary."

"Talking of Mary" interrupted Alan. "Did you know she came to the synagogue to see us married?"

"No, not at all, I didn't see her, Oh how I wish I had. How terribly sad that she did not come to the reception, I really wanted her to come for the meal and join in the festivities. However, I truly can see her point of view, lies simply breed more lies."

Alan thought that the time was now right to hand over the package.

"My darling, Mary gave Samuel a little packet to give to you. There it is also a little handwritten note that accompanied the gift."

Sarah read Mary's letter to Samuel and then slowly untied the twine and opened the parcel, inside was a piece of soft tissue paper, she carefully unwrapped the paper which had yellowed with age, nestling inside was a pendant on a gold chain, a perfectly plain gold Star of David. There was also a small card written in faded copperplate writing which read.

> *My dearest darling Agnes,*
> *Thank you for my beautiful twins.*
> *I love you, Ben.*

Sarah started to cry, no comforting from Alan would stop her tears from falling, a wedding present not only from her unknown mother but from her father who had died so tragically when she was little more than a tiny baby.

Eventually her sobbing ceased, she fingered the beautiful Star of David and turned to Alan, saying.

"Alan please fasten on my faith and a reminder of where I have come from, I intend to wear this beautiful symbol for the rest of my life."

Alan gently fastened the gold pendant around Sarah's neck then gently kissed his new bride.

CHAPTER 31
November 1926

While Sarah and Alan had been enjoying their Honeymoon on the Cornish Riviera and settling into their new home in Whitecraigs, all their hopes and dreams, and choices of soft furnishings, before them; Sarah's half sister was seeing all her dreams and hopes diminish by the day.

McInnes's illness progressed quicker than even the doctor's most pessimistic prognosis. He tried to use every day as fully as he could, carefully dismantling the business of his life and his small Drysaltery Empire of three shops.

Throughout the desperately sad weeks and months Hugh Mason was McInnes's rock. Even although he thought that the closing of the Main Street shop could be the end of his working life, and more than that, his reason for living, Hugh never gave McInnes the slightest indication of how he really felt.

Hugh was businesslike and did what he knew the boss would want, treated him simply as a human being who was winding up a business. Neither of them could have borne mawkish sentimentality.

The Airdrie shop was the smaller of the three but the property was owned outright by McInnes, together with a small flat above the shop. This was quickly sold as a profitable operating business, together with an owners residence. The money for this sale McInnes used to pay off the mortgage on his Glasgow flat and he banked the balance.

The two businesses in Coatbridge were in leased property, when he came to dealing with them McInnes offered Hugh the tenancy of

Main Street and promised him the stock, fitments and fittings as his parting gift.

Hugh was touched beyond words at McInnes's thoughtfulness, he accepted, as much because he wanted to secure the employment of his men, as for himself.

McInnes intended to do the same for Jessie in Bank Street, for Jessie he also proposed to will a substantial amount of money and his flat in the West End of Glasgow, so that he could pass away in the knowledge that his Lieutenant Hugh and his great love were both well provided for, financially if not emotionally.

For McInnes each day seemed to be shorter than the previous one, so much to do and so little time. Meetings with accountants; lawyers; banks; landlords; together with teaching Jessie the financial side of the business.

In between all this McInnes and Jessie did manage to have a few weeks together when they did their best to simply enjoy their final moments and dwell on their love.

One day in late October, everything was still far from being finalised, McInnes was attending a meeting with his accountant, when he simply doubled up in agony.

Mr Irvine, his accountant of many years, realising the seriousness of the situation promptly telephoned for an ambulance and McInnes was taken to Glasgow Royal Infirmary. He never left.

After the immediate crisis was over McInnes sent for his brother, Fraser and asked him to help finalise his wishes, he signed a power of attorney and asked Fraser to act on his behalf. He could now die content in the knowledge he had done everything he could to leave behind security for those he loved and cared for and that all his affairs were in order.

One day, while laying in bed with his eyes closed, he heard two young nurses in conversation.

"Do you see that man, Mr McInnes in the end bed Ina? He is only in his thirties and he looks seventy, he must be in some terrible pain, he looks so old and emaciated."

At that moment McInnes knew he never wanted to see his beloved Jess, his Princess of the Brig, ever again.

That afternoon he asked the nurse to give him paper and his fountain pen. McInnes then started a correspondence with Jessie which amounted to some thirty letters. Some days he could only manage to write a few words, others pages, but the outpouring of love within those pages was to warm Jessie's heart and last her for the remainder of her days as a reminder of the meaning of pure love.

While Jessie's heart was breaking another member of the Law family was also very unhappy in his relationship.

Mary had finished her housework for the day and given her mother some lunch. Now her intention was to take a walk over to Coatbridge with Rags, just for the exercise and some quiet thinking time, perhaps also buy some fish for the evening meal.

As she left the house James caught sight of her and ran to catch up with his elder sister.

"Mary a word, I've been trying to get you on your own but my Maw or Jessie, one of the boys always seem to be about."

Mary replied. "That's what life is like at number twelve James, I never get a minute to myself, that's why I'm walking over to the 'Brig for some shopping, I need a bit of time to think.

Now what problem do you want to discuss with me because sure as eggs is eggs it's not going to be good news."

"You're right there Mary" agreed James. "You know marrying Margaret was the biggest mistake of my life. And, don't say we all told you so, I know you did and that doesn't make it one whit easier.

I have found out through her brother that she was pregnant a couple of months back and had an abortion, apparently she did not want to lose her looks. Can you imagine Mary killing a wee baby, my wee baby, all because she wanted to keep her waistline.

I am disgusted with her, what with that and the debts. My Maw would go mad if she knew the number of debt collectors who have been at our door. I just don't know what to do, Mary have you any ideas, because sure as God I don't."

"James Law this is not the moment" exclaimed Mary. "Your sister Jessie is mindless just now; every few days another letter arrives from McInnes, they are tearing her apart. He refuses to see her, and in a way I can understand him, but poor Jessie she is brokenhearted.

You got yourself into this Margaret business with your eyes fully open, sort it out yourself.   I know that sounds hard but at the moment nobody in number twelve can deal with yet another crisis. Besides my Maw's only advice would be 'marry in haste, repent at leisure'.

I'm sorry James, but that is the way it is, now away into your fancy house with it's never never furnishings and think on.   The only way for you to get out of this pickle is for you to be the man of the house."

CHAPTER 32
December 1926

Jessie came home from work, dripping with snow and cold beyond thinking. Her first words as she entered the house were;
"Any letter from Glasgow?"
While helping her off with her snow sprinkled hat and coat Mary replied.
"No word at all. Don't you think maybe you should go to the Royal Infirmary and see him yourself. You can't keep going through this torture day after day, waiting for yet another letter from Glasgow."
"Look Mary, he doesn't want to see me. It doesn't mean he doesn't love me, it means he cannot bear to be reminded of what should have been and of all our times together, planning our business, our family, our home, laughing and just being in love. This should be the happiest time in my life and it is the worst, my life is over."
Jessie's words spilled into tears.
There was a loud knock at the door. Mary opened the door foreboding in her heart. The 'Telegraph Boy' handed her a brown envelope saying. "Telegraph for Miss Law, mam." Mary opened her purse and gave the boy a penny. She stared at the envelope for a few seconds before taking a deep breath and returning to the living room where Jessie was now sitting warming herself by the fire.
Mary handed her the envelope. "Jessie, it's a telegraph for you." her usual voice reduced to a whisper.
Jessie held out her hand, to take the missive from Mary. Jessie knew in her heart what the telegraph would say, but even that knowledge did not prepare her for the starkness of the words.

Thomas Anderson McInnes died today of rectal cancer.
signed: Fraser McInnes, Brother

No sympathy, no address at which to contact Fraser McInnes, no instruction regarding she shop, nothing.   Nothing but a stark end to all Jessie's hopes and dreams for the future.

The McInnes family, Fraser, his wife Francis and his two sisters, Alice and Effy, had gathered at the flat belonging to their brother in Glasgow's West End. Like Jessie, They had known for some months what the eventual outcome of Anderson's illness would be. However, unlike Jessie they had been planning and plotting as to how they were going to gain from their brother's death.

"I suppose we will need to invite her to the funeral?" said Fanny, the wife of Fraser.

"Yes," her husband replied "I don't think we have any option on that one but we will make it clear we four are the family, she is the outsider.

Can you imagine a girl from folks like that becoming part of our family.   I heard that the father was completely illiterate, couldn't read or even write his name. I don't know what Anderson was thinking about, the kindest thing I can say is that it must have been his illness working on him, that's what let his defences down.

We are not going to let the little money grubber get a penny.   I have his Power of Attorney and I've already spoken with the Solicitor and the Accountant, everything will be done and dusted before Anderson's funeral."

It was early in the morning of 11th December.   Jessie sat in front of the fire that she had just kindled.   She simply could not believe that she had been allowed to know such love and happiness only for it to be taken from her in such a cruel fashion.

Tears dripped down her face as she sat with her Mother's old plaid shawl around her shoulders for warmth.

Mary brought her a cup of tea and said.

"What are you going to do about the shop?"

Torn from her thoughts Jessie said.

"To be honest I have no idea.   McInnes sold the Airdrie shop when he found out he was ill but he said he would give Hugh the Main Street shop and the Bank Street shop would be mine, to ensure I had a steady income, he also said I would be well provided for financially.

He made sure I knew how to do the accounts, prepare the wages for the painters, negotiate with suppliers, everything. Then his illness progressed at such a speed and he was taken into hospital.

As you well know he refused to see me at the last and I only have his letters.

I suppose I should contact his family to see what is to be done and to find out about the funeral arrangements."

Jessie composed a telegram and Mary walked through the snow to Sunnyside Post Office to send it for her.

Back in Glasgow, Fraser McInnes answered the door and received the brown enveloped telegram from the young lad on his doorstep. He opened the envelope and read the contents aloud.

"When would you like to meet me to discuss Anderson's funeral service and the shops in Coatbridge?" Regards, Jessie Law."

"What do you think of that Frances." He addressed his long suffering wife?

"As if we have anything to discuss with that woman. I have a tenant lined up for the Coatbridge shops, he will take over everything lock, stock and barrel. All the proceeds from the sale will be included in the estate and divided equally between the three remaining siblings.

As soon as the funeral is past, Anderson's so called fiancé, will be given a weeks wages in lieu of notice and that will be the end of Jessie Law in this family and that other fellow, what's his name, Mason, Hugh Mason.

I suppose I'd better write a telegram with the funeral details." He quickly scribbled a few lines on a piece of vellum watermarked paper, then instructed his long suffering wife.

"Nip down to the post office right away and get it sent off, would you Frances dear."

Later that day a telegram arrived in the Long Row.   Mary decided to open it in the absence of Jessie, who had decided to go into the shop that morning, if only to tell Stanley the news.

Mary read the stark words.

A small private family funeral for Thomas Anderson McInnes will be held at The Barony Church, Glasgow followed by internment at Glasgow Necropolis on December 16th at 3.00pm.
Signed: Fraser McInnes.

"Well Maw, there is no warmth or welcome there for Jessie.   I think I had better go with her to the funeral, she'll needs some family support."

"You are right Mary, as usual, you certainly had better go with her.   You are always the strength and support in this family, even with all your health problems, you have more gumption than the rest of us all put together."

When Jessie arrived home from work, eyes red rimmed from crying, Mary had no option but to show her the telegram, saying,

"Don't worry Jessie, I'll come with you for some family support.   You can't go into the lions den alone."

"Thanks Mary, I must admit I am terrified of taking on the McInnes Clan.   Anderson promised me the shop, so at least I'll still have a job, but I expect there are still some legal things to sort out. If you want the truth I just want to sit in a corner and cry, and never leave this house again."

"Well you can't Jessie" said the ever practical Mary.   "No matter how upset you are you have to make sure you keep your interest in the business.

With James married there is one less wage coming into the house.   Alexander is only working for an apprentice rate, which will scarcely feed him. I don't mean to sound harsh but we need your wages from the shop. Robert's wage isn't enough to cover everything, and the bits and pieces I earn don't amount to very much.

The day of the funeral dawned.   Mary got out her dark blue

coat which was deemed suitable to wear to a funeral. Jessie owned a black skirt and jumper but as she had no mourning clothes to keep out the cold, Jessie Johnstone, who was about the same size gave her a loan of her Sunday black coat and hat.

The two sisters walked gloomily to Blairhill station. Jessie, to bury her hopes and dreams. Mary, knowing full well that her role was as Jessie's protector in whatever lay ahead.

They reached the Glasgow Necropolis at around two thirty, it was cold, wet and the sky had darkened. Hugh Mason joined the two Law girls, he put his arms around Jessie, she cried for her love, he cried for a son.

Eventually from under their umbrellas they saw the cortège approach, with the entire McInnes family following in a black car, which was traveling at a walking pace   The occupants of the car clearly saw Jessie, Mary and Hugh at the side of the path but didn't stop to offer them a lift. The three walked soberly behind the family, who were protected from the rain in the comfort of their black limousine.

Mary was seething with rage, red, beyond anger. As she walked she thought 'What gives these people the right to treat my sister in this high handed way? Status? Education? Money? We might be poor but there is more respect and support to be found in the Rows of Gartsherrie when a family suffer a bereavement, than in all their posh sandstone Glasgow houses.'

As they walked Jessie was not angry. Her and Hugh were possibly the only members of the assembled company who were genuinely grieving for the man that was Anderson McInnes. Jessie cried for the children they would not have; for the business they would not build; for the house they would not furnish; for the love that would never be consummated.

As she cried, occasionally her thoughts would flash back to a happy moment, like a glorious colourful happy picture, surrounded by a frame of darkness and pain. Jessie knew the only way to retain her sanity was to focus on the bright pictures.

Hugh cried for the man he felt like a father towards but he also cried for Jessie, during their time working together he had grown to care deeply for the young lass and he knew how happy she had made McInnes.

Mary's anger grew with every step.

After the internment the McInnes party; Fraser, his wife Francis together with his two perjink sisters, walked towards the black car, with it's smart chauffeur.

The three women got into the car but Fraser McInnes waited outside. He accosted Hugh and Jessie.

"You two will be anxious to know what is happening about the shops you currently manage, well I will now enlighten you both. The new owner takes over next Monday. He wants to engage his own staff so I will have to pay off all the employees. The accountant will make up the wages and I will bring them out to Coatbridge on Saturday first, you two will also receive an additional payment of a weeks wages in lieu of notice.

I have attended to all my brothers affairs and this is my final word on the arrangements. Goodbye to you both."

He immediately jumped into the car and was off before they even had an opportunity to question him.

Hugh did not mourn for a lost business, he owned his small cottage, he had some money in the bank and he fully intended to spend it all on good Scotch whisky until the day came when he could join his loved ones again. He had suffered too much sorrow for any man in one life.

Jessie, almost collapsed at Fraser's speech. Mary, on the other hand, was not in the least surprised, she had been fully expecting something of this sort from McInnes's brother.

Somehow or other the threesome got back to Coatbridge, separating at Coatbridge Railway Station. Hugh to head for Carnbroe and his little cottage, where he had a fine Glenmorangie malt in his kitchen press, a malt which he had intended for Jessie and McInnes's wedding. The bottle would be opened today and Hugh intended to attempt to drown his sorrow in the fine malt whisky.

Jessie and Mary caught a blue Baxter's bus back to Gartsherrie, on arriving home Mary gave her sister some hot milk, containing a tot of whisky, and put her to bed.

The following day, back in Gartsherrie Mary felt as though the troubles of the world were resting entirely on her shoulders. James had privately owned up to her that his marriage to Margaret had been a huge mistake, although he would not admit it to his brothers.

Since the appendicitis operation Mary's own health had not been good. Although she mainly suffered in silence she worried about who would take care of the household if she was once again to be incapacitated. Especially since Agnes seemed to be doing less and less in the home these days.

Since Rab had died Agnes had developed a new role for herself, that of the family matriarch, and that role did not seem to include helping Mary with housework or shopping.

Robert and Alexander were both working, thank God, but their wages were not great and Robert would be finishing his apprenticeship soon. Although this would mean a large increase in his money it also increased the probability that he would marry and set up his own household.

However her major worry was Jessie. Now that the McInnes family had done their worst she had no job, no business, no reason to get up in the morning and go out and face the world. Mary feared she would sink into a deep depression from which there would be no return, unless she could take some action.

Mary did what she often did, she discussed it with her maker. Putting on her coat, she put on Rag's lead and they headed down to the Store to buy some eggs and sugar.

However, she was not thinking of the messages she would purchase, she was inwardly praying to her personal God to give her strength and a solution to her problems.

That evening, as she was cooking a bite of dinner, inspiration suddenly struck. A thought flashed into her head, where no thought had been before. I must write to Samuel and ask him if the McInnes clan really can take the shop away from Jessie.

The decision made Mary enjoyed the best nights sleep she could remember in many months.

The following morning she got out her writing paper and wrote.

Dear Samuel,

I am sure you will have heard from Sarah that life
has been very hard in Gartsherrie these past few
months.

You once said if I ever needed any help I should
contact you.   Well Samuel, I would like to ask for
your help on behalf of my sister Jessie.

Her fiancé, Anderson McInnes has recently passed
away.   McInnes promised Jessie one of his shops and
financial security, and I believe he took steps to organise this for her before his illness took hold.

Unfortunately the McInnes family seem to be very
powerful and they have arranged things so that Jessie
gets nothing.

Jessie is so full of grief that she does not realise the
seriousness of the situation.   We need the income from
her employment to make ends meet.

I have enclosed all the paperwork Jessie can find.
Would you please be good enough to read it and give
me your opinion.   Does Jessie have a case against the
McInnes family?

Any advice you can give will be gratefully received.
I hope all is well with you and you are happy and
healthy.

Your friend and sister
Mary

A week passed before Mary received a reply.

My dear Mary,

Firstly, I was very sorry to hear from Sarah that you
had to undergo such a serious operation.   It was very
frustrating not to be able to contact you but I did not
want to risk correspondence being opened by another
member of your family.

I was also very sorry to hear of the predicament Jessie

finds herself in, due to the greed of the McInnes family.
My apologies for the delay in replying to your letter
but I wanted to carry out some detailed investigations
before contacting you.

Regrettably Jessie's fiancé was hospitalised before he
had completed all the legal paperwork. He placed his
trust in his brother to do the right thing by Jessie and
Mr Mason. Unfortunately Fraser McInnes has
not behaved as a man of honour.

I am sorry Mary, there is absolutely nothing I can
do to help. Jessie would never succeed in a court case
and the cost of trying would be prohibitive.

However, on a more positive note. A friend of mine,
Mr John Dickson owns a number of drysaltery shops
throughout Glasgow. He is looking for a competent
manageress for his shop in Shettleston, and he is willing to give Jessie a trial. I have explained to him
that I don't want my name involved, as far as Jessie is
concerned.

I have therefore suggested that he puts a small adver-
tisement into the Evening Citizen on Friday first.
Your role in this Mary is to spot the advert and make
sure Jessie applies for the job.

I am so sorry I could not do more to help but I am
afraid Jessie does not stand a chance against a clever
and ruthless man, who did not have it in his heart to
carry out his brother's dying wishes.

Mary I know you are fiercely independent but if you
need any help financially please let me know. I
would be very upset if I ever found out that I was in a
position to help you and you did not call on me to do so.
I think of you often and wish you and all the family
well

Your brother
Samuel

Mary got out her writing box and immediately replied.

Dear Samuel,
Very many thanks for your letter and the investigations
you have carried out on Jessie's behalf.
I rather suspected the McInnes family would win out,
they have power and money. Jessie only had love.
I will certainly buy the Evening Citizen and push
Jessie in the right direction. You have no idea what a
relief it is to me to think of Jessie, not only earning, but
getting out of the house every day with a real purpose.
On behalf of Jessie and myself thank you from the bot-
tom of my heart.
With all good wishes
Your sister, Mary

The following Friday Mary bought a copy of the Evening Citizen and carefully read the advertisements for shop workers. As suggested by Samuel, Mary pointed out the arranged advert to Jessie.

"Jessie, have you seen this advert. Someone is looking for a manageress for a drysalters shop in Shettleston. Am I right in thinking Shettleston is on the rail line into Glasgow from Blairhill?"

"Yes, I think it is." replied Jessie, "but it seems ridiculous to apply for a job when I had my own shop with McInnes."

Mary took hold of her sisters hand, saying.

"Jessie, look I understand you are very upset at losing McInnes and his family have treated you despicably but life has to go on; the rent has to be paid; the food has to be bought. You need to work and contribute to the household.

The job in the paper sounds not too bad and you are very well qualified. Write an application now and I will go down to the box and post it off to Mr Dickson."

Reluctantly Jessie penned the letter and Mary took it down to the post box before she could change her mind.

A few days later a letter arrived addressed to Jessie, asking her to go to the shop in Shettleston, the following day, for an interview.

The letter brought on more tears from Jessie, and threats not to attend the interview.

Knowing the job opportunity was entirely due to Samuel's involvement made Mary even more determined that Jessie should not only put on a brave face but give a good account of herself.

Mary spoke sternly to her sister.

"Jessie, I do understand you are in mourning but you are not Queen Victoria. You don't have the luxury of being able to leave the practicalities of life to others, nobody is going to serve you breakfast or pay for the rent and the gas. If we are to survive as a family you have to make a good impression on this Mr Dickson get offered the job and negotiate the best wage you can from him. Remember you are also going to have to pay train fares, you won't be able to walk to and from work if you get a job in Glasgow.

Now my girl, I'm going to say no more but tomorrow morning I expect you to dress nicely, put on some lipstick and impress this Mr Dickson. Remember, 'must do is a good master'."

The following morning Jessie rose early, washed and waved her hair, carefully applied a little make up and at ten o'clock left for Blairhill railway station, dressed in her heavy, lovat green, winter coat.

At one o'clock Mary was in the scullery about to prepare a boiled egg for her mother's midday meal.

Jessie arrived home from Shettleston, she shook out her umbrella, took off her coat and announced.

"Well Mary, I've got the job. I start next Monday on two pounds five shillings a week. Tuesday is my half day, two weeks holiday, hours nine to five thirty, five o'clock on a Saturday.

As jobs go it is absolutely fine but it won't be my own business. McInnes and I had such plans for the future and now I will only be managing a shop belonging to someone else, with an assistant and a young junior.

The painting side is all run from one of the other shops so all we have to do is take note of the enquiries and pass them on to the Parkhead branch.

Mary was greatly relieved at her sister's news. But it wasn't in her nature to fuss, she simply said.

"Go through to the kitchen and tell Maw your news.   I'll make you some egg and toast."

Later in the afternoon Mary found half an hour to herself, between finishing the washing and starting the supper, she wrote to Samuel.

> *My dear brother,*
> *You will probably have heard that your friend, Mr*
> *Dickson, has employed Jessie on very generous terms.*
> *I am more grateful than you can possibly imagine for*
> *your intervention.*
> *Please accept my sincere thanks.*
> *Your sister, Mary*

In a few days time it would once again be Hogmanay.   The bells would ring in the year 1927, and with the New Year a new chapter in the lives of all the members of the Law, Fischer and Johnstone families.

THE END

Retired and looking for a new interest, like many of my generation, I started to research my family tree.

I was saddened to find that Gartsherrie, a place that my mother had greatly loved, appeared to have been almost wiped from the pages of history.

With the demolition of Wm. Baird Iron & Steel Works and the flattening of the Rows to make way for new council housing the history of Gartsherrie and its people, during the years when it was so closely affiliated to Wm. Baird & Sons, appears to have simply vanished.

My best efforts on the internet turned up very little information. Even Gartsherrie Primary School and the Carnegie Library have now fallen into neglect and are up for sale.

The Laws of Gartsherrie is my attempt to re-awaken memories of Gartsherrie and the hard working, decent people who lived out their lives within the Rows.

Alexandra J Morris

www.AJMorris.me.uk

Printed in Great Britain
by Amazon